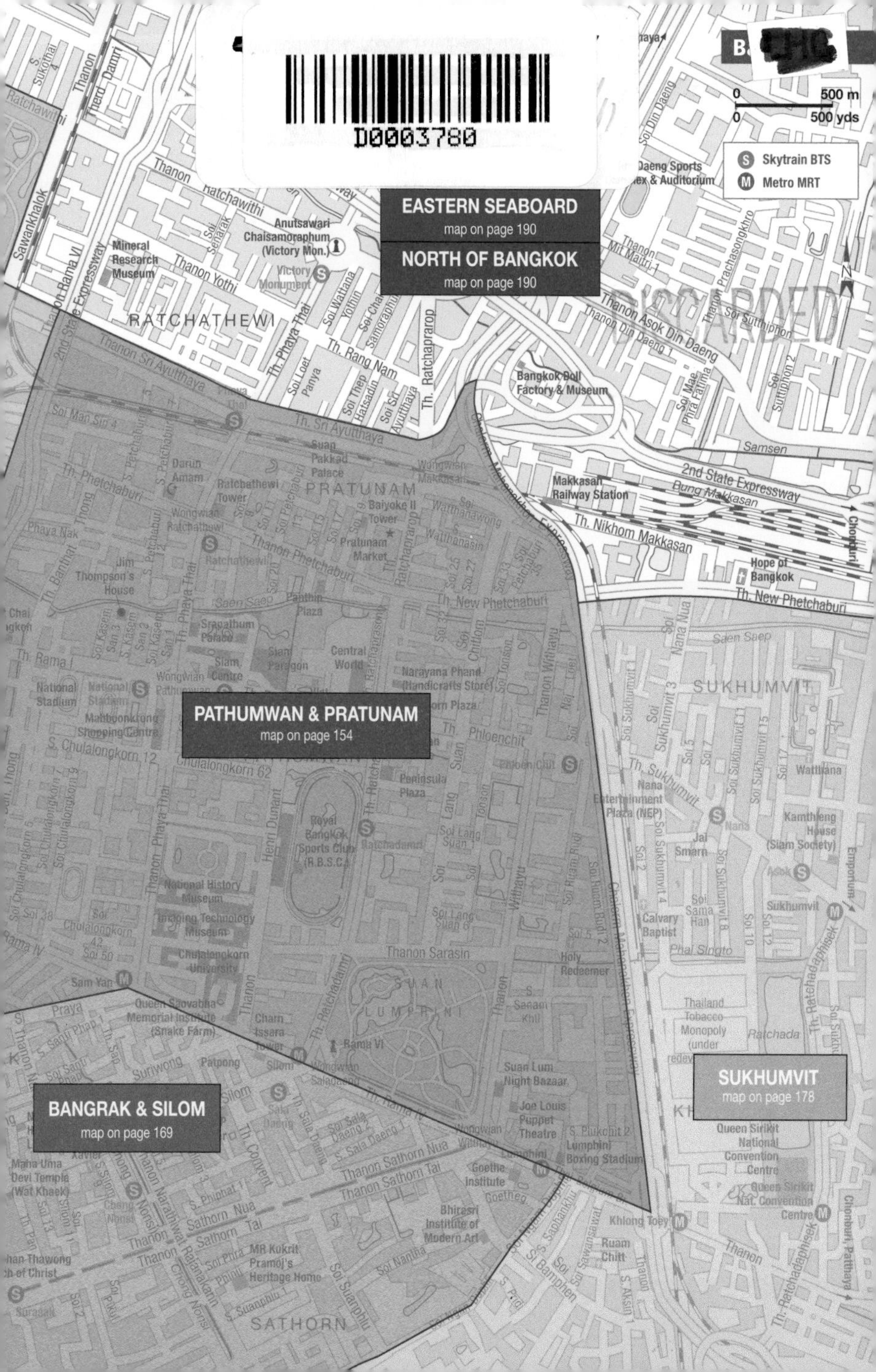
D0003780
DISCARDED
0 500 m
0 500 yds
Skytrain BTS
Metro MRT
EASTERN SEABOARD
map on page 190
NORTH OF BANGKOK
map on page 190
PATHUMWAN & PRATUNAM
map on page 154
BANGRAK & SILOM
map on page 169
SUKHUMVIT
map on page 178
RATCHATHEWI
PRATUNAM
SUKHUMVIT
SATHORN
Anutsawari Chaisamoraphum (Victory Mon.)
Victory Monument
Mineral Research Museum
Bangkok Doll Factory & Museum
Makkasan Railway Station
2nd State Expressway
Th. Nikhom Makkasan
Hope of Bangkok
Th. New Phetchaburi
Suan Pakkad Palace
Baiyoke II Tower
Pratunam Market
Ratchathewi Tower
Jim Thompson's House
Srapathum Palace
Siam Paragon
Central World
Siam Centre
National Stadium
Mahboonkrong Shopping Centre
Narayana Phand (Handicrafts Store)
Peninsula Plaza
Royal Bangkok Sports Club (R.B.S.C.)
National History Museum
Imaging Technology Museum
Chulalongkorn University
Thanon Sarasin
Queen Saovabha Memorial Institute (Snake Farm)
Rama VI
Suan Lum Night Bazaar
Joe Louis Puppet Theatre
Lumphini Boxing Stadium
Goethe Institute
Bhirasri Institute of Modern Art
MR Kukrit Pramoj's Heritage Home
Maha Uma Devi Temple (Wat Khaek)
Nana Entertainment Plaza (NEP)
Kamthieng House (Siam Society)
Calvary Baptist
Holy Redeemer
Thailand Tobacco Monopoly
Queen Sirikit National Convention Centre
Thanon Phetchaburi
Th. Sukhumvit
Thanon Sathorn Nua
Thanon Sathorn Tai
Thanon Rama IV
Chonburi, Pattaya

INSIGHT GUIDES

BANGKOK

APA PUBLICATIONS
Part of the Langenscheidt Publishing Group

How to Use This Book

This book is carefully structured both to convey an understanding of the city and its culture and to guide readers through its attractions and activities:

◆ The Best Of section at the front of the book helps you to prioritize. The first spread contains all the Top Sights, while the Editor's Choice details unique experiences, the best buys or other recommendations.

◆ To understand Bangkok, you need to know something of its past. The city's history and culture are described in authoritative essays written by specialists in their fields who have lived in and documented the city for many years.

◆ The Places section details all the attractions worth seeing. The main places of interest are coordinated by number with the maps.

◆ Each chapter includes lists of recommended shops, restaurants, bars and cafés.

◆ Photographs throughout the book are chosen not only to illustrate geography and buildings, but also to convey the moods of the city and the life of its people.

◆ The Travel Tips section includes all the practical information you will need, divided into five key sections: transport, accommodation, activities (including nightlife, events, tours and sports), an A–Z of practical tips and a handy Thai phrasebook. Information may be located quickly by using the index on the back cover flap of the book.

◆ A detailed street atlas is included at the back of the book, with all restaurants, bars, cafés and hotels plotted for your convenience.

Places and Sights

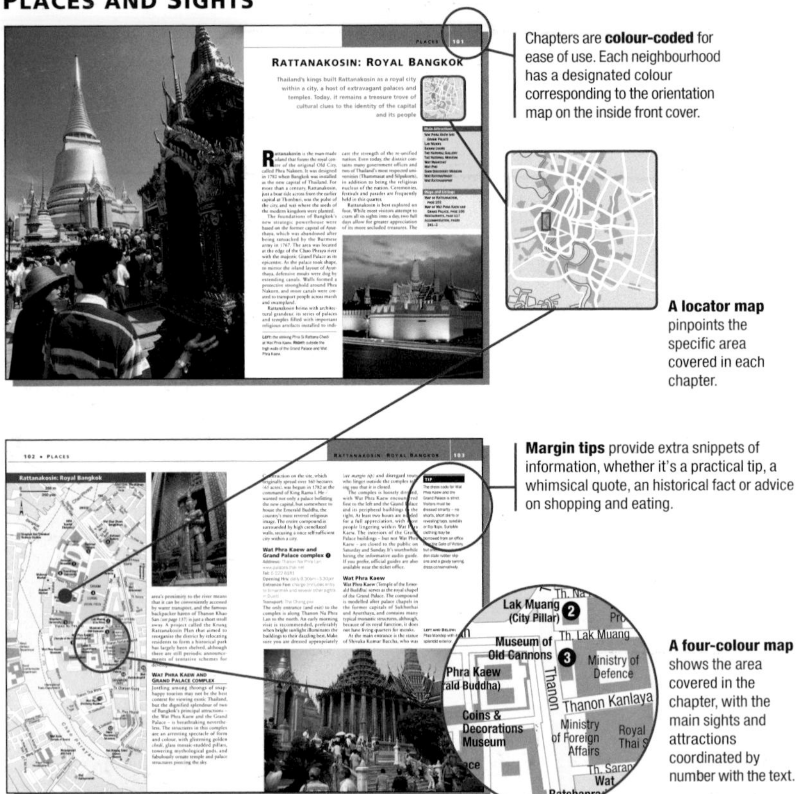

PHOTO FEATURES

164

JIM THOMPSON'S HOUSE • 165

JIM THOMPSON'S THAI HOUSE

In a city increasingly dominated by Western architecture, this fine museum offers a glimpse of Thailand's rich cultural heritage

THE KING OF THAI SILK

The Essentials

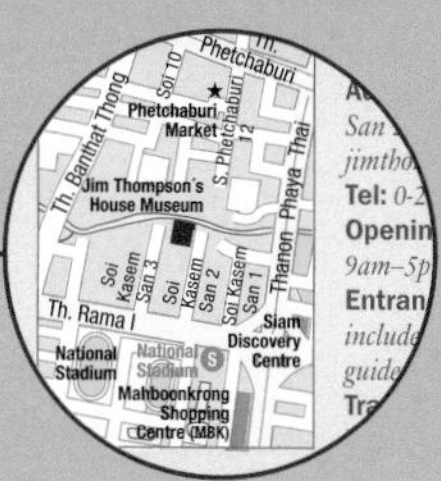

Photo features offer visual coverage of major sights or unusual attractions. Where relevant, there is a map showing the location and essential information on opening times, entrance charges, transport and contact details.

SHOPPING AND RESTAURANT LISTINGS

SUKHUMVIT 179

SHOPPING

162 • PLACES

BEST RESTAURANTS AND BARS

Shopping listings provide details of the best shops in each area. **Restaurant listings** give the establishment's contact details, opening times and price category, followed by a useful review. Bars and cafés are also covered here. The coloured dot and grid reference refers to the atlas section at the back of the book.

Japanese

Shin Daikoku

Fl 2, InterContinental Hotel, Th Ploenchit. Tel: 0-2656 0096/7. Open: daily L and D. **$$–$$$** (44) p275, C1

Dine on high-quality *sushi* and *sashimi*,

TRAVEL TIPS

234 • TRAVEL TIPS

TRANSPORT • 235

TRANSPORT

GETTING THERE AND GETTING AROUND

By Airport Bus

The Airport Bus passes the ma hotels in downtown Bangkok. Yo must first get on the free airport shuttle to the Public Transportation Centre, which is separate from the main terminal building. Buses depart every 15 minutes from 5.30am to 12.30am, and the cost is B150 per person.

Airport Bus Routes:

AE-1 – to Silom via Pratunam, Thanon Phetchaburi, Thanon Ratchadamri, Thanon Silo on Surawong

Travel Tips provide all the practical knowledge you'll need before and during your trip: how to get there, getting around, where to stay and what to do. The A–Z section is a handy summary of practical information, arranged alphabetically.

Contents

Introduction

History

Features

Insights

MINI FEATURES

PHOTO FEATURES

Places

LEFT: Wat Arun.

Travel Tips

Maps

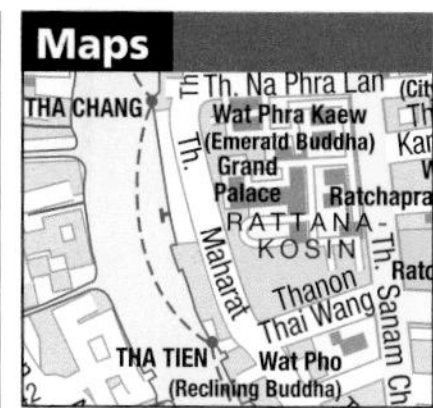

The Best of Bangkok: Top Sights

At a glance, the attractions in and around Bangkok that you can't afford to miss, from fairytale temples to flea markets and ancient ruins to idyllic beaches

◁ **Ayutthaya** Thailand's former capital until the Burmese destroyed it in 1767, ancient Ayutthaya is now a Unesco World Heritage Site, where the ruins offer a glimpse into the city's glorious past. *See pages 220–6.*

▽ **Islands of the Eastern Seaboard** From the small islands off Pattaya to Ko Samet and Ko Chang, there are white sand beaches with diving, sailing and delicious barbecue parties with succulent fresh seafood. *See pages 209–17.*

▽ **Chatuchak Market** Join the 100,000 shoppers at "the world's largest flea market". Search hard and you'll find what you are looking for; follow your nose and you'll discover unimagined treasures. *See pages 184–5.*

△ **Ancient City** Leave Bangkok for the bucolic surrounds of this Thailand-shaped park with near life-size, and painstakingly accurate, replicas of important temples and palaces, including some lost centuries ago. *See pages 209–10.*

△ **Khao Yai** You probably won't see a tiger in Thailand's first national park, but you will see macaques, and possibly bears, and the waterfall from the film *The Beach*. And then you can tour wine country. *See pages 228–9.*

◁ **The Mandarin Oriental** The "Old Lady of Bangkok" has provided lodgings since the 19th century. Guests have included many famous writers, who are honoured in its colonial-style Author's Wing, a lovely spot for afternoon tea. *See page 168.*

▷ **Wat Phra Kaew** The fairytale royal temple attached to Bangkok's Grand Palace glitters golden in the sun. It contains several important religious buildings and the most sacred Buddha image in Thailand, over which *yaksha* (demon) statues stand guard. *See pages 102–4.*

△ **Erawan Falls** Climb the seven tiers to the top of this most famous of waterfalls, and you'll be rewarded with stunning views over the national park countryside towards the border with Burma (Myanmar). *See page 201.*

◁ **Wat Pho** Bangkok's oldest temple is known as Thailand's first university, and it is still the main centre for learning Thai massage. It also holds the stunning Reclining Buddha image. *See pages 114–5.*

The Best of Bangkok: Editor's Choice

Setting priorities, saving money, unique attractions... here, at a glance, are our recommendations, plus some tips and tricks even Bangkokians won't always know

Best for Families

These attractions are popular with children, though not all will suit every age group.

- **Dusit Zoo**. Kids love the lions and tigers and monkeys swinging through the trees. Boating on the lake provides respite when they get tired. *See page 142.*
- **Crocodile Farm and Zoo**. Visitors shriek as handlers wrestle with large crocodiles and stick their heads between the snapping jaws of these monstrous reptiles. *See page 210.*
- **Dream World**. There are good views from the cable cars at this adventure park and stomach-churners like the Grand Canyon water ride. They even have snow to cool you down. *See page 186.*
- **Rose Garden Riverside Resort**. Traditional dancers, Thai boxing and other folk culture are performed in a garden setting outside Bangkok. *See page 193.*
- **Samphran Elephant Ground**. Learn about the pachyderm's role in Thailand, with fun elephant rides and re-enactments of battles. *See page 194.*
- **Siam Ocean World**. A giant aquarium with over 30,000 marine creatures and glass-bottomed boat rides will leave kids spellbound. *See page 156.*

Only In Bangkok

- **Canal Cruising**. Hop aboard a longtail boat and glide along canals *(khlong)* for a slice of Bangkok's past. *See page 238.*
- **Extreme Makeover**. On holiday, why not have a tummy tuck, nose-job, or even a gender reassignment? Bangkok is a world hub for medical tourism with 5-star care at bargain prices. *See page 259.*
- **Jumbo Queen**. See a charitable beauty pageant open to only heavier women. *See page 194.*
- **Ladyboy Cabaret**. Bangkok's Vegas-style shows by elaborately costumed transvestite performers are now travelling the world. *See pages 86 and 252.*
- **Motorcycle Taxis**. Fast and furious, these waistcoat-wearing madmen weave through the city's gridlock at knee-trembling speeds. Helmets optional, courage essential. *See page 237.*
- **Thai Boxing**. Punishing and brutal, this ancient martial art is more than just sport, with drinking and gambling on the sidelines. *See page 254.*
- **Tuk-Tuk**. An icon of the city, these noisy three-wheelers should be experienced at least once. *See page 237.*

BEST WALKS

- **Banglamphu**. A district of old shophouses, grand mansions, colourful backpacker bars and a riverbank park. *See page 136.*
- **Chinatown**. This is Bangkok at its visceral best: narrow lanes awash with local colour and mercantile bustle. *See page 145.*
- **Lumphini Park**. The city's favourite green lung buzzes to life at dawn and dusk with both exercise fiends and those content to just watch them. *See page 159.*
- **Rattanakosin**. The capital's historic heart brims with architectural grandeur. Royal palaces and devotional tributes abound in this old neighbourhood. *See page 101.*
- **The Old City**. Experience the slower, calmer side of the city with traditional crafts, Buddhist shops, amulet markets and views from the Golden Mount. *See page 129.*

BEST FESTIVALS AND EVENTS

- **Bangkok Film Festival**. A chance to view acclaimed local- and foreign-produced flicks and mingle with stars at the film screenings. Jan/Feb. www.bangkokfilm.org
- **Chinese New Year**. Get into the action in Chinatown where loud firecrackers, boisterous lion and dragon dances and festival foods herald in the start of the new year for Bangkok's Chinese. Jan/Feb. *See page 250.*
- **King's Birthday**. Known as Thailand's Father's Day, key streets in Bangkok are magically lit up in the colours of the national flag while fireworks pierce the night sky. 5 Dec. *See page 251.*
- **Loy Krathong**. Expect a visual treat as Bangkokians honour water spirits by lighting candles and incense and setting them afloat on tiny baskets along the city's waterways. Full moon day, Nov. *See page 251.*
- **Songkran**. Pack water pistols (along with a sense of humour) for a three-day soaking. The Thai Lunar New Year is the nation's largest and wettest celebration. 13–15 Apr. *See page 250.*

FAR LEFT: Dream World bumper car ride. **LEFT TOP:** frenetic Thai boxing, or *muay thai*. **LEFT:** tuk-tuk.

LEFT: the Temple of the Emerald Buddha (Wat Phra Kaew) in Rattanakosin. **ABOVE:** Damnoen Saduak Floating Market.

BEST MARKETS

- **Chatuchak Weekend Market**. The mother of all markets, pulling in nearly half a million people every weekend. An unbeatable shopping experience; it has it all and then some. *See page 184.*
- **Damnoen Saduak Floating Market**. This century-old market has become a bit of of a circus, with tourists clambering to photograph fruit-laden boats paddled by women in straw hats. Nevertheless, it's worth seeking out. *See page 197.*
- **Pak Khlong Talad**. A 24-hour riot of colour and fragrance; this is where Bangkok gets all its floral garlands for temple offerings. *See page 131.*
- **Patpong Night Market**. Surrounded by sleaze and neon, the location is as much the attraction as the piles of counterfeit watches, bags, clothes and general tourist tat. *See page 171.*

ABOVE: embroidered cushion cover. **BELOW:** lighting candles in honour of the water spirits during the Loy Krathong festival.

Best Bars and Clubs

- **Bed Supperclub**. A futuristic oval pod with white-on-white furnishings where you recline on beds in the restaurant section to watch multimedia floor shows. *See pages 181 and 251.*
- **Club Culture** Set in a reclaimed traditonal Thai theatre, this club attracts international DJs with a funky edge. Eclectic music range. *See page 251.*
- **Niu's on Silom**. All clubby leather armchairs, top local jazz players and occasional very hot imported musicians. *See page 253.*
- **Distil**. This 64th-floor wine bar with heart-stopping views rises taller than any of the city's other fresh-faced nightspots. Part of State Tower's opulent Dome. *See page 175.*
- **Q Bar**. Modelled after a New York lounge bar, this dark and seductive two-floored venue plays some of the hippest dance tracks. *See page 251.*
- **Tapas**. Located at Silom Soi 4's party strip, sit outside to ogle passers-by or head inside for the funkiest DJ-spun house grooves. *See page 252.*

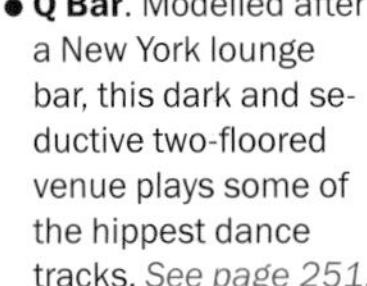

Above: bring on the champagne. **Right Top:** shopping at Siam Square. **Right Middle:** Suan Lum Night Bazaar. **Right Bottom:** lacquerware. **Below:** the futuristic interior of Bed Supperclub.

Best Shopping Experiences

- **MBK**. Lots of fun at this old-school Thai-style mall with stalls in the corridors and everything from cameras to copies of master artworks. *See page 155.*
- **Siam Square and Siam Paragon**. A study in contrasts: the former is one of the city's last surviving low-rise street shopping enclaves (popular with pimply adolescents), while the latter, just across the road, is a luxury mall filled with designer goods and the city's high society. *See pages 155–6.*
- **Panthip Plaza**. Tech-geeks should make a beeline for Bangkok's mecca for computer gadgetry. Stocks both legitimate hard and software as well as pirated games, software, DVDs and VCDs. *See page 161.*
- **Suan Lum Night Bazaar**. More sanitised, but also more easily navigable (and infinitely cooler) alternative to Chatuchak. Stocks souvenirs, clothing, handicrafts, antiques and home decor. *See page 159.*
- **Central World**. Bangkok loves big shopping and this is the biggest mall in the country, full of restaurants, beauty shops, fashion and two department stores. *See page 156.*

BEST SPAS AND MASSAGES

- **Devarana**. Located at the luxury Dusit Thani hotel, ethereal Devarana is a million miles away from the frenetic city. Calming Zen mood with private treatment suites and a range of therapies that will ease away urban strain. *See page 90.*
- **Divana**. A well-regarded local spa chain with the full range of treatments at reasonable prices. The Sukhumvit Soi 35 outlet is the most popular. *See page 90.*
- **The Mandarin Oriental Spa**. In the historic Oriental, this atmospheric luxury spa sits in a century-old teakwood house on the banks of the Chao Phraya river. *See page 90.*
- **Wat Pho**. In the city's oldest temple, this famous no-frills traditional massage school has blind masseuses giving vigorous rubdowns for next to nothing. *See pages 90 and 115.*

ABOVE AND TOP RIGHT: luxury Thai spa and herbal compress treatment. **RIGHT:** Thai *lakhon* dancer in traditional costume.

BEST CULTURAL DINING

- **Loy Nava**. Take a wooden barge dinner cruise along the Chao Phraya river, with Thai dancing and traditional music on board. *See page 253.*
- **Studio 9**. Thai contemporary theatre at its best, presented by thespian Patravadi Medchudhon. Dinner shows take place on Friday and Saturday nights with drama, puppetry and music. *See page 249.*
- **Sala Rim Nam**. At the Oriental's riverside restaurant, sit around low tables on cushions and feast on Thai food while watching a condensed history of Thai dance and drama. *See page 249.*
- **Siam Niramit**. A visual spectacle that presents Thailand's rich history and culture in three acts. Pre-show dinner buffet is optional. *See page 249.*

MONEY-SAVING TIPS

Bargaining for Best Deals While department stores have fixed prices, it's common to bargain at markets and at some small shops. If a shopowner offers to give the "best price", then negotiations are thrown open *(see text box on page 73)*. Remember to keep a sense of humour while bargaining.

Counterfeit Goods Even the most morally upright go weak in the knees when faced with the onslaught of quality knock-offs at Bangkok's markets, from watches and bags to clothing. If you succumb, remember: you get what you pay for *(see text box on page 74)*.

Hit the Happy Hour Afternoon and early evening drinking isn't part of the Bangkok scene, so to draw customers many bars offer incredible happy hour deals – like cheap drinks from noon till 9pm or two-drinks-for-one promotions.

Keep Your Ticket Hold onto your Grand Palace/Wat Phra Kaew entry ticket as it also gets you into most of the Dusit Park sites (like Vimanmek Mansion and Abhisek Dusit Throne Hall, to name a few) for free.

No Invite, No Matter Check the daily newspapers and monthly listings magazines for upcoming social events, art openings and promo parties. The city's freeloaders always turn up for free buffets, drinks and entertainment. It's a great way to rub shoulders with the city's elite and fill up for free.

VAT Refunds Before making significant purchases, ask if the shop offers VAT refunds (7 percent) to tourists. Refunds *(see page 262)* can be claimed on single items of B2,000 or more, as long as your overall shopping exceeds B5,000. Allow time at the airport to process claims.

CENTER

WHITE HOT BANGKOK

Still sprawling and steamy hot, Bangkok is reinventing itself for the 21st century. The Asian Tiger economy brought unimagined riches and booming construction but, in old markets and golden temples, glimmers of history poke tantalisingly from behind the modern malls

Bangkok hurtles into the 21st century at time-travel pace; a city where it sometimes feels you can live 200 years in a single day. Downtown, booming construction leaves pockets of tradition concealed in its wake. Glass-and-steel shopping malls glint in the sun, dwarfing the wooden trestles of next-door markets; kosher Gucci and fake Rolex just a stone's throw apart. Businessmen savour Fine de Claire oysters in posh restaurants outside which office girls giggle over spicy aromatic salads at a noisy street-side dinners. These days they increasingly travel by the underground Metro or elevated Skytrain, as, below, vendors weave their pedal carts between the lines of traffic, where the steamy heat envelopes you like a blanket.

There's a noticeable change of pace in Chinatown, with thrusting commerce in narrow lanes that haven't changed much since the early 19th century. In the Old City the golden spires of fairytale temples overlook 100-year-old shophouses where monks search for lucky amulets and Buddha statues down tiny alleyways. Walk ten minutes north and you're in the cosmopolitan backpacker warren of the Khao San Road, a pedestrian-friendly block of guesthouses, bars and clubs, where people make new friends before heading to the islands.

Thais live for *sanuk* (fun), and after sunset there's something for everyone: rice whisky at country music halls; designer cocktails at funky dance clubs; cheap beers in a bar with no walls; or flutes of champagne served up with 200-metre (656ft) -high rooftop views of the city.

Bangkok is modern Asia, its all-too-recent traditional life breathing strong inside a thrilling new adventure. ❑

PRECEDING PAGES: tuk-tuk; gleaming towers of Bangkok. **LEFT:** Thai boxing match at the MBK centre. **ABOVE LEFT:** door detail at the Phra Nakhon Khiri Historical Park, Phetchaburi. **ABOVE RIGHT:** blue and yellow taxis.

PEOPLE

The furious pace of growth has caused huge disparities between Bangkok's residents. Well-heeled "hi-sos" sip champagne in nightclubs, as northeastern migrants down rice whisky at boondock barns. Both, though, buy garlands from kids on the street. And binding all is a ubiquitous sense of fun

The Bangkokian appears in many guises. Sitting behind the darkened windows of a chauffeur-driven Mercedes is the high-society lady on her way to a VIP gala function. Hurrying up the steps of the Skytrain station is the young and smartly dressed office manager, late for a meeting. Slicing up a watermelon on his cart in front of a towering office block is the fruit vendor busy with the lunchtime crowds. Bangkok is a city of contrasts – between wealth and poverty, east and west, the old and the new. The city's inhabitants dwell on all sides of these delineations, with many creatively straddling more than one divide.

City on the move

Bangkok is forever shifting, always adapting to Western trends and outside influences. The cityscape is in a constant state of renewal, with old wooden buildings frequently demolished to make way for modern office and shopping complexes. For the most part, Bangkokians are creatures of this environment, enthusiastically embracing all things new. Trends spread through the city like wildfire, from the craze for fitness gyms to Starbucks copy-cat cafés. Clubs and restaurants open and close at a bewildering rate as they fall in and out of fashion.

Though the capital's official population hovers around 6 million, the large number of migrant workers bring most estimates closer to 12 million. Bangkok's biggest growth spurt has taken place during the economic boom years

LEFT: four generations of a Thai family. **RIGHT:** passing the time in a Bangkok café.

COOL HEARTS

The essential ingredient to surviving the stresses of daily life in the hot and humid streets of Bangkok is the Thai concept of *jai yen* (literally, "cool heart"). *Jai yen* is about taking obstacles in your stride. It is the antithesis of out-of-control tempers and sudden anger. This very Thai concept ensures that an oasis of calm exists inside every Bangkokian; differences of opinion rarely escalate to fistfights, and misunderstandings are countered with a smile. The accompanying phrase that answers to all of life's vicissitudes is *mai pen rai*, or "never mind". Make use of both these concepts and Bangkok will seem a little less difficult.

A Nation Divided

Thailand has been torn by the political crisis surrounding former Prime Minister Thaksin Shinawatra. Thaksin is roundly regarded as a self-serving politician who changed laws to further his business interests. But this is far from unusual in Thailand, and he also introduced policies such as affordable health care that made real changes to poor people's lives. They elected him with a huge majority. When the army overthrew Thaksin in 2006 his supporters saw it as the Bangkok hierarchy forcibly removing "their" national leader.

In the years following the coup the anti-Thaksin Yellow Shirts and pro-Thaksin Red Shirts infiltrated every aspect of daily life. Hundreds of thousands marched on both sides; people defined themselves as "red shirt" or "yellow shirt", dividing offices and homes; Thais discussed politics like never before.

Grass-roots movements, previously a mess of disparate causes, have united behind the Red Shirts, who by February 2010 consisted of 459 affiliated organisations from around the country. The media claimed the coup instigators were "the traditional ruling elite". The cost for them of removing Thaksin could be a long-term change in the political landscape. As one Red Shirt leader said about the coup makers: "They have turned Thaksin the big capitalist into Thaksin the revolutionary."

from the 1980s, during which the Bangkok dream has become a reality for many. As glass-and-chrome condos rise into the sky, Western fast-food outlets take over the streets, along with glitzy nightclubs and swanky restaurants.

This perennial change is oiled by the generally accepting Thai nature *(see Cool Hearts, page 19)* and the Buddhist concept of non-attachment. Historically, rather than resisting outside influences, Thailand has always welcomed them, and traditionally chooses compromise over conflict. Which is why the ongoing, sometimes violent, political struggle of recent years has taken many by surprise *(see above)*. While there are those who deride Bangkok as not representing the "real" Thailand, the city stubbornly retains a sense of Thai-ness. Beneath the yellow arches of McDonald's you'll find women threading fragrant jasmine garlands and next to every modern skyscraper is an old shrine where the spirits of the land are still appeased each day.

Sanuk means fun

The city is infused with the Bangkokian's search for *sanuk*, a Thai word meaning fun. The quantity and quality of *sanuk*, whether in work or play, determines if something is worth pursuing. Checking out anything new – the latest movie, a recently opened restaurant or shopping mall – is a sure-fire *sanuk* activity. Gatherings of friends

The concept of sanuk *(fun) is always close to the surface in Bangkok. Thais seemingly never crave solitude, preferring to gather in groups for drinks and laughter-filled meals of shared food.*

always have high *sanuk* value, whether it's an evening beneath the gaudy chandeliers of a karaoke club, or huddled around a tin table on the pavement quaffing whisky.

Doing anything alone is generally considered *mai sanuk* (not fun). Thailand's culture and society have traditionally been centred on agriculture, an activity that nurtures a sense of community. The shift to urban life has changed much of the countryside's ways, but it is a rare Thai who does not enjoy getting together with friends. Most are puzzled by Westerners who dine or holiday alone, as they do not understand the occasional need for solitude. The *sanuk* quota of any given event can usually be gauged by the number of people involved: the general rule being "the more, the merrier". A Bangkokian's mobile phone is never silent for long.

FAR LEFT: Buddhism is a way of life for many Thais.
LEFT: the traditional Thai greeting known as the *wai*.
ABOVE: a game of *takraw*, or kick volleyball.

Hi-So and Lo-So

Bangkok society is fiercely hierarchical. At the top of the pyramid are the "hi-so", a Thai slang abbreviation for high society. The phrase and its counterpart, "lo-so" (for low society), are used to boost or deride a person's standing: "She's *very* hi-so", or, "Oh no, he's too lo-so". The city's hi-so tribe is not limited only to aristocratic Thai families; the economic boom has created a significant *nouveau riche* class; being hi-so is as much about glamour and wealth as it is about pedigree. The hi-so are pictured in the society pages of newspapers and magazines (like the English-language *Thailand Tatler*), with the women sporting big hair and big jewels. Hi-so life is a seemingly endless whirl of lunches, cocktail parties and shopping.

Many members of the hi-so are Sino-Thai. The Chinese knack for entrepreneurial know-how has ensured that Sino-Thai families control much of Bangkok's wealth. Chinese traders have lived in the Bangkok area since the 18th

century, and have been assimilated, to a remarkable degree, into the life of their adopted land. Chinese and Thais have intermarried freely and there is no outward anti-Chinese bias in Thailand, and racial conflicts like those found in neighbouring countries have been very rare. While some estimates state that a quarter of Bangkok's population is Chinese, it is now hard to differentiate between Chinese and Thais as most second and third generation immigrants are Thai citizens and no longer speak Chinese.

All over the city are billboards advertising the *moo bahn*, or housing estates, that litter the outskirts of Bangkok. Depicting Western-style houses complete with two children and a dog playing in the garden, they appeal to Bangkok's burgeoning middle-classes. Residing on cheaper land at the city's edge, though, means a long daily commute to work.

Mixed races and migrants

A Bangkok phenomenon of recent years is the rise of the *luk kreung*, literally "half child". *Luk kreung* are mixed-race children, mostly with one Thai and one Caucasian parent. The *luk kreung* "look" is astoundingly popular with Bangkokians and many Bangkok celebrities are *luk kreung* TV presenters, pop stars, soap opera actors and actresses, or models. The *luk kreung* epitomises Bangkok's hybrid culture: Thai, but also a little bit Western. It is a blend that infuses everything from the mix-and-match style of pop music to the city's creative takes on fusion cuisine.

Of other minorities in the city, Indians make up the second largest group after the Chinese. There are around a million Muslim Thai-Malays who are fairly well integrated into Thai society, despite the many killings on both sides

in the last decade of separatist unrest in the Muslim provinces of the Deep South. There are also significant groups of expatriates living in Bangkok, working mostly for international companies. Among them are some 25,000 Westerners, known as *farang* or foreigner in Thai, and around 50,000 Japanese, whose "Little Tokyo" is centred around Sukhumvit Soi 33/1.

Less integrated with Bangkok society are the illegal immigrants fleeing poverty in Cambodia and Burma (Myanmar). They provide the city with low-cost labour and are forced into the jobs no one else wants: on construction sites, refuse collection and in factories and brothels. Of the estimated one million migrant workers in Thailand, 800,000 are from Burma.

> *The admirably named radio station "Let's Get Together and Help People" was established to do just that. People phone in with problems and the listeners rally round to help them.*

Rising above and beyond all these social divisions is the king and the Thai royal family. Even to cultured urbanites, His Majesty King Bhumibol *(see page 45)* is still the much-loved and revered figurehead of the nation. Portraits of the king and queen hang in almost every office, shop and restaurant. At cinemas, the audience stands while the national anthem is played before each film. In many ways, the king acts as a moral arbiter for all Bangkokians; while the city races helter-skelter towards all that is new, the monarch stands as a symbol of Thai tradition and old-world values.

Asian influence

Thailand, like many other countries, in the past looked to the dominant West for direction in fashion, music and film. But the last decade has seen a shift as the internet generation, many educated abroad, have found a new confidence in Thai and Asian styling, particularly in clothes fashions and interiors. Foreign influences in music and youth trends are as likely to be Japanese or Korean as Western, and bands from both these countries (J-Pop and K-Pop) have huge numbers of fans. Japanese manga comics, meanwhile, are the biggest read for teenagers; Thai-language Japanese TV series are on the rise; and magazines carry stories on sushi and tea drinking ceremonies. In 2008, the Ministry of Culture ordered the seizing of Japanese comics about gay male relationships that had become a fad with young readers calling themselves "Y-Girls". The Y-Girls, in their own version of fan fiction, liked posting clips of their favourite pop stars on YouTube and imagining them as gay couples.

Bangkok as a village

The most neglected Bangkokians are the poor, hundreds of thousands of whom live in inner-city slums. The largest, at Klong Toey, has been bought for huge sums, causing armed pitched battles from 2009 between developers and resi-

LEFT TOP: spectacular views from the Vertigo Grill – popular with the hi-so. **LEFT BOTTOM:** taxi driver. **ABOVE:** teashop in Chinatown. **RIGHT:** girls at a Japanese-style costume role-play in Bangkok.

dents, who do not want to leave. Slum life is fuelled by *yaa baa* (the Thai word for amphetamines, meaning, literally, "crazy medicine") and desperation forces many people into crime and prostitution. Many are migrants escaping rural poverty in Isaan, northeastern Thailand, where a tenant farmer may earn as little as B30,000 a year. Though the Bangkok dream has yet to filter into their lives, the city would surely collapse without them. Manpower from the northeast provides the city with a crucial task force of taxi and tuk-tuk drivers, construction workers, cleaners and security guards. Many find work in the streets as roving vendors or rubbish-collectors.

Living away from the air-conditioned world of shopping malls and nightclubs, these rural migrants bring a touch of the village to the capital. The outskirts of the city especially have many barn-like halls where bands play regional music like *morlam* to hundreds of Isaanites fuelled by rice whisky.

Despite its wide variety of residents, Bangkok retains many of the traditional communal elements of Thai village life. Proof comes in the form of one of the most popular radio stations, Ruam Duay Chuay Kan, or "Let's Get Together and Help Each Other". The radio station is broadcast live, 24-hours-a-day, and its concept is simple: a person calls in with a problem and the presenters muster all the forces of good in the city to solve it. Bureaucratic tangles are untied, lost relatives are reunited and even Bangkok's steaming gridlock can be moved when drivers hear that a screaming woman in labour is trying to get to hospital. The radio show emphasises the familiar sense of community inherent in village life. Through it, Bangkokians can share practical advice, help out in times of trouble and, of course, stick their noses into other people's businesses. Most of all, though, the station is proof that the big bad city has a heart of gold. ❑

Sin City Bangkok

Bangkok has a complex historical relationship with its sex workers: the trade is both illegal and openly tolerated, a source of shame to some, and of income to others

Thailand made prostitution illegal in 1960, although the law is rarely enforced, and sex is openly for sale in the capital's many girlie bars, brothels and massage parlours. In part this is because it is an accepted and common practice for Thai men to patronise prostitutes or have a *mia noi*, literally "little wife" or mistress on the side. They will usually patronise more discreet brothels or, at the higher end, plush members-only clubs, while foreign tourists go for the brash red lights of Patpong and Nana Entertainment Plaza *(see pages 171 and 176)*.

Sex tourism escalated with American troops taking R&R during the Vietnam War, and, by the 1980s, planeloads of men were flying in for the purpose. Most Bangkok sex workers, both male and female, come from northeast Thailand, where incomes are the lowest in the country. They regularly send money home to support their families. Many cross-cultural marriages have started in a Bangkok brothel, and government figures often cite foreign husbands in northeastern villages as being significant contributors to GDP.

NGOs estimate there are between 200,000 and 300,000 sex workers in Thailand, and, having found that few are motivated to leave the business, no longer focus their primary efforts on extricating them. Organisations such as Empower instead educate bar girls and boys about the dangers of HIV, and teach them English so they are less likely to be exploited by their clients.

The non-voluntary side of the sex trade is infinitely more grim. There are an estimated 60,000 child prostitutes in Thailand, many willingly sold by their parents, against whom convictions are very rare. Young women and girls are also trafficked from neighbouring Laos, Burma and Cambodia. Lured by promises of factory jobs or waitress work, they unwittingly sell themselves into lock-up brothels, where they must work until they have earned back the price the brothel-owner paid for them. Thailand is also an established transit point for trafficking to other countries.

The highly visible nature of sex work in Thailand is at odds with the otherwise high moral code of behaviour in the country. Women especially are expected to deport themselves modestly, and the Ministry of Culture (much to the outrage of many) is constantly making edicts about appropriate behaviour and dress. (Websites that criticise the ministry have been closed down, although at the time of writing a Facebook page, "We're sick of Ministry of Culture in Thailand" (sic), was still running.) The discrepancy between the requirement for modesty and the prominent profile of sex work is often attributed to the Thais' general high tolerance for other lifestyles. ❑

LEFT TOP AND BOTTOM: children in the Klong Toey slum area. **ABOVE:** bartop dancers in Patpong.

Decisive Dates

Pre-Thai Civilisation

3600–250 BC
Ban Chiang culture flourishes in northeastern Thailand.

4th–8th centuries AD
Influence of Mon and Khmer empires spreads into Thailand.

9th–13th centuries
The Khmer empire is founded in Angkor. Thai people migrate south from Yunnan Province in China into northern Thailand.

The Sukhothai Era

1238
Khmer power wanes. Kingdom of Sukhothai founded by King Intradit.

1277–1318
Reign of Ramkamhaeng, often called Thailand's "Golden Age", with flourishing arts and the first use of Thai script.

1296
Lanna kingdom founded at Chiang Mai. King Mengrai eventually controls much of northern Thailand and Laos.

The Kingdom of Ayutthaya

1350
Phya U-Thong founds the kingdom of Ayutthaya, proclaims himself Ramathibodi I, and soon rules areas belonging to Sukhothai and the Khmer empire.

1390
Ramathibodi's son King Ramesuen captures Chang Mai.

1393
Ramesuen seizes Angkor, base of the Khmer empire, in Cambodia.

1448–88
Reign of King Trailok, who finally unites the Lanna (Chiang Mai) and Ayutthaya kingdoms.

1569
Burmese seize Ayutthaya.

1584
Naresuen declares the independence of Siam.

1590
Naresuen becomes king and defeats Burmese. Ayutthaya expands rapidly at the expense of Burmese and Khmer empires.

1605–10
King Ekatotsarot develops significant economic ties with Europeans.

1610–28
Reign of King Songtham. British arrive and obtain land for a trading factory.

1628–55
Reign of Prasat Thong. Trading concessions expand and regular trade with China and Europe is established.

1656–88
Reign of King Narai. British influence expands. The reputation of Ayutthaya as a magnificent city and a remarkable royal court spreads in Europe.

1678
Constantine Phaulkon arrives at Narai's court and gains great influence; French presence expands.

1688
Narai dies and Phaulkon is executed.

1733–58
Reign of King Boromakot. Ayutthaya enters a period of peace; the arts and literature flourish.

1767
Burmese King Alaungpaya captures and sacks Ayutthaya, destroying four centuries of Thai civilisation.

LEFT TOP: a French map of Siam (old Thailand), dating from 1686. LEFT BOTTOM: King Narai, ruler of Ayutthaya, 1656–88. RIGHT: 17th-century lacquer painting depicting delegates of Louis XIV in the Kingdom of Siam.

Seven months later General Phya Taksin returns, expels the Burmese and moves the capital from Ayutthaya to Thonburi, near Bangkok.

BEGINNING OF CHAKRI DYNASTY

1767
Phya Taksin crowned as King Taksin.

1779
Generals Chao Phya Chakri and Chao Phya Surasi conquer Chiang Mai, expel the Burmese from what is now Thailand and take control of most of the Khmer and Lao kingdoms. The statue of the Emerald Buddha is brought from Vientiane in Laos, to Thonburi.

1782
Taksin is deposed, and Chao Phya Chakri is offered the throne, founding the Chakri dynasty and assuming the name Ramathibodi (later Rama I). Capital is moved across the river to Bangkok. Under Rama I, Siam consolidates and expands its strength. Rama I revives Thai art, religion and culture. Work begins on the Grand Palace and Wat Phra Kaew in Bangkok.

1809–24
Reign of Rama II, known as the poet king. His famous Boat Songs were often odes to his favourite foods. The king reopens relations with the West, which had been suspended since the time of King Narai.

1824–51
Reign of Rama III, who continues open-door policy

with foreigners. Encourages American missionaries to introduce Western medicine to Siam.

1851
King Mongkut (Rama IV) ascends the throne. He is the first Thai king to understand Western culture and technology.

1868
Chulalongkorn (Rama V) ascends the throne, reigning for the next four decades. Schools, infrastructure, military and government modernised. Slavery is abolished.

1910–25
Reign of Vajiravudh (Rama VI), an Oxford-educated and Westernised ruler, who made Thai people adopt surnames.

1925–35
Reign of Prajadhipok (Rama VII). Economic pressures from the Great Depression rouse discontent among Thais.

Modern Thailand

1932
A coup ends the absolute monarchy and ushers in a constitutional monarchy.

1939
Siam's name is officially changed to Thailand, "Land of the Free".

1941
Japan invades Thailand with the acquiescence of the military government.

1946
King Ananda (Rama VIII) is killed by gunman; Bhumibol Adulyadej (Rama IX) ascends the throne.

1973–91
Bloody clashes between the army and students bring down the military government; political and economic blunders bring down the subsequent civilian government three years later. Various military-backed and civilian governments come and go for the next 20 years.

1992
Another clash between military forces and civilian demonstrators results in the military leaving government to civilian politicians. Thailand begins five years of unprecedented economic growth.

1996
King Bhumibol celebrates his golden jubilee of 50 years on the throne.

1997
Thailand's economy crashes. Start of the Asian economic crisis.

2001
Populist leader Thaksin Shinawatra is elected prime minister.

2004
Tsunami hits southern Thailand and causes widespread devastation.

2005
Thaksin is elected for a second term as prime minister in February.

2006
Mass Bangkok demonstrations after Thaksin sells a company and pays no tax. The protestors unite under the People's Alliance for Democracy (PAD) banner. In September, a bloodless coup removes Thaksin, who remains in exile. Retired general Surayud Chulanont appointed interim premier.

2007
Thaksin is banned from politics. His followers, the United Front for Democracy Against Dictatorship (UDD), launch protests. A Thaksin proxy, the People Power Party (PPP), wins the December election.

2008
The PAD occupies Government House and seizes the airport. In December, the courts disband the ruling party. The Democrat Party leader Abhisit Vejjajiva becomes prime minister.

2009
In April, UDD protests disrupt the ASEAN Summit in Pattaya, causing several heads of state to be airlifted to safety; Songkran riots erupt in Bangkok; PAD leader Sondhi Limthongkul is shot, but survives.

2010
In February the courts find Thaksin guilty of abuse of power and confiscate assets of B46 billion. April and May see thousands of Red Shirt demonstrators occupy various parts of the city, closing parliament for days and Pathumwan shopping malls for several weeks. Eighty-five people are killed and nearly 1,500 injured in clashes with the army on 10 April and 19 May, while banks, department stores and other major buildings are torched in the battles. Thaksin, still abroad, is charged with terrorism.

FAR LEFT TOP: General Suchinda Kraprayon, leader of the 1991 military coup. FAR LEFT BOTTOM: Chulalongkorn (Rama V) and his wife. ABOVE: anti-government Red Shirt protester. LEFT TOP: tsunami warning sign. LEFT BOTTOM: PAD protesters at the airport in 2008 celebrate the news that the ruling party has been disbanded.

A CITY OF ANGELS

Whatever you call it – Bangkok, The Big Mango, Krung Thep or the City of Angels – this thriving metropolis dominates Thailand. It has been transformed from a sleepy riverside village where wild plum trees grew to a cosmopolitan community more than 30 times larger than any other city in the kingdom

Bangkok's history as a town began in the 16th century when a short canal was dug across a loop of the Chao Phraya river to cut the distance between the sea and the Siamese capital at Ayutthaya. Over the years, monsoon floods scoured the banks of the canal until it widened to become the main course of the river. On its banks rose two towns – originally trading posts along the river route to Ayutthaya, 85km (55 miles) north – Thonburi on the west and, on the east, Bangkok. At the time, Bangkok was little more than a village *(bang)* in an orchard of wild plum trees *(kok)*. Hence, the town's name, Bangkok, which translates as "village of the wild plum".

Ayutthaya prospered as the capital of Siam (the name of old Thailand) for more than four centuries, but in 1767 it was captured by the Burmese after a 14-month siege. The Burmese killed, looted and set fire to the whole city, plundering Ayutthaya's many rich temples and melting down all the gold from images of the Buddha. Members of the royal family, along with some 90,000 captives and the accumulated booty, were removed to Burma.

Despite their overwhelming victory, the Burmese didn't retain control of Siam for long. A young general named Phya Taksin gathered a small band of followers during the final Burmese siege of the Thai capital. He and his comrades broke through the Burmese encirclement and escaped to the southeast coast. There, Taksin assembled an army and a navy. Only seven

LEFT: mural of the Grand Palace in Bangkok. **RIGHT:** European impression of 17th-century Ayutthaya.

THE LONGEST PLACE NAME EVER

In 1782, King Rama I decided the name Bangkok was insufficiently noble for a royal city so he renamed it *Krungthep mahanakhon amonrattanakosin mahintra ayutthaya mahadilok popnopparat ratchathani burirom udomratchaniwet mahasathan amonpiman avatansathit sakkathattiya visnukamprasit.* In English this means: "Great City of Angels, City of Immortals, Magnificent Jewelled City of the God Indra, Seat of the King of Ayutthaya, City of Gleaming Temples, City of the King's Most Excellent Palace and Dominions, Home of Vishnu and All the Gods". Most Thais, however, refer to Bangkok by just two syllables, Krung Thep, or "City of Angels", in everyday speech.

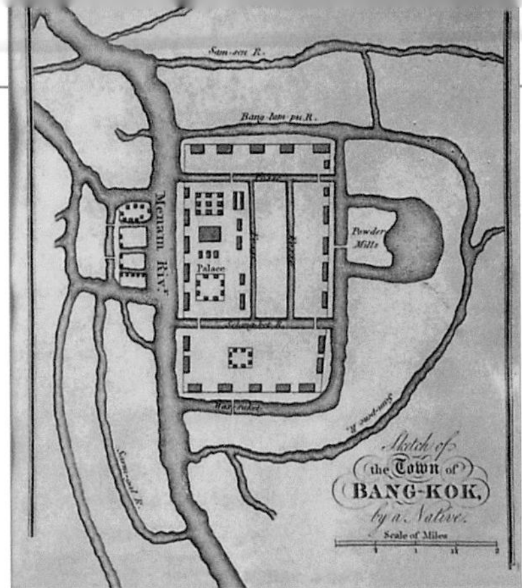

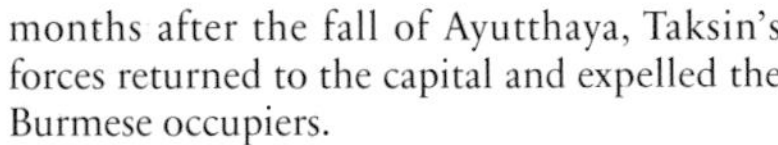

months after the fall of Ayutthaya, Taksin's forces returned to the capital and expelled the Burmese occupiers.

Move to Thonburi

Taksin had barely spent a night at Ayutthaya when he decided to transfer the site of his capital to Thonburi. Here he ruled until 1782. In the last years of his reign, he relied heavily on two trusted generals, the brothers Chao Phya Chakri and Chao Phya Surasi, who were given absolute command in their military campaigns. Meanwhile at Thonburi, Taksin's personality underwent a slow metamorphosis, from strong and just to cruel and unpredictable. When a revolt broke out in 1782, Taksin abdicated and entered a monastery, but was executed shortly thereafter.

Start of the Chakri Dynasty

The official who engineered the revolt offered the throne to Chao Phya Chakri on his return from Cambodia. General Chakri assumed the kingship on 6 April – a date still commemorated as Chakri Day – thereby establishing the still reigning Chakri dynasty. On assuming the throne, Chakri took the name of Ramathibodi. Later known as Rama I, he ruled from 1782 until 1809. His first action as king was to transfer his capital from Thonburi to Bangkok.

Rama I was an ambitious man eager to re-establish the Thai kingdom as a dominant civili-

sation. He ordered the digging of a canal across a neck of land on the Bangkok side, creating an island and an inner city. Rama I envisioned this artificial island as the core of his new capital. Within its rim, he would concentrate the principal components of the Thai nation: religion, monarchy and administration. To underscore his recognition of the power of the country's principal Buddha image, he called this island Rattanakosin *(see pages 101–17)* or the "Resting Place of the Emerald Buddha".

> *After his abdication Taksin was executed in the traditional royal manner – with a blow to the neck by a sandalwood club concealed within a velvet bag.*

To dedicate the area solely to statecraft and religion, he formally requested that the Chinese living there move to an area to the southeast. This new district, Sampeng *(see pages 145–50)*, soon sprouted thriving shops and busy streets, becoming the commercial heart of the city in what is now known as Chinatown.

Rama I then turned his attention to constructing the royal island's principal buildings. First was a home for the Emerald Buddha, the most sacred image in the realm, which, until then, had been resting in a temple in Thonburi. Two years later, in 1784, Wat Phra Kaew was completed. A palace was next on his agenda; the Grand Palace was more than a home, it contained buildings for receiving royal visitors and debating matters of state. The last building to be constructed, the Chakri Maha Prasat, was not erected until late in the 19th century. Until 1946, the Grand Palace was home to Thailand's kings. The palace grounds also contain Wat Pho, the National Museum, prestigious Thammasat University, the National Theatre, and various government offices.

Rama II and Rama III

Rama I's successors, Rama II and Rama III, completed both the consolidation of the Siamese kingdom and the revival of Ayutthaya's arts and culture. If Rama I laid the foundations of Bangkok, it was Rama II who instilled it with the spirit of the past. Best remembered as an artist, Rama II (ruled 1809–24), the second ruler of the Chakri dynasty, was responsible for building numerous Bangkok temples and repairing others, most famously Wat Arun *(see page 122)*, the Temple of Dawn, which was later enlarged to its present height by Rama IV. He is also said to have carved the great doors of Wat Suthat, throwing away the chisels so his work could never be replicated.

Far Left Top: Bangkok canal in the late 19th century. **Left Top:** early map of Bangkok's waterways. **Left:** French Jesuit ambassadors arriving in the Kingdom of Siam in the 17th century. **Above:** artist's impression of King Mongkut (Rama IV). **Right:** King Mongkut (Rama IV) and his wife.

Rama II reopened relations with the West, which had been suspended since the time of former King Narai, and allowed the Portuguese to open the first Western embassy in Bangkok.

Rama III (ruled 1824–51) continued to open Siam's doors to foreigners. A pious Buddhist, Rama III was considered to be "austere and reactionary" by some Europeans. But he encouraged American missionaries to introduce Western medicine, such as smallpox vaccinations, to Siam.

Mongkut (Rama IV)

With the help of Hollywood, Rama IV (ruled 1851–68) became the most famous king of Siam. More commonly known as King Mongkut, he was portrayed by Yul Brynner in *The King and I* as a frivolous, bald-headed despot – but nothing could have been further from the truth. He was the first Thai king to understand Western culture and technology, and his reign has been described as the bridge spanning the new and the old.

The younger brother of Rama III, King Mongkut spent 27 years as a Buddhist monk prior to his accession to the throne. This gave him a unique opportunity to roam as a commoner among the populace. He learned to read Buddhist scriptures in the Pali language; missionaries taught him Latin and English. As a monk, Mongkut delved into many subjects: history, geography and the sciences, but he had a particular passion for astronomy. Mongkut instituted a policy of modernisation, and England was the first European country to benefit from this, when an 1855 treaty granted extraterritorial privileges, a duty of only 3 percent on imports, and permission to import Indian opium duty-free. Other Western nations followed suit with similar treaties. When Mongkut lifted the state monopoly on rice, it rapidly became Siam's leading export.

In 1863, Mongkut built Bangkok's first paved road – Thanon Charoen Krung (Prosperous City) or, as it was known to foreigners, New Road. This 6km (4-mile) -long street, running from the Grand Palace southeast along the river, was lined with shops and houses. He also introduced new technology to encourage commerce. The foreign community moved into the areas opened by the construction of New Road. They

Bangkok's Pig Shrine

Close by Wat Ratchabophit in downtown Bangkok is an unusual shrine in the likeness of a golden pig. It is dedicated to the chief consort of King Chulalongkorn, Queen Saowapha (1864–1919), who was born in the Chinese zodiacal Year of the Pig. The "pig shrine" is also an early monument to the women's movement in Thailand. In 1897, Queen Saowapha founded a college of midwifery in Bangkok. She also founded the Thai Red Cross Society, and built schools for girls in Bangkok and in the provinces. Her court was recognised as a centre for fine arts; young girls attached to the Siamese court attained the equivalent of a university education.

> *King Chulalongkorn, who was just 15 when he ascended the throne, went on to abolish slavery and completely modernise Thailand's institutions, improving both education and health care.*

built their homes in the area where the Mandarin Oriental Hotel now stands, and along Thanon Silom and Thanon Sathorn, both rural retreats at the time.

Chulalongkorn (Rama V)

Mongkut's son, Chulalongkorn (Rama V), was only 15 when he ascended the throne in 1868. The farsighted king immediately revolutionised his court by ending the ancient custom of prostration, and by allowing officials to sit on chairs during royal audiences. Chulalongkorn's reign was truly revolutionary. When he assumed power, Siam had an under-equipped military force, few roads, and no schools, railways or hospitals. He brought in foreign advisors and sent his sons and other young men to be educated abroad. He also founded a palace school for children of the aristocracy, following this with other schools and vocational centres. During his reign, Chulalongkorn abolished the last vestiges of slavery and, in 1884, introduced electric lighting. He hired Danish engineers to build an electric tram system 10 years before the one in Copenhagen was completed, and encouraged the import of automobiles about the same time they began appearing on American streets.

Left Top: Chulalongkorn (Rama V) poses with the Crown Prince and other young students. **Left Bottom:** Chulalongkorn with his son Vajiravudh. **Above:** procession of royal barges along the Chao Phraya River at Prajadhipok's (Rama VII) 1925 coronation.

Chulalongkorn changed the face of Bangkok. By 1900, the city was growing rapidly eastward. In the Dusit area, he built a palace, the Vimanmek Mansion *(see page 141)* and constructed roads to link it with the Grand Palace. Other noble families followed, building elegant mansions. In the same area, he constructed Wat Benjamabophit *(see page 143)*, the last major Buddhist temple built in Bangkok.

In the area of foreign relations, however, Chulalongkorn had to compromise and give

up parts of his kingdom in order to protect Siam from foreign colonisation. When France conquered Annam in 1883 and Britain annexed Upper Burma in 1886, Siam found itself sandwiched between two rival expansionist powers. Siam was forced to surrender to France its claims to Laos and western Cambodia. Similarly, certain Malay Peninsula territories were ceded to Britain in exchange for renunciation of British extraterritorial rights in Siam. By the end of Chulalongkorn's reign, Siam had given up sizeable tracts of fringe territory. But that was a small price for maintaining the country's peace and independence. Unlike its neighbours, Siam has never been under colonial rule.

Vajiravudh (Rama VI)

King Chulalongkorn's successor, his son Vajiravudh, started his reign (1910–25) with a lavish coronation. He was educated at Oxford and was thoroughly anglicised, and his Western-inspired reforms aimed at modernising Siam had a profound effect on modern Thai society.

One of the first changes that Vajiravudh instituted was a 1913 edict which demanded that his subjects adopt surnames. In the absence of a clan or caste system, genealogy was virtually unheard of in Siam at that time. Previously, Thais had used first names, a practice that the king considered uncivilised. The law generated much initial bewilderment, especially in rural areas, and Vajiravudh personally coined patronymics for hundreds of families. To simplify his forebears' lengthy titles, he invented the Chakri dynastic name, Rama, to be followed by the proper reign number. He started with himself, as Rama VI.

To bring Thai ideals of femininity into line with Western fashions, women were encour-

From Siam to Thailand

The man partly responsible for the end of Thailand's centuries-old absolute monarchy, Luang Phibulsongkhram, or Pibul, tried to instil a sense of mass nationalism in the Thais when he was elected PM in 1938. With tight control over the media and a creative propaganda department, Pibul whipped up sentiment against the Chinese. Chinese immigration was restricted, Chinese workers were barred from certain jobs, and state enterprises were set up to compete in Chinese-dominated industries. By changing the country's name from Siam to Thailand in 1939, Pibul intended to emphasise that it belonged to Thai ethnic groups and not to the Chinese.

aged to grow their hair long instead of having it close-cropped, and to replace their *dhoti*, or wide-legged Thai trousers, with the *panung*, a Thai-style sarong. Primary education was made compulsory throughout the kingdom; Chulalongkorn University, the first in Siam, was founded, and schools for both sexes flourished during Vajiravudh's reign.

Vajiravudh preferred individual ministerial consultations to summoning his appointed cabinet. His regime was therefore criticised as autocratic and lacking in coordination. His extravagance soon emptied the funds built up by Chulalongkorn; near the end of Vajiravudh's reign, the national treasury had to meet the deficits caused by his personal expenses.

The king married late. His only daughter was born one day before he died in 1925. He was succeeded by his youngest brother, Prajadhipok, who inherited the problems created by the brilliant but controversial former ruler.

Prajadhipok (Rama VII)

Prajadhipok's prudent economic policies, combined with the increased revenue from foreign trade, amply paid off for the kingdom. In the early years of his reign, communications were improved by the advent of a wireless service, and Don Muang Airport began to operate as an international air centre. It was also during the course of his reign that Siam saw the establishment of the Fine Arts Department, the National Library and the National Museum, institutions that continue today as important preservers of Thai culture.

The worldwide economic crisis of 1931 affected Siam's rice export and the government was forced to cut the salaries of junior personnel, and retrench officers in the armed services. Discontent brewed among army officials and bureaucrats. In 1932, a coup d'état ended absolute rule by Thai monarchs. The coup was staged by the People's Party, a military and civilian group masterminded by foreign-educated Thais. The chief ideologist was Pridi Banomyong, a young lawyer trained in France, who is now often cited as "The Father of Thai Democracy". On the military side, Capt. Luang Phibulsongkhram (Pibul) was responsible for gaining the support of important army colonels.

With only a few tanks, the 70 conspirators sparked off the "revolution" by occupying strategic areas and holding the senior princes hostage. Other army officers stood by as the public watched. At the time, Prajadhipok was in Hua Hin, a royal retreat to the south. Perceiving he had little choice and to avoid bloodshed, he agreed to accept a provisional constitution by which he continued to reign.

The power of Pibul and the army was further strengthened in October 1933 by the decisive defeat of a rebellion led by Prince Boworadet, who had been the war minister under King Pra-

Left: 1947 coronation of King Bhumibol Adulyadej. **Above:** Vajiravudh (Rama VI). **Right:** Thai school children in the late 1940s.

jadhipok. The king had no part in the rebellion, but had become increasingly dismayed by quarrels within the new government. He moved to England in 1934 and abdicated in 1935. Ananda Mahidol (Rama VIII), a 10-year-old half-nephew, agreed to take the throne, but remained in Switzerland to complete his schooling.

After a series of crises and an election in 1938, Pibul became prime minister. His rule, however, grew more authoritarian. While some Thai officers favoured the model of the Japanese military regime, Pibul admired – and sought to emulate – Hitler and Mussolini. Borrowing many ideas from European fascism, he attempted to instil a sense of mass nationalism in the Thais *(see text box, page 36)*.

Post World War II

On 7 December 1941, the Japanese bombed Pearl Harbor and launched invasions throughout Southeast Asia. Thailand was invaded at nine points. Despite a decade of military build-up, resistance lasted less than a day. Pibul acceded to Japan's request for "passage rights", signed a treaty with Japan and declared war on the Allies. Thailand's ambassador in the US, MR Seni Pramoj, famously collaborated with the Americans, who refused to accept the declaration of war. Seni formed a Free Thai movement. In Bangkok, Pridi Banomyong, who had been marginalised by Pibul due to his attempted reforms, which were perceived as Communist, established a local resistance movement, the Seri Thai.

By 1944, Thailand's initial enthusiasm for its Japanese partners had evaporated. The country faced runaway inflation, food shortages, rationing and black markets. The assembly forced Pibul out of office.

Pridi Banomyong's struggle for power with Pibul and later Seni Pramoj lasted several years, and he became prime minister in 1946. In the same year, while on a visit to Thailand from school in Europe, the now adult King Ananda was found shot dead in his palace bedroom. Of the many rumours and conspiracy theories surrounding this incident, one of the most significant claimed that Pridi was involved. He resigned and the following year fled to Singapore after his house was attacked during a military coup. After a failed armed rebellion against the Pibul government in 1949, Pridi left for China, and never returned. The protracted murder trial of King Ananda's alleged killers finally convicted and sentenced to death three palace aides for conspiracy, although a gunman was never formally identified. The circumstances of the king's death have still not been satisfactorily explained; the incident is still discussed and most people have their own theories.

> *When Thailand, then an ally of Japan, declared war on the US in 1942, the Americans refused to accept it, and a Thai resistance movement, the Seri Thai, was formed.*

King Ananda was succeeded by his younger brother, Bhumibol Adulyadej (Rama IX), the present monarch *(see page 45)*, who returned to Switzerland to complete law studies. He did not, however, take up active duties until the 1950s. By then, Thailand had been without a resident king for 20 years.

In 1957, a clique of his one-time protégés overthrew Pibul. Their leader, General Sarit Thanarat, and two cohort generals, Thanom Kittikachorn and Prapas Charusathien, ran the government until 1973, employing martial law.

Left Top: King Prajadhipok in 1926. **Left Bottom:** Prajadhipok visits Berlin in 1934. **Above:** King Ananda Mahibol (Rama VIII) and Louis Mountbatten, the Allied Supreme Commander in South East Asia. **Right:** billboard, *c.*1950.

Traffic Woes

The 1980s and '90s saw the vertical growth of Bangkok. Its skyline changed dramatically but along with it came congested roads and notorious traffic jams. In the early 1980s, various government officials suggested solutions to ease Bangkok's traffic problem. Eventually the ideas evaporated, mired in corruption or woefully poor cooperation between competing agencies – only to be recycled a year or two later. Thankfully, the situation has improved vastly with the construction of a complex network of elevated expressways. To ease traffic further, in 1999, Bangkok's first mass transit system, the Skytrain, started operations, and in 2004 a metro line opened.

The military, which had steadily been gaining power, reached its peak of influence during these years. The generals' ascendancy coincided with America's involvement in the Vietnam War. Large infusions of money flowed from the US to Thailand, America's staunchest ally, resulting in a burgeoning economy. Health standards improved; the business sector expanded; construction boomed; the population swelled in response to new jobs; and a middle class began to emerge. And the generals, now called "The Three Tyrants", used their power to amass huge personal fortunes. But the socio-economic changes also brought new aspirations to the population.

The October 1973 uprising

Following the arrest of student leaders for distributing anti-government leaflets, protests broke out around the country, including 400,000 people at Bangkok's Democracy Monument. Clashes on 14 October 1973 between troops and students left many students dead (the official figure was 77, press estimated 400). Under pressure from several influential factions, The Three Tyrants fled to the US.

Two subsequent elections produced civilian governments, but the fledgling democracy was hampered by the diverse interests of new political parties, labour unions and farming organisations. The middle class, originally strongly supportive of the student revolution, along with some of the upper class, came to fear that total chaos or a Communist takeover would emerge.

The 1976 return of General Thanom, ostensibly to become a monk, sparked more student protests. After two were garrotted, allegedly by police, students occupied Thammasat University. On 6 October, police, troops and paramilitary organisations stormed the grounds, raping

and killing many people. Within hours the army had seized power in a coup. Self-government had lasted but three years. Ironically, the civilian judge appointed to be prime minister, Thanin Kraivichien, turned out to be more brutal than any of his uniformed predecessors. Yet another military coup ousted Thanin in October 1977. For the next decade there was relatively moderate military rule, and under General Prem Tinsulanond the foundations were laid for new elections, which ushered in a civilian government.

Another military coup

After a bloodless military coup in 1991, spearheaded by General Suchinda Kraprayoon, the junta installed a businessman and ex-diplomat, Anand Panyacharun, as a caretaker premier until elections planned the following year. Anand earned plaudits for running the cleanest government in memory and is still a highly respected figure in Thai politics.

A political party newly formed by the junta won the most seats at the election, but General Suchinda unseated the intended prime minister and installed himself as leader. The middle classes protested, gathering at rallies, inspired by former Bangkok Governor Chamlong Srimuang, a figure who would have great impact on Thai politics into the new millennium. More than 70,000 people alone met at Sanam Luang on 17 May 1992. Late in the evening, soldiers fired on unarmed demonstrators. Killings, beatings, riots and arson attacks continued sporadically for the next three days. The Thai broadcast media, controlled by the government, were obliged to impose a news blackout, but owners of satellite dishes, along with viewers around the world, watched the coverage of "Bloody May". The crisis ended when King Bhumibol intervened. A little later, the unrepentant Suchinda bowed out and left the country. The Democrat Party and other prominent Suchinda critics prevailed in the September 1992 re-elections.

Democracy prevails

Prime Minister Chuan Leekpai, considered honest but ineffectual, persisted for almost three years from 1992 to 1995, a record for a civilian government. Setting another record, he was not toppled by a coup. But by the end, Chuan had lost much of the goodwill of the pro-democracy groups that had lifted him to power.

Chuan battled constantly to keep his coalition working together. It finally disintegrated when some members of Chuan's own party were implicated in a land-reform scandal. Elections in July 1995 brought an old-style politi-

Left Top: Field Marshal Thanom Kittikachorn at a news conference in 1971. **Left Bottom:** soldier occupying Thammasat University during the 1976 student protests. **Above and Right:** protesters march through the streets and are later forced to the ground when government troops open fire, in the "Bloody May" crisis of 1992.

cian, Banharn Silpa-archa, to the premiership. As the Thai press phrased it at the time, both Banharn and his party, Chart Thai, had a strong "reputation" for corruption.

Economic crisis

The Thai economy, which registered phenomenal annual growth rates for over a decade to emerge as one of the famous "Tiger" economies of Southeast Asia, suddenly saw the good times come to an end. By late 1996, inflationary pressures, a widening current account deficit and slower economic growth led to a censure motion against the 14-month-old government led by Banharn Silpa-archa. Elections held in November 1996 saw a coalition headed by the New Aspiration Party come to power. NAP leader Chavalit Yongchaiyudh became Thailand's 22nd prime minister, but many of his partners in government were the same as in the previous administration and little was done to stem the economic rot that had set in.

By February 1997, ratings agency Moody's had downgraded Thailand's credit rating. A few months later, the government ordered the closure of 16 finance companies that were in the red. The final straw came shortly afterwards, on 2 July, when the Chavalit administration decided to drop the traditional currency peg in favour of a "managed float". This had the disastrous double effect of sending the currency down in a devaluation spiral and making the foreign debts of local corporations skyrocket.

The pressure to float the baht was partly caused by aggressive attacks by foreign hedge funds; enormous sums from the country's foreign exchange reserves were spent in its defence. In the end, the government was forced to ask the IMF for US$17 billion to help keep the country afloat. The crisis saw businesses go bankrupt and many thousands lose their jobs, due to closures or downsizing.

Amid all this, changes to Thailand's constitution were promulgated on 11 October 1997 by the Chavalit government. It set up positive new measures for Thai democracy, including a bicameral legislature and independent bodies to monitor the government. The new document, however, was not enough to save the government, and Chavalit stepped down under intense public pressure in September 1998 as the country's economic gloom deepened.

This brought in a Democrat government headed by Prime Minister Chuan Leekpai. After over a year of hard work, the economy, which had bottomed out, began showing gradual signs of recovery. The process was helped along by a banking reform package in August 1998 that helped boost confidence in the country among foreign investors. The government also pushed forward business laws to help speed up corporate debt restructuring.

LEFT: leader of the New Aspiration Party, Chavalit Yongchaiyudh, who became Prime Minister in 1996. **ABOVE:** Prime Minister Chuan Leekpai casts his vote in the 1995 elections. **RIGHT:** street celebrations in honour of the King's 80th birthday.

The Thaksin administration

In 2001, general elections installed the populist billionaire entrepreneur Thaksin Shinawatra and his newly formed Thai Rak Thai (Thai Love Thai) party.

Thaksin's governance proved almost immediately controversial. He faced, and successfully defended, charges of corruption; he was widely condemned after hundreds were killed in his "War on Drugs"; and he was slammed for suppressing the media. But his leadership was a breath of air to many. His "populist" approach saw loans and cheap health care for the poor, and he brought a swagger and confidence to Thailand's self-perception on the world stage, famously dismissing international criticism on one occasion by declaring: "The UN is not my father". However, as he became wildly popular in poorer rural areas, particularly in the north and northeast, his "CEO style" of government was increasingly annoying traditional powers in the country, centred in Bangkok.

In 2005, an alliance of opposition interests formed, led by Chamlong Srimuang and former Thaksin supporter Sondhi Limthongkul. They united under the name the People's Alliance for Democracy (PAD), and began anti-Thaksin street demonstrations. They adopted the colour yellow to show allegiance to the monarchy. The movement intensified after Thaksin, already the richest man in Thailand, sold his telecommunications company to an arm of the Singapore government for US$1.9 billion and paid no tax.

Yet another coup

In response, Thaksin announced a snap election in April 2006. Opposition parties boycotted the process, and although Thaksin won again, he resigned as prime minister in the face of mass protests, appointing his deputy, Chidchai Wannasathit, as the new caretaker premier. Thaksin was plagued by claims of rigged bids for the new Suvarnabhumi Airport, *lèse majesté* against the beloved King Bhumibol, alleged vote-buying and a worsening Muslim insurgency in the south, which by then had claimed over 2,000 lives.

Following months of protests, the army staged a bloodless coup on 19 September 2006, when Thaksin was in New York attending a United Nations summit. Following up on charges of election irregularities, the new authorities banned 111 Thai Rak Thai officials from politics, including Thaksin, and froze his bank accounts in the country. As Thaksin lived

in exile in London, his followers, calling themselves the United Front for Democracy Against Dictatorship (UDD), and wearing red shirts, launched protests against the military government. A Thaksin proxy, the People Power Party (PPP), won the next general election in December 2007, and Thaksin returned the following year, only to later skip bail on corruption charges and flee once again to London.

Red Shirt, Yellow Shirt

Meanwhile, the yellow shirt PAD demonstrations resumed. During late 2008, they occupied Government House, sometimes clashing violently with Thaksin supporters, and finally seized the airport, bringing the country to a standstill. In December that year, the courts disbanded the ruling party, and, in a deal largely seen as being brokered by the army, some key Thaksin allies jumped ship. The Democrat Party took office with Abhisit Vejjajiva as prime minister.

As befits a telecoms tycoon, Thaksin mobilised his followers with a series of satellite phone-ins and video links, launched internet sites, and began twittering on a daily basis. In April 2009, Red Shirt protests intensified. They disrupted the ASEAN Summit in Pattaya, causing several heads of state to be airlifted to safety, and Songkran riots erupted in Bangkok. In the same month, PAD leader Sondhi Limthongkul was shot, but survived the assassination attempt.

In a provocative twist, and revealing his links with regional powers were still significant, Thaksin was appointed as financial advisor to the Cambodian government late in the year. Tensions between Thailand and Cambodia were already high over the disputed lands around the Preah Vihear Temple on the Cambodian border. Troop numbers were increased and ambassadors recalled by both countries.

As the New Year approached, commentators were increasingly debating the possibility of civil war breaking out at some level, particularly as factions either within the army, or with strong army connections, began to reveal themselves as Thaksin supporters.

In February 2010, outstanding corruption charges against Thaksin were finally heard. The courts found him guilty of abuse of power and confiscated assets of B46 billion. Still immensely rich, Thaksin vowed to fight on. ❑

Above: anti-government "red shirt" protesters in Bangkok's main shopping district, April 2010.

The Monarchy

Thailand is officially a constitutional monarchy, but the king's importance in the nation's life is apparent everywhere, from official buildings to people's homes

Although an army-led bloodless coup in 1932 removed the absolute powers of Thailand's King Prajadhipok (Rama VII), the monarchy remains one of the most influential institutions in the land, and is omnipresent.

The monarchy is represented by the blue bar of the Thai tricolour (red stands for the nation, white is religion), while photographs of the current King Bhumibol Adulyadej adorn government buildings and public spaces, and legal regard is enshrined in *lèse majesté* laws, which carry a maximum penalty of seven years imprisonment for anyone convicted of insulting the royal family.

King Bhumibol ascended the throne in 1946, following the death, in mysterious circumstances, of his brother King Ananda Mahidol (Rama VIII), and is the world's longest-reigning monarch. Respect for the king is enhanced by a sense of his morality and representation of traditional Thai values in the face of corrupt governments. He was seen as the ameliorating figure in the turbulent conflicts of 1973, 1976 and 1992, when the army and police killed many civilians. In recent years he has endured pockets of unprecedented criticism from some supporters of Thaksin Shinawatra, who believe the king and other elements of the traditional elite were involved in the overthrow of the fugitive ex-prime minister. The *lèse majesté* laws have been used more widely than usual during recent years.

Books and films about King Mongkut based on the memoirs of Anna Leonowens, titled *The English Governess at the Siamese Court*, are all banned in Thailand. These include the Hollywood favourite *The King and I*, starring Yul Brynner. Leonowens was a tutor of the royal children, but is regarded as having misrepresented both her role and life in the palace.

Radio and TV stations play the national anthem regularly, as do cinemas and railway and bus stations, when people will stand respectfully for the duration. Indeed, his subjects have a famed love of the king and will generally take offence at anyone speaking ill of the monarchy. Photographs of King Bhumibol are widespread in shops and homes, along with those of his predecessors, particularly King Mongkut and King Chulalongkorn, who were the modernisers of Thailand in the late 19th and early 20th centuries.

Right: King Bhumibol and Queen Sirikit.

King Bhumibol is also seen as a man of the people, particularly through his work in the King's Project, which is concerned with the development of small agricultural communities. His subjects are also genuinely proud of his achievements in the field of jazz *(see box, page 84)*; the king has penned many tunes, including the humorously named "HM Blues". The nation's monarchist fervour sees crowds turn out in huge numbers for the king's birthday celebrations in Sanam Luang *(see page 109)* each December. ❑

RELIGION

Buddhism is central to the lives of most Thais, as shown by the many rituals and practices that are part of daily routine. Yet a strong thread of animism persists: people wear amulets to ward off bad luck, while buildings have tiny "spirit houses" to appease previous occupants

Though it is predominantly Buddhist, Thailand has historically been tolerant of other religions. According to the government census, 94 percent of the population are Theravada Buddhists, 3.9 percent are Muslims, 1.7 percent Confucians and 0.6 percent Christians (mostly hill-tribe people living in the north). Buddhism – a philosophy, rather than a religion – has played a profound role in shaping the Thai character, particularly in the way in which people react to events. The Buddhist concept of the impermanence of life and possessions, and of the necessity to avoid extremes of emotion or behaviour, has done much to create the relaxed, carefree charm that is one of the most appealing characteristics of the Thai people.

Theravada Buddhism

Most of the Thai population subscribe to Theravada Buddhism, which is also the main Buddhist form practised in neighbouring countries like Laos, Cambodia and Burma (Myanmar), as well as Sri Lanka. Nevertheless, even a casual visitor to temples in these countries will quickly see differences between them. As they have done with most outside influences – Khmer temple decorations and Chinese food, for instance – the Thais have evolved a Buddhism of their own cast over the centuries.

Theravada Buddhism is a mixture of Buddhist, Hindu and animistic beliefs, and, as the oldest of all Buddhist faiths, it is the only one to trace its origins directly back to the 6th century BC teachings of Siddhartha Gautama, the Indian prince who gave up his royal privileges to follow an ascetic life, and became the Buddha. The central doctrines are based on *dukkha* (stress, misery), *anicca* (impermanence) and *anatta* (the absence of self).

The Buddha taught that the craving for self-worth and possessions creates misery, and that because everything is impermanent and cannot be possessed, the exercise is in any case senseless. If we suppress desire and practise detachment we will no longer be unhappy.

To reach this state, Gautama advocated a method of living he called the Middle Way

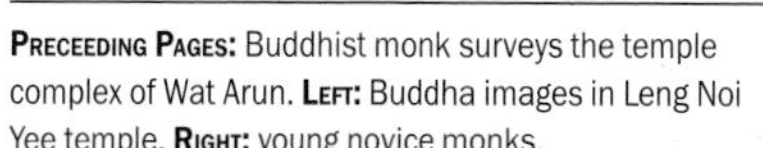

PRECEEDING PAGES: Buddhist monk surveys the temple complex of Wat Arun. **LEFT:** Buddha images in Leng Noi Yee temple. **RIGHT:** young novice monks.

(or Eightfold Path), which leads to enlightenment. At the time of enlightenment, Gautama became the Buddha and ascended into Nirvana, an event now represented by reclining Buddha statues and celebrated on Visakha Puja Day, each May *(see page 250)*.

Adherents believe the Buddha lived 500 lives, and that they themselves will be reincarnated (an idea adopted from Hinduism) and finally, if they live a good cycle of lives, will reach Nirvana. Living a good cycle requires rightful and mindful actions and thoughts, and is significantly aided by *tham boon* (merit making). People can make merit in many ways. A man who spends some part of his life as a monk will earn merit by living in accordance with the strict rules governing monastic life. So, too, a person who supports the monks on a daily basis by donating food, or who visits a temple to pray for a sick person. People can also make merit by releasing birds or fish, which market stalls sell for the purpose. And a donation to a worthy cause is always helpful.

The Buddha image in front of which prayers are offered provides only a formal background for these activities. The image and the Buddha himself are there as inspiration rather than objects to be worshipped.

Mahayana Buddhism

In addition to Theravada Buddhism, there is Mahayana Buddhism that is practised by those of Chinese descent. Visitors are likely to spot Mahayana temples in Bangkok's Chinatown. Mahayana literally means "Greater Vehicle"; the defining belief, according to this doctrine, is that those who have attained Nirvana return to help others reach the same state. The various Buddhist sects and practices that predominate in China, Tibet, Taiwan, Japan, Korea and Vietnam are classified as Mahayana.

Chinese Buddhism, at least that practised in Thailand, primarily consists of incense, lucky charms, and heaps of other folk practices. The visitor entering a *sanjao,* or inner shrine, of such a temple will have a chance to shake sticks out of a canister, from which a fortune can be told. At funerals, paper money and doll-size cardboard houses (complete with paper Mercedes Benz cars) are burned to assist the deceased in his or her next life.

Temple life

Most of Thailand's 300,000 or so monks live in *wat* (temples), practising and teaching the rules of human conduct laid down by the Bud-

LEFT: making a request at Erawan Shrine.
ABOVE: garlanded flower offerings at Erawan.
RIGHT: monks over prayers at Wat Pho temple.

A little over 90 percent of the Thai people are Buddhist, but religious tolerance is extended to other religions. Around 3.9 percent of Thais are Muslim, with the remainder Christian, Hindu and Sikh.

dha. There are literally hundreds of Buddhist temples in the city and suburbs, usually sited in serene pockets of densely packed neighbourhoods and serving as hubs for the spiritual and social life of the community.

The term *wat* defines a large, walled compound made up of several buildings, including a *bot* or hall where new monks are ordained, and one or more *viharn* where sermons are delivered. It may also contain a belltower, a *ho trai* (library) and *guti*, or monk meditation cells, as well as a domed edifice, called *chedi* in Thailand, or *prang* in Cambodia, and *stupa* or *pagoda* in other countries. *Chedi* contain the ashes or relics of wealthy donors, emulating the Buddha, whose ashes and relics were placed according to his instruction in a mound of earth.

Tradition requires that every Buddhist male enter the monkhood for a brief period before marriage, and companies customarily grant paid leave for male employees wishing to do so. The entry of a young man into monkhood is seen as repayment to parents for his upbringing, and as bestowing special merit on them, particularly his mother. Unlike other Buddhist countries, women cannot be ordained in Thailand. It is thus popularly believed that a son, as a monk, can earn merit for his mother and other female relatives.

BRAHMAN BELIEFS

Many of the Thais' non-Buddhist beliefs are Brahman in origin, and even today Brahman priests officiate at major ceremonies. The Thai wedding ceremony is almost entirely Brahman, as are many funeral rites. The rites of statecraft pertaining to the royal family are presided over by Brahman priests. One of the most popular of these, the Ploughing Ceremony (Raek Na), takes place each May in Bangkok. To signal the start of the rice-planting season, sacred oxen are offered a selection of grains. Astrologers watch the events carefully, as the grains the oxen choose will determine the amount of rainfall to come and the success or failure of the crops in the year ahead.

For all its spartan life, however, a Buddhist *wat* in Thailand is by no means isolated from the real world. In addition to the schools that are attached to most *wat* (for centuries, the only schools were those run by monks), the *wat* has traditionally been the centre of social and communal life in the villages. Monks serve as herbal doctors, psychological counsellors and arbitrators of disputes. They also play an important part in daily life, such as blessing a new building, or at birthdays and funerals.

Spirits and amulets

When Buddhism started in what is now Thailand in the early years, it promised a better life for farmers. But as it provided little assistance with the unfathomable tragedies of daily life, and certainly no answer to the questions of the supernatural, the people continued to worship their old deities and spirits to fill in what they saw as gaps in Buddhism.

The variety of *phi* (spirits) in Thailand is legendary. A seductive female *phi*, believed to reside in a banana plant, is said to torment young men who come near it. Another bothersome one takes possession of her victims and forces them to remove their clothes in public. (For some reason, the most destructive spirits seem to be female.)

To counteract the spirits and potential dangers in life, protective spells are cast and kept in small amulets *(see page 132)* mostly worn around the neck. Curiously, the amulets are not bought, but rather rented on an indefinite lease from "landlords", often monks considered to possess magic powers. There are amulets that offer protection against accidents while travelling or against bullet and knife wounds; some even boost sexual attraction.

All this has no more to do with Buddhism than the protective blue-patterned tattoos sported by some Thais to ward off evil. But some monasteries have been turned into highly profitable factories for the production of amulets. In 2007 a great cult following grew around idols called Jatukam Ramathep, which were believed to be particularly powerful. Thousands all over the country exchanged hands for ever-increasing prices, and many people saw an opportunity to make a fast profit. But the bubble burst and some temples were left in financial difficulties because they had over-stocked.

Spirit houses

No building in Thailand, not even the humblest wooden hut, will be seen today without a "spirit house", or at least a house altar. In ordinary residences, the small doll-like house may resemble a Thai dwelling; in hotels and offices, it is usually an elaborately decorated mini-temple. In either case, these spirit houses serve as the abodes of the resident spirits. As it is within their power either to favour or plague the human inhabitants of the actual house or building, the spirit house is regularly adorned with placatory offerings of food, fresh flowers and incense sticks.

If any calamity or ill luck befalls the members of the compound, it may be necessary to call in an expert to consult the spirit to determine what is wrong.

One of the most famous spirit houses in Bangkok is the Erawan Shrine, at the intersection of Ratchadamri and Ploenchit roads *(see page 156)*. This shrine, honouring the Hindu god Brahma, was erected by the owners during the construction of the original Erawan Hotel in the 1950s, after several workers were injured in mysterious accidents. The shrine soon acquired a widespread reputation for bringing good fortune to outsiders as well.

A less well-known shrine sits in the compound of Bangkok's Lai Nert Park Hotel *(see page 242)*, known as the Chao Mae Tuptim shrine. Its offerings consist entirely of phalluses, ranging from small to gargantuan, sculpted from wood, wax, stone or cement, and with fidelity to real life. They are left by women hoping to conceive a child. ❑

Some idols blessed by monks are believed to be so powerful that cult followings develop around them. Fortunes can be won and lost depending on the state of the market in these talismans.

Left Bottom: miniature Buddha statue. **Left Top:** offerings of food at a Buddhist temple. **Above:** a spirit house. **Right:** phalluses at the Chao Mae Tuptim shrine in the grounds of the Lai Nert Park Hotel.

Temple Art and Architecture

The temple *(wat)* plays a vital role in every community, large or small; for many visitors Thailand's temples are the country's most enduring sights

A typical Thai *wat* (temple) has two enclosing walls that divide it from the secular world. The monks' quarters are situated between the outer and inner walls. In larger temples the inner walls may be lined with Buddha images and serve as cloisters for meditation. This part of the temple is called *buddhavasa* or *phutthawat*. Inside the inner walls is the *bot* or *ubosot* (ordination hall), surrounded by eight stone tablets and set on consecrated ground. This is the most sacred part of the temple and only monks can enter it. The *bot* contains a Buddha image, but it is the *viharn* (sermon hall) that contains the principal Buddha images. Also in the inner courtyard are the bell-shaped *chedi* (relic chambers), as well as towering Khmer-style spires called *prang*, which are a variation of *chedi* and similarly contain the relics of either the Buddha or pious or distinguished people. *Salas* (pavilions) can be found all around the temple; the largest of these areas is the *sala kan prian* (study hall), used for saying afternoon prayers. Apart from Buddha images, various mythological creatures *(see page 106)* are found within the temple compound.

Above: the cloisters at Wat Suthat are lined with Buddha statues, these portrayed in the "Subduing Mara" position, denoting a renunciation of worldly desire.

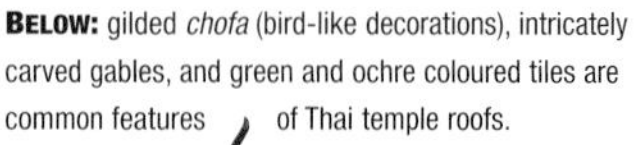

Below: gilded *chofa* (bird-like decorations), intricately carved gables, and green and ochre coloured tiles are common features of Thai temple roofs.

Above: temple exteriors are often very ornate, such as that of the *bot* of the Emerald Buddha at Wat Phra Kaew. Gold tiles, glass mosaic, lacquer and mother-of-pearl are some of the materials used.

BELOW: Thai temple murals are created on a background that has been prepared and dried before the artist paints on it using coloured pigments mixed with glue. Often featured on the interior of temple walls, such murals depict the classic subjects of Thai painting, including tales from the *Jataka* (Buddha's birth and previous lives) and other Buddhist themes, and also vignettes of local life. During the reign of Rama III (1824–51), mural painting reached its peak, with artists not only following the principles of traditional Thai art but also introducing new elements, like Western perspective. The mural below, from Wat Suthat in Bangkok, is an example of the late 18th-century art style (better known as the Rattanakosin Period).

BELOW: the gleaming Phra Si Rattana *chedi* at Wat Phra Kaew is bell-shaped with a ringed spire and a three-tiered base – a feature of Sri Lankan reliquary towers. Close-up inspection will reveal a surface made up of thousands of tiny gold mosaic pieces.

BELOW: these towering *chedi* at Wat Pho sit on square bases and have graceful and elegant proportions, remininscent of the Lanna-style architecture of north Thailand. Decorated with coloured tiles, the *chedi* are memorials to the first four Chakri kings.

BELOW: Wat Arun features five rounded *prang* – reflecting Cambodian-Khmer influence – encrusted with thousands of broken porcelain pieces. These porcelain shards were leftover ballast from Chinese ships which visited Bangkok in its early days.

THE CREATIVE ARTS

While Thailand's traditional dance-dramas are an enticing part of the Thai experience for visitors, its young indie movie industry, cutting-edge contemporary theatre and dance, and modern artists and sculptors are fast gaining international attention

Like most of Southeast Asia, Thailand's traditional cultural symbols and aesthetics are often most keenly appreciated by people outside the country. Abroad, for instance, Thai dance-drama is recognised as among the world's most dazzling and stylistically challenging; in Thailand performances are relatively rare outside tourist centres.

While the various forms of traditional artistry are delightful to watch, and enforce perceptions of exotic Thailand, it is also worth trying to catch some of Thailand's contemporary art scene, which is fast gaining recognition in international circles. The capital's modern art galleries, cutting-edge theatre and indie movies directed by a new breed of imaginative young directors are all part of the historical creative process that appears in traditional dance-drama and the faded beauty of temple murals.

Thai dance-drama

The origins of traditional Thai theatrical arts are entwined with court ceremony and religious ritual, some of which can still be seen today in Bangkok's Erawan Shrine *(see page 156)* or at the Lak Muang *(see page 109)*, where performers are hired to dance as a means of thanksgiving to the spirit gods. Drama and dance are inseparable as the dancer's hands and body express the emotions that the silent lips do not, with the storyline and lyrics provided by a singer and chorus on the side of the stage. A *phipat* orchestra *(see page 58)* creates not only the atmosphere, but also an emotive force.

It is thought that the movements of dance-drama originated in *nang yai* (shadow puppet) performances of the 16th and 17th centuries. Huge buffalo hides were cut into the shapes of characters from the *Ramakien*. Against a torch-lit translucent screen, handlers manipulated puppets, using their silhouettes to tell complex tales of good and evil. As they moved the figures across the screen, the puppeteers danced the emotions they wanted the stiff figures to convey. These movements gradually evolved into an independent theatrical art.

The most identifiable form of dance-drama is *khon*, historically performed by a

LEFT AND RIGHT: *lakhon* dancers perform scenes from the epic *Ramakien*.

large troupe of male dancers wearing beautifully crafted masks. The performances were originally staged for the royal court. These days a condensed version of several episodes from the *Ramakien* – based on the Hindu epic *Ramayana* – is adapted into a short medley of palatable scenes for tourist dinner shows *(see page 249)*; the entire *Ramakien* would take 720 hours to perform. The colourful masks depict beasts and demons from the epic tale, with each performer trained to portray the particular character of each creature through gestures and actions.

The most graceful dance is the *lakhon*. There are two forms: the *lakhon nai* ("inside" *lakhon*), once performed only inside the palace walls by women, and the *lakhon nawk* ("outside" *lakhon*), performed beyond the palace by both sexes. Garbed in costumes as elaborate as their movements, the performers glide slowly about the stage, their stylised choreography conveying the plot. *Lakhon*'s rich repertoire includes scenes from the *Ramakien*, and tales like *Inao*, with its romantic storylines.

There have always been two cultures in Thailand: palace and village. The village arts are often parodies of the palace arts, but more burlesque, with pratfalls and bawdy humour. *Likay* is the village form of *lakhon*, played out against

gaudy backdrops to an audience that walks in and out of the performance at will, eating and talking, regardless of what happens to the performers on stage.

Puppet theatre

Traditional puppet theatre, like dance-drama, has also lost most of its Bangkok audiences to television. One troupe struggling to survive is

Thai Classical Music

To the uninitiated, classical Thai music sounds like a jarring and ear-piercing mishmash of contrasting tones without any pattern. The key is to listen to it as one would jazz, picking out one instrument and following it, switching to another as the mood moves one. Thai music is set to a scale of seven full steps, with a lilting and steady rhythm. Each instrument plays the same melody, but in its own way and seemingly without regard to how others are playing it. Seldom does an instrument rise in solo; it is always being challenged and cajoled by the other instruments of the orchestra.

A classical *phipat* orchestra is made up of a single reed instrument, the oboe-like *phinai*, and a variety of percussion instruments. The pitch favours the treble, with the pace set by the *ching*, a tiny cymbal, aided by the drums beaten with the fingers. The melody is played by two types of *ranad*, a bamboo-bar xylophone, and two sets of *gong wong*, tuned gongs arranged in a semi-circle around the player.

Another type of orchestra employs two violin-like instruments, the *saw-oo* and the *saw-duang*, and is usually heard accompanying a Thai dance-drama. A variation of the *phiphat* orchestra can be found performing at Thai boxing *(muay thai)* matches to spur the sinewy combatants to action.

the Joe Louis Theatre at the Suan Lum Night Bazaar. The company, which won the Best Performance Award at the World Festival of Puppet Arts in 2008, stages a *hun lakhon lek* puppet show nightly *(see also pages 86, 159 and 249–50)*. Visually mesmerising and based on *khon* masked dance-drama, the performance requires three puppeteers who manipulate sticks attached to the marionettes to bring them to life. This endangered art form was revived by

> *In traditional puppetry, the handlers also danced as they moved their puppets. Their complex choreography developed into the separate art form of Thai classical dance.*

the late Sakorn Yangkeawsot, who went by the moniker Joe Louis.

He succeeded in updating *hun lakhon lek*, without diluting its origins, by allowing freer movement and more detailed costuming, and by incorporating contemporary themes based on social issues and modern speech.

Modern theatre and dance

Sadly, this is one area where modern innovation has been stifled, compounded by language barriers (for international appreciation) and budget limitations.

The only venue left that regularly stages and produces quality modern productions is Patravadi Theatre, in Thonburi. The open-air venue is run by Patravadi Mechudhon, whose adaptations of classic Thai tales meld traditional local dance and theatre with modern Western styling. Some of its works fuse elements of Asian dance forms like Japanese *butoh* and Indonesian *wayang kulit*. Patravadi Theatre *(see also pages 86 and 250)* stages its acclaimed shows both in the open-air theatre and in the riverside Studio 9 on Saturday and Sunday nights.

Some productions tour overseas – notably the landmark *Sahatsadecha*, a mix of *khon* and *nang yai*, which played at the Biennale de la Danse, in Lyon, France. Recent works have included *Monster*, a contemporary Japanese piece inspired by the artworks of Francis Bacon, and *The Ministry of Truth*, a performance described as discomfiting, in which German dancers and Thai lady-

LEFT TOP: *saw-duang* player. **LEFT BOTTOM:** Hanuman is a key character in the *Ramakien*. **ABOVE:** the Joe Louis puppet troop performing the *khon* classical dance.

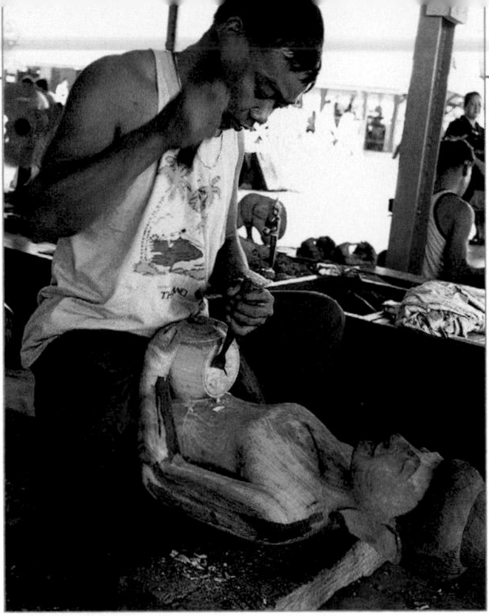

boys explored the human need to control and be controlled. Patravadi Theatre also hosts the annual Fringe Festival of dance, drama and music in both Bangkok and Hua Hin.

Classical literature

Thais have always placed a heavy emphasis on oral tradition. Unfortunately, most of the country's classical written literature was destroyed when the Burmese sacked Ayutthaya in 1767. At the heart of Thai literature is the *Ramakien*, the Thai version of the Indian *Ramayana*. The enduring story has found a home in the literature, dance and drama of many Asian countries. Familiarity with the *Ramakien* enables one to comprehend a variety of dramatic forms, its significance for the Thai monarchy and its role as a model for exemplary behaviour.

The *Jataka* tales are also of Indian origin, telling of Buddha's reincarnations prior to enlightenment, though some are probably based on tales that existed before the Buddha lived. The first tales were translated from Pali script to Thai in the late 15th century. They have generated many other popular and classic stories, such as *Phra Aphaimani*, written by Sunthorn Phu, the 18th-century poet laureate.

Modern literature

It wasn't until the 1920s that Thai novels were published, with themes mainly touching on social or political issues. In the 1950s, however, censorship became so heavy and writers so harshly persecuted that quality fiction practically disappeared for 20 years. Thai writers since the 1980s have enjoyed a measure of political freedom. While they remain social critics, there are efforts to write fiction of literary merit. Many landmark Thai books were translated into English in the early 1990s.

BUDDHA IMAGES

The focal point of the *bot* and *viharn* (ordination and sermon halls) of a Thai temple is the Buddha image. The image is not considered a representation of the Buddha, but is meant to serve as a reminder of his teachings. Buddha images cast in bronze, or carved in wood or stone, constitute the bulk of classic Thai sculpture. They epitomise the zenith of sculpting and employ some of the finest artistry (and some of the highest prices) of any arts. Superb examples of bas-relief sandstone carving can be seen around the base of the *bot* of Bangkok's Wat Pho *(see page 114)*. Delicately executed, the dozens of panels depict scenes from the *Ramakien*.

Buddha images conform to aesthetic rules, including being placed in one of four positions – sitting, standing, walking or reclining – and possessing distinguishing features *(laksanas)*, such as slender fingers and long eyelashes. The hand positions *(mudras)* are also significant, and are sometimes adopted by Buddhists to help focus during meditation. For instance, the hands in the lap, pointing up, indicate a disciplined mind. The *mudras* relate to events in the Buddha's life. The thumb and forefinger joined to make a circle represents the Buddha's first sermon after enlightenment. It signifies the Wheel of Dharma (Buddhist teachings).

The late prime minister and cultural advocate Kukrit Pramoj's *Many Lives*, for instance, gives a good introduction to the Buddhist way of thinking. His *Four Reigns* is a fictional yet accurate account of court life in the 19th and 20th centuries. Also of note are Kampoon Boontawee's *Children of Isan* and Botan's *Letters from Thailand*.

The highlight of the literary calendar is the SEA Write awards, held every August/September. Recent Thai winners have included Uthis Haemamool for the novel *Laplae, Kaeng Khoi*, and Prabda Yoon, who stirred things up with the old establishment by penning works that connect to Thai youth.

Expatriate writers like Jake Needham and Christopher Moore bring a Western perspective to life in the kingdom, mainly using the hard-boiled detective genre to focus on the seedier aspects of the capital's nightlife. The most widely acclaimed has been John Burdett with *Bangkok 8*.

Far Left: visitors to the Bangkok International Book Fair. **Left:** a Thai woodcarver. **Above:** *Ramakien* murals in the walls surrounding Wat Phra Kaew. **Right:** mother-of-pearl inlay on door at Wat Ratchabophit.

Traditional art

The inner walls of the *bot* (ordination hall) and *viharn* (sermon hall) in Thai temples are traditionally covered with murals *(see page 55)*. In the days before public education, the temple was the principal repository of knowledge for the common person. Monks were the teachers, and the interior walls of the temples were illustrated lectures. The principal themes are the life of Bud-

dha, with the back wall generally depicting the *Maravijaya*, in which all earthly temptations are united to break the meditating Buddha's will and prevent his achieving Nirvana.

The murals at Buddhaisawan Chapel in Bangkok's National Museum are among the finest examples of Thai painting. Others include the murals at Wat Suthat and the 19th-century paintings at Wat Bowonniwet. Although restored several times with less than perfect accuracy, the *Ramakien* murals on the walls surrounding Wat Phra Kaew include wonderful scenes of village and palace life.

Traditional art is also executed in the form of lacquer and gold paintings found on the shutters of most Thai temples. The best examples of lacquer painting can be found on the walls of the Lacquer Pavilion at Suan Pakkad Palace. Equally stunning is the intricate mother-of-pearl work by Thai artisans.

Contemporary art

At the turn of the 20th century, King Chulalongkorn commissioned several European artists to embark on projects in Bangkok, a trend the government continued in 1923 when they invited Italian sculptor Corrado Feroci to teach sculpture at the Fine Arts Department of the Ministry of Palace Affairs. The Florentine artist proved catalytic in the development of modern Thai art right through the 1960s; locals even gave him the adopted name of Silpa Bhirasri. He is regarded as the forefather of modern art in Thailand, and established the country's first school of fine arts, which later became Silpakorn University.

Spirituality and Buddhism have been, and still are, major precepts in contemporary art – whether created by neo-traditionalist painters like Thawan Duchanee and Chalermchai Kositpipat, whose late 20th-century paintings reinvigorate traditional perceptions of Thai identity, or the meditative installations in the 1990s by the late Montien Boonma. Rising artist Sakarin Krue-on uses spiritual metaphors as his basis, appropriating traditional imagery to question the blind adoption of Western trends.

Aside from the spiritual, since the 1997 economic collapse, many local artists have begun to question the effects of globalisation on the Thai populace. Rebellious artist Vasan Sitthiket blurs his art with faux political campaigning to highlight his contempt for national policies, while conceptual photographer Manit Sriwanichpoom ridicules the Thai urbanite's consumerist compulsions with his satirical *Pink Man* series.

The 11-storey Bangkok Arts and Culture Centre, despite political infighting and being a less than perfect space, is already the most significant exhibition centre in the city, and has run several major shows with both local and international artists since it opened in 2008.

Cinema

Like most places in the world, Hollywood blockbusters dominate the cinemas. Of late however, a few talented Thai directors have been receiving acclaim for their works on the international film circuit. Leading the charge is the new wave director Apichatpong Weerasethakul, whose 2002 film *Blissfully Yours* was awarded the *Prix un certain regard* at the Cannes Film Festival, followed by his atmospheric 2004 film *Tropical Malady* (*Sud Pralad*), which also picked up a special prize at Cannes. Apichatpong's 2004 collaboration with Thai–American artist Michael Shaowansai on the hilariously campy *The Adventures of Iron Pussy* – about a cross-dressing superhero – is proof that Thai cinema is engaging and provocative to both domestic and international audiences. Another Thai filmmaker to watch is Pen-Ek Ratanaruang who has produced two successful films, *Last Life in the Universe* (2004) and *Invisible Waves* (2006), starring the Japanese superstar actor Tadanobu Asano.

However, many such films don't get the airing they deserve in Bangkok – the only real indie cinema is House on RCA, with occasional screenings at Lido in Siam Square. Additionally, there are film festivals, including the World Film Festival, EU Film Festival, and the big one, the Bangkok International Film Festival. ❑

LEFT TOP AND BOTTOM: contemporary Thai art. **ABOVE:** scene from the award-winning film, *Last Life in the Universe*. **RIGHT:** Michael Shaowanasai, the star of the musical comedy, *The Adventures of Iron Pussy*.

CUISINE

Thai cuisine is not just about tongue-numbing spices. Distinct regional, ethnic–migrant and Thai-fusion styles create a fabulous variety of complex flavours that appeal to the serious gourmand. And if you want a change from Thai, the city abounds with international restaurants

Thai food is expanding faster globally than any other cuisine, and it's easy to see why. Less a dining experience than a sensory attack, it's one of the few cuisines in the world capable of drawing people to a country purely on its own merits.

It's the explosive spiciness of Thai food that initially overwhelms, but what's most impressive is the extraordinary complex balance of flavours that lie underneath. And contrary to what most people think, it's not all blatantly spicy: most Thai meals will include a sampling of less aggressive dishes, some subtly flavoured with only garlic and herbs.

The variation of foods and cooking styles is immense, as each of Thailand's four regions has a distinct cuisine of its own. The northeast is influenced by Laos, the south by Malaysia and Indonesia, the central area by the cuisine of the Royal Thai kitchens of the capital (the one people are most familiar with) and the north by Burma and Yunnan. All types are available in Bangkok, and often at street stalls and markets serving the city's migrant communities. As usual, the busiest spots have the best food.

Thai chefs are adept at adapting foreign influences for local cooking styles. China, Malaysia, Laos, and even Portugal, have left their tastes on the Thai dinner table.

LEFT: eating out in Bangkok: the busiest places are usually the best. **RIGHT:** massaman curry, a creamy dish of Persian origin.

But Bangkok offers far more than Thai food. It's fast emerging as an international culinary hot-spot, with options that include Mexican, Italian, Lebanese, Spanish and even the franchise of a hip Michelin-starred French restaurant. Adding excitement is a clutch of new-wave fusion restaurants that are boldly experimenting with Thai and Western ingredients and methods of preparation.

How to eat Thai food

Most Thai meals have dishes placed in the middle of the table to be shared by all; the larger

ORIGINS OF ROYAL THAI CUISINE

Royal Thai cuisine has hugely influenced the food of the Central Plains, with dishes such as green curry and the hot and sour shrimp soup *tom yum goong.* The great-grandson of King Rama IV, MR Sorut Visuddhi, co-owner of Bangkok's Thanying (www.thanying.com), a royal Thai restaurant that serves the recipes of his mother, Princess Sulap-Walleng Visuddhi, explains: "In the palace it was considered bad manners to perspire at the table or to eat foods that had strong smells. So we would use coconut milk to cut down on these tastes. This had a big influence on Central cooking."

The Grand Palace had many residences where each princess cooked what was called *ahaan chawang* (food for the palace people). These recipes spread through the wealthy classes via palace finishing schools and publications such as *Mae Krua Hua Baak*, the country's first cookbook, written by Thanpuying Pliang Pasonakorn, a descendant of King Rama II.

Later, when the royal families moved out of the palaces, the kitchen hands they hired learnt the recipes and started cooking them at home. A number of royally connected Thai restaurants began to open from the 1980s, but few authentic ones remain today. The intricate fruit and vegetable carving seen at fine Thai restaurants – like the Sala Rim Naam at the Oriental hotel – is also a legacy of Royal Thai cuisine.

the group the more dishes you can try. Heap a little rice onto your plate, together with small portions of various dishes at the side (it's polite to take only a little at a time). Eat with a fork and spoon, using the fork to push food onto the spoon. Chopsticks are only for Chinese and noodle dishes.

Rice is the staple; in the past it sustained workers throughout the day, with just small portions of chilli, curry or sauce added for flavour. Even now, rural Thais eat large helpings of rice with just morsels of dried or salted fish. Thankfully, jasmine-scented Thai rice is one of the most delicious in Asia, regarded as being so valuable that the government has patented its genetic code.

Condiments on the table usually include dried, ground red chilli, sliced chilli with vin-

Thai cooks use several types of chilli (prik), *both red and green, some relatively mild, and some very fiery. When sliced and served in fish sauce* (nam pla) *as a condiment, it's called* prik nam pla.

egar, sliced chilli with *nam pla* (fish sauce), and white sugar. These are mainly used to add extra flavour to noodle dishes. Many visitors are surprised to find that the peanut sauce condiment used in many Thai restaurants in Western countries is of Malaysian or Indonesian origin; in Thailand it's only used as a dip for satay.

Northern cuisine

This is the mildest of Thai foods. Northerners generally eat *khao nio* (sticky rice), kneading it into a ball to dip into sauces and curries such as the Burmese *kaeng hanglay*, a sweet and tamarind-sour pork dish. *Khao soi* is also found in Burma, but is possibly of Chinese origin. Usually made with chicken, it has fresh egg noodles swimming in a mild coconut curry, with crispy noodles sprinkled on top.

FAR LEFT: noodle stand in Talad Kao Market.
LEFT: hot green chillis, a key ingredient of many dishes.
ABOVE: exquisitely presented dishes at the Sala Rim Naam restaurant, at the Mandarin Oriental Hotel.

Other northern Thai specialities include sausages, such as the spicy pork *sai oua* (roasted over a coconut husk fire to impart aroma and flavour) and *naem* (fermented raw pork and pork skin seasoned with garlic and chilli). *Laab* is a salad dish of minced pork, chicken, beef or fish, served with mint leaves and raw vegetables to cool the spices. It's also common in the northeast.

Dipping sauces include *nam prik ong* (minced pork, mild chillies, tomatoes, garlic and shrimp paste) and the potent northern classic, *nam prik noom* (grilled chillies, onions and garlic). Both are eaten with the popular snack called *khaep moo* (crispy pork rind).

Northeastern cuisine

Northeastern (Isaan) food is simple, generally spicy, and eaten with mounds of sticky rice kept in bamboo baskets. Hot dishes include the legendary *som tam* (shredded green papaya, garlic, chillies, lime juice, and variations of tomatoes, dried shrimp, preserved crab and fermented

fish) and a version of *laab*, which is spicier and sourer than its northern sister.

But perhaps the most popular Isaan food is not hot at all. *Gai yang* is chicken grilled in a marinade of peppercorns, garlic, fish sauce, coriander and palm sugar, and served with both hot and sweet dipping sauces.

Southern cuisine

The south – notable for Thailand's hottest dishes – also has gentler specialties such as *khao yam*, an innocuous salad of rice, vegetables, pounded dried fish and a southern fish sauce called *budu*. Slightly spicier are *phad sataw*, a stir-fry usually with pork or shrimp, and *sataw*, a large lima bean look-alike with a strong flavour and aroma. *Khao moke gai* is roasted chicken with turmeric-seasoned yellow rice – like an Indian *biryani*, often sprinkled with crispy fried onions.

Hot dishes include *kaeng tai plaa*. Fishermen who needed food that would last for days at sea are said to have created it by blending the fermented stomachs of fish with chillies, bamboo shoots and vegetables together with an intensely hot sauce. Even hotter is *kaeng leuang* (yellow curry), a variant of the central Thai *kaeng som*, with fish, green papaya and bamboo shoots or palm hearts in an explosive sauce.

Central cuisine

Central cuisine, which has been influenced by the royal palaces *(see text box page 66)*, includes many of the dishes made internationally famous at Thai restaurants abroad. It's notable for the use of coconut milk and even modern garnishes such as grapes, which mellow the chilli heat and add a little sweetness. It's still fiery, though, so

Thai Chinese Cuisine

Many ethnic Chinese in Thailand still speak the Teochew dialect of their southern Chinese ancestry, and most Chinese restaurants serve Teochew or Cantonese food. Especially famous are goose feet cooked in soy sauce, Peking duck, a wide variety of steamed and fried fish dishes, and the bite-sized lunchtime snacks called *dim sum*. Poultry, pork, seafood and mushrooms are ubiquitous items along with noodles or rice, while piping-hot Chinese tea is an integral part of every meal. Chinatown is awash with dining options although it has surprisingly few actual restaurants. Most people choose to eat at streetstalls or in tiny shophouse cafés.

take care. Trademark dishes include *tom kha gai*, a soup of chicken, coconut milk and galangal, the celebrated hot and sour shrimp soup *tom yum goong*, and *kaeng khio waan* (green curry), with chicken or beef, basil leaves and pea-sized green aubergines. Stir-fries and noodle dishes are everywhere, due to the large Chinese presence in the central region.

Common dishes to try

Kaeng is usually translated as curry, but it covers a broad range, from thin soups to near-dry dishes like the northern *kaeng ho*. Many *kaeng* are made with coconut cream, like the spicy red curry *(kaeng pet)* and *kaeng mussaman*, a rich, sweetish dish of Persian origin with meat, potatoes and onions. *Kaeng* without coconut milk include "jungle curries", which are very spicy.

Fish and seafood have featured largely in Thai cooking since ancient times. *Haw mok talay* is mixed seafood in a curried coconut custard and steamed in a banana-leaf cup or coconut shell. Other delicious choices to try are *poo pat pong karee* (steamed chunks of crab in an egg-thickened curry sauce with crunchy spring onion) and *hoi malaeng poo op maw din* (mussels in their shells, steamed in a clay pot with lime juice and aromatic herbs).

Meat – usually chicken, pork or beef – is cooked in all manner of styles, such as pork fried with garlic and black pepper *(muu thawd kratiam prik Thai)* or the sweet and sour *muu pad prio waan*, probably of Portuguese origin, brought to Thailand by Chinese immigrants. *Neua pad nam man hoi* is a mild, delicate dish of beef fried with oyster sauce, spring onions and mushrooms. The popular and very spicy *pat pet pat bai kaprao* dishes include meat stir-fried with chillies, garlic, onions and holy basil *(bai kaprao)*. Main ingredients to note are: chicken *(gai)*, pork *(muu)*, beef *(neua)*, duck *(ped)*, seafood *(talay)* and shrimp *(goong)*.

Noodles and rice

Noodles – a Chinese import – have a place in Thai restaurants. The ubiquitous street-side noodle shop sells two types: *kuay tiaw*, made from rice flour, and *ba mee*, from wheat flour. Both can be ordered broad *(sen yai)*, narrow *(sen lek)* or very narrow *(sen mee)*, and with broth *(sai naam)* or without *(haeng)*.

Common dishes are *kuay tiaw raad naa* (rice noodles flash-fried and topped with sliced meat

LEFT: an array of curries at a food market. **ABOVE:** street-side noodle stalls are ubiquitous in some areas of the city. **RIGHT:** typical Isaan dishes from northeastern Thailand, including *som tam* and *gai yang*.

and greens in a thick, mild sauce) and *paad thai* (narrow pan-fried rice noodles with egg, dried and fresh shrimp, spring onions, tofu, crushed peanuts and bean-sprouts). In *mee krawp*, the rice noodles are fried crispy, tossed in sweet-and-sour sauce and topped with sliced chillies, pickled garlic and slivers of lime rind.

Many lunchtime rice dishes are of Chinese origin. They include *khao man gai* (chicken with rice cooked in chicken broth), *khao moo daeng* (with Chinese red pork) and *khao kaa moo* (with stewed pork leg and greens). At night and in the early morning, two soup-like rice dishes are favoured. *Khao tom* comes in the water it was boiled in (with additions such as garlic-fried pork, salted egg or pickled ginger) and the close relative *joke*, which is porridge-like rice seasoned with minced pork, coriander and slivers of fresh ginger. Crispy *pathongko* (fried dough) pieces float on top.

Thai desserts

In Bangkok, *khanom* (desserts) come in bewildering variety, from light concoctions with crushed ice and syrup, to custards, ice creams and little cakes, and an entire category based on egg yolks cooked in flower-scented syrups.

THE KING OF FRUIT

The notorious durian, often avoided by foreigners for a smell they liken to toilets, is so prized by Thais they call it the King of Fruit. The outer appearance is like a large, spiky green rugby ball, while inside it has a creamy flesh with a unique, slightly burning sweetness that tastes much better than it smells.

Of the many varieties, which are in season from May to August, Chanee and Monthong are said to be the best, and those grown in Nonthaburi the best of all. Some upmarket restaurants now include durian ice cream and durian cheesecake on their menus, which entice more foreigners to their charms.

The heavier Thai confections are rarely eaten after a big meal. After-meal desserts, served in small bowls, are generally light and elegant. *Kluay buat chee* has banana slices in sweetened and salted warm coconut cream. *Kluay kaek* uses bananas sliced lengthwise, dipped in coconut cream and rice flour, and deep-fried until crisp. Other favourites are *taap tim krawp* (water chestnut pieces covered in red-dyed tapioca flour and served in coconut cream and crushed ice) and *sangkhaya ma-praoawn*, a coconut cream custard steamed in a young coconut or a small pumpkin.

Many desserts are startlingly inventive – you may finish a rich pudding before realising that

its tantalising flavour comes from crisp fried onions. Look out for market vendors who sell "roof-tile cookies" *(khanom beuang)*, crispy shells filled with strands of egg yolk cooked in syrup with shredded coconut, sweet and spicy dried shrimp, coriander and coconut cream. But, if you sample nothing else in Thailand, don't miss the heavenly *khao niao ma-muand* (mango with sticky rice and coconut cream).

Thai fusion cuisine

There have been foreign influences in Thai food for centuries (even chilli, which is another Portuguese import), but recent years have seen the growth of a dedicated style of Thai-fusion dishes. It often takes the form of Italian–Thai blends such as Thai-style spaghetti with anchovies and chilli, served at modern cafés like Greyhound (several branches in the city).

Other modern Thai restaurants, like Mahanaga for instance, use non-traditional ingredients such as lamb and salmon, and plate their essentially Thai dishes Western style.

FAR LEFT: Singha beer, popular with Thais and *farang* alike. **LEFT:** mango with sticky rice and coconut cream, a truly sumptuous dessert. **ABOVE:** fresh-juice stall.

When international Thai restaurant chain The Blue Elephant opened its Bangkok branch, it introduced several fusion items, including salmon *laab*. The new hot shot is Long Table, where ex-Bed Supperclub chef Dan Ivarie works interesting combinations like foie gras with dried shrimp and tamarind. And at Breeze they incorporate Thai flavours into their pan-Asian menu with delicious flare.

Refreshments

With meals Thais drink locally brewed beers such as Singha, Kloster and the stronger Beer Chang. Foreign brands brewed on licence include Heineken. The middle-class obsession with French wines is waning, and there is now a decent selection available from the New World. Thailand itself is even producing its own wines *(see page 228)*.

Among the working classes, the rice whisky brands Maekhong and Saeng Thip are popular, usually served as a "set" with ice, soda and lime. Note: fresh fruit and ice drinks will often get a splash of syrup (and salt) unless you request otherwise. ❑

• *Restaurant recommendations are listed at the end of each chapter in the Places section.*

SHOPPING

Brush up your bargaining skills and fill your pockets with baht, because Bangkok is a retail heaven. Colourful markets sell everything from cheap clothes to snakes and violins, while gigantic high-gloss malls take care of the Gucci crowd

Bangkok is one of the shopping capitals of the world. It's a city where you can sniff out an antique treasure under the sweltering awnings of an outdoor market or pick up an Hermès handbag from a luxury marble-clad mall. If you know where to look for it, just about anything is available – from Siamese pottery and hand-woven silks to cutting-edge home furnishings and funky street wear. The city caters to both spendthrifts and penny pinchers, with shops open seven days a week. Bangkok's Skytrain conveniently connects the best shopping areas and you can glide above the traffic in air-conditioned comfort from Emporium, a glitzy shopping mall offering brands like Prada, Versace and Chanel, to the rough and ready Chatuchak Weekend Market, where thousands of stalls sell everything from hill-tribe clothing to quirky home accessories.

The main shopping areas converge around Thanon Rama I and Thanon Ploenchit and are linked by the Skywalk – a covered walkway beneath the Skytrain tracks – which connects the Chidlom, Siam Square and National Stadium Skytrain stations. This means you can walk from mall to mall without ever touching terra firma. Just a stone's throw from Siam Square, a warren of market stalls and shops catering to a trendy teenage clientele, is the high-end Siam Discovery Centre, as well as Mahboonkrong (MBK), a multi-storey bargain-hunter's heaven. Nearby is the gargantuan Siam Paragon mall, are

LEFT: dazzling colours in a Thai silk shop. **RIGHT:** night markets are great places to pick up unusual and inexpensive souvenirs.

THE ART OF BARGAINING

First, don't start bargaining unless you really want to buy. Stage One involves asking the price. At Stage Two you say it is too much, and they will (99 percent of the time) lower the original price, signalling they are open to offers. Then you offer your first price, which is always too low, and from there the volley of bargaining begins until the final price is agreed. It's a good idea, if you can, to watch local shoppers to see what price they get. And walking away is a good tactic. You may be called back with a better price, and if not you've at least established some groundwork for trying at another stall (many stock the same items).

COUNTERFEIT CITY

Bangkok has long had an unwelcome reputation for its fakes, from Louis Vuitton handbags to pirated copies of the latest Hollywood movies. For a fraction of the price of the real thing you can buy reproductions of Rolex, Cartier or Tag Heuer watches. Bear in mind that some reproductions are better than others – a dud "Rolex" may stop running a few weeks after purchase. Clothes are a safer bet. Popular knock-offs include Nike, Hilfiger, Armani, dkny and Ralph Lauren. The quality can vary tremendously, so inspect each garment carefully.

With increasing pressure from international companies, the Thai government musters half-hearted crackdowns on counterfeit goods from time to time, but the trade is fairly open. Sporadic government raids only mean that watches, DVDs or audio cds are sometimes sold more surreptitiously. The covers of pirated DVDs, for instance, are displayed in albums at street-side stalls; once buyers have made their choices, vendors will disappear to a hidden stash nearby and minutes later return with the merchandise.

Fake goods can be found almost anywhere in Bangkok's markets and shopping malls, but they proliferate mainly around the Thanon Silom and Patpong night markets, MBK Centre and the stalls that spring up along Thanon Sukhumvit (Soi 5 to Soi 11) each evening.

peppered with high-end boutiques, cafés, and even a giant aquarium and a Ferrari showroom. Further down the road is the even bigger Central World mall. At the other end of the Skywalk is luxury shopping at Gaysorn Plaza and Erawan Bangkok, which boasts funky fashion from the likes of Galliano and Yamomoto.

Other good areas for shopping are Chinatown, where the maze of crowded streets gives a taste of old Bangkok without the tacky tourist goods; Thanon Khao San, catering to its backpacker clientele, so shops there specialise in tattooing, hair-braiding, funky clothes, used books and silver jewellery; and Pratunam for its interesting market and also for Panthip Plaza, where various shops sell computers, software, games and DVDs.

The best times to shop

Shops in the main downtown and tourist areas open daily, usually from 10am to 10pm, but in the Old City and Chinatown they will normally close on Sundays. Bangkok hosts a number of seasonal sales that offer unique items, such as the twice-yearly prison sale of wooden furniture made by Thai prisoners. Check the local English-language newspaper listing sections for details. Also worth attending are the annual export sales events such as Made in Thailand, the Bangkok International Gift Fair (BIG) and the Bangkok

International Houseware Fair (BIH). Every June–July and December–January, major department stores and malls take part in the Thailand Grand Sales, though many also offer a 5 percent tourist discount year-round – simply show your passport at the point of purchase. Additionally, you can claim the 7 percent VAT refund at the airport *(see page 262)*.

Traditional Thai products

Thailand is famous the world over for the fine quality of its traditional handicrafts, and there is an extraordinary variety on offer.

Northern silversmiths pound out bowls coated with an extract of tamarind to enhance their sheen. Teakwood is carved into practical items such as breadboards and salad bowls, as well as more decorative trivets and statues of mythical gods, angels and elephants. Bronze statues of classical drama figures like the recumbent deer from the *Ramakien* make elegant decorations. Brassware, like the large noodle cabinets which street vendors sling on bamboo poles, can double up as small side tables. Natural fibre woven into placemats, laundry baskets and handbags also make great buys.

Thai craftsmen excel at lacquerware, the art of overlaying wooden or bamboo items with glossy black lacquer, then painting scenes in gold leaf on this black "canvas". Bowls and trays are the main items sold. One of Thailand's lesser-known arts is nielloware, which involves applying an amalgam of black metal onto etched portions of silver or, to a lesser extent, gold. Thai craftsmen are also supremely skilled at setting oyster shells aglow in black lacquer backgrounds to create scenes of enchanting beauty.

Thais have been crafting pots for over 5,000 years with great skill. While original antiques are rarities, most ceramics are still thrown in the same

FAR LEFT: lacquerware at Chatuchak market. **LEFT AND ABOVE:** elaborate wood carvings of fiery dragons and a scene from the *Ramakien*. **RIGHT:** kitsch trinkets.

shapes and designs as their age-old counterparts. Among the best-known are Sangkhaloke ceramic plates from ancient Sukhothai, with their distinctive twin-fish design. Celadon is a beautiful stoneware with a light jade green or dark-brown glaze, and is used to make dinnerware, lamps and statuary. *Bencharong* originated in China and was later developed by Thai artists. Its name describes its look: *bencha* is Sanskrit for five, and *rong* means colour. The five colours of *bencharong* – red, blue, yellow, green and white – appear on delicate porcelain bowls, containers, ashtrays and decorative items. Popular blue-and-white porcelain, which also originated in China, has been produced extensively in Thailand for centuries.

Thai handicrafts are found in shops and markets all over the city, and some of the more specialist shops are worth seeking out. If pressed for time, head for Nayarana Phand in Thanon Ratchadamri, a one-stop shop for all things Thai.

Export Permits

The Thai **Department of Fine Arts** prohibits the export of all Thai Buddha images, images of other deities and fragments (hands or heads) of images dating before the 18th century. All antiques must be registered with them. The shop will usually do this for you, or you can take the piece yourself to the office at Thanon Na Prathat (tel: 0-2226 1661) together with two postcard-sized photos of it. The export fee ranges from B50 to B200 depending on the antiquity of the piece. Fake antiques do not require export permits, but airport customs officials are not art experts and may mistake these for genuine pieces. If it looks authentic, clear it at the Department of Fine Arts to avoid problems later.

Antiques

Thai and Burmese antiques are among the finest in Asia, although the real thing is hard to find these days. The tenacious and well-informed can still unearth treasures, but the rule of thumb is to take claims of antiquity with a pinch of salt unless you really know what you're doing; things are not always what they seem. The centre of the city's antiques trade is located on the upper floors of River City, an array of shops selling genuine antiques as well as lookalike *objets d'art*. Note: the Fine Arts Department maintains strict control over the export of religious antiques *(see box, left)*; dealers are usually able to clear buyers' purchases by obtaining export permits and shipping them abroad.

Gems and jewellery

Thailand mines its own rubies and sapphires from the eastern coast city of Chantaburi, and also acts as a conduit for stones from Burma and Cambodia. Globally, Thailand is a major player in the international jewellery market, and Bangkok is home to the world's leading cutters of coloured gems. Rubies range

Thailand has one of the world's leading markets in gemstones and jewellery products, with all aspects of the trade covered in the country, from mining to the finished product.

from pale to deep red (including the famous "pigeon's blood" red); sapphires come in blue, green and yellow, as well as in the form most associated with Thailand – the star sapphire. Thai jewellers can turn gold, white-gold, silver and platinum into delicate jewellery settings and are able to produce both traditional and modern designs.

Be careful when shopping for gems and jewellery; on streets and in some small shops, the stones may not be of the quality and weight advertised. The Tourism Authority of Thailand has joined hands with gem-trading organisations to provide quality control through the Jewel Fest Club – look for the ruby-ring logo on shop fronts.

Left Top: ornate lacquer jewellery. **Left Bottom:** toy cars made from recycled beer cans. **Above:** the place to go for a tailor-made silk suit.

Textiles and tailoring

The potential glamour of Thai silk was recognised in the late 1940s by American entrepreneur Jim Thompson. He promoted it abroad where it quickly gained wide acceptance for its bumpy texture and shimmering iridescence. Today, silk has become a major Thai industry. While the Jim Thompson shop offers an excellent range of coloured silks and ready-made products, bargains can also be gleaned from the lesser-known Jim Thompson Factory Outlet.

Also worth buying is *mudmee*, a northeastern silk characterised by subtle zigzagging lines and in more sombre hues such as dark blue, maroon and deep yellow. Dazzling embroidery can be found in the modern-day versions of *teen chok* – a method with which women of the ancient Lanna kingdom in the north of Thailand symbolically wove their family histories into their sarongs. The country's northern hill-tribes each have their own distinctive patchwork and embroidery designs, mainly in bright blues, magentas and yellows. At the Siam Centre's Mae Fah Luang shop – a royal initiative to pro-

mote the livelihood of Thai villagers through traditional means – you can purchase hand-woven silks and cottons in lengths, or ready-made into cushion covers and clothes.

Using local and imported fabrics, Bangkok's excellent tailors can whip up perfectly fitted three-piece suits for men as well as elegant dresses with appliqué and beadwork for women. Choose designs from catalogues, conjure up your own creations or have your old favourites copied. If using your own material, rummage at Bangkok's famous fabric market on Sampeng Lane in Chinatown. Though some shops offer a 24-hour service, it's always best to return for at least one fitting to ensure the best results.

Cutting-edge Thai

Thai craftsmanship and creativity extends far beyond the realm of the traditional, and Bangkok is fast becoming a hub for cutting-edge design. Keep an eye out for some of Thailand's up-and-coming homegrown fashion labels such as the flamboyant offerings from Fly Now and Jaspal, or the more understated designs from Greyhound. Thai designers are also making waves in the area of home decor. Propaganda (at Siam Discovery Centre and Emporium) produces innovative accessories, while Ayodhya (at Gaysorn Plaza) offers a line of chi-chi throws and water hyacinth furniture. Thai cosmetics companies, such as Harnn, are also reinventing natural Thai beauty products like jasmine rice soap and tamarind facial scrubs, and packaging them in elegant rattan baskets.

Even the shopping experience is being repackaged; if you get bored with the city's seemingly limitless supply of department stores and malls, you can sample more eclectic boutique shops like It's Happened to Be a Closet (Emporium mall), where customers are encouraged to mix-and-match vintage dress designs with homeware products and accessories, before dining in their coffee shop or popping into their hair stylist. ❑

• *For more recommended shops and markets, see the Shopping listings in the Places section chapters.*

Bangkok Bazaar

Markets are an essential Bangkok experience. In fact, they're hard to avoid: shops spill onto every street, and vendors hawk goods off metal carts and tarpaulin sheets

The colours, noise and pungent aromas of Bangkok's markets *(talad)* are a tantalising assault on the senses. And Bangkok has a market for just about every neighbourhood, and every hour of the day or night.

The ultimate bazaar is **Chatuchak Weekend Market** *(see page 184)* affectionately dubbed "JJ" due to the alternative Thai spelling, Jatujak. Some 15,000 stalls offer a mind-boggling variety of goods. From pedigree pooches to hill-tribe fabrics, old Thai movie posters and handmade paper... you name it, it's here.

There are numerous markets tucked around the shopping malls and department stores of central Bangkok. **Pratunam Market** *(see page 159)* rivals Chatuchak for its selection of clothing. At midday the stalls at **Soi La Lai Sap** (literally "lane which melts your money away") sell shoes, handbags and myriad accessories. **Thanon Khao San** *(see page 137)* is lined with stalls offering backpacker requisites such as silver jewellery, hand-painted cards and second-hand books.

For a real flavour of **Chinatown** *(see page 145)* wander the length of **Soi Itsaranuphap**, passing spice shops, a fish market and stores selling religious paraphernalia. At its river end, **Talad Kao** *(see page 149)* sells fresh produce. Also in Chinatown, at the so-called "Thieves Market" *(see page 148)*, where in the past residents would look for items burgled from their homes, you find musical instrument shops and antiques. Retaining more of its traditional atmosphere is **Faichai**, or Flashlight Market, held on Saturday evenings along the labyrinth of streets around Central Hospital near Chinatown. It sells a variety of goods and bric-a-brac. **Pahurat Market** has all things Indian, from saris to henna dyes, and don't miss the 24-hour **Flower Market**, which spills into the clothes and accessories stalls of **Saphan Phut Market** come nightfall.

For more nighttime shopping, head to **Suan Lum Night Bazaar** *(see page 159)*. With stalls selling handicrafts, clothes and furniture, it's a smaller version of Chatuchak without the midday heat and crowds. Other evening markets, like those along **Thanon Silom** and in **Patpong** *(see page 171)*, as well as the stalls along **Thanon Sukhumvit** (roughly Soi 5 to Soi 11), are a treasure-trove of counterfeit goods and souvenirs, and are open until midnight. **Damnoen Saduak**, the most famous floating market, selling vegetables and fruit *(see page 197)* on the outskirts of Bangkok, is now mainly a tourist attraction, but still worth a visit. ❑

LEFT TOP: funky stationery at the Propaganda store. **LEFT BOTTOM:** window display at cutting-edge fashion store, Fly Now. **RIGHT:** Sukhumvit night market.

ENTERTAINMENT
KING'S GROUP
G.T. COLOR LAB

BANGKOK AFTER DARK

Bangkok struts to live jazz, rock and indie music with a thriving scene full of hip clubs and cool bars. You can sip champagne cocktails on a rooftop 63 storeys up, or down cheap beers in a bar with no walls. There really is something here for everyone

Many visitors' expectations of Bangkok nightlife extend no further than the much-hyped Patpong go-go bar scene, but this cosmopolitan city has plenty of options for entertainment once the sun goes down. The Thai craving for *sanuk* (fun) has in recent years seen booms in everything from microbreweries and bars offering Cuban cigars and art on the walls to clubs specialising in music as diverse as jazz, Latin, hip hop, house and mind-numbing techno, often all on the same street. In addition, there is traditional dance, theatre, opera, classical music, indie films and evening sports aplenty. Bangkok really comes alive under the cover of darkness, and never before has it offered so much choice to the nighttime reveller.

Nightlife zones

Officially, for the purposes of nightlife entertainment, Bangkok is divided into three zones: Thanon Silom, Thanon Ratchadaphisek and Royal City Avenue (RCA), where venues with valid dance licences can stay open until 2am. The rest should close by 1am. This system was introduced early this century, following a clampdown on drugs, underage drinking and inappropriate behaviour close to temples and schools. But habits die hard: Bangkok has long had a party atmosphere, and although the zones survive, the restrictions in other areas are less strictly enforced. If anything, the extra regulations merely provide extra opportunities for the local police to collect bribes. A venue may or may not close according to law, and there are generally places to carry on drinking if you follow your nose. One lingering effect of the crackdown is that you have to be over 20 to enter clubs and almost all require you to show ID, whatever your age. Best to carry a photocopy of your passport, rather than the original.

The Silom zone includes the famous Patpong red-light district as well as numerous pubs and restaurants, but little in the way of dance clubs outside Soi 2 and Soi 4. Thanon Ratchadaphisek has been the traditional stomping ground for huge gentlemen's clubs and even larger massage parlours, visited mainly

LEFT: the night comes alive at infamous Patpong.
RIGHT: racing through the streets of Bangkok on a tuk-tuk.

THAI ROCK AND COUNTRY

Three types of music dominate Thai-style rock and country clubs. The rock-format *plaeng puer cheewit* (Songs For Life) is played in countless Bangkok clubs notable for their kitschy decor of cowboy hats, buffalo horns and Confederate flags from the US Civil War. The music has its roots in the record collections of American GIs stationed in Thailand during the Vietnam War, and the lyrics developed as protest songs during Thailand's student uprisings of the early 1970s. The most famous practitioner of this music form is Ad Carabao, who still plays gigs with his band Carabao.

Luk thung (Child of the Rice Fields), as the name suggests, is Thai country music and mainly appeals to the working class. Its lyrics recount "real life" issues, ranging from unrequited love to poverty and despair. The genre of music is so popular it has spawned several magazines and TV programmes, and even a few films.

Morlam (Master Rap) is an upcountry form sung in the Lao dialect by singers sometimes dressed in ornate costumes inspired by the royal courts. The lyrics are usually improvised and are usually highly sexual or political. You'll hear *luk thung* and *morlam* played on taxi drivers' radios and in clubs primarily located on the outskirts of town where Isaan migrant communities congregate. Spicy food and copious amounts of local rice-based whiskies are the fuel for any of these gigs.

by Thais and Asian tourists, but there's also a clutch of smaller bars and live music venues that attract young Thais. You'll occasionally find imported bands here as diverse as heavy metallists Lamb of God and the Indie folk duo Kings of Convenience, who appeared within weeks of each other in 2010.

Of the three zones, it is RCA that has developed into the most focused club scene in town, with a stretch of hip bars and clubs that people flit in and out of. Dedicated restaurants are scarce in the area, but most bars and clubs in Bangkok have some provision for food, and there are reasonable Thai menus at most places on the strip. Current hot spots with dance floors include Route 66 and 808, the latter of which has a regular influx of international DJs.

The club scene

Bangkok's club scene is constantly expanding. Dance music has evolved from ear-bashing

LEFT: Bangkok has no shortage of cocktail bars.
ABOVE: renowned live music venue, Overtone.
RIGHT: party time at Q Bar.

techno to include hip-hop, deep house, jungle, Indian vibes, and countless variations led by cutting-edge dance clubs like Bed Supperclub and Q Bar (both Sukhumvit Soi 11), and Club Culture (Thanon Sri Ayutthaya), all of which draw multinational crowds. All these spots regularly import international DJs like Goldie, Judge Jules and Joachim Garraud, in addition to hosting an increasingly confident posse of local DJs who go by names like Dragon, Seed and Funky Gangster.

The lanes off Soi Thonglor have popular bars and clubs such as Demo that draw Thais and expats from around town. A Thai scene also flourishes in the backpacker quarter near Thanon Khao San, with hot venues like Café Democ and The Club.

Even some of the city's hotels are getting funky, with great wine-and-dine monthly specials with electronic sounds at Barsu, in the Sheraton Grande, and fashion shows and film nights at Met Bar, in The Metropolitan Hotel.

Live music

Front-line international acts of many genres stop off at Bangkok on Asian tours. Recent visits include Placebo, who headlined the annual Tiger Translate Festival in 2010, sax giant Chris Potter at the boutique Niu's Bangkok Jazz Festival, and Eric Clapton, who threw out some blues at Impact Arena.

Local music in bars varies tremendously. The huge Tawandaeng German Brewhouse on Thanon Narathiwat features local band Fong Nam, led by American classical avant gardist Bruce Gaston. They fuse a traditional Thai *phiphat* orchestra with rock in a quirky, highly costumed night of cabaret. Thai rock and country *(see box opposite)* features in barn-like venues, usually on the outskirts of town, and there's a good helping of R&B, blues, rock and jazz *(see text box page 84)*, by local, visiting and expat musicians all over the city. Good live jazz and blues venues include Ad Here, Saxophone and Niu's on Silom; axe-hero rock appears at Overtone, on RCA; while Brick Bar, on Khao San Road, stages rock, ska and reggae.

T-pop (Thai pop music), like its Western counterpart, is a PR-heavy package of cute faces and bubblegum tunes, often fronted by *luk kreung* (half-Thai, half-Western) stars like Tata Young. Indie labels like Hualampong Riddim and Panda Records provide recording opportu-

nities outside the mainstream, and their bands play regular gigs. Look out, too, in the local press for Indie promoters Mind the Gap, who hold regular events featuring various genres like electronica, thrash and grunge around the city. Every November, Bangkok's coolest radio station, Fat Radio (104.5FM), stages its two-day Fat Festival at various venues.

Bars and pubs

Upmarket bars with international sensibilities are found all over central Bangkok. Try sky-high champagne and caviar (both in price and altitude) at the rooftop Sky Bar and Distil, both with astonishing views of the city, in the State Tower on Thanon Silom, or cocktails at the exquisite modern Thai restaurant Mahanaga (Sukhumvit Soi 29) or Face Bar (Sukhumvit Soi 38). The Conrad Bangkok has one of the coolest hotel lobby bars imaginable in the Diplomat Bar, while the Sofitel Silom offers reasonably priced bottles of wine with 37th-floor city panoramas at V9. And, as high fliers sip their fine champagne and cocktails, lo-sos head for Cheap Charlie's – nothing more than a bar (no roof, no walls) – on Sukhumvit Soi 11. The hip Thai scene constantly shifts with the whims of local image mavens, but increasingly centres on Soi Thonglor, in venues like To Die For.

The English and Irish pub scene is mainly concentrated on Thanon Silom and Thanon Sukhumvit, with notable venues being the Bull's Head (Sukhumvit Soi 33) and Molly Malone's (Soi Convent, off Thanon Silom). There are also a few American-style sports bars, such as The Roadhouse (Thanon Surawong), which has great Buffalo wings, and microbreweries like the Londoner Brew Pub (corner of Sukhumvit Soi 33). All these places have variations on the usual pub grub and games formula.

Blue-blooded Jazz Player

King Bhumibol is a keen sax player and jazz composer – he's jammed with virtually all the jazz musicians who have visited Bangkok, including Stan Getz and Benny Goodman – and the city organises jazz festivals each year to commemorate his birthday. Regular gigs around town include Niu's on Silom and the Living Room (Sheraton Grande hotel), both of which attract fine resident bands and visiting guests like sax player James Carter. The Oriental Hotel's Bamboo Bar has an excellent Russian jazz quartet which backs foreign singers, while Saxophone, on Thanon Phayathai, is the pick of the city's stand-alone venues, with Latin and big band outfits as regulars.

The gay scene

Whether tolerance towards gays and lesbians is increasing or decreasing in Thailand often depends on the nuances of context, but either way the scene is thriving and very visible. Clubs and bars around Silom Soi 2 and Soi 4 cater to a variety of gay tastes, be it quiet drinking and Thai dining at Sphinx (Soi 4), boozy cruising

Increasingly bars, promoters and record companies are massaging the creative forces of Bangkok's non-mainstream musicians. Electro, grunge and metal bands are plugging in all over town.

at Balcony (Soi 4) or hard dance at DJ Station (Soi 2). Soi 2 has a pretty much exclusively gay crowd, while Soi 4 is more of a free-for-all, its street-side tables hosting people of varying sexual inclinations watching the world go by. Gay sex shows and gay pick-up joints with go-go boys are located around Thanon Surawong, particularly on Soi Tawan and Duangthawee Plaza. The iconic Bangkok Gay Pride Festival (www.bangkokpride.org/en) is an on–off event pencilled in every November as a year-end climax of parades and celebration around the Silom–Patpong area.

FAR LEFT: live jazz at the Saxophone. **LEFT:** the spectacular view from Dome at the State Tower. **ABOVE:** a night club in the Nana Plaza red-light district. **ABOVE:** transsexual cabaret performers.

Red-light entertainment

As titillating foreign press headlines so readily paint Bangkok as a city of sleaze, it surprises visitors to find how small the red-light zone really is. The go-go bars that cater to *farang* (foreigners) in Patpong 1 and Patpong 2, and Nana Entertainment Plaza and Soi Cowboy on Thanon Sukhumvit, are largely neon-lit

strips with a (usually) gentle hustle from girls hanging outside. Transsexual "ladyboys" (*katoey*) can be more aggressive, particularly after hours around Soi Nana. Tourists who prefer more discreet adult entertainment seek out the bars along Sukhumvit Soi 33. Asian men often make a beeline for the massage parlours of Thanon Ratchadaphisek and Thanon Petchaburi; Soi Thaniya in Silom caters largely to Japanese.

Most bars feature pole-dancing girls gyrating in bikinis, although a few illegal "upstairs" shows offer full nudity and sex acts, either simulated or real. The infamous shows where girls use their genitalia for assorted juggling of bananas, darts and ping pong balls still appear on menu cards handed out in Patpong.

Prostitution, however, extends beyond the borders of these places; most clubs and bars around town will have freelance working girls (and boys) roaming the dance floors.

Kathoey cabaret

Thailand's famous transsexual cabaret shows have become an international staple, as these entertaining acts now travel to global events like the Edinburgh Festival. Mambo, on Thanon Rama III, and New Calypso Cabaret at Asia Hotel, on Thanon Phayathai, are the main Bangkok venues. The shows feature saucy (and sometimes risqué) lip-synching song and dance routines performed by a revue of sequinned and feather boa'ed artistes at various stages of sex-change surgery.

Theatre and dance

Thespian Patravadi Mejudhon stages modern dance and drama that is often inspired by traditional and Buddhist themes at her open-air Patravadi Theatre in Thonburi. Performances are usually in Thai, but as they are music and dance oriented, they are often accessible to foreigners.

There are short performances of the classical *khon* dance-drama at tourist venues and restaurants, while more serious performances are held at Sala Chalerm Krung Theatre each weekend.

The recently opened Aksra Theatre and the Joe Louis Theatre, at Suan Lum Night Bazaar, which has won many international awards, both stage *hun lakhon lek*, a traditional puppet theatre based on the *khon* dance-drama.

Above and Right: cabaret performers, from the sublime to the ridiculous. **Far Right:** a frenetic bout of *muay thai*.

Opera and classical music

Multi-talented Cambridge graduate Somtow Sucharitkul, who has written Hollywood horror scripts and several books in English, including the excellent *Jasmine Nights*, set up the Bangkok Opera in 2002. Among its three or four yearly productions of classics, like *The Magic Flute*, are Somtow's own works (written in English) such as *Mae Naak*, which is based on a Thai ghost story. Among their ambitious projects they intend to complete the entire *Ring Cycle* over the next few years. The concerts are mainly staged at the Thailand Cultural Centre, off Thanon Ratchadapisek.

> Kathoey, *or ladyboy, cabaret shows are now taking their sequins and lip-synching routines to international festivals, but two of the best companies, Mambo and New Calypso Cabaret, entertain every night in Bangkok.*

The Bangkok Symphony Orchestra, as well as providing many of the musicians for the Bangkok Opera, plays regular concerts throughout the year, also at the Thai Cultural Centre and on Sundays during the cool season in Lumphini Park.

The International Festival of Dance and Music brings international acts for a season of opera, classical music, contemporary dance and ballet every September to October.

Nighttime sports

Bangkok at night isn't all booze and boogie. You might want to try disco bowling – to music and flashing lights – at several bowling alleys in the city, or RCA has an indoor go-kart track. There's even night golf, and snooker clubs that open into the small hours.

Nobody who comes to Thailand should miss the sport of *muay thai*, frenzied kickboxing accompanied by the wailing of traditional music and animated betting on the outcome. Lumphini Stadium remains the world mecca of *muay thai*, which has not been relocated despite several attempts in the past few years. Another venue at which to watch the sport is the Art Deco Ratchadamnoen Stadium in the Dusit area. ❑

• *Recommendations for pubs and bars are listed at the end of each Places section chapter. See also Travel Tips (see pages 251–3) for more information on nightlife.*

SPAS AND WELLNESS CENTRES

One of the world's great spa centres, Thailand has a penchant for pampering rooted in its ancient history of traditional Thai massage. And Bangkok is packed with plush spas to relax both body and mind

Thailand is renowned as the spa capital of Asia, and with good reason. Many treatments we now associate with modern spa "pampering" have their origins in the ancient healing methods brought to Thailand as part of Buddhist philosophy. They have existed here for nearly 2,000 years, so Thai therapists have a knowledge of practices that have been handed down through generations. Thai massage is one of the great pleasures of visiting Thailand, and it is available cheaply at small shophouses all over Bangkok, although signs offering services such as "soapy massage" promise a very different kind of experience. These days, of course, you can also opt for a more luxurious environment and a wider choice of treatments at hotel spas.

The spas draw on natural healing practices such as traditional Thai massage, herbal compresses and herbal steams and baths that have long been provided in the country's temples, which served as doctor and hospital to local communities.

The famed warmth of Thai people extends to masseuses and therapists, so the spa visit here tends to be not only gentle and relaxing, but also a highly personalised experience. In fact there is a Buddhist concept of giving on the part of the masseur that, in the best instances, ensures this personal connection.

Traditional Thai massage

Perhaps the most unique spa treatment for visitors to Thailand is the traditional Thai massage, or *nuad paen boran* (ancient massage), which is as old as the name suggests. Buddhist monks brought the practice with them from India when they arrived in Thailand in the 2nd or 3rd century AD. They taught that Shivakar Kumar Baccha, the Buddha's personal medical advisor, developed it from Indian Vedic treatments. Temples were traditional places of healing as well as worship, and as Buddhism spread through Thailand, so did Thai massage.

Thai massage technique is linked to the ancient Indian yoga philosophy which holds that our life energy is supplied along 72,000 meridian lines that run through our bodies. This is why some of the stretching actions of Thai massage resemble the stretching poses of

yoga. Thai massage focuses on 10 key energy lines (*sip sen*), and uses pressure to release the blocked energy along those lines.

There is also a spiritual element to Thai massage. It is believed that the masseuse is healing the recipient by offering loving care through his or her hands. In ancient times, the masseuse would say a prayer to centre the mind in a meditative mood before performing a healing massage, and some will still do this today. This meditative awareness enables the masseuse to sense the energy flow and blockages in the recipient's body, thus providing optimum healing to the affected areas. When done properly, the masseuse should feel as relaxed as the recipient, because Thai massage is supposed to be a spiritual act that nourishes both the giver and the recipient.

> *The ancient healing art of Thai massage was initially considered a spiritual practice, a meditative application of loving kindness. It is based on the concept of invisible energy lines that run throughout the body.*

Left: stress-relieving yoga meditation at Devarana Spa.
Above: the sumptuous River Private Spa suite, at the Bangkok Peninsula Hotel.

Unlike Western massage, Thai massage does not make use of oils or lotions, apart from occasional heating balms on areas of particular tightness, and the recipient remains fully clothed. The client is supplied with loose-fitting cotton pyjamas and the massage is done on a mattress laid on the floor. The masseuse uses his or her thumbs, arms, elbows, knees and feet, and may climb all over your body and even walk on your back.

The masseuse uses a combination of pressure and stretching techniques, done in a rhythmic and rocking motion that usually lasts for between one and two hours. The deep tissue kneading can be initially painful and towards the end of the massage, expect to be twisted and stretched into yoga-like poses.

Shophouse operations all over Bangkok, particularly in tourist areas, offer Thai massage from around B200 an hour with little more than a mattress and a curtain as decor. In hotels and, increasingly, independent urban spas the treatment has gone upmarket, joining the likes

Hotel and Day Spas in Bangkok

For the ultimate in pampering, head for **The Mandarin Oriental Spa** in the Oriental Hotel. It is the pioneer of Thai spas and is designed in the style of a Thai teak house (48 Oriental Avenue; tel: 0-2233 9630; www.mandarinoriental.com). A few doors down is the equally stunning **Peninsula Spa** in the Peninsula Hotel (333 Thanon Charoennakorn; tel: 0-2861 2888; www.bangkok.peninsula.com). In the Business District, try the exquisite Thai-style **Devarana Spa** at the Dusit Thani Hotel (946 Thanon Rama 4; tel: 0-2636 3600, ext. 7006; www.devarana.com), which is imbued with the feeling of a light and airy Thai temple, or the **Shambala Spa** at the ultra-chic Metropolitan Hotel (27 Thanon Sathorn Tai; tel: 0-2625 3357; www.metropolitan.com.bz). Equally tempting is the exotic **Chi Spa** at the luxury Shangri-La Hotel (89 Soi Wat Suan Plu; tel: 0-2236 7777; www.shangri-la.com).

Bangkok's growing number of day spas are located all over town, often in renovated old houses. Popular is the **Divana** spa chain (8 Sukhumvit Soi 35, tel: 0-2661 4818; 7 Sukhumvit Soi 25, tel: 0-2261 6784; 103 Soi Thonglor 17, tel: 0-2712 8986; www.divana-dvn.com). Or try **Rasayana Retreat** (57 Soi Sukhumvit 39; tel: 0-2662 4803-5; www.rasayanaretreat.com), which also has Thailand's only raw-food restaurant offering organic meals.

of Swedish massage and reiki on wide-ranging, pampering menus that can cost thousands of baht. If you want to take things further, Wat Pho Thai Traditional Massage School (2 Thanon Sanam Chai; tel: 0-2622 3550; www.watpomassage.com; daily 10am–6pm) teaches traditional massage and meditation for those who want to learn the art.

Steams, saunas and compresses

A number of other treatments offered in Thai spas stem from the same ancient healing tradition. The use of heat therapies combined with herbal ingredients is a distinguishing trait of traditional Thai healing practices. One of the most popular is the Thai herbal steam or sauna. Their healing secret lies in the use of indigenous Thai herbs like turmeric, *prai*, lemongrass, camphor and kaffir lime. Aside from providing an overall health and skin booster, practitioners claim that Thai herbal steam can result in weight loss if done consistently over an extended period of time.

Another ancient Thai healing therapy is the

use of hot herbal compresses made of medicinal herbs wrapped in a tight bundle, steamed for several hours, and then pressed against trouble areas of the body, like tense shoulders or rheumatic joints. The key to healing lies in the combination of medicinal herbs and heat.

Spa options

While Thailand is well known for its self-contained resort spas complete with accommodation and set in scenic areas, Bangkok also offers a bewildering number of spas that are popular with visitors as well as locals. The most luxurious establishments are hotel spas. These welcome the public as well as hotel guests, and usually spare no expense on design and fittings – with prices to match. Less extravagant but with a charm of their own are the many day spas around Bangkok, usually located in renovated old houses and set among well-tended gardens. Day-spa prices veer towards the mid-price range, and the treatments are just as good as hotel spas.

New on the scene is the medical spa, combining hospital health services with holistic spa therapies. Here, Western health practices such as medical check-ups and laser cosmetic surgery are offered in the same place as traditional Thai massage and Chinese acupuncture – to both fix and pamper your body at the same time. Patients can select from a variety of slimming, rejuvenation and detox fasting programmes, tailored to individual needs. ❑

Far Left: welcome to the River Private Spa, at the Bangkok Peninsula Hotel, one of the city's most luxurious spas. **Left:** relaxing massage at Divana spa. **Above:** an energetic yoga workout.

Medical Spas

The centrally located **S Medical Spa** is chic and well thought out. It has physicians, dermatologists, and even psychiatrists on site for clients. A wide choice of treatments is available, and includes use of steam rooms, hydrotherapy pools, jacuzzi and other facilities (2/2 Phakdi Building, Thanon Withayu; tel: 0-2253 1010; www.smedspa.com).

The **Bangkok Dermatology Centre** (SCB Park Plaza; tel: 0-2937 5455; www.bkkdermato.com) puts the focus on beauty, with a dermatology clinic offering laser surgery, plus spa rooms for sessions of pampering body massages, scrubs and reflexology treatments.

0-2287-3004-8
13
HONDA

U2
HONDA

PLACES

A detailed guide to the entire city and its surroundings, with principal sites numbered and clearly cross-referenced to the maps

Modern Bangkok, much of which just 60 years ago was empty land, has grown rapidly and largely unplanned. As a result, Thailand's capital can seem a bewildering maze of old and new, exotic and humdrum. But there are recognisable areas, each with its own character.

The city's layout began when King Rama I dug a canal at a bend in the Chao Phraya river to form the artificial island of Rattanakosin. Its glittering highlights, including the Grand Palace and Wat Pho, are an essential part of any tour.

Surrounding Rattanakosin, but still within the capital's original walls, is the Old City, with important temples like Wat Suthat, and shops devoted to religious materials, frequented by monks. Also part of the Old City is Banglamphu, a hub for budget travellers, especially around Thanon Khao San and the Khao San Road.

In the 20th century, the monarchy moved north to Dusit, where the Ananta Samakom Throne Hall is the centrepiece of several European-influenced palaces around royal Dusit Park.

East of Rattanakosin, along the river, are the enclaves where foreigners originally settled: Chinatown and Bangrak, an early home to the European community. Thanon Silom and Thanon Sathorn dominate Bangrak today, and comprise the main business district. The infamous Patpong red-light area is at Silom's eastern end. North of here are the shopping malls of Pathumwan, where Thanon Rama I continues east to Sukhumvit, a major middle-class residential area full of nightlife and restaurants.

All of these are along one bank of the Chao Phraya river. On the opposite, southern bank is Thonburi, which was briefly the royal capital. While it too is an ill-considered urban sprawl, it has the attraction of canals that thread past old wooden houses and temples to give a glimpse of a traditional life perhaps less confusing than that of today. ❑

PRECEDING PAGES: spectacular views from Sirocco, the world's highest outdoor restaurant; motorcycle taxis waiting for passengers. **LEFT AND ABOVE RIGHT:** Bot of the Emerald Buddha. **ABOVE LEFT:** night-time skyline.

BANG PHLAD
Soi Charan Sanit Wong 40
Nonthaburi
Thanon Somdet Phra Pin Klao
Soi Suwannin
Amarin
Soi Suwichandamri
THA THEWET
National Library
Wat Thewarat Kunchon
Th. Samsen
Th. Uthong Nok
Soi Samsen 12
Th. Ratchasima
Vimanmek
National Assembly (Parliament)
Abhisek Dusit Throne Hall
Ananta Samakhom (Royal Throne Hall)
SUAN SAT DUSIT
Dusit Zoo
DUSIT
Uthong Nai Gate
Th. Sri Ayutthaya
Th. Phitsanulok
Parusakkawan Palace
King Chulalongkorn
AMPORN PARK
Prem Prachakon
Thanon Rama V
Chitralada Palace
Rama VIII Saphan
Chao Phraya
Th. Wisut Kasat
THA WISUTHI KASAT
Wat Indra Wiharn
Soi The Wet 1
Th. Krung Kasem
Th. Luk Luang
Nok
Wat Dao Wadung
Th. Arun
Wat Sam Phraya
Wat Mai Amatarot
Wat Benjamabophit (Marble Temple)
Th. Nakhon Pathom
Thanon Sri Ayutthaya
National Museum of Royal Barges
PHRA PIN KLAO BRIDGE
THA PHRA ATHIT
Wat Sangwet
Soi Samsen 4
Wat Mongkrut
Government House
Royal Turf Club
Ansorel Sunnah
UNICEF
Th. Phra Athit
Th. Chakrabongse
Banglamphu
Th. Prachathipathai
Krasat Thiyaram
Ratchadamnoen Boxing Stadium
Thanon Phitsanulok
Bangkok Noi
Saphan Phra Pin Klao
Wat Chai Chana Songkhram
Th. Phra Sumen
Wisut Kasat
Wat Sommanat
Phadung Krung Kasem
Thanon Sawan
Bangkok Noi/Thonburi Railway Station
THON BURI
Banphak Rotfai
National Museum
National Theatre
National Gallery
Th. Chao Fa
Th. Khao San
Th. Tanao
Wat Bowonniwet
Th. Dinso
Th. Parinayok
Thanon Ratchadamnoen
Thanon Nakhon Phaniang
Th. Luk Luang
Museum of Forensic Medicine
Thammasat University
Th. Na Phra That
SANAM
Th. Ratchadamnoen Klang
Democracy Monument
Loha Prasat
Thanon Lan Luang
Th. Lan Luang
Thanon Phranok
THA PHRANNOK
Th. Wang Lang
Th. Phra Chan
Maharat
Th. Atsadang
Th. Rachini
Wat Mahathat
LUANG
Wat Mahan
City Hall
Wat Ratchanatda
Thanon Damrong Rak
Chakkaphatdi Phong
Th. Khlong Lan Pak
Th. Krung Kasem
Soi Ban Chang Lo
Th. Arun Amarin
Wat Rakhang
THA CHANG
Th. Na Phra Lan
Lak Muang (City Pillar)
Sao Ching Cha (Giant Swing)
Th. Maha Chai
Th. Boriphat
Wat Saket
Phu Khao Thong (Golden Mount)
Saen Saep
Wat Phraya Yang
Wat Phra Kaew (Emerald Buddha)
Grand Palace
Th. Kanlaya Namit
Th. Ban Baat
Th. Rong Liang Dek
Th. Anantanak
Wat Boromniwat
Wat Ratchapradit
RATTANAKOSIN
Th. Fuang Nakhon
Th. Ti Tong
Wat Suthat
Ban Baat
Thanon Barum Muang
Wat Chamni Hatthakan
Dev Mandir Temple
Th. Luang
Th. Wora Chak
Th. Ditsamak
Th. Yukhon 2
S. Yotsi
Th. Rama I
Thanon Thai Wang
Th. Sanam Chai
Wat Ratchabophit
Th. Charoen Krung
Thanon Arun Amarin
Th. Maharat
Thanon Itsaraphap
THA TIEN
Wat Pho (Reclining Buddha)
Nakhon Kasem (Thieves Market)
Th. Chakrawat
Th. Chao Khamrop
Th. Suapa
Phla Chai
Wat Thepsirin
Th. Luang
Wat Phlapphla Chai
Th. Phlab
S. Itsaraphap 42
Wat Arun (Temple of Dawn)
Siam Discovery Museum
Sri Guru Singh Sabha
Pahurat Market
Th. Chak Phet
Th. Ban Mo
Wat Mangkon Kamalawat
Th. Yaowarat
Maitri
Thanon Rong Muang
Th. Rama
Soi 40
Wang Doem
Pak Khlong Talad (Flower Market)
Th. Chakkaphet
Soi Wanit 1
Wat Chakrawat
CHINATOWN
(New Road)
Talad Mai
Talad Kao
Chit
Hualamphong Railway Station
Thanon Charu Muang
Vichaiprasit (Old Fort)
THA RAJINI
Th. Saphan Phut
MEMORIAL BRIDGE
Wat Ratchburana
Saphan Pra Pokklan
Thanon O-Sathahon
Th. Song Sawat
(Sampeng Lane)
Thanon Songwat
Wat Kalayanamit
Wat Traimit
Rama IV
Hualamphong
THA RATCHAWONG
S. Itsaraphap 28
Th. Thetsaban Sai 1
Wat Prayunwongsawat
S. Somdet Chao Praya 3
Th. Songwat
Th. Traimit
Th. Kao Lan
Th. Maha Phruttharam
Th. Thetsaban Sai 2
Th. Thetsaban 2
Th. Tha Din Daeng
S. Tha Din Daeng 18
Wat Pathuma Kongkha
S. Charoen Phanit
S. Itsaraphap 21
Thanon Itsaraphap
Th. Somdet Chao Praya
Wat Thong Thammachat
Th. Chiang Mai
HARBOUR DEPT.
Th. Charoen Krung (New Rd)
Thonburi Christian Hall
Soi 15
Bangkok Yai
Soi 10
S. Somdet Chao Praya 12
Thanon Prachathipok
River City Shopping Complex
Bang Sakae
Khang Rong Rap Chamnan
Patchamid Fort
THA SI PHRAYA
Royal Orchid
BANGRAK
Wat Yai Si Suphan
Th. Itsaraphap
Th. Tha Din Daeng
Thanon Phet Kasem
Thanon Lad Ya
Soi 13
Soi 3
Soi 2
Soi 5
Th. Charoen Nakhon
Chao Phraya
Charoen Krung 43
Th. Inthraraphitak
Wongwian Yai (King Taksin Mon.)
Soi Wiset San
Thanon Charoen Rat
Soi 3
Soi 2
Soi 1
Soi 2
KHLONG SAN
Soi 8
Soi 10
Soi 7
Soi 9
THA WAT MUANG KAA
Th. Suriwong
Th. Mahasak
Thanon Thoet Thai
Wongwian Yai Railway Station
Soi 4
Tr. Yenchit
Wat Thong Phleng
Wat Suwan Ubasikaram
Oriental
THA ORIENTAL
Assumption Cathedral
Th. Silom
Suanphlu
S. Saksin
Soi 1
Soi 3
Soi Charoen Nakhon 14
THA SHANGRI-LA
Soi 13
Soi 15
2nd State Expressway
S. Surasak
Soi Silom 21
THONBURI
Soi 4
Thanon Krung Thonburi
Shangri-La
Th. Charoen Krung
Wongwain Yai
Krung Thon Buri
Soi Saraphi 3
Wat Phothi Nimit
Thanon Somdet Phra Chao Taksin
Soi Charoen Nakhon 18
Saphan Taksin
THA SATHORN
Th. Sathorn
Th. Sathorn Tai

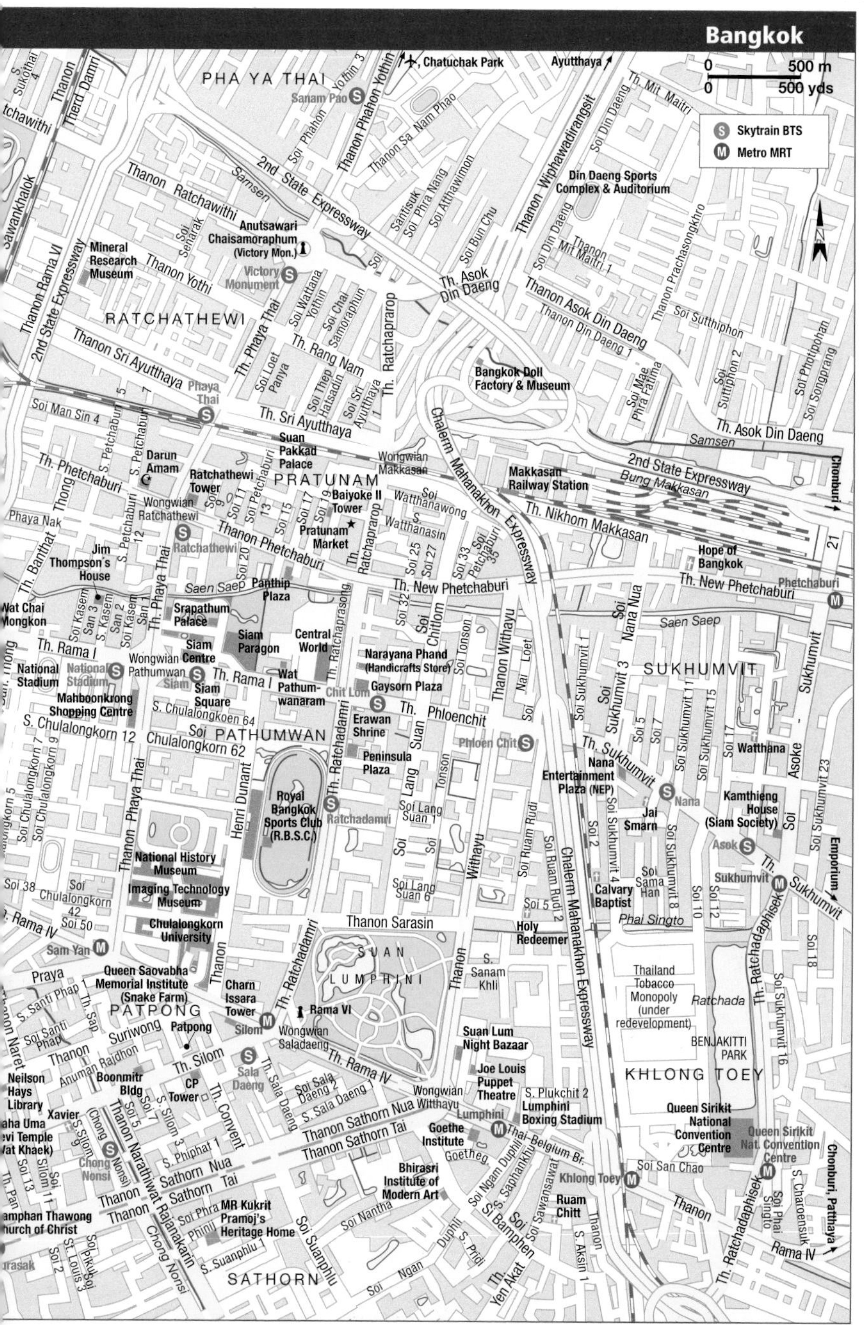
Bangkok
0 500 m
0 500 yds
Skytrain BTS
Metro MRT
Chatuchak Park
Ayutthaya
PHA YA THAI
Sanam Pao
Thanon Phahon Yothin
Thanon Sa Nam Phao
2nd State Expressway
Thanon Ratchawithi
Samsen
Anutsawari Chaisamoraphum (Victory Mon.)
Victory Monument
Mineral Research Museum
Thanon Yothi
RATCHATHEWI
Thanon Sri Ayutthaya
Phaya Thai
Th. Phaya Thai
Th. Rang Nam
Th. Ratchaprarop
Th. Asok Din Daeng
Thanon Wiphawadirangsit
Din Daeng Sports Complex & Auditorium
Thanon Asok Din Daeng
Thanon Din Daeng 1
Thanon Prachasongkhro
Soi Sutthiphon
Bangkok Doll Factory & Museum
Th. Sri Ayutthaya
Suan Pakkad Palace
Wongwian Makkasan
Chalerm Mahanakhon Expressway
Th. Asok Din Daeng
2nd State Expressway
Bung Makkasan
Makkasan Railway Station
Th. Nikhom Makkasan
Chonburi
Darun Amam
Th. Phetchaburi
Ratchathewi Tower
PRATUNAM
Baiyoke II Tower
Pratunam Market
Wongwian Ratchathewi
Ratchathewi
Thanon Phetchaburi
Jim Thompson's House
Hope of Bangkok
Th. New Phetchaburi
Phetchaburi
Saen Saep
Panthip Plaza
Wat Chai Mongkon
Srapathum Palace
Siam Paragon
Central World
Narayana Phand (Handicrafts Store)
Th. Rama I
Siam Centre
National Stadium
Wongwian Pathumwan
Siam
Siam Square
Wat Pathum-wanaram
Chit Lom
Gaysorn Plaza
Th. Phloenchit
Thanon Withayu
SUKHUMVIT
Mahboonkrong Shopping Centre
S. Chulalongkoen 64
Soi PATHUMWAN
Chulalongkorn 62
Erawan Shrine
Peninsula Plaza
Phloen Chit
Th. Sukhumvit
Nana
Entertainment Plaza (NEP)
Watthana
Royal Bangkok Sports Club (R.B.S.C.)
Ratchadamri
Henri Dunant
Soi Lang Suan 1
Jai Smarn
Kamthieng House (Siam Society)
Asok
National History Museum
Imaging Technology Museum
Chulalongkorn University
Soi Lang Suan 6
Calvary Baptist
Sukhumvit
Emporium
Phai Singto
Thanon Sarasin
Holy Redeemer
Sam Yan
SUAN LUMPHINI
Queen Saovabha Memorial Institute (Snake Farm)
Charn Issara Tower
Thailand Tobacco Monopoly (under redevelopment)
Ratchada
BENJAKITTI PARK
PATPONG
Patpong
Silom
Rama VI
Wongwian Saladaeng
Suan Lum Night Bazaar
Th. Silom
Th. Rama IV
Joe Louis Puppet Theatre
KHLONG TOEY
Neilson Hays Library
Boonmitr Bldg
CP Tower
Sala Daeng
Wongwian Witthayu
Lumphini Boxing Stadium
Queen Sirikit National Convention Centre
Xavier
Thanon Sathorn Nua
Thanon Sathorn Tai
Lumphini
Goethe Institute
Thai-Belgium Br.
Queen Sirikit Nat. Convention Centre
Chong Nonsi
Thanon Narathiwat Rajanakarin
Khlong Toey
Soi San Chao
Chonburi, Pattaya
Bhirasri Institute of Modern Art
Ruam Chitt
Thanon Rama IV
Sathorn Nua
Sathorn Tai
Kamphan Thawong Church of Christ
MR Kukrit Pramoj's Heritage Home
SATHORN
Th. Ratchadaphisek

RATTANAKOSIN: ROYAL BANGKOK

Thailand's kings built Rattanakosin as a royal city within a city, a host of extravagant palaces and temples. Today, it remains a treasure trove of cultural clues to the identity of the capital and its people

Main Attractions

WAT PHRA KAEW AND GRAND PALACE
LAK MUANG
SANAM LUANG
THE NATIONAL GALLERY
THE NATIONAL MUSEUM
WAT MAHATHAT
WAT PHO
SIAM DISCOVERY MUSEUM
WAT RATCHAPRADIT
WAT RATCHABOPHIT

Maps and Listings

MAP OF RATTANAKOSIN, PAGE 102
MAP OF WAT PHRA KAEW AND GRAND PALACE, PAGE 105
RESTAURANTS, PAGE 117
ACCOMMODATION, PAGES 241–2

Rattanakosin is the man-made island that forms the royal centre of the original Old City, called Phra Nakorn. It was designed in 1782 when Bangkok was installed as the new capital of Thailand. For more than a century, Rattanakosin, just a boat ride across from the earlier capital at Thonburi, was the pulse of the city, and was where the seeds of the modern kingdom were planted.

The foundations of Bangkok's new strategic powerhouse were based on the former capital of Ayutthaya, which was abandoned after being ransacked by the Burmese army in 1767. The area was located at the edge of the Chao Phraya river with the majestic Grand Palace as its epicentre. As the palace took shape, to mirror the island layout of Ayutthaya, defensive moats were dug by extending canals. Walls formed a protective stronghold around Phra Nakorn, and more canals were created to transport people across marsh and swampland.

Rattanakosin brims with architectural grandeur, its series of palaces and temples filled with important religious artefacts installed to indicate the strength of the re-unified nation. Even today, the district contains many government offices and two of Thailand's most respected universities (Thammasat and Silpakorn), in addition to being the religious nucleus of the nation. Ceremonies, festivals and parades are frequently held in this quarter.

Rattanakosin is best explored on foot. While most visitors attempt to cram all its sights into a day, two full days allow for greater appreciation of its more secluded treasures. The

LEFT: the striking Phra Si Rattana Chedi at Wat Phra Kaew. **RIGHT:** outside the high walls of the Grand Palace and Wat Phra Kaew.

Rattanakosin: Royal Bangkok

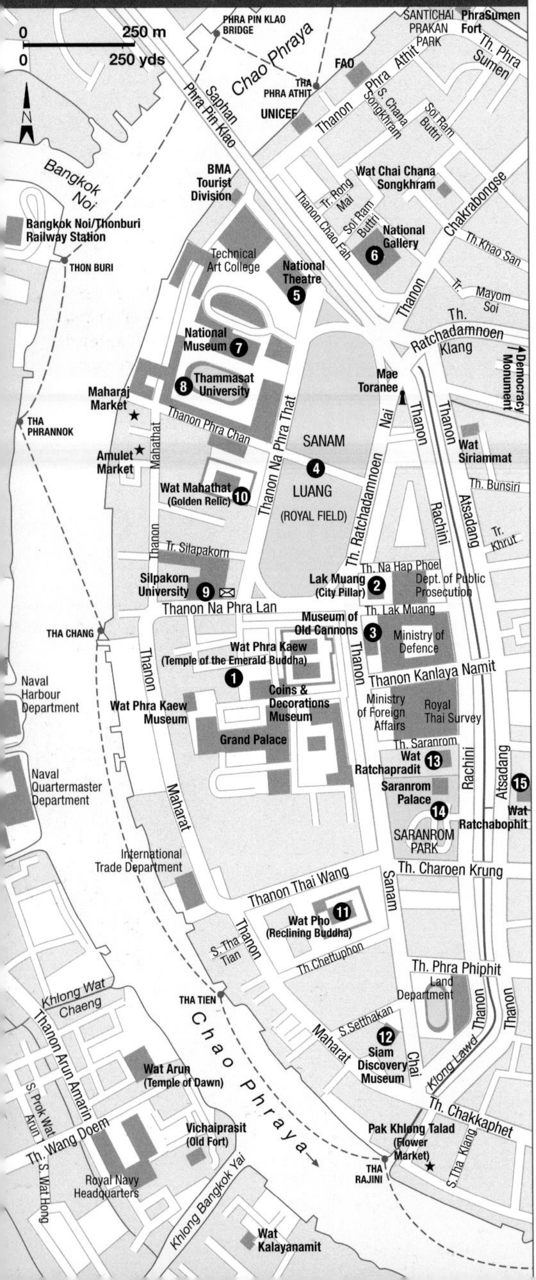

area's proximity to the river means that it can be conveniently accessed by water transport, and the famous backpacker haven of Thanon Khao San *(see page 137)* is just a short stroll away. A project called the Krung Rattanakosin Plan that aimed to reorganise the district by relocating residents to form a historical park has largely been shelved, although there are still periodic announcements of tentative schemes for development.

Wat Phra Kaew and Grand Palace Complex

Jostling among throngs of snap-happy tourists may not be the best context for viewing exotic Thailand, but the dignified splendour of two of Bangkok's principal attractions – the Wat Phra Kaew and the Grand Palace – is breathtaking nevertheless. The structures in this complex are an arresting spectacle of form and colour, with glistening golden *chedi*, glass mosaic-studded pillars, towering mythological gods, and fabulously ornate temple and palace structures piercing the sky.

Construction on the site, which originally spread over 160 hectares (65 acres), was begun in 1782 at the command of King Rama I. He wanted not only a palace befitting the new capital, but somewhere to house the Emerald Buddha, the country's most revered religious image. The entire compound is surrounded by high crenellated walls, securing a once self-sufficient city within a city.

Wat Phra Kaew and Grand Palace complex ❶

Address: Thanon Na Phra Lan, www.palaces.thai.net
Tel: 0-222 8181
Opening Hrs: daily 8.30am–3.30pm
Entrance Fee: charge (includes entry to Vimanmek and several other sights in Dusit)
Transport: Tha Chang pier

The only entrance (and exit) to the complex is along Thanon Na Phra Lan to the north. An early morning visit is recommended, preferably when bright sunlight illuminates the buildings to their dazzling best. Make sure you are dressed appropriately *(see margin tip)* and disregard touts who linger outside the complex telling you that it is closed.

The complex is loosely divided, with Wat Phra Kaew encountered first to the left and the Grand Palace and its peripheral buildings to the right. At least two hours are needed for a full appreciation, with most people lingering within Wat Phra Kaew. The interiors of the Grand Palace buildings – but not Wat Phra Kaew – are closed to the public on Saturday and Sunday. It's worthwhile hiring the informative audio guide. If you prefer, official guides are also available near the ticket office.

Wat Phra Kaew

Wat Phra Kaew (Temple of the Emerald Buddha) serves as the royal chapel of the Grand Palace. The compound is modelled after palace chapels in the former capitals of Sukhothai and Ayutthaya, and contains many typical monastic structures, although, because of its royal function, it does not have living quarters for monks.

At the main entrance is the statue of Shivaka Kumar Baccha, who was

TIP

The dress code for Wat Phra Kaew and the Grand Palace is strict. Visitors must be dressed smartly – no shorts, short skirts or revealing tops, sandals or flip-flops. Suitable clothing may be borrowed from an office near the Gate of Victory, but unless you want to don stale rubber slip-ons and a gaudy sarong, dress conservatively.

LEFT AND BELOW: Phra Mondop with its splendid exterior.

TIP

For an explanation of the architectural features of Thai temples, see Temple Art and Architecture, pages 54–5.

reputed to be the Buddha's private physician, and on the upper terrace to the left are the gleaming gold mosaic tiles encrusting the Sri Lankan-style circular **Phra Si Rattana Chedi** Ⓐ. Erected by King Mongkut (Rama V), the *chedi* is said to enshrine a piece of the Buddha's breastbone.

In the centre is **Phra Mondop** Ⓑ (Library of Buddhist Scriptures), surrounded by statues of sacred white elephants (the white elephant is the symbol of royal power). The library was erected to hold the holy Buddhist scriptures called *Tripitaka*. The original library was destroyed by fire, ignited by fireworks during festivities to celebrate its completion. Phra Mondop is a delicate building, studded with blue and green glass mosaic, and topped by a multi-tiered roof fashioned like the crown of a Thai king.

Adjacent to it is the **Prasat Phra Thep Bidom** Ⓒ (Royal Pantheon), This contains life-sized statues of the Chakri kings and is open to the public only on Chakri Day, 6 April. Around the building stand marvellous gilded statues of mythological creatures, including the half-female, half-lion *aponsi*. The original pantheon was built in 1855, but was destroyed by fire and rebuilt in 1903. Flanking the entrance of the Prasat Phra Thep Bidom are two towering gilded *chedi*.

RIGHT: worshipper outside the Bot of the Emerald Buddha. **BELOW:** gilded garuda images encircle the exterior of the Bot of the Emerald Buddha.

Behind Phra Mondop is a large, sandstone model of the famous Khmer temple of Angkor Wat in Cambodia. The model was built during King Rama IV's reign when Cambodia was a vassal Thai state. Just behind, along the northern edge of the compund, is the **Viharn Yot** (Prayer Hall), flanked by the **Ho Phra Nak** (Royal Mausoleum) on the left and **Ho Phra Montien Tham** (Auxillary Library) on the right.

The walls of the cloister enclosing the temple courtyard are painted with a picture book of 178 murals telling the *Ramakien* epic, the Thai version of the Indian *Ramayana*. Originally painted during the reign of King Rama III (1824–50), they have been meticulously restored.

Around the cloisters, six pairs of towering stone *yaksha* (demons), again characters from the *Ramakien*, stand guard, armed with clubs, protecting the Emerald Buddha. At the complex's eastern edge are eight *prang* structures, which represent Buddhism's Eightfold Path.

The Emerald Buddha

Finally you come to Wat Phra Kaew's most sacred structure, the **Bot of the Emerald Buddha** **D**. Outside this main hall, at the open-air shrine, the air is always alive with the supplicants' murmured prayers and heavy with the scent of floral offerings and joss sticks. Remove your shoes before entering the hall.

At the top of the elaborate golden altar, in a glass case and protected by a nine-tiered umbrella, sits the country's most celebrated image, the diminutive 75cm (30ins) tall **Emerald Buddha**, which, surprisingly, is not made of emerald but carved from a solid block of green jade. Many non-Buddhists may be disappointed by the size of the Emerald Buddha statue, but the belief in its power and importance are apparent from the demeanour of the pilgrims inside the hall. This gets particularly busy on weekends and holidays when worshippers fill the main sanctuary, prostrating themselves on the marble floor before the temple's 11-metre (36ft) -tall altar. Photography is forbidden and it's hard to get a clear view of the statue from ground level.

ABOVE: the multi-tiered roof of the Bot of the Emerald Buddha at Wat Phra Kaew.

Three times a year, at the beginning of each new season, the Thai king presides over the changing of the Emerald Buddha's robes: a golden, diamond-studded tunic is used for the hot season, a gilded robe flecked with blue for the rainy season, and a robe of enamel-coated solid gold for the cool season.

According to legend, the Emerald Buddha was carved in India, but stylistically its design is 13th- or 14th-century Thai. It was discovered in 1434 in Chiang Rai, where, for unknown reasons, it had been hidden in a *chedi* in a temple also known as Wat Phra Kaew, until the *chedi* was struck by lighting during a storm. In the mid-16th century, the invading Lao army

Wat Phra Kaew and Grand Palace

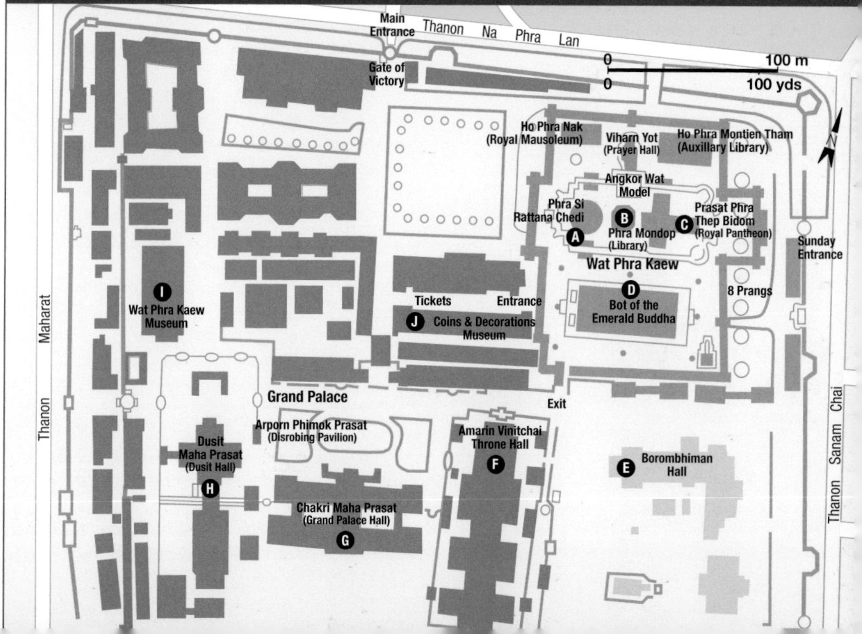

Main Entrance
Thanon Na Phra Lan
Gate of Victory
0 100 m
0 100 yds
Ho Phra Nak (Royal Mausoleum)
Viharn Yot (Prayer Hall)
Ho Phra Montien Tham (Auxillary Library)
Angkor Wat Model
Phra Si Rattana Chedi
A
B
Phra Mondop (Library)
C
Prasat Phra Thep Bidom (Royal Pantheon)
Sunday Entrance
Wat Phra Kaew
D
Bot of the Emerald Buddha
8 Prangs
I
Wat Phra Kaew Museum
Tickets
Entrance
J
Coins & Decorations Museum
Thanon Maharat
Grand Palace
Exit
Arporn Phimok Prasat (Disrobing Pavilion)
Amarin Vinitchai Throne Hall
F
Dusit Maha Prasat (Dusit Hall)
H
E
Borombhiman Hall
Chakri Maha Prasat (Grand Palace Hall)
G
Thanon Sanam Chai

A Mythical Zoo

All around Bangkok are images of strange creatures that have migrated from the tales of Hindu mythology to the stuff of everyday life. These are the most common

Garuda: Considered the most powerful creature of the Himaphan Forest, this half-eagle, half-man demigod is the mount of the Hindu god Vishnu. *Garuda* is the sworn enemy of the magical water serpent *naga*. *Garuda* is often depicted with *naga* caught in his talons. Since Ayutthayan times the *garuda* has been a symbol for the Royal Seal, and today, brightly coloured representations are emblazoned across official documents as well as the facades of royally approved banks and corporations.

Naga: Brother and nemesis of *garuda*, the *naga* is a semi-divine creature with multiple human heads and serpent tails. The snake has special symbolism to most of the world's faiths and cultures, and in Buddhism a great *naga* is said to have provided shelter to the meditating Buddha. A resident of the watery underworld, the *naga* is associated with water's life-giving force, as well as acting as a bridge between the earthly and divine realms. *Naga* are typically represented along steps leading into temples.

Erawan: The magical elephant *erawan* was the steed for Indra, the Hindu king of the gods. The gigantic pachyderm has 33 heads, each with seven tusks so long that thousands of angels live inside them. Obviously, with such a gargantuan beast, a more modest three-headed version is usually represented. For proof of *erawan*'s importance to Thais, head to Erawan Shrine *(see page 156)* at one of Bangkok's busiest intersections, where wooden elephants are presented as offerings.

Kinnaree and **Aponsi:** This exotic looking belle has the head and body of a woman with the tail and legs of a swan. Known for her talent in song and dance, beautifully crafted *kinnaree* sculptures can be seen at Wat Phra Kaew. Perhaps a distant relative, *aponsi* is similarly portrayed as half-female, half-lion. The Golden Kinnaree is the Thai film industry equivalent of the Oscar.

Hongsa: This bird-like creature has similarities to the swan and goose, and is a prevalent motif in traditional arts and crafts. In Hindu mythology, the *hongsa* is the mount of Brahma, the god of creation. Take a drive along Utthayan Avenue in Bangkok's southern suburb of Puttha Monthon, and you will see some 1,000 golden *hongsa* birds decorating the tops of lampposts.

Yaksha: These giant half-demon, half-god creatures, which appear so forbidding as they guard the entrances to the temple structures at Wat Phra Kaew and Wat Arun, are actually protectors of earthbound wealth. Led by Kuvera, they are worshipped as symbols of fertility and are also believed to protect newborn infants. ❑

LEFT: *yaksha* protector at Wat Phra Kaew. **ABOVE:** a seven-headed *naga* at the Prasat Phra Thep Bidom.

took the figure to Vientiane, Laos. It was seized back by the Thais in 1779. King Rama I eventually brought the statue to Bangkok from Thonburi in 1784 after the city was established as the new capital. The Emerald Buddha is claimed to bestow good fortune on the kingdom that possesses it.

The Grand Palace

Adjoining Wat Phra Kaew is the **Grand Palace**. Embodying Thailand's characteristic blend of temporal and spiritual elements, the Grand Palace has been added to or modified by every Thai king, so that today the complex is a mélange of architectural styles, from traditional Thai, Khmer and Chinese to British, French and Italian Renaissance. In the early 20th century, the royal abode shifted to the more private Chitralada Palace in Dusit district *(see page 140)*, with the Grand Palace now reserved for special ceremonies and state visits.

Palace buildings

Exit from Wat Phra Kaew. On your left and tucked behind a closed gate guarded by sentry is the French-inspired **Borombhiman Hall Ⓔ**. It was built in 1903 as a residence for King Rama VI but is now reserved as a state guesthouse for dignitaries.

To the right lies the **Amarin Vinitchai Throne Hall Ⓕ**, part of the three-building Phra Maha Montien complex. Originally a royal residence, it contained the bedchamber of Rama I, with the main audience hall beyond. Today, the audience hall is used for coronations and special ceremonies. By tradition, each new king also spends the first night after his coronation here.

Next to it in a large courtyard stands the triple-spired royal residence – and the grandest building in the complex – the **Chakri Maha Prasat Ⓖ** (Grand Palace Hall). This two-storey hall set on an elevated base was constructed during King Chulalongkorn's reign (1868–1910) to commemorate the 100th anniversary of the Chakri dynasty in 1882. An impressive mixture of Thai and Western architecture, the building was designed by British architects.

ABOVE: Chakri Maha Prasat Hall, Grand Palace. **BELOW:** sentry guard on duty outside the Chakri Maha Prasat.

ABOVE: Chinese-style statue outside the Dusit Maha Prasat.
BELOW: Thai national flag and coat of arms, Grand Palace complex.

The Thai spires, however, were added at the last moment, following protests that it was improper for a hallowed Thai site to be dominated by a European-style building.

The top floor contains golden urns with ashes of the Chakri kings; the first floor still functions as an audience chamber for royal banquets and state visits, while the ground floor is now a **Weapons Museum**.

The central hall contains the magnificent **Chakri Throne Room**, where the king receives foreign ambassadors on a niello throne under a nine-tiered white umbrella, originally made for King Chulalongkorn. Outside, the courtyard is dotted with ornamental ebony trees pruned in Chinese *bonsai* style. Beside the hall, a closed-off door leads to the **Inner Palace**, where the king's many wives once lived. The king himself was the only male above the age of 12 allowed to enter the area, which was guarded by armed women.

The next building of interest is the **Dusit Maha Prasat** **H** (Dusit Hall), built by King Chakri (Rama I) in 1789 to replace an earlier wooden structure. A splendid example of classical Thai architecture, its four-tiered roof supports an elegant nine-tiered spire. The balcony on the north wing contains a throne once used by the king for outdoor receptions. Deceased kings and queens lie in state here before their bodies are cremated on Sanam Luang.

To its left stands the exquisite **Arporn Phimok Prasat** (Disrobing Pavilion). It was built to the height of the king's palanquin, so that he could alight from his elephant and don his ceremonial hat and gown before proceeding to the audience hall.

Opposite, do not miss the superb collection of small Buddha images made of silver, ivory, crystal and other materials at the **Wat Phra Kaew Museum** **I**. On the way out, next to the ticket office is the **Coins and Decorations Museum** **J**. It has a collection of coins dating from the 11th century and also royal regalia, decorations and medals made of gold and precious stones.

Park Life

Contemporary accounts record that when King Rama I was cremated at Sanam Luang in 1809, the congregation included 10,000 monks and the atmosphere resembled a festival. Alongside the solemnity there were theatre performances, fireworks and boxing matches and the crowds was showered with money buried in limes. Today, one of the most important events is the Royal Ploughing Ceremony each May. This Brahman festival, which dates to the Sukhothai era nearly 1,000 years ago, sees a pair of sacred cows led to a choice of seven foodstuffs, such as rice, green beans and liquor. Whichever they consume first prophesises what kind of harvest farmers will have that year.

Lak Muang ❷

Address: Thanon Sanam Chai
Tel: 0-222 9876
Opening Hrs: daily 5am–7pm
Entrance Fee: free
Transport: Tha Chan pier

Every Thai city is supposed to have a foundation stone, around which the city's guardian spirits gravitate, protecting and bringing supposed good fortune to worshippers and the municipality. Bangkok was officially born into the world in 1782, when King Rama I erected the **Lak Muang** (City Pillar), to mark the official centre of the capital.

Located just across Thanon Sanam Chai from the eastern wall of the Grand Palace, this is a gilded wooden pillar sheltered by a Khmer-style *prang*. Resembling the Hindu Shiva *lingam*, which represents potency, it is accompanied by the taller Lak Muang of Thonburi, which was moved here when the district (and former capital) became part of Bangkok. The pillar is considered the city's spiritual core, and is watched over by a pavilion containing several golden spirit-idols. Devotees thankful their prayers have been answered usually hire resident classical *lakhon* dancers to perform here.

Museum of Old Cannons ❸

Clearly visible across the street from the Lak Muang is a battalion of antique armoury that menacingly protects the imposing Ministry of Defence. Of passing interest to those with a military bent is the **Museum of Old Cannons** (daily 24 hours; free). On the lawn in front of the 19th-century European-style former barracks are displays of battle-worn and bulky cast-iron cannons.

Sanam Luang ❹

North of the Wat Phra Kaew and Grand Palace, the large oval turf of **Sanam Luang** (Royal Field) is where royal cremations and important ceremonies are held. It is particularly lively on the King's and Queen's birthdays; during the Songkran festival; the kite-flying competition

ABOVE: the Royal Thai Navy stand guard at the King's 82nd birthday at Sanam Luang. **BELOW:** Mae Toranee, or the Earth Goddess, was one of the protectors of the meditating Buddha.

season (Feb–Apr) – which attracts contestants from all around the country and abroad – and for the Ploughing Ceremony, a Brahman ritual held in May to predict the state of the coming harvest. When not in official use, the field becomes a general recreation and market stall area, also used by fortunetellers. The park was closed for renovations during 2010, when the homeless, who found a place to lay their heads here, and traders were moved on, and thousands of pigeons were relocated to Chiang Mai. Time will tell whether they return.

Previously, Sanam Luang was a racecourse, a golf course and home to a Sunday market, until it moved to Chatuchak in 1982 when the grounds were prepared for the Bangkok Bicentennial.

Northeast of Sanam Luang, opposite the Royal Hotel, is an elaborate public drinking fountain in the shape of **Mae Toranee** (Earth Goddess). Erected by King Chulalongkorn in the late 19th century, the ornate statue depicts the goddess wringing torrents of water out of her hair to wash away evil spirits trying to corrupt the meditating Buddha. It is an apt symbol, perhaps, in a city that is still sometimes flooded by overflowing waters from the monsoon-swollen Chao Phraya river.

ABOVE: inside the Thai National Museum. **BELOW:** National Museum exterior.

National Theatre 5

North of Sanam Luang, next to the traffic-clogged Saphan Phra Pin Klao bridge along Thanon Rachinee is the **National Theatre** (tel: 0-2244 1342; open only during performances). Unfortunately, this large white modern Thai edifice does not open its doors as frequently as it used to. It has weekly and monthly performances of folk and classical Thai music, dance and drama. Occasionally it showcases highbrow concerts and theatre from abroad. Call ahead for schedules.

National Gallery 6

Address: Thanon Chao Fa
Tel: 0-2281 2224
Opening Hrs: Wed–Sun 9am–4pm
Entrance Fee: charge
Transport: Phra Athit pier

On the opposite side of the Saphan Phra Pin Klao bridge is the **National Gallery**, which has seen better days as an exhibition space, with little renovation since the 1970s. Situated within a fine old colonial-style building that used to function as the Royal Mint, the gallery's permanent collection of traditional and contemporary Thai art isn't particularly outstanding. However, the annexe on both sides of the gallery holds interesting monthly exhibitions, mainly by local groups, veteran Thai artists or the odd cutting-edge youngster, and occasional international exposes.

National Museum 7

Address: Thanon Na Phra That, www.thailandmuseum.com
Tel: 0-2224 1333

Opening Hrs: Wed–Sun 9am–4pm
Entrance Fee: charge (guided tours at 9.30am Wed and Thur)
Transport: Phra Athit pier

To the west of Sanam Luang is the **National Museum**. Besides housing a vast collection of antiquities from all over Southeast Asia, the museum has an interesting history of its own *(see photo feature on pages 118–9)*. Its grounds and some of the principal rooms were part of the former Wang Na (Front Palace) of the king's second-in-line, the Prince Successor, a feature of the Thai monarchy until 1870.

The oldest buildings in the compound date from 1782, including the splendid **Buddhaisawan Chapel**. Built by the Prince Successor as his private place of worship within the palace, it contains some of Thailand's most beautiful and best-preserved murals, depicting 28 scenes from the Buddha's life and dating from the 1790s. Above the windows, five bands of angels kneel in silent respect to Thailand's second most sacred Buddha image, the famous Phra Buddha Sihing. According to legend, the bronze image came from Ceylon, but art historians attribute it to 13th-century Sukhothai. The image is paraded through the streets of Bangkok each year on the day before Songkran *(see page 250)*.

To the left of the entrance is the **Sivamokhaphiman Hall**, originally an open-sided audience hall that now houses a prehistoric art collection. It displays bronzes and some of the painted earthenware jars found in northeast Thailand. The front of the building is devoted to the Thai History Gallery, documenting the country's history from the Sukhothai period (13th century) to the present Rattanakosin period (1782 onwards). Most of the exhibits are weak on contextual information, so buy a copy of the museum guidebook.

Also on site is the **Red House** (Tamnak Daeng), an old golden teak dwelling that once belonged to King Rama I's elder sister. Built in the Ayutthaya style, the house has an ornate wood finish and elegant early Bangkok-style furnishings.

ABOVE: statue of Dr Pridi Banomyong, founder of Thammasat University.
LEFT: schoolboy studies a mural in the Thai National Museum.

TIP

Arts buffs should visit the Silpakorn University Gallery (Mon–Fri 9am–7pm, Sat 9am–4pm; free). It displays interesting works of art by both teachers and students as well as those by visiting artists.

SHOP

Amulets are associated with fortune, both good and bad, so in the lanes around the Wat Mahathat amulet market you'll also find astrologers working in palmistry, Thai astrology and tarot. There are several more at Pra Chan pier.

The central audience hall of the Wang Na is divided into rooms containing various ethnological exhibits of elephant *howdah*, wood carvings, ceramics, palanquins, royal furnishings, weapons, *khon* masks, musical instruments and other artefacts. Temporary exhibits are displayed in the Throne Hall.

Adding to the museum's ambience are the inner courtyards, embellished with ponds and shady trees, providing spots for reflection. Mingling among armies of curious young local students, the museum feels more inviting than more austere museums elsewhere.

Thammasat University ❽

Adjoining the National Museum at Thanon Phra Chan is **Thammasat University**, Thailand's second most prestigious educational establishment (after Chulalongkorn University). The university was founded in 1934 to educate people in the new political constitution, which had been introduced two years earlier. Thammasat scholars have a reputation for being vocal in their strong political beliefs and in the past have been labelled as radicals.

The university's darkest days came in October 1973 and 1976, when students peacefully protesting for greater democracy were brutally suppressed by the military, police and rightist thugs. Hundreds of innocent students were slain. Inside the university gates are two small but pertinent memorials to the bloody crackdowns, hidden reminders of Thailand's chequered past and the continuing might of the Thai military.

RIGHT: Wat Pho's main *chedi* are dedicated to Bangkok's monarchs. **BELOW:** monk at Wat Mahathat's amulet market.

Silpakorn University ❾

North of the Grand Palace and Wat Phra Kaew complex is **Silpakorn University**. The oldest and most prestigious art institution in Thailand, Silpakorn was originally the site of Tha Phra Palace, once occupied by the royal grandchildren. A few of the old buildings still stand, now part of the university campus.

The art school is attributed to the vision of Italian sculptor Corrado Feroci, known as Silpa Bhirasri to locals and dubbed "the father of Thai modern art". During the 1920s, Feroci was invited to work as a sculptor in Thailand, where he executed key public commissions like the design for the Democracy Monument.

The university's Fine Arts Department operates a **Hall Of Sculpture** (Mon–Fri 8.30am–4.30pm; free). It displays a collection of original plaster casts of statuesque monuments to royal, religious and other important dignitaries, whose originals stand tall throughout the kingdom. The university galleries also hold decent monthly exhibitions by students, teachers, alumni and visiting artists.

Wat Mahathat ⑩

Address: Sanam Luang
Opening Hrs: daily 7am–8pm
Entrance Fee: free
Transport: Tha Chang pier

Nestled between Silpakorn and Thammasat universities is **Wat Mahathat**. You will enter through the gates of the earth-toned Thawornwatthu building, a former royal funerary hall donated to the temple as a library for monks. Compared to other sites in the vicinity, Wat Mahathat, although an important temple, has little visual appeal to capture tourist attention. Founded in the 1700s, the temple houses the **Maha Chulalongkorn Rajavidyalaya University**, one of the two highest seats of Buddhist learning in the country, and where King Rama IV spent almost 25 years studying as a monk before taking the throne in 1851.

Wat Mahathat exudes a more genuine, working-temple atmosphere compared to the more ceremonial temples in the area, with locals swarming here to receive spiritual tutelage. Apart from an outdoor herbal medicine market, an **amulet market** *(see margin note, page 112)* has stalls along Trok Silpakorn, an alley between the temple and Silpakorn University, all the way to the riverside Thanon Mahathat.

You might also be able to get in tune with your inner self at the temple's **International Buddhist Meditation Centre**, which conducts regular classes in English (tel: 0-2623 5881; www.mcu.ac.th/ibmc).

ABOVE: Wat Mahathat.
BELOW: amulets come in myriad forms and serve a variety of purposes, from religious or spiritual to the more practical, such as ensuring sexual potency.

Wat Pho ⓫

Address: Thanon Thai Wang
Tel: 0-2222 5910
Opening Hrs: daily 8am–5pm
Entrance Fee: charge
Transport: Tha Tien pier

South of the Grand Palace and Wat Phra Kaew complex is the much visited **Wat Pho**, Bangkok's largest and oldest surviving temple. The site retains a more casual ambience than the younger and more dominant Wat Phra Kaew. Apart from its historic significance, visitors come to Wat Pho for two things: to pay homage to the monumental Reclining Buddha, and to unwind at the city's best traditional massage centre.

Also known to Thais as Wat Phra Chetuphon, the temple dates back to the 16th century. However, it did not achieve real importance until the establishment of Bangkok as the capital. Wat Pho was a particular favourite of the first four Bangkok kings, all of whom added to its treasures. The four towering coloured *chedi* to the west of the *bot* (ordination hall) are memorials to the monarchs, and around the hall are 90-plus other *chedi*. The temple cloisters contain 394 bronze Buddha images, retrieved from ancient ruins in Sukhothai and Ayutthaya. One of the most important was the Reclining Buddha, added by King Rama III in 1832. This king also converted the temple into the country's earliest place of public learning and instructed that the walls be inscribed with lessons on astrology, history, morality and archaeology, leading locals to fondly call it the kingdom's first university.

Wat Pho's gigantic **Reclining Buddha**, 46 metres (150ft) long and 15 metres (50ft) high, and made from brick, plaster and gilded in gold, depicts the resting Buddha passing into nirvana. The flat soles of the Buddha's feet are inlaid with mother-of-pearl designs, illustrating the 108 *laksana* (distinctive marks of a Buddha). Also numbering 108 are the metallic bowls that span the wall; a coin dropped in each supposedly brings goodwill to the devotee. With the building's pillars preventing full view, the head and feet are the best vantage points.

The temple's main hall is considered to be one of Bangkok's

ABOVE AND BELOW: the giant Reclining Buddha.

most beautiful. Girding its base are superbly carved sandstone panels depicting scenes from the *Ramakien*. The striking doors are also devoted to *Ramakien* scenes, brilliantly rendered in some of the finest mother-of-pearl work found in Asia. The ashes of Rama I are interred in the pedestal base of the hall's principal Buddha image. Standing beside the inner doorways, pairs of large stone *farang* (foreigner) guards are striking for their Western characteristics.

Wat Pho massage school

Address: Thanon Thai Wang, www.watpomassage.com
Tel: 0-2221 2974
Opening Hrs: daily 10am–6pm
Entrance Fee: charge
Transport: Tha Tien pier

Wat Pho became, and still is, the place to learn about traditional medicine, particularly massage and meditation. The medicine pavilion displays stone tablets indicating beneficial body points for massage. Skirting the temple grounds are several small rock gardens which contain statues of hermits striking poses; these were used as diagnostic aids. Many of the old shophouses that fringe the temple walls today still peddle a range of traditional herbal remedies.

Traditional Thai massage *(see page 88)* is based on Indian yoga philosophy, and originated from millennia-old Indian therapies that aim to release blocked energy. In Thai massage, strong thumbs dig deep into tense muscles and the body's energy points. The masseurs also bring their full body weight to bear as they stretch the recipients' bodies into yoga-like poses. The **Wat Pho Thai Traditional Massage School** offers cheap hour-long massages, and also offers courses for those wanting to learn the art. Many masseurs around the country claim to have received tuition here, and the hands-on training has proved a staple career option for many of Thailand's blind population.

ABOVE: the walls of Wat Ratchabophit are decorated with brightly patterned Chinese ceramic tiles called *bencharong*.
LEFT: Wat Pho.

ABOVE AND BELOW: modern exhibits in the Siam Discovery Museum.

Siam Discovery Museum ⓬

Address: Thanon Sanam Chai
Tel: 0-2622 2599
Opening Hrs: Tue–Sun 10am–6pm
Entrance Fee: charge
Transport: Tha Tien pier

Southeast of Wat Po, the interactive multimedia displays and tableaux at the **Siam Discovery Museum** explain what it is to be "Thai". Starting from the ancient ethnic groups that populated the Southeast Asian region 2,000 years ago, when it was known as Suvarnabhumi (Golden Land) – the name adopted by Bangkok's main airport – the exhibits run through historical periods and population shifts, including the periods of Khmer, Sukhothai and Ayutthayan dominance. The museum is housed in a handsome listed building that was previously the Ministry of Commerce.

Wat Ratchapradit ⓭

Address: Thanon Saranrom
Tel: 0-2223 8215
Opening Hrs: daily 5am–10pm (chapel 9–9.30am, 5–7pm)
Entrance Fee: free
Transport: Tha Tien pier

Wat Ratchapradit, located next to Saranrom Park on Thanon Saranrom, is less grand than many other temples in this royal district, but it offers a more intimate appreciation of a monarch's connection with religious buildings. King Mongkut ordered its construction on a reclaimed coffee plantation in 1864, and some of its unusual interior murals depict the king, an avid astronomer, observing a solar eclipse in 1868 in the fishing village of Wa Kor, south of Bangkok. On the trip, the king contracted malaria and later died. His remains are held beneath the main Buddha statue here. The quaint grey marble-clad temple is an example of his, and later King Chulalongkorn's, interest in mixing Thai and Western architecture.

Saranrom Park ⓮

Just behind Wat Ratchapradit, the manicured landscape of **Saranrom Park** (daily 5am–8pm; free) is the perfect place to wind down after a full day of palace and temple tours. The park was originally a garden attached to Saranrom Palace, which was supposed to have been the retirement retreat for King Mongkut. However, he passed away before the palace was completed. Enhanced by bridges, ponds, a European-style cherub-spouting fountain and a Chinese pagoda, this green space has been open to the public since the 1960s. At the park's centre is a memorial erected by King Chulalongkorn for his wife Queen Sunanda, who tragically drowned in a boating accident in 1880. At the park's main gates, drink vendors sell freshly-squeezed juice to the legion of joggers – so grab a seat on a park bench and cool off with a drink.

Wat Ratchabophit ⓯

Address: Thanon Fuang Nakhon
Tel: 0-2222 3930
Opening Hrs: daily 5am–8pm (chapel 9–9.30am, 5.30–6pm)
Entrance Fee: free
Transport: buses 1, 508

Although it is located on the opposite bank of Khlong Lord canal and Rattanakosin, **Wat Ratchabophit** is easily accessed from Saranrom Park. This infrequently visited sanctuary is recognisable for its characteristic amalgamation of local temple architecture and period European style. It has an unusual design that places the main circular *chedi* and its circular cloister in the centre. Started in 1869 by King Chulalongkorn (Rama V), the complex took well over two decades to complete.

The *bot* (ordination hall), built into the northern side of the yellow tile-clad cloister, is covered in brightly patterned Chinese ceramic tiles, known as *bencharong*. The windows and entrance doors to the hall are exquisite works of art, with tiny pieces of mother-of-pearl inlaid in lacquer, in an intricate rendition of the insignias of the five royal ranks. The doors open into one of the most surprising temple interiors in Thailand, with a Gothic-inspired chapel of solid columns that looks more like a medieval cathedral than a Thai temple. The courtyard doors are carved in relief with jaunty-looking soldiers wearing European-type uniforms. Wat Ratchabophit was built before King Chulalongkorn made his first trip to Europe, so its design is all the more remarkable. ❑

ABOVE: Wat Ratchabophit.

BEST RESTAURANTS

Thai

Ch Prathumthong
11 Th Na Phra Lan. Tel: 0-2221 3556. **$** ❶ p268, B4
Right opposite the Grand Palace, with just six tables inside and out. The large menu, consisting of fried rice, noodles, curries and salads, is cheap and tasty. At night it's a bar hangout for Thammasat and Silpakorn students.

Coconut Palm
394/3–5 Th Maharaj. Tel: 08-1827 2394. Open: daily 10am–7pm. **$** ❷ p272, B1
Family-style restaurant with better meals than its Western-style fast-food interior suggests. The small range of soups and curries (red, green, *tom yam* and the coconut soup, or *tom kha gai*) disappear by lunchtime. They also serve up rice noodles with spicy and sour sauce.

The Deck
Arun Residence, 36–8 Soi Pratoo Nok Yoong. Tel: 0-2221 9158. www.arunresidence.com **Open: Mon–Thur 11am–10pm; Fri–Sun 11am–11pm; bar open from 6pm. $$–$$$** ❸ p272, B1
Just two minutes walk from Wat Pho, in the Arun Residence boutique hotel *(see page 241)*, this cute place has outdoor seating and river views of Wat Arun. A mixed Thai and Euro-fusion menu features plates such as carpaccio of tea-smoked duck. There is a separate Turkish-style bar, Amorosa, on the third floor.

Poh Restaurant
Tha Tien pier. No phone. **$** ❹ p272, B1
The lovely setting at this wooden-shack pierside café compensates for its ordinary menu. Sit upstairs for the best view across the river to Wat Arun. Serves squid, mussels and shrimp with rice or noodles, a few curries and numerous fish dishes.

Price per person for a three-course meal without drinks.
***$** = under B300, **$$** = B300–800, **$$$** = B800–1,600, **$$$$** = over B1,600.*

The National Museum

Bangkok's National Museum, one of the largest in Southeast Asia, is a good place to learn more about Thailand's history and culture

The National Museum's three main galleries are spread over a handful of old and new buildings. Thai history from the Sukhothai period (13th–14th centuries) to the Rattanakosin period (1782–the present) is covered in the Sivamokhaphiman Hall, while behind the hall, the Prehistoric Gallery has 5,000 year-old exhibits from the Ban Chiang archaeological site in the northeast. The south wing exhibits Buddha images and artefacts from the Srivijaya and Lopburi periods, while the north wing displays exhibits from the Lanna, Sukhothai, Ayutthaya and Rattanakosin periods. The rooms in the Wang Na, or Front Palace *(see opposite)*, display fine art masterpieces, mostly from the Rattanakosin period, with treasures in the form of gold, carvings, enamelware, musical instruments, ceramics, clothes, weapons and palanquins.

In front of the old palace is the Buddhaisawan Chapel, once the private chapel of the Prince Successor and a good example of Rattanakosin architecture. Today, it houses the second holiest image in Thailand, Phra Buddha Sihing, a Sukhothai-style Buddha image. Beautiful murals cover the wall of this chapel.

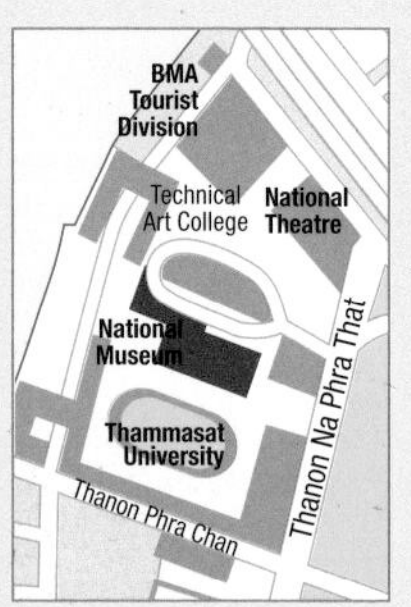

The Essentials

Address: *Thanon Na Phra That, www.thailandmuseum.com*
Tel: *0-2224 1333*
Opening Hrs: *Wed–Sun 9am–4pm*
Entrance Fee: *charge (guided tours at 9.30am Wed and Thur)*
Transport: *Phra Athit pier*

LEFT: a chariot fitting of a bronze Garuda holding a Naga. In Hindu and Buddhist mythology, Garudas are half-man half bird mounts of Vishnu; Nagas are serpents.

ABOVE: puppets used in the now disappearing art of *hun lakhon lek*, which recounts legends from the Thai epic *The Ramakien*, based on the Indian Ramayana.

ABOVE: the murals in the Buddhaisawan Chapel surround the Phra Buddha Sihing, Thailand's second most sacred Buddha image.

THE FIRST THAI MUSEUM

King Chulalongkorn, or Rama V established the country's first public museum in 1874 in the Grand Palace. The collections were based on those of his father, King Mongkut (Rama IV). In 1926 the museum was moved to what was the Wang Na (Front Palace), the abode of the second-in-line to the throne, called the "second king" or the Prince Successor. This vast palace, dating from 1782, once extended across Khlong Lot up to the Grand Palace and included a large park. When his heir-apparent attempted a violent overthrow, Chulalongkorn abolished the office in 1887 and tore down most of the buildings. The Wang Na is one of the remnants of the original palace and today it houses a variety of artefacts in Rooms 4–15. Room 6 contains a beautifully carved *howdah*, or elephant seat, made of ivory.

Chulalongkorn's statue can be found in the Issaretrachanusorn Hall, which also exhibits the beds of Phra Pin Klao, the thrones of King Chulalongkorn and King Vajiravudh, and intricate Chinese and European-style furniture.

ABOVE: King Chulalongkorn was Thailand's great moderniser. He introduced railways, mapping and the postal service, and reformed education and health care.

ABOVE: the National Museum entrance is in a culturally rich area, next to the National Theatre and opposite the royal ceremonial grounds of Sanam Luang.

BELOW: a statue of the reclining Buddha. It represents the moment the Buddha ascends into Nirvana, having completed the cycle of birth and rebirth and attained Enlightenment. The event is celebrated on Visakha Bucha Day.

THONBURI

Thonburi had a brief moment of glory as the country's capital in the 18th century, and the royal connection left a legacy of important temples. Some are still best reached via winding canals, which offer respite from the hustle of the modern city

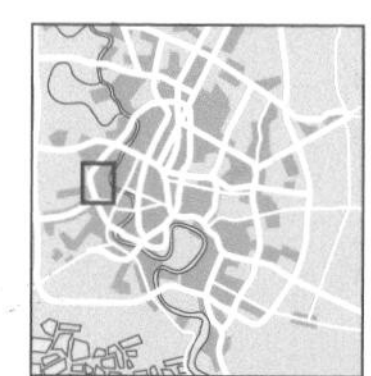

Main Attractions

WAT ARUN
WAT RAKHANG
MUSEUM OF FORENSIC MEDICINE
NATIONAL MUSEUM OF ROYAL BARGES
WAT SUWANNARAM
WAT KALAYANAMIT
SANTA CRUZ CHURCH

Maps and Listings

MAP OF THONBURI, PAGE 122
RESTAURANTS, PAGE 125
ACCOMMODATION, PAGE 241

After the fall of Ayutthaya in 1767, King Taksin established **Thonburi** as Thailand's third capital, which it remained for 15 years until Bangkok's ascendance in 1782. Taksin spent most of his reign fighting rebel factions that coveted the throne, leaving time only late in his reign to embellish his city.

Thonburi, which means "Town of Riches", remained a separate town until 1971, when it was incorporated into the Bangkok Metropolis. You can reach it by numerous bridges, the oldest of which is **Memorial Bridge** (Phra Buddha Yodfa). The area has only recently seen the growth of riverside condos and it has only a few high-end hotels, although these benefit from having views to the city across the river. Its tourist attractions are largely confined to the areas close to the old palace grounds. One of the most pleasing activities in Bangkok is a tour of Thonburi's canals *(see pages 126–7)*.

The canals worth exploring include **Khlong Bangkok Noi**, which winds into **Khlong Bangkok Yai** downstream, as well as connecting to **Khlong Om** upstream. Once a source of fresh produce for local communities, the floating markets at **Wat Sai** and **Taling Chan** now function mainly as tourist souvenir stops, so much so that several similar markets have been revived in Bangkok. The further down the canals you venture, the narrower and calmer the waterway becomes. With rickety teak houses, vendors selling produce from boats, fishermen dangling rods out of windows and kids frolicking in the water, the sights along Thonburi's canals are reminiscent of a more peaceful bygone era.

Canal and river cruising

The major canals are serviced by public **longtail boats** *(see text box, page*

LEFT: Wat Arun. **RIGHT:** riverside food stall.

TIP

One of the best times to visit Wat Arun is late afternoon, when there are fewer visitors. Later, take the ferry across the river to Tha Tien pier where you will enjoy great sunset views of Wat Arun from the popular but rundown bar-shack called Poh on the wooden pier.

123). But as the experience can be hectic at certain times of the day – most commuters travel into the city in the mornings and return in the afternoons – it might be better to hire your own private longtail boat for a more leisurely exploration.

Getting from pier to pier along the Chao Phraya river is best on the **Chao Phraya Express** boats, which operate from the southern outskirts up to Nonthaburi in the north. For shuttling from one side of the river to the other, make use of the cheap **cross-river ferries**, which you can board at the many jetties close to the Chao Phraya Express boat piers *(see page 237)*.

Wat Arun ❶

Address: Thanon Arun Amarin
Tel: 0-2891 2185
Opening Hrs: daily 8.30am–5.30pm
Entrance Fee: charge
Transport: Wat Arun pier

Also known as The Temple of Dawn, this temple gets its confusing nickname – the sun actually sets, not rises, behind the temple – from the arrival of King Taksin, who led the remnants of the Siamese armies here in 1767 after their defeat by the Burmese in the siege of Ayutthaya. The king first viewed **Wat Arun**, at dawn, and chose the area, Thonburi, as the new capital of Siam.

Taksin incorporated the temple – then called Wat Magog – into his palace compound, renamed it Wat Jaeng (Temple of Dawn), and housed the greatly revered Emerald Buddha here. King Rama I later moved it to Wat Kaew, near the Grand Palace. Rama II (1809–24) officially changed Wat Arun's name to Wat Arunratchatharam, and Rama IV (1851–68) later chose Wat Arunratchawararam.

After renovations of the temple by several kings of the Chakri dynasty, the main Khmer-style *prang* (spire) now stands at 79 metres (259ft). Rama III introduced the colourful fragments of porcelain that cover most of the tem-

BELOW: detail of a porcelain-encrusted *prang* of Wat Arun.

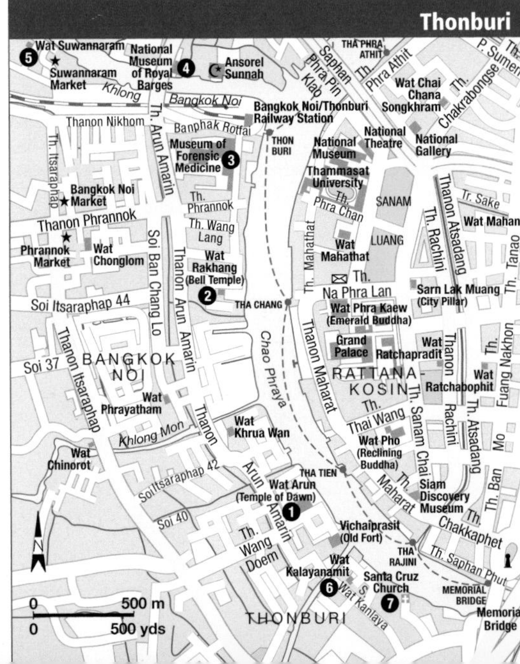

Touring by Longtail Boat

Some of the sights in this chapter are best visited by private longtail boat. Longtail boat operators (found at major piers like Tha Thien and Tha Chang) are notorious for overcharging tourists, so be prepared to bargain hard and set a price before embarking; B500–700 an hour (per boat) is a rough guide. Discuss beforehand where you want to visit and how much time you want to spend at each place. Bear in mind that once underway, it may be difficult to switch itineraries as boat drivers speak little or no English. Ask for a slow ride so that photos can be taken and the scenery enjoyed. Sit near the front of the boat, away from the noisy rear engines.

ple's exterior, recycling piles of broken ceramic that was leftover ballast from Chinese merchant ships. When builders ran out of porcelain the king asked his subjects to contribute broken crockery to complete the decoration. Artisans fashioned the pieces into flowers or used them to embellish the costumes of the gods and mythical figures that ring each tier.

The great *prang* represents the Hindu–Buddhist Mount Meru, home of the gods, with its 33 heavens. It is topped by a thunderbolt, the weapon of the Hindu god Indra. Four smaller *prang* stand at each corner of the temple, each with niches containing statues of Nayu, god of the wind, on horseback. Between the minor *prang* are four beautiful smaller towers, or *mondop*. In niches at the foot of each stairway, Buddha images portray the four key events of his life: birth, meditation (while sheltered by a seven-headed *naga* serpent), preaching to his first five disciples, and death/enlightenment. Mythical giants called *yaksha*, similar to those that protect Wat Phra Kaew, guard the complex.

Wat Rakhang ❷

Address: Thanon Arun Amarin
Tel: 0-2411 2255
Opening Hrs: daily 8.30am–5.30pm
Entrance Fee: charge
Transport: Sirirat pier

Further upriver, directly across from the Grand Palace complex, this temple has a lovely collection of bells. King Taksin liked the chime of the original temple bell and had it moved to Wat Phra Kaew, donating five bells as replacement.

Hidden at the rear of Wat Rakhang is the red-painted *ho trai* (wooden library), a three-part stilted building that King Rama I lived in as a monk before becoming king and when Thonburi was the capital. The late 18th-century building is considered an architectural gem and is decorated with murals from the *Ramakien*.

ABOVE: numerous small bells hang from Wat Rakhang's temple towers and gently chime in the afternoon breeze, adding a musical ambience to this riverside temple. **BELOW:** roof detail at Wat Rakhang.

The Museum of Forensic Medicine ❸

Address: 2/F, Adulaydejvigrom Building, Sirirat Hospital, 2 Thanon Phrannok
Tel: 0-2419 7000
Opening Hrs: Mon–Fri 8.30am–4.30pm

SHOP

Between the Museum of Royal Barges and Wat Suwannaram, ask your boatman to stop at Ban Bu, where a short alley leads to a workshop making hand-beaten alms bowls called *khan long hin*. You can watch the process and buy these beautiful bronzeware items from around B700.

Entrance Fee: free
Transport: Sirirat pier

To the north of Wat Rakhang, several museums are located within the Siriraj Hospital complex, the best known of which is this one. Green arrows point the way from the hospital grounds to the museum, located on the 2nd floor of the Forensic Department. The stomach-churning exhibits are definitely not for the queasy. Mummified corpses of Thailand's most notorious criminals, deformed foetuses in formaldehyde and a gallery of disturbing post-mortem photographs are among the exhibits here.

National Museum of Royal Barges ❹

Address: Khlong Bangkok Noi, off Chao Phraya river, Thanon Arun Amarin, www.thailandmuseum.com
Tel: 0-2424 0004
Opening Hrs: daily 9am–5pm
Entrance Fee: charge (photography fee extra)
Transport: longtail boat to museum pier

On the north bank of the Khlong Bangkok Noi canal is the **National Museum of Royal Barges**. A crammed canal bank community nearby provides a stark contrast to the regal opulence of the wooden barges. The dry-dock warehouse displays eight vessels from a fleet of over 50 that are only put to sail on auspicious occasions.

Their last outing – to celebrate the king's 80th birthday in 2007 – saw 2,000 oarsmen, musicians and guards in traditional dress sailing in a 52-barge procession to Wat Arun for a *khatin* ceremony, in which robes are presented to monks. Of the six barges displayed in dry dock here, pride of place goes to *Suphannahongse* (Golden Swan), named after the mythical steed of the Hindu god Brahma and in which the king travels on a gold-coloured throne. It's 50 metres (164ft) long – the largest vessel in the world to be crafted from a single piece of wood. Barge processions date to the Ayutthaya period, but the original *Suphannahongse* was built in the reign of King Rama I (1782–1809). King Rama VI launched the current version in 1911.

Also displayed are old figureheads from boats damaged by World War II Allied bombs aimed at the nearby Bangkok Noi Railway Station, which the Japanese used to ship supplies to and from western Thailand via the infamous Death Railway to Burma *(see page 199)*. Around the museum are glass cases with models of traditional canal transport, Ayutthaya-era drawings, photos of barge construction and gold ornamental cloths that adorn the barges.

RIGHT: Santa Cruz Church. **BELOW:** seven-headed *naga*, or serpent, adorning the prow of the *Anantanaganaj* barge at the Museum of Royal Barges.

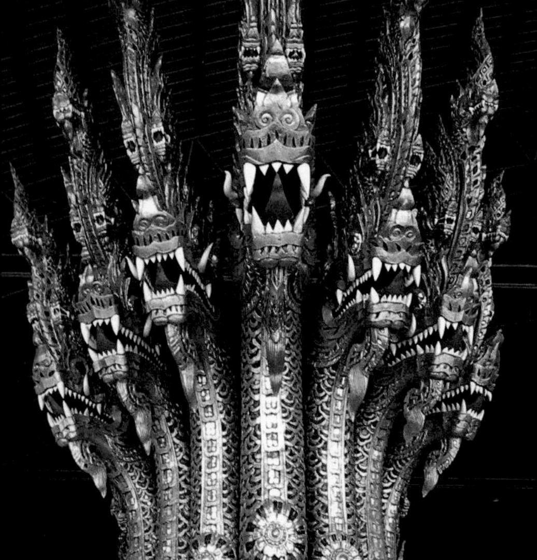

Wat Suwannaram ❺

Address: 33 Charan Sanit Wong Soi 32
Tel: 0-2434 7790
Opening Hrs: daily 6am–5pm
Entrance Fee: free
Transport: longtail boat to wat's pier

From the museum pier, it's a five-minute boat journey up Khlong Bangkok Noi canal to this historic temple on the opposite bank to the museum. Have a look at the grand murals contained within **Wat Suwannaram's** main building. If the building is locked, look for a monk, who may open the doors and windows to reveal the magnificent, if slightly deteriorated, paintings that tell the story of the Buddha's previous 10 lives. The intricate artwork, which adorns every corner of the temple's interior, was commissioned by King Rama III and is considered to be among the finest examples of 19th-century painting.

Wat Kalayanamit ❻

Address: 371 Soi Wat Kanlaya
Tel: 0-2466 5018
Opening Hrs: daily 8am–5pm
Entrance Fee: free
Transport: Wat Arun pier

South of Wat Arun, at the mouth of Khlong Bangkok Yai canal, are two sights worth visiting. The first is this 19th-century temple with Chinese-style embellishments. Built at the behest of Rama III, the tall main *vihara* (sermon hall) contains an impressive seated Buddha image. This is the largest of its kind in the country, as is the large bronze bell in the grounds.

Santa Cruz Church ❼

Address: 112 Thanon Thetsaban Soi 1
Opening Hrs: Mon–Sat 5–8pm, Sun 9am–8pm
Entrance Fee: free
Transport: Santa Cruz Church pier

From the temple head for **Santa Cruz Church**, the spire of which is visible from a couple of streets away. The pastel-coloured church, topped by an octagonal dome, has been rebuilt twice since it was first constructed in the 18th century. The present edifice dates from 1913. The neighbourhood surrounding the church was once part of a flourishing Portuguese district that migrated here after Ayutthaya was abandoned. ❑

ABOVE: Buddha image at Wat Kalayanamit.

BEST RESTAURANTS

Thai

Krua Rakang Thong
306 Soi Wat Rakhang, Th Arun Amarin, Sirirat. Tel: 0-2848 9597. Open: daily 11am–11pm. $ ❺ p268, A4
This old-style riverfront restaurant with views of the Grand Palace is a good sunset spot for king prawns in sweet and sour tamarind sauce, spicy northeastern salads, exploded catfish, diced and fried till crumbly, then added to coconut soup.

Patravadi Restaurant
Patravadi Theatre 69/1 Soi Wat Rakhang, Th Arun Amarin, Sirirat. Tel: 0-2412 7287-8. www.patravaditheatre.com Open: Mon–Fri 11am–9pm, Sat–Sun 11am–10pm. $ ❻ p268, A4
Garden café, located within Bangkok's premier fringe theatre near Wat Rakhang, with views of performances. Serves curries and a long list of vegetarian dishes. Enjoy coffee, tea or fruit juice with blueberry pie or brownies.

Sirirat Market
Th Phrannok. Open: daily 7am–8pm. $ ❼ p268, A4
Rough and ready food stalls in this general goods market offer local street fare: spicy sausages, perfect satay, flavoursome deep-fried chicken, aromatic stir-fries and steaming noodles. A small shop called Paa Sidaa, next to a sign reading Wienna, is one of Bangkok's most famous *som tam* sellers.

Studio 9
69/1 Soi Wat Rakang, Th Arun Amarin. Tel: 0-2866 2144. www.patravaditheatre.com Open: daily 11am–10pm. $$. ❽ p268, A4
The riverside restaurant of the Patravadi Theatre has dishes like paprika chicken with rice and spare ribs in pepper and garlic, which you can sample as you take in a dance performance (Sat and Sun). During the week you could see the company rehearsing as you dine.

Price per person for a three-course meal without drinks.
$ = under B300, $$ = B300–800, $$$ = B800–1,600, $$$$ = over B1,600.

LIFE ON THE CHAO PHRAYA RIVER

The river offers respite from Bangkok traffic, and gives an alternative view of a city that grew up along its banks

Many people enjoy travelling on the Chao Phraya River, not only to escape the roads, for the cool breeze and the cleaner air, but because numerous sites are best seen from the water. The city grew up along the river, so its banks are full of interesting old buildings. In the east are beautiful colonial-style structures and early European churches, and drifting towards the Old City are temples such as Wat Arun *(see page 122)*, which rises atmospherically on the Thonburi side.

Many of the riverside wooden dwellings hark back 100 years; there are back doors to markets, where waterborne goods are still loaded from boats; and not very far north you are into the green countryside. The river is not just a means to get from A to B; it can be a very satisfying tour in itself and well worth an hour or two of your time. There is a variety of water transport, from express boats – which travel up and down the length of the river – to cross-river ferries and longtail taxi boats (which link from the river into the *khlongs*, or canals). See pages 237–8 of Travel Tips for more details.

BELOW: as old wooden houses in this rapidly developing city disappear, those on waterways offer the best glimpse of Bangkok's traditional dwellings.

ABOVE: in pockets of Bangkok, boats remain the prime means of transport. Some are floating shops, selling everything from rice and beer to postal services.

ABOVE: the truly authentic Thai floating market is more or less a thing of the past. Head for the floating market at Damnoen Saduak *(see page 171)* keeping in mind that much of it is staged for tourists.

BELOW: the rapidly developing river skyline is particularly fine at night, especially when the hotels coordinate firework displays.

HOW THE *KHLONGS* DEVELOPED

Bangkok's origins date back to the 16th century when a canal was dug across a loop of the Chao Phraya River to cut the distance between the sea and the then Thai capital at Ayutthaya, 85km (55 miles) north. Over the years, monsoon floods scoured the banks of the canal until it widened to become the main course of the river. On its banks rose two towns, Thonburi on the west and Bangkok on the east. The abandoned river loop became Khlong Bangkok Noi and Khlong Bangkok Yai, the principal canals that run through Thonburi. Bangkok's founding king, Rama I, established Rattanakosin as the nucleus of the new capital in 1782 by digging three concentric canals, turning it into an easily defensible island. Houses were built on bamboo rafts and people travelled primarily by boat. In the mid-20th century, Bangkokians began leaving boats for cars. Canals were filled in to make roads, and houses were built on land. The congested streets that are sweltering in the hot season become flooded in the monsoon season. Some canals, though, remain, and Khlong Saen Saep still ferries people right across town from the Old City to Bangkok's eastern fringes.

LEFT AND BELOW: with few bridges and heavy road traffic, people rely on river ferries, both across river and along it. Luckily, they operate every few hundred metres.

THE OLD CITY

Bangkok's Old City retains some of its historic calm and charm, and is one of the easiest areas to tour on foot. There are many temples and Buddhist shops, and to the north, lively Khao San Road is where backpackers party until dawn

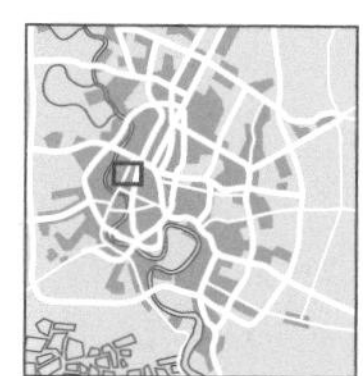

Main Attractions

WAT SUTHAT
PAK KHLONG TALAD
DEMOCRACY MONUMENT
WAT BOWONNIWET
LOHA PRASAT
KING PRAJADHIPOK MUSEUM
GOLDEN MOUNT
SOI BAN BAAT
THANON KHAO SAN

Maps and Listings

MAP OF THE OLD CITY, PAGE 130
SHOPPING, PAGE 137
RESTAURANTS, BARS AND CAFÉS, PAGES 138–9
ACCOMMODATION, PAGES 241–2

Dominated by the wide boulevard of Thanon Ratchadamnoen, the "Old City" contains all the peripheral buildings and temples that lie just outside Rattanakosin island. The area once marked the outskirts of the city, with the canals of Khlong Banglamphu and Khlong Ong Ang ferrying in supplies from the surrounding countryside. At the turn of the 20th century, hardly any roads cut into the landscape, with the neighbourhood occupied by traditional craftspeople and performing artisans. Devotional structures were the main protrusions on the skyline.

Time has drastically altered the area's visual appeal, yet there is still a strong sense of the past, making this one of the city's most pleasant areas to explore. Aside from tourist attractions, most foreigners head to the district of Banglamphu for cheap accommodation and entertainment in the well-known backpackers' haven of Thanon Khao San.

Thanon Bamrung Muang

Thanon Bamrung Muang, an old elephant trail, was one of the city's first paved tracks. This area is full of temples, and this street is typical for its shops selling accoutrements for Buddhist worship and funeral rites. Monks in orange robes mingle with housewives and businessmen placing orders for ceremonial candles, tiered umbrellas, temple drums, bells and gongs, incense and sparkling lanterns, and it's not unusual to see pickup trucks driving around with 3½-metre (12ft) gold Buddha statues strapped to the back.

Giant Swing ❶

Thanon Bamrung Muang intersects a large square with City Hall

LEFT: Buddha images lining the cloisters at Wat Suthat. **RIGHT:** the Giant Swing.

ABOVE: the Democracy Monument.

at its northern end and Wat Suthat and the **Giant Swing** opposite. Bangkok's original Giant Swing (Sao Ching Cha), erected by King Rama I in 1784, was based on one in Ayutthaya that had been brought to Thailand by Brahman priests in the 16th century. It was used to observe Triyampawai, the Brahman New Year Ceremony, during which four young men in a gondola would swing ever higher trying to catch purses of gold hanging from poles. The ceremony was banned in 1931 after several accidents. The swing itself has been removed, leaving just the tall red-painted teak frame as a marker. There have been recent discussions as to whether the old ritual can be restored.

Wat Suthat ❷

Address: 146 Thanon Bamrung Muang
Tel: 0-2224 9845
Opening Hrs: daily 8.30am–9pm
Entrance Fee: charge
Transport: buses 10, 12, 42

Standing tall behind the Giant Swing, this is one of the country's six principal temples. Begun by Rama I in 1807, it took three reigns to complete. The temple is notable for its enormous *bot*, or ordination hall, said to be the tallest in Bangkok, and for its equally large *viharn* (sermon hall), both of them surrounded by cloisters of gilded Buddha images.

The 8-metre (26ft) -tall Phra Sri Sakyamuni Buddha is one of the largest surviving bronze images from Sukhothai, and was transported by boat all the way from the former northern kingdom. The base of the image contains the ashes of King Ananda Mahidol (Rama VIII), older brother of the present king. The murals date from the reign of King Rama III; most intriguing are the depictions of sea monsters and foreign ships on the columns.

Accounts vary, but it is said that

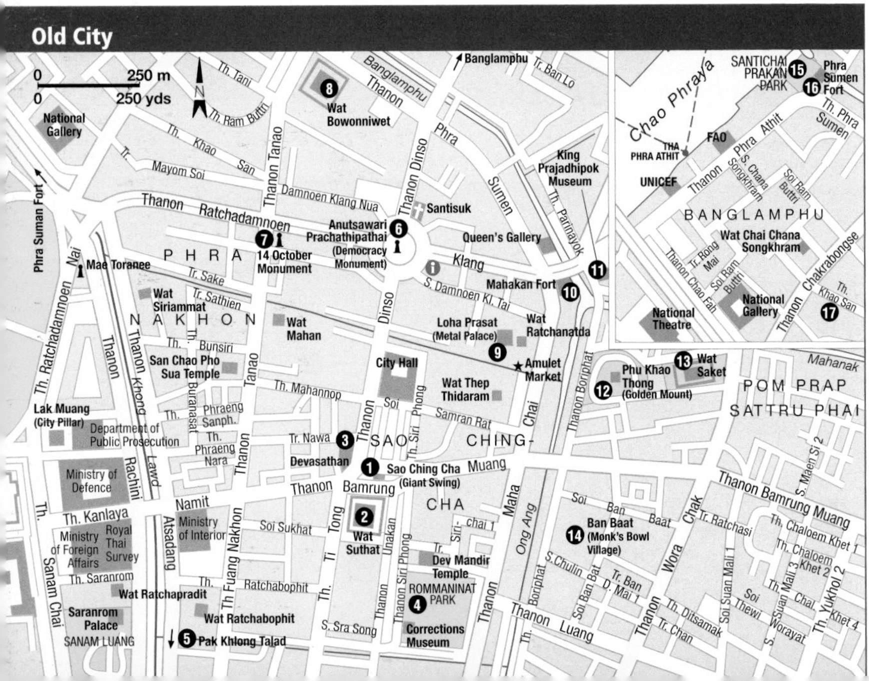

Old City

0 250 m
0 250 yds
National Gallery
Th. Tani
Th. Ram Buttri
Th. Khao San
Tr. Mayom Soi
Wat Bowonniwet
Banglamphu Thanon
Banglamphu
Tr. Ban Lo
Phra Sumen
Thanon Tanao
Thanon Dinso
Damnoen Klang Nua
Thanon Ratchadamnoen
Santisuk
King Prajadhipok Museum
Th. Parinayok
Anutsawari Prachathipathai (Democracy Monument)
14 October Monument
Queen's Gallery
Klang
Mahakan Fort
S. Damnoen Kl. Tai
Phra Suman Fort
Mae Toranee
PHRA NAKHON
Tr. Sake
Tr. Sathien
Wat Siriammat
Wat Mahan
Loha Prasat (Metal Palace)
Wat Ratchanatda
Amulet Market
Th. Bunsiri
San Chao Pho Sua Temple
City Hall
Wat Thep Thidaram
Th. Mahannop
Soi
Samran Rat
Th. Ratchadamnoen
Thanon Khong
Th. Buranasat
Lak Muang (City Pillar)
Department of Public Prosecution
Th. Phraeng Sanph.
Th. Phraeng Nara
Tr. Nawa
Devasathan
SAO CHING-CHA
Sao Ching Cha (Giant Swing)
Muang
Thanon Bamrung
Ministry of Defence
Rachini
Lawd
Th. Kanlaya
Ministry of Foreign Affairs
Royal Thai Survey
Th. Saranrom
Namit Ministry of Interior
Atsadang
Th Fuang Nakhon
Soi Sukhat
Tong
Wat Suthat
Unakan
Siri Phong
Tr. Dev Mandir Temple
Ti Tong
Th. Ratchabophit
Wat Ratchapradit
Wat Ratchabophit
Saranrom Palace
SANAM LUANG
Th. Sanam Chai
Pak Khlong Talad
S. Sra Song
ROMMANINAT PARK
Corrections Museum
Maha Chai
Ong Ang
Thanon Boriphat
Phu Khao Thong (Golden Mount)
Wat Saket
Mahanak
POM PRAP SATTRU PHAI
Soi Ban Baat
Ban Baat (Monk's Bowl Village)
Chak Wora
Tr. Ratchasi
Thanon Bamrung Muang
Th. Chaloem Khet 1
Th. Chaloem Khet 2
S. Chulin
Tr. Ban D. Mai 1
Soi Ban Bat
Thanon Luang
Th. Ditsamak
Tr. Chan
Soi Suan Mali 1
Soi Thewi
Th. Suan Mali 3
Th. Chai
Worayat
Th. Yukhol 2
Khet 4
S. Maen Si 2
SANTICHAI PRAKAN PARK
Phra Sumen Fort
Chao Phraya
THA PHRA ATHIT
FAO
UNICEF
Thanon Phra Athit
S. Chana Songkhram
Soi Ram Buttri
BANGLAMPHU
Wat Chai Chana Songkhram
Tr. Rong Mai
Soi Ram Buttri
Thanon Chao Fah
National Theatre
National Gallery
Thanon Chakrabongse
Th. Khao San
Th. Phra Sumen

Rama II himself carved the ornate teakwood doors of the *bot.* Incised to a depth of 5cm (2ins), they follow the Ayutthaya tradition of floral motifs, with tangled jungle vegetation hiding small animals. The temple courtyard is a virtual museum of statuary, with stone figures of Chinese generals and scholars, which came as ballast in 18th century rice ships returning from deliveries to China.

Devasathan ❸

West of the Giant Swing along Thanon Dinso is a row of three adjoining Brahman shrines called **Devasathan** (daily 9am–5pm, chapel Thur and Sun only 10am–4pm; free). Built in 1784 at the same time as the Giant Swing and recently renovated, the three chapels house images of Shiva, Ganesha and Vishnu. Although Thais are largely Buddhists, certain Brahman beliefs have been retained from historical ties with Angkor *(see margin, right)*.

Rommaninat Park ❹

Southwest of Wat Suthat, a short walk along Thanon Siri Phong brings you to **Rommaninat Park** (daily 5am–9pm; free). Formerly the grounds of a prison built in 1893, this became a public park in 1992 to celebrate Queen Sirikit's birthday. The original watchtowers are still standing, and some of the former prison buildings now house the small **Corrections Museum**, with displays of old methods of punishment (Mon–Fri 8.30am–4.30pm; free). Other features include ponds, fountains, a children's play area, jogging tracks and a large bronze sculpture of a conch shell.

Pak Khlong Talad ❺

South of the park, on Thanon Chakraphet, the atmospheric **Pak Khlong Talad** (Flower Market) sits by the riverfront at the mouth of Khlong Lord. It's a convenient location for supplying funeral wreaths for use in the Old City temples. The market, busy 24 hours a day, spills from covered warehouses onto streets lined with stalls selling roses, carnations, sunflowers and myriad orchids. It is best visited after nightfall, when the surrounding area also heaves with the

Long-haired, white-robed Brahman priests have been a fixture of Thai royal life since the 14th century. They are in charge of royal statecraft and rite-of-passage ceremonies. They have also introduced Hindu gods, such as Shiva, Brahma, Indra and others, who appear in Thai art and architecture.

LEFT: detail of wall mural at Wat Suthat.
BELOW: the Devasathan shrine has strong Hindu influences.

ABOVE: roses at Pak Khlong Talad.
BELOW: the 14 October Monument is a shrine to the people who died in the 1973 demonstrations against Thailand's military dictatorship.

youthful clothes and accessory stalls of Saphan Phut Market.

Democracy Monument ❻

Moving north, the **Democracy Monument** lies beyond City Hall. Designed with four elongated wings by Italian sculptor Corrado Feroci (also known as Silpa Bhirasri), the 1939 monument is a celebration of Thailand's 1932 transition from absolute to constitutional monarchy. Almost every detail and measurement of the monument has symbolic relevance, and the central metal tray contains a copy of the original Constitution of the Kingdom of Thailand. A rallying point for civil discontent in October 1973 and May 1992, the monument became the scene of bloodbaths after the army violently suppressed peaceful demonstrations against military dictatorships. Officially nearly 200 protesters were killed during the two incidents.

14 October Monument ❼

A short walk west from Democracy Monument, along Thanon Ratchadamnoen Klang, brings you to the **14 October Monument.** This chiselled granite edifice is a sombre memorial to the victims of the 1973 mass demonstrations against the dictatorship of the "Three Tyrants", led by Prime Minister Thanom Kittikachorn. A small amphitheatre surrounds the central spire, which has the names of 73 of the victims inscribed in Thai. Beneath are an exhibition room, meeting rooms and a minitheatre. Given the government's past denial of this tragic event, it was a major victory for survivors and victims' families when this tribute was erected in 2002.

Wat Bowonniwet ❽

Due north of the 14 October Monument along Thanon Tanao is **Wat Bowonniwet**, a modest-looking temple with strong royal bonds (daily 8am–5pm; free). Built in 1826 during the reign of Rama III, King Mongkut (Rama IV) served as abbot of the temple for a small portion of his 27 years

Armed with Amulets

The thriving amulet market in the forecourt of Wat Ratchanatda *(see page 134)* reflects the Thai belief in a mix of talismanic powers based on animism as well as Brahman and Buddhist beliefs. The market deals in amulets of all shapes and sizes, along with prayer beads, Buddha images and totems of revered monks. They are worn for religious or spiritual purposes or for more practical reasons, such as keeping the wearer safe or attracting fortune in love or money. Look out for wooden *palad khik* (phalluses), which are believed to ward off evil spirits. Many will have been blessed by monks for use in exorcism. There is another famous amulet market close to Wat Mahathat *(see page 113).*

as a monk. More recently the present King Bhumibol (Rama IX) donned saffron robes here after his coronation in 1946.

Home to Thailand's second Buddhist university, the temple is known for its extraordinary murals painted by innovative monk-artist Khrua In Khong. Krua had never travelled outside Thailand, but had looked at Western art reproductions and understood the concept of perspective. Unlike the flat, two-dimensional paintings of classical Thai art, these recede into the distance and are characterised by muted, moody colours. Also interesting are the subjects: pre-Civil War American mansions, horse-racing tracks and people dressed in the fashions of 19th-century America.

Thanon Ratchadamnoen

Stretching all the way from the Grand Palace to the Dusit Park area, the wide **Thanon Ratchadamnoen** (Royal Passage) splits into three sections and is modelled after Paris's famous boulevards. Built at the turn of the 20th century, the tree-lined avenue has some of the city's widest and least cluttered pavements.

The somewhat austere-looking 1930s buildings that line both sides of Thanon Ratchadamnoen Klang have been given a lick of paint and public benches have been added along the pavements to offer rest for the weary. On royal birthdays, the area is turned into a sea of decorative lights, flags and royal portraits. Don't be surprised if all traffic and pedestrians are abruptly halted by legions of police – it means a royal cavalcade is on its way.

Queen's Gallery

Towards the eastern end of Thanon Ratchadamnoen Klang, on the corner of Thanon Phra Sumen, is the modern, cream-coloured **Queen's Gallery** (tel: 0-2281 5360/1; www.queengallery.

ABOVE: the pointed metal spires of the Loha Prasat. **BELOW:** Mahakan Fort, one of only two remaining watchtowers that guarded the old city walls of Bangkok.

ABOVE: during World War II, the Golden Mount served as a watchtower, with guards armed with signal flags to warn of enemy invaders. **BELOW:** the climb to the Golden Mount is rewarding for its views of the Rattanakosin area.

org/en; Thur–Tue 10am–7pm; charge). This five-floor gallery exhibits modern and contemporary paintings, predominantly by local artists.

Loha Prasat and Wat Ratchanatda ❾

Address: 2 Thanon Maha Chai
Tel: 0-2224 8807
Opening Hrs: daily 9am–5pm
Entrance Fee: charge
Transport: buses 2, 12, 42

Just before the point where Thanon Ratchadamnoen Klang crosses Pan Fah Bridge over the canal and veers left into Ratchadamnoen Nok are several noticeable structures on the right. The **Loha Prasat** (Metal Palace), evocative of Burmese temple structures, is the main attraction in the grounds it shares with **Wat Ratchanatda**. The Loha Prasat is a step pyramid construction modelled on a Sri Lankan temple from the 3rd century BC. King Rama III ordered it built in 1846. Its 37 black spires, each topped with an umbrella embellishment called a *hti*, depict the virtues needed to attain enlightenment. You can climb a spiral staircase past corridors of meditation cells right onto the roof itself, where a tower holds a sacred bell. Dizzying views include the Golden Mount.

The *viharn* at Wat Ratchanatda has lovely murals depicting heaven and hell on its interior walls. Outside the entrance is a manicured forecourt with the **Mahachesdabodin Royal Pavilion**. The ornate wooden pavilion is actually just over a decade old, one of the first additions in a grand scheme to redevelop the area. Its rich, gleaming embellishments have made it an appropriate setting for special ceremonies. Just behind the temple is a thriving amulet market *(see page 132).*

Mahakan Fort ❿

Across Thanon Maha Chai from Wat Ratchanatda is one of only two surviving remnants of the 14 original fortified watchtowers that once protected the old city wall. With development having consumed most of the wall and other towers, the white octagonal turret of **Mahakan Fort** survives along with Banglamphu's larger Phra Sumen Fort *(see page*

Fun of the Fair

Bangkok's most famous temple fair *(ngan wat)* is held at Wat Saket each November. Temple fairs are an annual feature in many Bangkok communities and villages across the country, often lasting several days. They are raucous occasions that bring all ages together to enjoy a mix of market stalls, fairground games, fortune telling, theatre and comedy shows, and to raise money for the temple. Young girls enter beauty contests and their brothers, sometimes as young as seven, might start a fledgling career in Thai boxing. Bands play all kinds of music, often all at once, and the night brings romantic liaisons forged over rice wine and plates of spicy food to a soundtrack of thunderous disco.

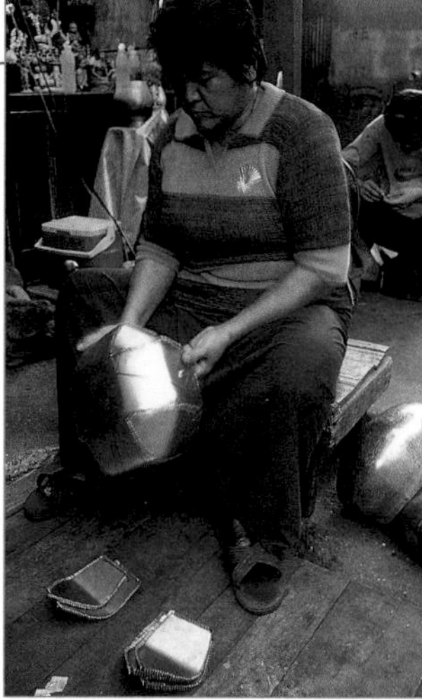

136). The cannons here were only recently disarmed. The site is closed to the public.

King Prajadhipok Museum ⓫

Address: 2 Thanon Lan Luang
Tel: 0-2280 3413
Opening Hrs: Tue–Sun 9am–4pm
Entrance Fee: charge
Transport: buses 2, 12, 42

Over the bridge from Mahakan Fort, this museum tells something of the intrigue behind the end of absolute monarchy in 1932, when King Prajadhipok (Rama VII) was Thailand's ruler. It portrays the king's life before, during and after his reign through photos, official documents, personal effects and audio-visual displays. They cover his school days at Eton and his coronation, plus significant public works, such as the construction of Memorial Bridge *(see page 121)*. The king abdicated in 1935 and lived the rest of his life in England. The white neoclassical building, dated 1906, was originally the John Sampson Store, an early Bangkok purveyor of Western clothes.

Golden Mount ⓬

Address: 344 Thanon Chakraphatdi Phong
Tel: 0-2223 4561
Opening Hrs: daily 7.30am–5.30pm
Entrance Fee: charge
Transport: buses 2, 12, 42

Standing tall, south of King Prajadhipok Museum, is the elevated spire of the **Golden Mount** (Phu Khao Thong). Started by Rama III as a huge *chedi*, the city's soft earth made it impossible to build and the abandoned site became an artificial hill overgrown with trees and shrubbery. In 1865, flat Bangkok got its then highest point when Rama IV added a golden *chedi* to the top, completing the 78-metre (255ft) high Golden Mount and giving it its name.

The *chedi*, a part of Wat Saket *(see below)*, is said to contain a Buddha relic from India. Visitors take the gentle climb past shrines, trees and rock gardens, ringing temple bells and enjoying 360-degree views of the city as the path spirals upwards. There's a refreshment stop halfway.

Wat Saket ⓭

At the bottom of the Golden Mount stands one of the capital's oldest temples, **Wat Saket** (daily 8am–5pm;

LEFT: skilled artisans hammering out alms bowls for monks at Soi Ban Baat. **ABOVE:** alms bowls, or *baat* are used by monks to collect food from faithful Buddhists every morning. **BELOW:** amulets for sale in the market behind Wat Ratchanatda.

TIP

Backpacker land Khao San Road has become so popular that it's even spawned its own website, www.khaosanroad.com. It's packed chock-a-block with tips on cheap guesthouses, food and nightlife, as well as offbeat advice on how to wash your dreadlocks.

free). Upon returning from Laos in 1782 with the Emerald Buddha, General Chakri stopped here and took a ceremonial bath before making his way back to Thonburi to be crowned King Rama I. The temple's name was later changed to Saket, which means "the washing of hair".

The temple is also associated with a more grisly history as it was used as the Old City's main crematorium. Disease epidemics broke out regularly during the 19th century, killing an estimated 60,000 people. The bodies of the dead were taken out of the city to the temple through the **Pratu Pii** (Ghost Gate) for cremation; if the families were too poor to pay for the ceremony, they were left for the vultures. Notable features are the fine murals in the main hall, and a beautiful wooden scripture library that dates to Rama I.

Monks' Bowl Village

Skirting the western edge of the Golden Mount is **Thanon Boriphat**, a street lined with timber merchants and wood carvers, chiselling away at doors, lintels and even birdcages. Further along the some road are the narrow alleyways that run off **Soi Ban Baat** 14. This area's name means **Monk's Bowl Village**. Although you still see monks carrying metal alms bowls *(baat)* around Bangkok's streets to this day, they are now mainly machine-made, and there are just five families remaining of the original community that moved here from Ayutthaya in the 18th century to make hand-beaten bowls in the new capital.

Saffron-robed monks walk barefoot along the streets at dawn collecting food offerings from merit-seeking alms-givers. The bowls are crafted from eight pieces of metal, representing the eight spokes in the wheel of Dharma. Cashing in on the tourist market, the community has posted signs in English guiding you towards the tap-tap of distant hammers. Finished in enamel paint, the bowls sell from about B500.

BELOW: streetside hair-braiding service at Thanon Khao San.

Banglamphu

Called the village *(bang)* of the *lamphu* tree, the **Banglamphu** district was originally settled by farmers who fled the old capital of Ayutthaya after it was abandoned. The riverbank once held several princely mansions for nobles, a few of which survive on Thanon Phra Athit as offices of large companies and international agencies like UNICEF.

The riverfront from Saphan Phra Pin Klao Bridge along the length of Thanon Phra Athit to **Santichai Prakan Park** 15 is one of the city's few easily accessible river paths. It offers sweeping views up towards the Rama VIII Bridge. This lovely bankside park (daily 5am–10pm), always busy with activity of some sort, fringes the whitewashed octagonal **Phra Sumen Fort** 16, and has the only surviving *lamphu* trees in the neighbourhood. The fort, built in 1873 and restored in 1999, is one of two remaining defences of the old

city wall *(see also page 134)*. It is not open to the public.

Nearby **Thanon Phra Athit** is a lively street of art bars, some frequented by budding artists from nearby Silpakorn University. These colourful and cosy venues, which hold regular exhibitions and cultural events, are far less hectic than the backpacker-crammed watering holes just a stone's throw away on Thanon Khao San.

Thanon Khao San ⓱

Since the early 1980s, **Thanon Khao San** (or Khao San Road as it's popularly referred to) has been a self-contained ghetto for the backpacking globetrotter. Once a rather seedy gathering of cheap guesthouses, rice shops and pokey bars, as portrayed in Alex Garland's best-selling novel *The Beach*, Banglamphu's nerve centre has undergone a significant upgrade in recent years, with the arrival of boutique hotels like Buddy Lodge *(see page 241)*, sleek bars and international chains like Starbucks.

In the late 1990s, after local film and TV shows began using the street as a location, young Thais craving a sympathetic ambience for their own growing indie lifestyle started opening their own places to hang out in. The result is a mix of East and West 20-something culture that now stretches over several blocks and is among the most vibrant areas of the city.

All the needs of the "alternative" traveller are here – tattooists, hair braiders and body piercers, jugglers and buskers, tarot readers, used books and dealers in fake IDs. And of course a perpetual party atmosphere. ❑

LEFT: Khao San, a magnet for budget travellers.

SHOPPING

The main shopping options are found around Thanon Khao San and therefore mainly cater to the needs of backpackers.

Accessories

Max Body Art
70/3 D&D Hotel, Th Khao San. Tel: 0-2629 1642. www.maxtattoobangkok.com p268, B/C3
One of the best-known tattoo parlours in an area packed with them, offering original designs, reworks and cover-ups.

Chuchep Poi Shop
Bayon Building, 249 Th Khao San. Tel: 08-1510 1611. p268, B/C3
A must-buy for many people as they head to the islands is their own set of juggling stuff. Chuchep Poi sells sticks, pois and batons to practise your moves on before you hit the beach.

Books

Shaman Books
71 Th Khao San. Tel: 0-2629 0418. p268, B/C3
A large collection of second-hand books, from best sellers and classics to travel guides and specialist subjects like philosophy, Buddhism and food. The books are mainly in English, but other languages are available.

Food

Nittaya Curry Shop
136-40 Th Chakrabongse. Tel: 0-2282 8212. p268, B3
Nittaya exports Thai curry pastes all over the world, and this small shop offers all the favourites – green, red and yellow – and lots more besides.

Jewellery

SP Silver
216/4 Th Khao San. Tel: 0-629 3313. p268, B/C3
One of the main draws for business-minded travellers is wholesale jewellery. Try SP but be sure to shop around. Also sells retail.

Markets

Banglamphu Market
Th Phra Sumen and Th Chakrabongse. p268, B3
A mini-mini Chatuchak with all the usual cheap stuff, ie everything.

BEST RESTAURANTS, BARS AND CAFÉS

Restaurants

Chinese

Yee Lao Tang Jua Lee
45–7 Th Kalayana Maitri. Tel: 0-2221 8447. Open: daily L and D. **$$**
⑨ p268, C4
Air-conditioned restaurant with only Thai script outside (look for the fish drawing). Serves Chinese specialities, including various *dim sum* and stir-fried scallops. Busy in the week with mainly office workers nearby, while Chinese families converge at weekends.

International

Primavera
56 Th Phra Sumen. Tel: 0-2281 4718, www.primavera-cafe.com Open: daily 9am–11pm. **$–$$**
⑩ p268, B2
European coffee shop interior of mainly dark woods. Top billing on a short menu goes to pizza, along with liver pâté and fried calamari as starters. Reasonable choice of ice creams and coffees.

Italian

La Casa
210 Th Khao San. Tel: 0-2629 1628. Open: daily noon–midnight. **$$**
⑪ p268, C3
Simple open-fronted trattoria with terrace seats ideal for watching the Khao San bustle. A few spicier dishes, such as the moreish sizzling squid with chilli, garlic and lime, enliven the ample menu of pastas, risottos and traditional plates like *osso bucco*.

Thai

Chote Chitr
Th Praengphutorn. Tel: 0-2221 4082. Open: Mon–Sat 10am–9pm. **$**
⑫ p268, C4
Five-table shophouse opened 90 years ago by a doctor of traditional medicine. They've served excellent food (and medicines) ever since. Try the dark, pungent wing bean salad, *mee krob*, or wonderful, sour and peppery "old-fashioned soup".

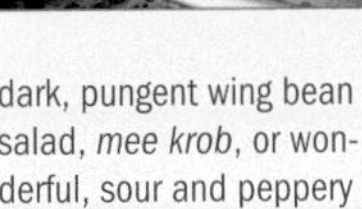

Krua Nopparat
130–2 Th Phra Arthit. Tel: 0-2281 7578. Open: Mon–Sat 10.30am–9pm. **$**
⑬ p268, B2
Don't be put off by the plain formica tables and wooden chairs, this tiny shophouse has relied on local customers for 30 years, and consequently serves very reliable traditional home cooking.

May Kaidee
117/1 Th Tanao. Tel: 0-2281 7137. www.maykaidee.com Open: daily 8am–11pm. **$**
⑭ p268, C3
Does vegetarian Thai standards like stir-fried basil with soya beans and mushrooms, and *massaman* curry with tofu, potatoes and peanuts. May also offer cooking lessons at a second outlet (33 Th Samsen).

Mayompuri
22 Th Chakrabongse. Tel: 0-2629 3883. www.mayompuri.com Open: daily 11am–1am. **$–$$**
⑮ p268, B3
This restaurant-bar occupies a spa-like venue with Greek pillars and fountains in several rooms around a terraced garden. The menu mixes Thai standards with international favourites like fish and chips. A laid-back atmosphere with trip-hop and Latin sounds.

Methavalai Sorn Daeng
78/2 Th Ratchadamnoen Klang. Tel: 0-2221 2378. Open: daily 10am–11pm.

LEFT: *paad thai* stall.
ABOVE: spicy noodle soup.

$$ 16 p268, C3
Popular, upmarket old-style Thai-Chinese restaurant with linen tablecloths and tacky salmon-coloured floral chairs. Decent food includes double-boiled duck soup with preserved lemon, and spicy banana flower salad. Right by the Democracy Monument roundabout.

Mitr Go Yuan
186 Th Dinso. Tel: 0-2224 1194. Open: Mon–Sat 11am–10pm, Sun 4–10pm. **$** 17 p268, C4
Traditional shophouse set-up that's busy at lunch and after 5pm with workers from the nearby City Hall. They rave about the *tom yum goong* (clear and spicy prawn soup) and spicy Thai salads.

Nan Faa
164 Th Dinso. Tel: 0-2224 1180. Open: daily 8am–8pm. **$** 18 p268, C4
Thai-Chinese café that specialises in slow roasted duck and goose basted with honey. Also has *dim sum* and traditional family dishes like stewed pig's ears and pig's feet. If it's full, go two doors away to Tien Song for similar food in air-conditioned surroundings.

Pen Thai Food
229 Soi Rambutri. Tel: 0-2282 2320. Open: daily 7am–7.30pm. **$** 19 p268, B3
Khun Sitichai has been here since 1980, before the first backpackers appeared. His menu has changed little – spicy curry, soups and deep-fried fish displayed outside in metal pots street-stall fashion – and at B20–40 each, neither have his prices.

Roti-Mataba
136 Th Phra Arthit. Tel: 0-2282-2119. Open: Tue–Sun 7am–10pm. **$** 20 p268, B2
An army of women here make Muslim-style breads by the hundreds in this incredibly busy shophouse. Dip the crisp *roti* into their delicious *massaman* and *korma* curries of fish, vegetable or meat. Just a few tables, so be prepared to wait.

Thip Samai
313 Th Mahachai. Tel: 0-2221 6280. www.thipsamai.com Open: daily 5.30pm–3.30am. **$** 21 p269, C4
A very basic but legendary café that does several versions (and nothing else) of *pad thai*, the fried noodle, dried shrimp, roasted peanut and bean sprout meal that is often claimed as Thailand's national dish.

Tom Yum Kung
Th Khao San. Tel: 0-2629 2772. www.tomyumkungkhaosan.com Open: daily 3pm–2am. **$** 22 p268, B3
Proof that Khao San is more than just backpackers and American breakfasts; this is perennially packed with young partying Thais in an old townhouse set back from the street. Popular are the eponymous soup, stir-fries and sizzling seafood hot plates.

Prices per person for a three-course meal without drinks:
$ = under B300
$$ = B300–800
$$$ = B800–1,600
$$$$ = over B1,600

ABOVE: the local vegetarian/vegan option.

Bars and Cafés

Baan Phra Arthit Coffee and More
102/1 Th Phra Arthit. Tel: 0-2280 7879. 1 p268, B2
Comfortable sofas with mochas and cappuccinos in a refined old house. Along with various gateaux are salads, snacks and mains.

Bangkok Bar
100 Soi Rambuttri. Tel: 0-2281 2899. www.bkkbar.com 2 p268, B3
New location for an old favourite, the busy BB now occupies a glass building and has live acoustic music by an outdoor pool, plus DJs and dining areas inside.

Café Democ
78 Th Ratchadamnoen. Tel: 0-2622 2572. www.cafe-democ.com 3 p268, C3
Progressive drum 'n' bass, and hip- and trip-hop are the music of choice at this bar-club, mixed by local celebrity DJs with the occasional international guest spinner.

Gulliver's Traveller's Tavern
Th Khao San. Tel: 0-2629 1988-9. www.gulliverbangkok.com 4 p268, B3
Perched at the end of the strip, this large alehouse is marked by a tuk-tuk above the door and usually teems with bleary-eyed tourists. Serves typical pub grub.

Phranakorn Bar & Gallery
58/2 Soi Damnoen Klang Tai. Tel: 0-2282 7507. Open: daily 6pm–1am. 5 p268, C3
Laid-back bar with rooftop views of Golden Mount, plus three other floors of art shows, decent Thai food and live music.

DUSIT

Bangkok's close-knit streets of fuming traffic are left far behind in royal Dusit, an expanse of wide parades and grandiose European architecture developed as a retreat by King Chulalongkorn. Museums galore sit in a tranquil park next to a zoo with boating on a lake

Main Attractions

STATUE OF KING CHULALONGKORN
ANANTA SAMAKHOM THRONE HALL
VIMANMEK MANSION
ABHISEK DUSIT THRONE HALL
DUSIT ZOO
WAT BENJAMABOPHIT

Maps and Listings

MAP OF DUSIT, PAGE 141
RESTAURANTS, PAGE 143
ACCOMMODATION, PAGES 241–2

The monarchy chose Dusit as the new area in which to build palaces and official buildings from the reign of King Chulalongkorn. The king was widely travelled and incorporated ideas he found abroad into all aspects of Thai life. Consequently, the royal quarter of Dusit is unlike any other area of Bangkok. The streets are modelled on the wide boulevards of Paris and the architecture rises in classical lines more associated with London or Rome.

Dusit Park

As Thanon Ratchadamnoen Klang leaves the Old City, it becomes Ratchadamnoen Nok, a pleasant, tree-lined boulevard leading to **Royal Plaza**, a broad square watched over by the bronze equestrian **Statue of King Chulalongkorn** (Rama V) ❶. Chulalongkorn was the first Thai monarch to venture to Europe and his travels left a lasting impression on the architecture and layout of this district, which was once a rustic royal retreat from the city and the Grand Palace.

The much revered king was also a great reformer and modern thinker. He abolished slavery and modernised many institutions, including the fields of medicine and education. People gather at the statue regularly, but particularly on 23 October, the anniversary of Chulalongkorn's death, to give offerings, including brandy, whisky or cigars which he particularly enjoyed, and wish luck for themselves in health, business and love. Royal Plaza hosts ceremonial occasions such as the Trooping of the Colour.

Ananta Samakhom Throne Hall ❷

Address: Thanon U-thong Nai
Tel: 0-2628 6300-9
Opening Hrs: daily 8.30am–4.30pm
Entrance Fee: charge (or free with Grand Palace entrance ticket)

Transport: buses 3, 72

Behind Chulalongkorn's statue is the monumental **Ananta Samakhom Throne Hall,** an Italian Renaissance-style hall of grey marble crowned by a huge dome. It is the tallest building within **Dusit Park**, which comprises a network of former royal gardens with canals, bridges, fountains and several small museums.

Built in 1907 by King Chulalongkorn as a grandiose venue for receiving visiting dignitaries, the hall is still used for state occasions. It was used for the first official meeting of the new parliament after Thailand became a constitutional monarchy in 1932. A Parliament House has since been built behind the throne hall. The highlights of the rich interior are frescoes on the domed ceiling depicting the Chakri monarchs from Rama I to Rama VI.

Vimanmek Mansion ❸

Address: 16 Thanon Ratchawithi, www.thai.palaces.net

Tel: 0-2628 6300

Opening Hrs: daily 9.30am–4pm

Entrance Fee: charge (free with Grand Palace entrance ticket); compulsory guided tours every 30 minutes; visitors dressed in shorts must wear sarongs that are provided at the door; shoes and bags have to be stowed in lockers

Transport: buses 18, 28, 110

Beyond Ananta Samakhom Throne Hall is the **Vimanmek Mansion**, billed as the world's largest golden teak building. Chulalongkorn had it built in 1868 as a summer palace on the east coast island of Ko Si Chang *(see page 212)*. However, he ordered the three-storey mansion dismantled and reassembled on the Dusit grounds in 1901. Made entirely from golden teak and without a single nail, the gingerbread fretwork and octagonal tower of this 72-room lodge looks more Victorian than period Thai. The king and his family lived here for only five years, during which time no other males were allowed entry. The mansion was

OPPOSITE: Vimanmek Mansion. **ABOVE:** Ananta Samakhom Throne Hall, which dates back to 1907, is more European than Thai in character. **BELOW:** meerkats at Dusit Zoo.

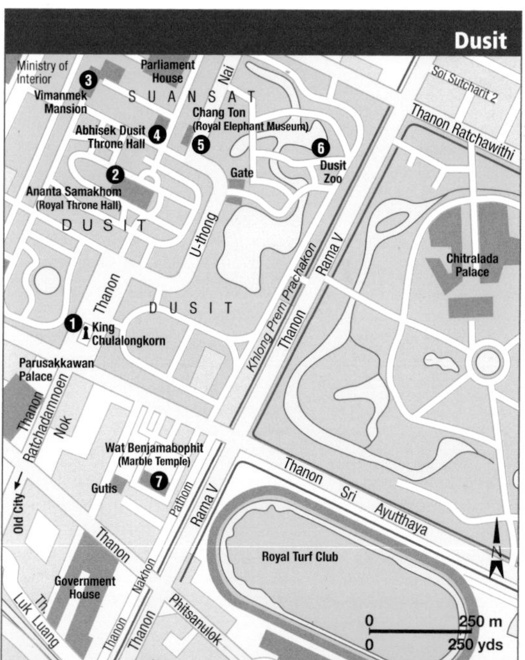

ABOVE: the Abhisek Dusit Throne Hall.

occupied on and off during the next two decades before being abandoned and used as storage space. It was restored for the Bangkok bicentennial in 1982 and given a new lease of life.

Vimanmek (meaning "Palace in the Clouds") offers an interesting glimpse into how the royal family of the day lived. Only 30 of the rooms are open to the public and the tour is rather brief given the fact that there are so many treasures to see. A highlight is the king's bedroom, which has a European-style four-poster bed, and the bathroom, which houses what was probably Thailand's first bathtub and flushing toilet. The plumbing, however, was in its early days – the waste had to be carried out on a spiral staircase hidden beneath. Among the porcelain and hunting trophies are rare finds like the first typewriter to have Thai characters.

Free performances of Thai dance and martial arts are held every day at 10.30am and 2pm in the pavilion south of the mansion.

Abhisek Dusit Throne Hall ❹

Address: 16 Thanon Ratchawithi
Tel: 0-2628 6300
Opening Hrs: daily 9.30am–4pm
Entrance Fee: charge (free with Grand Palace entrance ticket)
Transport: buses 18, 28, 110

In the garden east of Vimanmek is the **Abhisek Dusit Throne Hall**. Constructed in 1903 for King Chulalongkorn as an accompanying throne hall to Vimanmek, the ornate building is another sumptuous melding of Victorian and Moorish styles. The main hall is now used as a showroom-cum-museum for the SUPPORT foundation, a charitable organisation headed by Queen Sirikit, which helps preserve traditional arts and crafts. On view are examples of jewellery, woodcarving, nielloware, silk and wicker products. Next to the museum is a shop selling the handiwork of village artisans.

TIP

Be sure to keep your admission ticket to Wat Phra Kaew and the Grand Palace *(see page 102)*. This allows you free access to many of Dusit's sights, such as the Ananta Samakhom Throne Hall, Vimanmek Mansion, Abhisek Dusit Throne Hall and the Royal Elephant Museum.

Royal Elephant Museum ❺

Further east is the **Royal Elephant Museum** or Chang Ton (daily 9.30am–4pm; charge, or free with Grand Palace entrance ticket). This is a former stable for white elephants, which, when found in the wild, automatically become the property of the king. It displays a large model of one of the present king's prized living pachyderms, plus tusks and charms used by elephant handlers *(mahouts)*, photos and articles about elephant capture and training, and a tableau of the Brahman ceremony conferring royal status on white elephants *(see text box below)*.

Dusit Zoo ❻

Address: 71 Thanon Rama V
Tel: 0-2281 2000
Opening Hrs: daily 8am–6pm
Entrance Fee: charge
Transport: buses 18, 28, 110

Continuing east, across a small road is **Dusit Zoo**. Originally King Chulalongkorn's private botanical gardens, it contains 300 animal species and a lake, with pedaloes for hire. Most of the animals are located around the

White Elephants

To the uninitiated, white elephants look nearly the same as everyday grey ones. It is only by a complicated process of examining skin colour, hair, eyes and genitalia that an elephant's albino traits can be determined. Historically in Southeast Asia, the number of white elephants a king owned was seen as a direct reflection of his wealth and power. But these rare animals had to be fed rare foods and housed in special quarters. If the king disliked a courtier for some reason, he might give him a white elephant. The courtier would go bankrupt trying to maintain it. Hence, the term "white elephant" denotes a gift that is less desirable than it seems.

park's edges, and include deer, gibbons, bears, hippos, lions, tigers and birds. The zoo is a favourite place for locals to hang out away from the heat and fumes of the city.

Chitralada Palace

Next to Dusit Zoo, a thick tree-shaded fence and moat protects the grounds of **Chitralada Palace**, the current king's permanent home. It was built in 1913 as a place where King Vajiravudh (Rama VI) found creative solitude away from court life at the Grand Palace. It is not open to the public, but keen observers might spot agricultural equipment along the fence perimeter, where King Bhumibol himself once conducted experiments in agricultural sustainability for the benefit of his people.

Opposite the palace on Thanon Sri Ayutthaya is the **Royal Turf Club** horseracing track. Races are held here every other week.

Wat Benjamabophit 7

Address: 69 Thanon Rama V
Tel: 0-2282 7413
Opening Hrs: daily 8.30am–4.30pm
Entrance Fee: charge (free with Grand Palace entrance ticket)
Transport: buses 3, 72

Further west , on the corner of Thanon Rama V, the Marble Temple was the last major temple built in central Bangkok and the best example of modern Thai religious architecture. Started by King Chulalongkorn at the turn of the 20th century, the *wat* was designed by the king's half-brother Prince Naris and Italian architect Hercules Manfredi, and completed in 1911. They incorporated Western elements to dramatic effect, most notably in the walls of Carrara marble from Italy, the cruciform shape and the unique European-crafted stained-glass windows depicting Thai mythological scenes. The *bot*'s principal Buddha image is a replica of the famous Phra Buddha Chinarat of Phitsanulok, whose base contains the ashes of Chulalongkorn.

A gallery behind the *bot* holds 53 original and copied significant Buddha images from all over Asia. Early in the morning merit-makers gather in front of the temple gates to donate food and offerings to monks, who line up here for alms. ❑

ABOVE: Ayutthayan-style Buddha image in the *abhaya mudra* (reassurance) posture at a gallery in Wat Benjamabophit.

BEST RESTAURANTS

Thai

In Love
2/1 Th Krung Kasem, Thewet pier. Tel: 0-2281 2900. Open: daily 11am–midnight. **$** 23 p269, E4
Many are in love with the river views at this pier-side diner as well as the plates of fried rice with chicken or prawns with coconut shoots. Singers with acoustic guitars entertain.

Kaloang Home Kitchen
2 Th Sri Ayutthaya, Dusit. Tel: 0-2281 9228/0-2282 7581. Open: daily 11am–10pm. **$–$$** 24 p269, C1
Located behind the National Library where Thanon Sri Ayutthaya ends amid riverbank boatyards, rustic Kaloang serves good Thai standards, particularly grilled fish and terrific seafood such as curried crab.

Kinlom Chom Saphan
11/6 Samsen Soi 3. Tel: 0-2628 8382-3. www.khinlomchomsaphan.com Open: daily 11am–2am. **$** 25 p268, C2
Sit on the open-air wooden terrace for leisurely meals of steamed shrimp in spicy sauce, curried crab and charcoal-grilled fish and views of the spectacular Rama VIII Bridge. A few Western dishes balance the menu.

Krua Apsorn
Th Samsen. Tel: 0-2241 8528. Open: Mon–Sat 11am–7.30pm. **$** 26 p269, D1
A plastic-table café owned by former royal cook Paa Daeng (Auntie Red). You won't go wrong with anything here, but the yellow curry with lotus shoots is legendary. There's no street number; find it just north of the National Library.

Wangwana Kitchen
Dusit Zoo. Tel: 0-2282 1491. Open: daily 11.30am–11.30pm. **$–$$** 27 p269, E1
This lakeside sala restaurant with walls open to the air is a good spot to watch the boating in Dusit Zoo while dining on steamed seafood coconut curry or jungle curry with sun-dried pork.

Price per person for a three-course meal without drinks.
***$** = under B300, **$$** = B300–800, **$$$** = B800–1,600, **$$$$** = over B1,600.*

TAXI
สก 3733

CHINATOWN

One of the oldest areas of the city, Bangkok's Chinatown retains narrow lanes of cluttered markets not much changed since its creation. Pungent food stalls, ornate Chinese shrines: loud, boisterous and frenzied, this is Bangkok at its visceral best

Main Attractions

SAMPENG LANE
WAT CHAKRAWAT
PAHURAT MARKET
WAT MANGKON KAMALAWAT
SOI ITSARANUPHAP
TALAD KAO
WAT TRAIMIT

Maps and Listings

MAP OF CHINATOWN, PAGE 146
SHOPPING, PAGE 148
RESTAURANTS, PAGE 151
ACCOMMODATION, PAGE 242

Bangkok's early Chinese inhabitants were brought to Thailand by King Taksin – himself half-Chinese – as labourers to work on his new capital at Thonburi across the river. They lived in what is now Rattanakosin, but were relocated further south by King Rama I when he built the Grand Palace in 1782. The migrants – who arrived, according to an old Chinese saying "with a mat and a pot" – settled on a riverside dirt track called Sampeng Lane. Chinatown was born.

In 1863, after King Mongkut built Bangkok's first paved street, Thanon Charoen Krung (New Road), Chinatown began mushrooming northwards. Later, a third artery, Thanon Yaowarat, appeared between Charoen Krung and Sampeng roads. It became Chinatown's main thoroughfare and the Thai name of the area. Plots of land here were also given to the Indian and Muslim communities.

The Chinese play an important role in Thailand's corridors of power, a position that matured during the Ayutthaya period, when merchants acquired powerful business positions and gained court influence through their daughters becoming royal concubines. In the Rattanakosin period Chinese businessmen gained concessions as tax collectors, and later used the riches they amassed to buy into rice mills, taking advantage of Thailand's greatest export. Modern examples of powerful Chinese include Thaksin Shinawatra, the ex-prime minister and formally Thailand's richest man, Chin Sophonpanich, a one-time labourer who went on to found Bangkok Bank, and Central Group, the country's largest retail chain, which started as a Chinatown magazine stall in the 1920s.

LEFT: night-time traffic in Chinatown.
RIGHT: Talad Kao market.

ABOVE: the golden-domed Sri Guru Singh Sabha temple is where Bangkok's Sikh community congregates.

Chinatown's narrow roads and lanes teem with traffic. Luckily it is relatively easy to explore on foot, which allows you to soak up the atmosphere. Away from downtown's plush mega-malls, Chinatown is a raw experience of Bangkok past and present: old shophouses, *godowns* (warehouses), temples and shrines, all swelling with activity.

Sampeng Lane ❶

The early Chinese immigrants toiled as labourers, rickshaw runners and dock workers at a time when the river was filled with wooden shops and houses floating on bamboo platforms. They ran two and three lines deep amid a clutter of trading vessels and cross river traffic. Trade with China was at the time Thailand's greatest revenue earner, and goods going both in and out of the country passed through **Sampeng Lane** (Soi Wanit 1). The little dirt lane was rich pickings for anyone with an entrepreneurial spirit, and there were plenty of those arriving by the boatload from southern China. Sampeng Lane was the trading ground for landlubbers, and though today many of the wares will be new, many haven't changed, and neither has the sense of chaos.

By 1900, Sampeng had a reputation as Sin Alley, with opium dens, gambling houses and buildings marked by *khom khiew* (green lanterns). A green-light district was like a Western red-light district, and while the lanterns have disappeared, the term *khom khiew* still signifies a brothel today.

Dodging scooters laden with crates here, you will pass dresses, bags, footwear, toys, party decorations, Thai flags, Chinese dice and scroll paintings, sparkling acrylic bracelets and stones for making your own jewellery. Most of it is available wholesale as well as retail. At the junction of Soi Mangkon (also

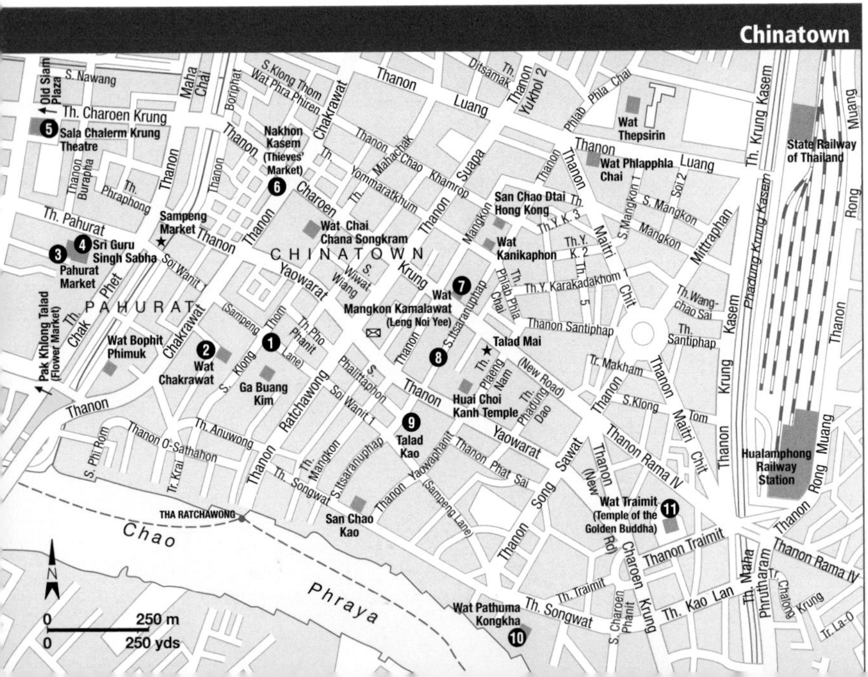

Chinatown

Old Siam Plaza
S. Nawang
Th. Charoen Krung
❺ Sala Chalerm Krung Theatre
Thanon Burapha
Th. Phraphong
Th. Pahurat
❹ Sri Guru Singh Sabha
❸ Pahurat Market
Sampeng Market
PAHURAT
Pak Khlong Talad (Flower Market)
Th. Chak Phet
Wat Bophit Phimuk
❷ Wat Chakrawat
❶ Ga Buang Kim
Sampeng Lane
Nakhon Kasem (Thieves' Market)
❻
Wat Chai Chana Songkram
CHINATOWN
Yaowarat
Mangkon Kamalawat (Leng Noi Yee)
❼ Wat
❽
Talad Mai
Huai Choi Kanh Temple
❾ Talad Kao
San Chao Kao
THA RATCHAWONG
Chao Phraya
Wat Pathuma Kongkha ❿
Th. Songwat
San Chao Dtai Hong Kong
Wat Kanikaphon
Wat Thepsirin
Wat Phlapphla Chai
Thanon Santiphap
Thanon Maitri Chit
Thanon Mittraphan
Thanon Rama IV
Wat Traimit (Temple of the Golden Buddha) ⓫
Thanon Traimit
Th. Kao Lan
Hualamphong Railway Station
State Railway of Thailand
Thanon Krung Kasem
Th. Maha Phrutharam
Thanon Charoen Krung (New Rd)
250 m
250 yds

called Sanjao Mai), on the right is the handsome facade of **Tang Toh Kang**, the oldest goldsmith in Bangkok. It originally opened around 1880, further down Soi Mangkon, and moved to these premises 90 years ago. It has a museum upstairs with gold items and examples of early crafting tools.

Wat Chakrawat ❷

Towards the western end of Sampeng Lane, cross Thanon Chakrawat and turn left to get to **Wat Chakrawat** (daily 8am–4.30pm; free). The temple comprises an odd amalgam of buildings. Dating from the Ayutthaya period, it has a small artificial hill topped by a *mondop* (square-based structure ususally topped with a spire) and a small grotto with a statue of a fat, laughing monk. According to legend, the statue was built to honour a devout but very handsome monk who was constantly pestered by women while deep in meditation. His devotion to Buddhism led him to gorge himself to obesity and the women soon lost interest. Also in the grotto is a curious black silhouette on the wall. Adorned with gold leaf, it is supposed to be Buddha's shadow.

Temples will often adopt stranded or unwanted animals, and this *wat* has a star attraction. In the mid-20th century the monks took in a crocodile nicknamed "One-Eyed Guy" that had been hunted down after terrorising bathers in the surrounding canals. He eventually died, but is preserved in a glass case above a small pond that is home to younger crocs.

Pahurat Market and Sri Guru Singh Sabha

West of Sampeng Lane is Bangkok's Little India at **Pahurat Market** ❸ (daily 9am–6pm), a two-level bazaar of tiny pathways, where Bangkok's main community from the subcontinent converged in the late 19th century. It is filled with Hindus and Sikhs selling all manner of fabrics, saris, Hindu deities and wedding regalia, together with traditional Thai dance costumes and accessories.

ABOVE: main entrance to Wat Chakrawat.

Off Thanon Pahurat and Thanon Chakraphet are cheap curry eateries such as the famous **Royal India** (tel: 0-2221 6565; daily 10am–10pm), as well as Indian tea and spice stalls, and confectionery shops.

Close to Pahurat Market, on Thanon Chakraphet, the four-storey, golden-domed Sikh temple of **Sri Guru Singh Sabha** ❹ is a focal point for the surrounding Indian–Thai community (daily 8am–5pm; free). It is said to be the second-largest Sikh temple outside India. The main shrine, draped with curtains and garlands of yellow flowers, is found on the top floor in a large open hall covered with rugs. Headscarves must be worn in the temple.

Sala Chalerm Krung Theatre ❺

North of Pahurat Market, at the corner of Thanon Charoen Krung and Thanon Tri Phet, stands **Sala Chalerm Krung Theatre** (box office: tel:

ABOVE: entrance detail from the Sala Chalerm Krung Theatre. **BELOW:** Thanon Yaowarat.

0-2222 1854). The theatre was opened as a gift to the Siamese people from King Rama VII in 1933 to mark the city's 150th anniversary. With its distinct Western Art Deco facade and Thai-style interior, it was once hailed as the biggest and grandest theatre in Asia. Sala Chalerm Krung was also the first Thai movie theatre to screen "talkies". In 1941, because of the scarcity of celluloid during World War II, the theatre was converted into a performance venue for traditional Thai *khon* (drama). In 1993, the theatre was renovated and today it hosts special film screenings, one-off concerts and traditional Thai dance-drama shows every weekend.

Old Siam Plaza

In the same vicinity is the three-floor **Old Siam Plaza** (daily 10am–9pm). Established in 1993 to replace the decaying Ming Muang Market, it is a faux-nostalgic shopping arcade with vendors dressed in traditional garb and wooden carts displaying a variety of handicrafts, including jewellery, silks, *khon* masks and traditional musical instruments. The architecture takes its cue from nearby Rattanakosin rather than Chinatown. It is a sanitised alternative to the market lanes of Chinatown and Pahurat. The ground floor has stalls with delicious traditional glazed fruits and sweets worth sampling.

Thanon Yaowarat and Nakhon Kasem ❻

Parallel to Sampeng Lane is Thanon Yaowarat, where the forest of neon signs makes it look in places much like a Hong Kong street. It is best known for its gold dealers, their shops painted gold and red for good luck, with daily prices scrawled on the windows. The gold is weighed in baht, an ancient unit separate from the Thai currency that is equal to 15 grams (about half an ounce).

At the western end, between Thanon Yaowarat and Thanon Charoen Krung, and on the corner of Thanon Chakrawat, is **Nakhon Kasem** or Thieves' Market (daily 8am–8pm). A few decades ago, this was a black market for stolen goods. It later developed into an antiques dealers' area, but today you are more

SHOPPING

Browse Chinatown's stalls and gold shops, but note most places close on Sundays.

Antiques

Chit Chai Antiques
124/33-34 Werng Nakhon Kasem. Tel: 0-2222 5576. p273, C1
Expect porcelain vases, jade, screens and forests of wooden furniture.

Jewellery

Hua Seng Heng
332-334 Th Yaowarat. Tel: 0-2225 0202. p273, D2
One of the most successful of the gold traders, selling jewellery, ornaments and gold bars.

Souvenirs

Lau Kwang Chiab Sia
41 Th Plaengnam. Tel: 0-2221 2768. p273, D2
Tiny shophouse with a small collection of traditional Chinese musical instruments.

Yin Shui Fung
58-60 Th Plaengnam. Tel: 0-2221 3498. p273, D2
This small shop sells temple decorations, and masks and costumes for use in Chinese Opera or the New Year Lion Dances.

likely to find items of a less glamorous description, such as run-of-the-mill household appliances. Nevertheless, it is still possible to find a few shops selling old grandfather clocks, musical instruments and Buddha images.

Wat Mangkon Kamalawat ❼

Address: Thanon Charoen Krung
Tel: 0-2222 3975
Opening Hrs: daily 8.30am–3.30pm
Entrance Fee: free
Transport: buses 4, 73

Near Soi Itsaranuphap is the imposing gateway of **Wat Mangkon Kamalawat**, also known as **Leng Noi Yee** (Dragon Flower Temple). The most revered temple in Chinatown, it is a constant swirl of activity and incense smoke from early morning onwards. As with the whole of this district, the temple is overrun at Chinese New Year.

The temple, built in 1871, is one of the most important centres for Mahayana Buddhism (most Thais practice Theravada Buddhism) in all of Thailand. Elements of Taoism and Confucianism are also prevalent. The dragon-crowned roof overlooks a courtyard containing several structures that house altars and images of gilded Buddhas, the Four Heavenly Kings and other Taoist deities.

Soi Itsaranuphap ❽

The most interesting lane in Chinatown is **Soi Itsaranuphap** (Soi 16), which runs south from Thanon Phlab Phla Chai and and passes a 19th-century Thai temple called **Wat Kanikaphon**, better known as Wat Mae Yai Fang, after the brothel madam who built it to atone for her sins (daily 6am–4pm; free).

Around the northern entrance to Soi Itsaranuphap are shops selling items made of folded paper that are burnt at the temple in *kong tek* ceremonies. They are offerings thought to provide comfort to deceased relatives, and include hell money, houses, Mercedes cars, mobile phones and furniture. Other shops sell red-and-gold-trimmed shrines for ancestor spirit worship in the home.

Talad Kao and Talad Mai

Soi Itsaranuphap has two of the city's best-known markets. Closer to the corner with Sampeng Lane is the two-century old **Talad Kao** ❾ (Old Market), while a little off Soi Itsaranuphap (closer to Thanon Charoen Krung) is the newer **Talad Mai** (New Market), which has been plying its wares for merely a century. The old market wraps up by late morning, while the newer one keeps trading until sundown. These fresh markets have a reputation for high-quality meat, fish and vegetables, and overflow during Chinese New Year. The raw and dried fish, pungent spices and boiling stoves here can overwhelm the senses.

Wat Pathuma Kongkha

Moving east along Sampeng Lane there are shops with Muslim names and merchants trading gems, and

ABOVE: bundles of "hell money" found at shops along Soi Itsaranuphap are legal tender only in the afterlife. **BELOW:** the main altar inside Wat Mangkon Kamalawat.

The Poh Teck Tung Foundation just off Thanon Phlab Phla Chai is a Sino-Thai charity whose workers respond to road accidents, picking up dead bodies and arranging funeral rites if no one claims them.

right at the end is **Wat Pathuma Kongkha** ⑩, also called **Wat Sampeng** (daily 8am–5pm; free). One of Bangkok's oldest temples, it dates to the Ayutthayan period, and was where criminals of noble birth were executed for crimes against the state.

Wat Traimit ⑪

Address: 661 Thanon Charoen Krung
Tel: 0-2225 9775
Opening Hrs: daily 8am–5pm
Entrance Fee: charge
Transport: (MRT) Hualamphong

Just east of where Thanon Yaowarat meets Thanon Charoen Krung, close to the Chinatown Gate at Odeon Circle, is **Wat Traimit**. The *wat* itself would be unremarkable except that it is the site of the world's largest solid gold Buddha and is consequently known also as The Temple of the **Golden Buddha**. On the left of the temple is a huge, 600-million-baht marble *mondop*, newly built to hold the 5.5-ton, 3-metre (10ft) Sukhothai-era statue. Believed to date from the reign of King Ramkhamhaeng the Great (*c.*1279–98), the Golden Buddha was probably first moved from Sukhothai to Ayutthaya, but by the time it reached Bangkok it had been covered in stucco, presumably to disguise its worth from Burmese invaders. Its true nature was only revealed in 1955, when an accident while moving it caused the surface to crack off.

The *mondop* is also the location of the **Yaowarat Chinatown Heritage Centre** (daily 8am–4.30pm; charge). The museum layout is preceded by a 3-D hologram show of a grandfather and his grandson discussing the past, which is only interesting for the comically "proper" English translation. The museum itself tells the story of Chinatown's beginnings through old photos, prints of period paintings and tableaux of various life situations, such as the interior of a junk and shops from old Sampeng Lane. The exhibits are well annotated, and it makes an interesting sideshow to the Golden Buddha.

RIGHT: the solid gold Buddha image at Wat Traimit was found purely by accident. **BELOW:** morning scene at Talad Kao.

Hualamphong Station

East of Wat Traimit is the city's main railway terminus, **Hualamphong Railway Station**, a fine example of Thai Art Deco style. King Chulalongkorn (Rama V) initiated Thailand's first rail line from here in 1891, carrying passengers the relatively short distance to Paknam. The Italian-designed structure was erected sometime between 1910 and 1916. A renovation in the late 1990s made the station far more comfortable. The MRT metro line terminates here. ❑

BEST RESTAURANTS

Chinese

Hong Kong Noodle

136/4 Trok Itsaranuphap. Tel: 02-623 1992. Open: daily 6am–6pm. **$**
28 p272, D1
You'll usually have to wait for a seat at this jammed shophouse where cooks-in-constant-motion ladle duck and pork on noodles. It's as chaotic as the market that surrounds it. For dessert, grab a custard tart at Hong Kong Dim Sum (no relation) next door.

Hua Seng Hong Yaowaraj

438 Th Charoen Krung Soi 14. Tel: 0-2627 5030. Open: daily 9am–9pm. **$–$$**
29 p272, D1
This is a former shophouse, now glassed-in, with marble-top tables and air-conconditioning. It's still a raucous Chinese lunch venue, though, selling all-day *dim sum* from an outside counter and all manner of *congee*, hot and sour soup and braised goose dishes inside.

Shangrila Yaowarat

306 Th Yaowarat. Tel: 0-2224 5933. Open: daily 10am–10pm. **$$**
30 p273, D1
Busy Cantonese place that does *dim sum* lunches, then brings out the tablecloths and napkins for dinner. Menu includes drunken chicken with jellyfish, smoked pigeon and seafood. Or choose from the displays of roasted duck and freshly baked pastries.

Tang Jai Yoo

85–9 Th Yaowapanit. Tel: 0-2224 2167. Open: daily 11am–2pm, 5–9pm. **$$**
31 p273, D2
Chinese seafood specialists in a couple of café-style rooms. They do a good line in baked oysters and steamed or baked crab with curry sauce or black pepper, whole fish and abalone. The suckling pig is also a big seller.

Thai Heng

50 metres/yds into Yaowarat Soi 8, opposite Wat Bamphen Chin Phrot. Tel: 0-2222 6791. Open: daily 10am–6pm. **$**
32 p273, D1
An 80-year-old café that some say makes the best Hainan chicken rice in Chinatown. It's simply chicken on rice soaked in chicken fat, served with spicy *nam jim* dip, but delicious. Also famed for Hainan sukiyaki: meat and veg in a peppery broth.

Yim Yim

89 Th Padsai. Tel: 0-2224 2203. Open: daily 11am–2pm, 5–10pm. **$$**
33 p273, D2
Old-style Chinese family restaurant with six tables nestled amid the household clutter. This is a Chinatown institution famed particularly for crab claws baked in a clay pot and Chinese sashimi, which comes with vegetables and sweet sesame sauce.

Indian

Punjab Sweets and Restaurant

436/5 Th Chak Phet. Tel: 0-2623 7606. Open: daily 8am–9pm. **$** 34 p273, C1
Pahurat's alleyways are crowded with tailors and tiny Indian cafés, of which this is one of the best. Its meat- and dairy-free food includes a choice of curries and *dosa* (rice-flour pancakes), plus Punjabi sweets wrapped in edible silver foil.

Thai

Laem Thong

894 Th Charoen Krung Soi 12. Tel: 0-2224 3591. Open: daily 8am–4pm. **$**
35 p273, D1
Non-Chinese Thai dishes are not that common in this part of town, so head here if you feel like red curry with pork or spicy fried chicken with ginger. The chairs are plastic and the walls are tiled, but its air-conditioning promises comfortable dining.

Thai Food Stalls

Soi Texas

Mouth of Th Padung Dao. Open: daily 6pm–2am.
36 p273, D2
One of Bangkok's most famous foodstalls sells great curried crab, plus seafood charcoal grilled or fried with garlic and chilli. Opposite, T & K is just as good. Bangkokians refer to them collectively as "Soi Texas seafood".

Prices per person for a three-course meal without drinks:
$ = under B300
$$ = B300–800
$$$ = B800–1,600
$$$$ = over B1,600

RIGHT: enjoying hot and sour soup in Chinatown.

PATHUMWAN AND PRATUNAM

Fashionable malls make this a great place to shop, but there's plenty to do if your bags are full, including traditional culture at Jim Thompson's House, a fun oceanarium, a puppet theatre and Bangkok's biggest art space

Main Attractions

JIM THOMPSON'S HOUSE MUSEUM
BANGKOK ART AND CULTURE CENTRE
SIAM SQUARE
MBK
SIAM PARAGON
ERAWAN SHRINE
SNAKE FARM
LUMPHINI PARK
SUAN LUM NIGHT BAZAAR
SUAN PAKKAD PALACE

Maps and Listings

MAP OF PATHUMWAN AND PRATUNAM, PAGE 154
SHOPPING, PAGE 160
RESTAURANTS AND BARS, PAGES 162–3
ACCOMMODATION, PAGES 242–3

The commercial heart of downtown Bangkok, **Pathumwan** is a string of shopping malls, all connected by the Skytrain. It's mainly a consumer's paradise, yet there are still plenty of sights more reminiscent of an older and more traditional Bangkok. The man-made canal **Khlong Saen Saep**, cleaved in the early 19th century, enabled the capital to spread east to **Pratunam** and beyond.

PATHUMWAN

Jim Thompson's House Museum ❶

Address: 6 Soi Kasem San 2, Thanon Rama I, www.jimthompsonhouse.com
Tel: 0-2216 7368
Opening Hrs: daily 9am–5pm
Entrance Fee: charge (includes compulsory tour of the museum)
Transport: (BTS) National Stadium

Just a short walk from the National Stadium Skytrain station is one of the finest traditional houses in the city, the **Jim Thompson's House Museum**. Jim Thompson *(see photo feature on pages 164–5)* was the American silk entrepreneur responsible for the revival of Thai silk. An architect by training, Thompson arrived in Thailand at the end of World War II, serving as a military officer. After the war he returned to Bangkok, where he became interested in the almost redundant craft of silk weaving and design.

Thompson mysteriously disappeared in the jungles of Malaysia's Cameron Highlands in 1967 but his well-preserved house still stands today near the banks of Khlong Saen Saep. Thompson was an enthusiastic collector of Asian arts and antiquities,

LEFT: Jim Thompson's House, viewed from the lush gardens. **RIGHT:** bustling shoppers at Mahboonkrong shopping centre.

ABOVE: window displays at Siam Square mainly target the young.

many of which adorn his traditional house-turned-museum. The surrounding garden is a luxuriant mini tropical jungle and an attraction in itself.

The museum comprises six teak structures, which were transported from Ayutthaya and elsewhere to the silk weaving enclave of Ban Khrua, just across Khlong Saen Saep, before being reassembled at its current spot in 1959. From the windows of the house, it's easy to imagine how scenic the view would have been some 40 years ago, looking across the lush gardens, or "jungle" as Thompson called it, to the canal and its daily life.

Next to the old house is a wooden annexe, housing a pond-side café with an elegant upstairs bar and restaurant, while opposite is the **Jim Thompson Art Centre**, a contemporary gallery that holds regular exhibitions of local and international art and crafts. Before leaving, be sure to stop by and pick up some silk accessories from the museum gift shop.

Pathumwan and Pratunam

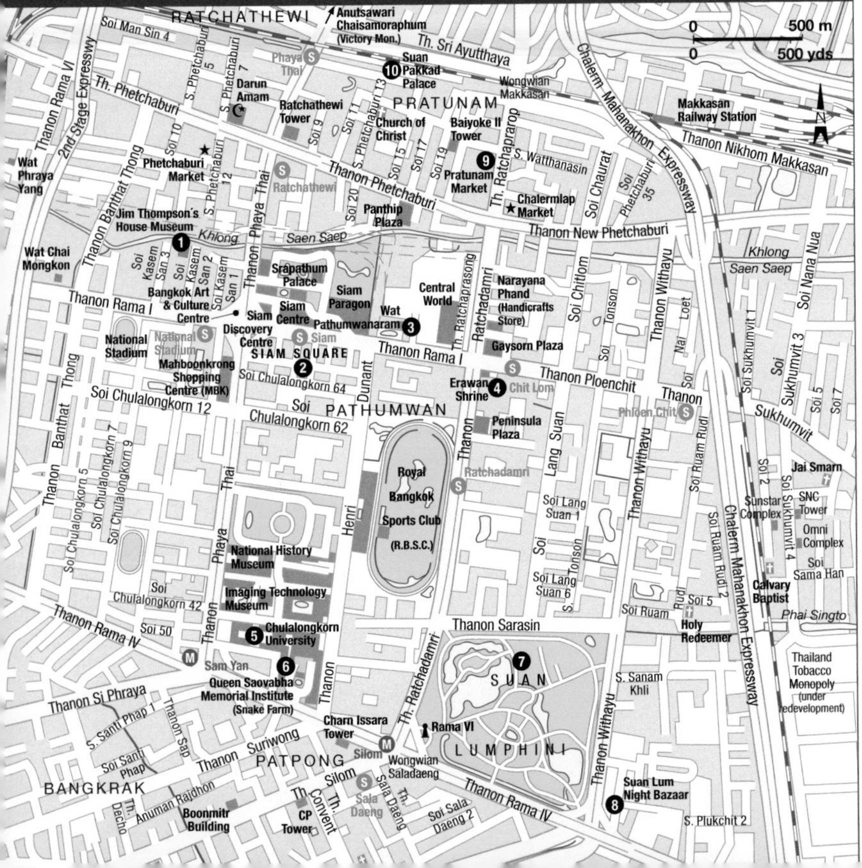

RATCHATHEWI
Anutsawari Chaisamoraphum (Victory Mon.)
Th. Sri Ayutthaya
0 500 m
0 500 yds
Soi Man Sin 4
Phaya Thai
Suan Pakkad Palace
Wongwian Makkasan
Thanon Rama VI
2nd Stage Expressway
Th. Phetchaburi
S. Phetchaburi 5
S. Phetchaburi 7
Darun Amam
Ratchathewi Tower
PRATUNAM
Church of Christ
Baiyoke II Tower
Th. Ratchaprarop
Chalerm Mahanakhon Expressway
Makkasan Railway Station
Thanon Nikhom Makkasan
Wat Phraya Yang
Thanon Banthat Thong
Soi 10
Phetchaburi Market
S. Phetchaburi 12
Ratchathewi
Soi 9
Soi 11
S. Phetchaburi 13
Soi 15
Soi 17
Soi 19
Pratunam Market
S. Watthanasin
Soi Chaurat
Soi Phetchaburi 35
Thanon Phetchaburi
Soi 20
Panthip Plaza
Chalermlap Market
Jim Thompson's House Museum
Khlong Saen Saep
Thanon New Phetchaburi
Wat Chai Mongkon
Soi Kasem San 3
Soi Kasem San 2
Soi Kasem San 1
Thanon Phaya Thai
Srapathum Palace
Siam Paragon
Central World
Th. Ratchaprasong
Ratchadamri
Narayana Phand (Handicrafts Store)
Soi Chitlom
Soi Tonson
Thanon Withayu
Nai Loet
Khlong Saen Saep
Soi Nana Nua
Thanon Rama I
Bangkok Art & Culture Centre
Siam Discovery Centre
Siam Centre
Wat Pathumwanaram
National Stadium
Siam
SIAM SQUARE
Thanon Rama I
Gaysorn Plaza
Soi Sukhumvit 1
Soi Sukhumvit 3
Mahboonkrong Shopping Centre (MBK)
Soi Chulalongkorn 64
Dunant
Erawan Shrine
Chit Lom
Thanon Ploenchit
Thanon Sukhumvit
Soi 5
Soi 7
Soi Chulalongkorn 12
Soi Chulalongkorn 62
PATHUMWAN
Phloen Chit
Peninsula Plaza
Thanon Banthat Thong
Soi Chulalongkorn 7
Soi Chulalongkorn 9
Soi Chulalongkorn 5
Thai
Royal Bangkok Sports Club (R.B.S.C.)
Ratchadamri
Lang Suan
Soi Ruam Rudi
Soi 2
Jai Smarn
Sunstar Complex
Soi Sukhumvit 4
SNC Tower
Omni Complex
Soi Lang Suan 1
Soi Ruam Rudi 2
Henri
Phaya
National History Museum
Soi Tonson
Soi Lang Suan 6
Soi Sama Han
Soi Chulalongkorn 42
Imaging Technology Museum
Calvary Baptist
Rudi Soi 5
Soi Ruam
Phai Singto
Thanon Rama IV
Soi 50
Chulalongkorn University
Thanon Sarasin
Holy Redeemer
Sam Yan
SUAN
Thailand Tobacco Monopoly (under redevelopment)
Queen Saovabha Memorial Institute (Snake Farm)
S. Sanam Khli
Thanon Si Phraya
S. Santi Phap 1
Thanon Sap
Thanon
Th. Ratchadamri
Charn Issara Tower
Rama VI
Soi Santi Phap
Thanon Suriwong
PATPONG
Silom
Wongwian Saladaeng
LUMPHINI
Thanon Withayu
BANGKRAK
Anuman Rajdhon
Th. Silom
Th. Convent
Sala Daeng
Th. Sala Daeng
Soi Sala Daeng 2
Thanon Rama IV
Suan Lum Night Bazaar
Th. Decho
Boonmitr Building
CP Tower
S. Plukchit 2

Bangkok Art and Culture Centre

Leaving Soi Kasem San 2 and turning left on Thanon Rama I brings you to the **Bangkok Art and Culture Centre** (tel: 0-2214 6630-8; www.bacc.or.th; Tue–Sun 10am–9pm; free). This 11-storey space has staged some of Bangkok's best art and multimedia shows, featuring both local and international artists, since it opened in late 2008. The retail outlets on its lower floors have imaginatively been issued to small independent galleries or organisations such as the Thai Film Foundation and Bangkok Opera. Art markets feature regularly on the concourse, and performances in a small auditorium on the ground floor.

Siam Square ❷

Diagonally across the main junction of Thanons Rama I and Phaya Thai is a grid of *sois* called **Siam Square**. The land is owned by Thailand's most prestigious educational institution, Chulalongkorn University, located on the southern edge of the square. Hence, it's packed with students and has a strong youth culture, including its own radio station with blaring street speakers that drown out the noise of the traffic. For many years it's been a hotbed of tyro fashion designers who pop out imaginative threads in boutique shops with eccentric names like It's Happened to Be a Closet. Continual rent hikes by the university, however, may signal the gradual demise of this creative zone.

ABOVE: monk at the main altar of Wat Pathumwanaram.

Silk Threads

Jim Thompson constructed his house opposite the canal-side Muslim village of Ban Khrua, where the population of specialist weavers were the descendents of 19th-century Cambodian immigrants. There are just two workshops still active, which you can visit by turning left from the Jim Thompson House, then left again along the canal. After 150 metres/yds, take the bridge over the water and walk on for 50 metres/yds to a small lane on the right. Twenty metres/yds along here, a handful of women at looms keep alive a traditional craft that once captivated the world. In the second shop, you may be lucky to catch owner Niphon Manuthas, who as a young boy knew Jim Thompson himself.

Malls along Thanon Rama I

Cross the footbridge over Thanon Phaya Thai from Siam Square and into **Mahboonkrong (MBK)** shopping centre. This huge, old-school Thai mall retains a market place ambience, with stalls scattered around the floor space selling goods including cosmetics, cameras, phones, clothes and jewellery. Art lovers head for the ground floor, where teams of painters copy masters from Titian to Klimt.

Leave MBK on the overhead skywalk to the interconnecting malls of **Siam Discovery Centre** and **Siam Centre** on Thanon Rama I.

SHOP

The main shopping areas in downtown Bangkok are linked by the Skywalk – a covered elevated walkway beneath the Skytrain tracks connecting Chidlom, Siam and National Stadium Skytrain stations along Thanon Rama I. This means you can walk from one mall to another under shade and without having to cross the streets.

The former, strong on home accessories, was slated for a revamp in 2010, scheduled to include the opening of Bangkok's own Madame Tussaud's waxworks museum at year's end. Siam Centre attracts teens, with local designer, sports and surf clothing.

Siam Paragon

Across the concourse east of Siam Centre is the swanky **Siam Paragon**, full of chi-chi designer labels from Apple to Ferrari, plus restaurants and an impressive aquarium called **Siam Ocean World** (tel: 0-2687 2000; www.siamoceanworld.com; daily 9am–10pm; charge), filled with over 30,000 marine creatures. Visitors here can ride in a glass-bottomed boat and dive with the sharks.

Wat Pathumwanaram ❸

Hidden to the rear of Siam Centre is **Srapathum Palace**, which is the home of Princess Sirindhorn, and closed to the public. The grounds include **Wat Pathumwanaram** (daily 8.30am–6pm; free), where the ashes of the king's parents are laid.

ABOVE: wooden elephants – which represent Brahma's elephant mount, Erawan – sold outside the Erawan Shrine (**BELOW**). In 2006, the shrine was destroyed by a mentally disturbed man, but was restored less than three months later. **RIGHT:** Gaysorn Plaza lobby.

Central World

Next door is **Central World**, which at 550,000 sq metres (5.9 million sq ft) is Bangkok's largest mall. It includes the department store **Isetan**, along with a staggering array of shops, restaurants and two enormous cineplexes, **Major Cineplex** and **SF World Cinema**. The adjoining **Centara Grand Hotel** has an open air restaurant, Red Sky, on the roof. Another department store here, **Zen**, was burnt to the ground during the 2010 Red Shirt protests.

Erawan Shrine ❹

Address: 494 Thanon Ratchadamri
Opening Hrs: daily 9am–5pm
Entrance Fee: free
Transport: (BTS) Chit Lom

After the chaotic junction with Thanon Ratchadamri, Thanon Rama I changes its name to Thanon Ploenchit. At the southeast corner of this junction an aromatic haze of incense hits you before you actually see the **Erawan Shrine**. This, the busiest of all Bangkok shrines, is dedicated to the four-headed Hindu god of creation, Brahma. It was erected in 1956 after an astrologer advised it would ward off bad luck plaguing construction of the Erawan hotel, after which it is named. Because the misfortune subsequently ceased, people believe the shrine has great powers. The hotel has since been replaced by the Grand Hyatt Erawan. Supplicants line up to buy garlands, joss sticks and other gifts as offerings in return for good fortune. Those whose wishes are granted might give thanks by paying the on-site dance troupe to perform.

The site is so revered that when a mentally disturbed man smashed the shrine with a hammer in 2006, he was beaten to death by an angry mob. Photographs of the shrine were displayed so that people could continue to worship until a new one was erected two months later. One thousand people attended the unveiling. Underlining the influence of supernatural belief in Thailand, an opposition leader accused supporters of then Prime Minister Thaksin Shinawatra of being responsible for the destruction, saying they wanted to maintain power over the country through black magic.

Thanon Ploenchit malls

Behind the Erawan Shrine, along Thanon Ploenchit, the boutique mall **Erawan Bangkok** is connected to the Grand Hyatt Erawan hotel. and offers a wellness and beauty centre alongside its fashion outlets. Across the street, **Gaysorn Plaza** is an expensive designer mall with tasteful arts and home decor stores and local designers like Stretsis and Fly Now.

North along Thanon Ratchadamri, **Narayana Phand** is a three-floor emporium of Thai arts and crafts, from classical musical instruments and ornate ceremonial headgear to paintings and silk purses.

Chulalongkorn University 5

South of Siam Square along both sides of Thanon Phaya Thai are the verdant grounds of **Chulalongkorn University**, the country's oldest and most prestigious institution of higher learning. Named in honour of King Chulalongkorn (Rama V), it combines Thai and Western architectural styles, and is located on two blocks of the city's most coveted real

BELOW AND ABOVE: Siam Square.

SHOP

There has been talk of closing down Suan Lum Night Bazaar for some time now (the land on which it stands is just too valuable for housing a casual market). No concrete plans have been announced, so enjoy it while you can. Prices are a little higher than the Chatuchak Weekend Market, but the bonus is that it's open every day and the atmosphere is a little less frenetic.

estate. The university holds regular campus events.

The campus grounds on the same side as MBK host two contemporary galleries. The **Jamjuree Gallery** (tel: 0-2218 3709; Mon–Fri 10–7pm, Sat 12–6pm; free) displays student shows as well as more experimental exhibits by rising artists, whereas the **Art Centre** (tel: 0-2218 2964; Mon–Fri 8am–7pm, Sat 9am–4pm; free), at the Centre of Academic Resources, holds exhibitions by Thailand's internationally recognised artists. The university's **Museum of Imaging Technology** by the lakeside may be of interest to photo buffs; it documents the development of photography in Thailand (tel: 0-2218 5581; Mon–Fri 9am–3pm; charge).

Royal Bangkok Sports Club

East of Chulalongkorn University along Thanon Henri Dunant is the members-only **Royal Bangkok Sports Club** (tel: 0-2255 1420 for race info). Dating from the early 1900s, the horse-racing club quickly became the favourite recreational spot for the city's upper class. The grounds also served as Bangkok's only airfield before Bangkok International Airport was eventually built. Non-members are only allowed through the gates on alternate Sundays for the races, which attract large crowds of feverish gamblers.

RIGHT: a young volunteer at the Snake Farm gingerly handles a python as he poses for a photograph. **BELOW:** bookstore in Siam Paragon.

Snake Farm ❻

Address: 1871 Thanon Rama IV
Tel: 02-252 0161-4
Opening Hrs: Mon–Fri 8.30am–4.30pm, Sat–Sun 8.30am–noon
Entrance Fee: charge
Transport: (MRT) Silom or Sam Yan

Travellers to the tropics often worry about encounters with dangerous beasts, and a visit to the **Queen Saovabha Memorial Institute**, popularly called the **Snake Farm**, will either enforce or allay such fears. Located south of Chulalongkorn University, it was founded in 1923 as the Pasteur Institute. Now operated by the Thai Red Cross, the institute's principal work lies in the research and treatment of snakebites and the extraction of antivenins. Venom-milking sessions (Mon–Fri 11am and 2.30pm, Sat–Sun 11am; slide show 30 mins before) are the best times to visit, when various snakes are pulled from the pit and generally goaded for a squealing audience.

Of Thailand's six species of venomous snake, the King Cobra is the largest and most common. A single yield of venom from the King Cobra is deadly enough to send some 50,000 mice to an early grave. Fortunately the King Cobra's basic diet is other snakes. Willing spectators can drape a snake around their necks for a one-of-a-kind photo memento.

Lumphini Park ❼

Green spots are few and far between in Bangkok, but in the heart of Downtown at the intersection of Thanon Rama IV and Thanon Ratchadamri is **Lumphini Park**, Bangkok's biggest outdoor retreat (daily 4.30am–9pm; free). Named after Buddha's birthplace in Nepal, the park was given to the public in 1925 by King Vajiravudh (Rama VI), whose memorial statue stands in front of the main gates.

It has lakes (with pedal boats for hire) and a Chinese-style clock tower. At sunrise or sunset you see *tai chi* practitioners, joggers, aerobic sessions, bodybuilders lifting weights at the open-air gym and youngsters kicking rattan balls in the sport of *takraw*.

Suan Lum Night Bazaar ❽

Across from Lumphini Park's gates at Thanon Withayu (Wireless Road), the **Suan Lum Night Bazaar** (daily 3pm–midnight) is a sanitised and cooler alternative to Chatuchak Weekend Market *(see page 184)*. Geared for tourists, but also full of locals, the open-air bazaar offers souvenirs, clothing, handicrafts, antiques, jewellery and home decor. There is also a large beer garden with live music and plenty of local and international food options, traditional massage and a German pub. Also found at Suan Lum Night Bazaar is the **Joe Louis Theatre** (tel: 0-2252 9683; www.joelouis-theater.com; nightly at 7.30pm; charge). Sakorn Yangkeawsot, who died in 2007, was better known as Joe Louis, and was responsible for reviving the fading art of *hun lakhon lek*, a unique form of traditional Thai puppetry *(see pages 58 and 250)*. The company won the Best Performance Award at the World Festival of Puppet Arts in 2008. A puppet gallery in the foyer is free to view.

PRATUNAM

North of Pathumwan, as you turn the corner left into Thanon Petchaburi, there are lots of cheap women's fashion items in the new, five-storey **Platinum Mall**, and in the narrow lanes on the other side of Phetchaburi is **Pratunam Market** ❾ (daily 9am–midnight). This bustling warren of stalls is more a lure for residents than tourists, but it has cheap piles of clothing, fabrics and shoes, and the abundance of African export traders makes for some interesting cafés.

The area is shadowed by Thailand's tallest building, **Baiyoke II**

ABOVE AND BELOW: Lumphini Park.

SHOPPING

Pathumwan is the location of Bangkok's big malls selling everything from cheap T-shirts to Jimmy Choo shoes.

Department Stores

Central Chidlom
1027 Th Ploenchit. Tel: 0-2655 7777. p275, C/D1
The best of the chain and one of Bangkok's top department stores. Has a great food court on the top floor.

Books

Kinokuniya
4th Fl, Siam Paragon, 991/1 Th Rama I. Tel: 0-2610 9500. p274, B1
This largest Bangkok outlet of a Japanese chain store has a comprehensive selection of mainly English books.

Electrical Goods

Panthip Plaza
604/3 Th Phetchaburi. Tel: 0-2251 9724. p270, C1
With 150 shops on five floors, this is Thailand's best-known marketplace for computers, software and cameras and anything to do with IT. They also do repairs.

Fashion

Fly Now
2nd Fl, Gaysorn Plaza, Th Ploenchit. Tel: 0-2656 1359, www.flynowbangkok.com p275, C1
Somchai Songwatana looms large in Thai fashion. Get accessories here like bags, wallet, belts and shoes, or have a classic modern dress made to order.

Jaspal
2nd Fl, Siam Centre, Th Rama I. Tel: 0-2251 5918, www.jaspal.com p274, B1
Stylish local fashion chain with branches in most shopping malls. Jaspal's designs are influenced by British and European styles, and his is a regular haunt of expat Westerners, because it has sizes that go up to XL.

Senada Theory
2nd Fl, Gaysorn Plaza, Th Ploenchit. Tel: 0-2656 1350. p275, C1
The flagship store of designer Chanita Preechawitayakul, whose smart "vintage romantic" designs are made of Thai silks and Chinese cottons. Flowing dresses share floor space here with savvy women's suits.

Home

Propaganda
4th Fl, Siam Discovery Centre Th Rama I. Tel: 0-2658 0430, www.propagandaonline.com p275, B1
Quirkily designed home decor items (think a Thai version of Alessi), including funky tableware and molar-shaped toothbrush holders.

Malls

Central World
Th Ratchadamri. Tel: 0-2255 9400, www.centralworld.co.th p274, C1
Bangkok's largest mall includes Isetan department store, hundreds of brand names, a cineplex, beauty services, yoga studios and restaurants. You could spend all day here.

Mahboonkrong (MBK)
444 Th Phaya Thai. Tel: 0-2217 9119. p274, B1
Thai-style market feel with shops and stalls scattered everywhere. Many bargains, including leather luggage, jewellery, software, phones and electronics.

Platinum Mall
222 Th Petchaburi. Tel: 0-2121 8000. www.platinumfashionmall.com p270, C4
Like an indoor Chatuchak with emphasis on women's fashion, this is five floors of bargain-basement prices available retail or wholesale. *Farang* women like it for larger-sized clothes.

Siam Discovery Centre
989 Th Rama I. Tel: 0-2658 1000. p274, B1
Packed with imported brands and big on interiors, you'll also find a decent musical instrument shop here and a good branch of Asia Books.

Siam Paragon
991/1 Th Rama I. Tel: 0-2610 9000, www.siamparagon.co.th p274, B1
An enormous mall, with top local and international clothing labels, an Apple shop, an excellent gourmet market and an aquarium, Siam Ocean World *(see page 156)*.

Men's Clothing

Embassy Fashion House
57/6-7 Th Withayu. Tel: 0-2251 2620. p275, D2
This place stands out for its relaxed service and wide range of local and imported fabrics. Staff from nearby embassies patronise it for made-to-measure, off-the-peg and casual wear.

Textiles

Mae Fah Luang Foundation
4th Fl, Siam Discovery Centre, Th Rama I. Tel: 0-2658 0424, www.doitung.org p274, B1
A royal initiative to promote the livelihood of Thai villagers through traditional means, MFL has traditional weaves infused with a funky modernity. Sells handwoven silks and cottons in lengths or ready made into cushion covers and clothes.

Tower, whose 84th-floor observation deck (daily 10am–10pm; charge) offers eye-popping views of the city and beyond.

If you're hungering for a byte, 200 metres/yds west on the other side of Thanon Petchaburi is **Panthip Plaza**, Bangkok's most famous mall devoted to IT. Frequented by more than just tech-heads, the competitively priced stores stretch over six floors, selling all manner of electronic devices, hard and software and entertainment discs (both genuine and counterfeit).

Suan Pakkad Palace ⑩

Address: Thanon Sri Ayutthaya; www.suanpakkad.com
Tel: 0-2245 4934
Opening Hrs: daily 9am–4pm
Entrance Fee: charge, includes guided tour
Transport: (BTS) Phaya Thai

Most tourists make a beeline for Jim Thompson's House, missing out on the equally delightful **Suan Pakkad Palace**. Located a short walk along Thanon Sri Ayutthaya from Phaya Thai Skytrain station, the quirkily named Suan Pakkad, or "Cabbage Patch", refers to its previous use as farmland before the palace was constructed in 1952. The former residence of the late Prince and Princess Chumbhot, who were prolific art collectors and gardeners, Suan Pakkad comprises five teak houses sitting amid a lush garden and lotus pond.

Converted into a museum, the wooden houses display an eclectic collection of antiques and artefacts, including Buddha images, Khmer statues, paintings, porcelain, musical instruments and ancient pottery from Ban Chiang. At the rear of the garden stands the mid 17th-century **Lacquer Pavilion**, which Prince Chumbhot discovered in a temple near Ayutthaya and carefully restored as a birthday present for his wife. The pavilion's black and gold leaf panels, considered masterpieces, depict scenes from the life of the Buddha, the *Ramakien* and the lifestyle of the period.

On the same grounds is the **Khon Museum**, a small but interesting exposé on the classic Thai dramatic art form of *khon*. ❑

ABOVE: Baiyoke II Tower. **BELOW:** Suan Pakkad Palace.

BEST RESTAURANTS AND BARS

Restaurants

International

Hyde & Seek
65/1 Athenée Residence, Soi Ruamrudee; Tel: 0-2168 5152; www.hydeandseek.com; Open: daily 11am–1am. **$$$** 37 p275, D1/2
A stylish gastro-bar with custom cocktails and European meals with an upmarket tweak. Try baby back ribs glazed with chocolate and chilli, or seabass with melted cabbage and shellfish emulsion. Eat inside or enjoy the garden terrace.

Red Sky
Centara Grand Hotel, 999/99 Th Rama I. Tel: 0-2100 6101. Open: daily L and D. **$$$$** 38 p274, C1
Alfresco rooftop restaurant with great views of Bangkok. Serves huge steaks of dry-aged New York strip loin, roast Boston lobster, Bresse pigeon stuffed with dried fruit and other expensive fare.

Tables
Grand Hyatt Erawan Hotel, 494 Th Ratchadamri. Tel: 0-2254 1234; www.bangkok.grand.hyatt.com Open: daily L and D. **$$$$** 39 p275, C1
Oxidised mirrors and waiters in white aprons complement the smart Parisian interior in this Tony Chi-designed restaurant. Billed as classic European, it has predominantly French stalwarts like lobster bisque and steak tartare.

Italian

Biscotti
Four Seasons Hotel, 155 Th Ratchadamri. Tel: 0-2255 5443. Open: daily L and D. **$$$** 40 p275, C2
A power-dining mecca of terracotta, marble and wood in another stylish Tony Chi-designed outlet. The large and busy open kitchen sets the tone for excellent Italian cuisine, while the open space is ideal for being seen, whether for business or society dinner.

Calderazzo
59 Soi Lang Suan. Tel: 0-2252 8108/9. www.calderazzobangkok.com Open: daily L and D. **$$–$$$** 41 p275, C2
Clever lighting and lots of wood, stone, metal and glass create a warm and exceptionally stylish atmosphere for good homey southern Italian food such as grilled vegetables in hazelnut pesto, hand-rolled "rag" pasta (torn rather than cut) with goat cheese sauce or lamb loin in red wine.

Gianni's
51/5 Soi Tonson. Tel: 0-2252 1619. Open: 6–11.30pm. www.giannibkk.com Open: daily L and D. **$$–$$$** 42 p275, D1
Larger-than-life Gianni Favro was perhaps Bangkok's first non-Thai celebrity chef. His restaurant in Soi Tonson serves all the classics – *vitello tonata*, *osso bucco*, tiramisu – in a large room with windows all along the street-side wall, and sunny murals along another.

Grossi
InterContinental Bangkok, 973 Th Ploenchit. Tel: 0-2656 0444. www.grossitrattoriabangkok.grossi.com.au Open: daily 9am–midnight. **$$$** 43 p275, C1
Trattoria franchise of star Aussie chef Guy Grossi with an elegant deli ambience. There's a floor of large black-and-white checks, marble counter displays of wines, bread and cold cuts. Has unusual items like pressed beef cooked with chocolate and orange zest.

Japanese

Shin Daikoku
Fl 2, InterContinental Hotel, Th Ploenchit. Tel: 0-2656 0096/7. Open: daily L and D. **$$–$$$** 44 p275, C1
Dine on high-quality *sushi* and *sashimi*, *matsuzaka* beef or *ishikarinabe* salmon and *enoki* mushrooms in *miso* soup. Modern bamboo cabinets divide the teppanyaki room from the restaurant proper. There's a second outlet on Sukhumvit Soi 19.

LEFT: Red Sky's stunning roof terrace.

Prices per person for a three-course meal without drinks:
$ = under B300
$$ = B300–800
$$$ = B800–1,600
$$$$ = over B1,600

Mexican

La Monita Taqueria
888/26 Mahatun Plaza, Th Ploenchit. Tel: 02-650-9581. Open: daily 11.30am–10pm. **$–$$** 45 p275, D1
A five-table Mexican diner with cheap decor, good food and a friendly atmosphere. It serves all the usual burritos, nachos, wings and Mexi or Cali tacos to wash down with mojitos and beer. Good smoky guacamole and free corkage.

Spanish

Rioja
1025 Th Ploenchit. Tel: 0-2251 5761-2. www.riojath.com Open: Mon–Fri L and D, Sat–Sun 11am–11pm. **$$** 46 p275, C1
This Spanish favourite offers options such as Iberico ham, along with dishes like shrimp carpaccio on sour cream with salmon roe, and Rioja-style oxtail stew. Of two dining rooms, the cellar-like *bodega*, with its stone floor and timber beams, is more appealing.

Thai

Coca
416/3–8 Th Henri Dunant, cnr Siam Square Soi 7. Tel: 0-2251 6337. www.coca.com Open: daily 11am–11pm. **$** 47 p274, B1
One of a chain offering communal dining from a pot of hot broth in the centre of the table for cooking morsels of fish, meat and vegetables, fondue-style. Served with bowls of sweet and spicy dips on the side.

Curries and More
63/3 Soi Ruam Rudi. Tel: 0-2253 5408. www.curriesandmore.com Open: daily L and D. **$$** 48 p275, D2
A branch of the famous Baan Khanitha (also at 69 Th Sathorn Tai and 36/1 Sukhumvit Soi 23), serving toned-down but tasty Thai food. The charming townhouse has sculptures, paintings and ceramics. International dishes include pasta, pies, crêpes and excellent apple crumble.

Gai Tort Soi Polo
137/1–2 Soi Polo, Th Witthayu. Tel: 0-2252 2252. Open: daily 7am–7pm. **$** 49 p275, D3
One of Bangkok's most famous fried chicken shops. The delicious *gai* is marinated in soy sauce, tamarind and pepper, and served piping hot, topped with fried garlic. Eat it with *som tam* (green papaya salad) and dipped in sweet-and-spicy and sour-and-spicy sauces.

Inter
432/1–2 Siam Sq Soi 9. Tel: 0-22551 4689. Open: daily 10am–10pm. **$** 50 p274, B1
Popular hangout for students and teachers from Chulalongkorn University. Spicy steamed shrimp with lemonade features on the menu with more usual fare such as crispy fried catfish salad and grilled mussels hot plate. Simple decor, but with two large windows.

Mah Boon Krong Food Centre
Top Fl, Mah Boon Krong, 444 Th Phyathai. Tel: 0-2217 9491. Open: daily 10am–9pm. **$** 51 p274, B1
Huge food court with a large variety of tasty local dishes (noodles, salads, desserts, vegetarian). Buy vouchers as you go in, choose from as many stalls as you like and sit anywhere. Redeem unused vouchers for cash on your way out.

Sara-Jane's
Gnd fl Sindhorn Bldg 130-132 Th Withayu. Tel: 0-2650 9992-3. Open: daily noon–10pm. **$** 52 p275, D2
American Sara-Jane, a long-time Bangkok resident, pulls off an authentic Isaan menu of the spicy salads and grilled beef staples of northeast Thailand. Locals into raucous dining pack this office-block outlet. Also offers a few less successful Italian dishes.

Savoury
Gnd Fl, Siam Paragon, Th Rama I. Tel: 0-2129 4353. Open: daily 11am–10pm. **$$** 53 p274, B1
Lemon-grass chicken with mixed fruits in a delicious hot-and-sour *som tam* dressing is typical of the inventive dishes served at this stylish café. Mouth-watering cakes and a range of teas and juices are also available.

Som Tam
392/2 Siam Sq Soi 5. Tel: 0-2251 4880. Open: daily 11.15am–9pm. **$** 54 p274, B1
This modern Isaan (north-eastern) restaurant is so popular that they put cushions outside for people waiting. The action whirls around an open kitchen where staff make a great fiery *som tam nua*, northeastern sausage, and other excellent dishes.

Bars

Bacchus
20/6-7 Soi Ruam Rudi. Tel: 0-2650 8986. www.bacchus.tv Open: daily 5pm–1am. 6 p275, D2
Located in the pleasant restaurant enclave of Ruam Rudi Village, this elegant four-storey wine bar sees a steady flow of creative and media types. Select from an impressive list of 250 wines and 200 liquors.

Diplomat Bar
Conrad Hotel, 87 Th Withayu. Tel: 0-2690 9999. www.conradhotels.com Open: Sun–Thur 10–1am, Fri–Sat 10–2am. 7 p275, D2
There are better jazz bands in town, but this beautiful bar of silks and teak, sculpted metal and cleverly concealed lighting has a far warmer ambience than most hotels achieve.

The Wine Pub
Pullman Hotel, 8/2 Th Rangnam. Tel: 0-2680 9999. www.pullmanbangkokkingpower.com Open: daily 6pm–2am. 8 p270, C3
Good prices here on tapas, pasta, cheese and cold cuts washed down with wine deals from the blackboard menu.

Jim Thompson's Thai House

In a city increasingly dominated by Western architecture, this fine museum offers a glimpse of Thailand's rich cultural heritage

Jim Thompson began his collection shortly after World War II, when Thai antiques were largely undervalued. It includes precious Buddha images, porcelain, traditional paintings, and finely carved furniture and panels collected from old homes and temples throughout Thailand. The traditional Thai houses where his collection is contained are painted with the red-brown hue characteristic of the country. The houses feature dramatic outward-sweeping roofs covered with rare tiles designed and fired in Ayutthaya. Gracefully curving in a *ngo* (peak), they allow the airy rooms to remain open all year long, sheltered from the downpours of the rainy season. The main structure, enveloped by lush tropical greenery, stands elevated a full storey above the ground as protection against flooding. The traditional family lived in several houses around a communal verandah, where they would eat on the floor. This is why people remove shoes before entering.

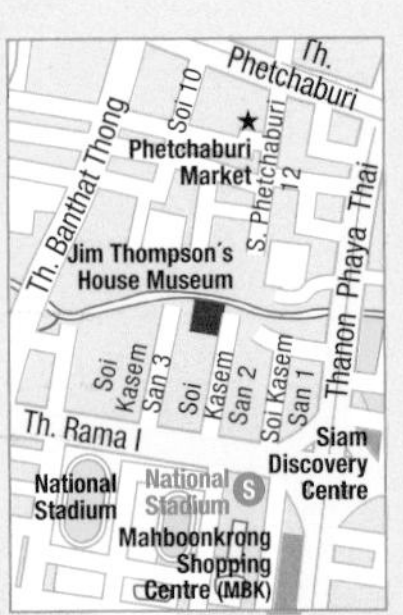

The Essentials

Address: *6 Soi Kasem San 2, Th Rama I, www.jimthompsonhouse.com*
Tel: *0-2216 7568*
Opening Hrs: *daily 9am–5pm*
Entrance Fee: *charge, includes compulsory guided tour*
Transport: *(BTS) National Stadium*

ABOVE: Jim Thompson's House, although not 100 percent authentic in detail, is one of the best examples of a traditional Thai dwelling in Bangkok. Its various elements were brought from around the country and reassembled here.

ABOVE: traditional houses are built without nails. On marriage, grooms would literally dismantle their bedroom and attach it their bride's family home.

THE KING OF THAI SILK

One Easter day in 1967 Jim Thompson went for a walk in the jungles of the Cameron Highlands in Malaysia and never came back. After years of speculation the mystery of his disappearance is still unsolved. Born in Delaware, USA, in 1906, Thompson worked as an architect before joining the army in 1939. He fought in Europe and Asia during World War II, and when the war ended, he served in Bangkok in the Office of Strategic Service (the forerunner of the CIA). Thompson later returned to Bangkok, where, inspired by swatches of silk he had collected during his trips in Thailand, he decided to track down traditional silk weavers. He found one lone community of Muslim weavers at the canalside Ban Khrua (he eventually built his own house just opposite the canal). Utilising new techniques and dyes that raised the silk's quality, he set up the Thai Silk Company, later exporting his creations around the world. Thompson is one of the most celebrated *farang* (Westerners) in Thailand and his silks remain a treasured part of Thailand's culture.

BELOW: Jim Thompson inspects a length of Thai silk. On the canal opposite the house there are still a couple of workshops operating today in the original Ban Khrua village where Thompson started his business in the 1950s.

ABOVE: the rooms and verandas in the house are full of antiques, and particularly strong on porcelain and religious art such as these two Buddha statues.

VISA CLUB
TEL. 02-2339694
JINA CLUB
Club Noa 5th fl.
Ginza Club 4F
0-2266-5821
ALBATROSS
888
スリーエイト
Excite Club
777 CLUB
THREE SEVEN
Tel. 233-6904, 4 TH Floor
Santa Lucia
ナイトクラブ
NIGHT CLUB MAWARI
ATESS
アテッ
6th Floor
3rd - 4th FLOOR
บริษัท
ธนิยะสปิริต
จำกัด
CHIVAS REGAL
12
HENNESSY
STIRS IT UP
VIP KARAO
6F
Tel. 632-

BANGRAK AND SILOM

Bangrak is one of the city's most modern areas, its gleaming glass condos and office blocks a testament to a Bangkok on the move. Yet there are rare glimpses of traditional life, and nighttime brings an earthier market trade around "the fleshpots of Patpong"

Main Attractions

MANDARIN ORIENTAL HOTEL
ASSUMPTION CATHEDRAL
STATE TOWER
MAHA UMA DEVI TEMPLE
PATPONG
MR KUKRIT PRAMOJ'S HERITAGE HOME

Maps and Listings

MAP OF BANGRAK AND SILOM, PAGE 169
SHOPPING, PAGE 170
RESTAURANTS AND BARS, PAGES 173–5
ACCOMMODATION, PAGES 243–4

During the mid 19th-century, Bangkok began to expand on a wave of canal and road construction. Thanon Charoen Krung (New Road), the city's earliest paved thoroughfare, runs parallel to the river, where the earliest communities formed. European traders settled around what is now Bangrak, close to the port entry to the city. Today, the waterside here is dominated by luxury hotels, but the quiet, easily navigable side streets still reveal elements of its history, such as colonial-style buildings that were once home to foreign banks, commercial and diplomatic offices, houses, and the capital's first lodging inns.

Thanon Silom, gravitating eastwards from the Chao Phraya River's premier real estate, is today the principal route that intersects the business district. It ends at Thanon Rama IV, with Lumphini Park beyond. Parallel to Silom are Sathorn, Surawong and Si Phraya roads. These four make up the district of **Bangrak**, with the first two now being full of high-rise glass and steel office blocks, condos and hotels.

But it's not all starchy commerce. After sunset, the upper end of Silom is alive with markets and nightlife, including a thriving gay scene and the infamous (and touristy) girlie bars of Patpong.

Holy Rosary Church ❶

Located behind the River City shopping centre and just off an alley housing a bustling market is the **Holy Rosary Church** or Wat Kalawa (daily 6am–9pm; free). Portuguese Catholics erected the original edifice in 1787 after they moved from the sacked capital of Ayutthaya. After a fire burnt down the wooden

LEFT AND RIGHT: Thanon Silom by night and day.

church, it was rebuilt around 1890. The neo-Gothic sanctuary features some of Thailand's best examples of stained glass.

Continue south past the River City shopping centre, and just next door to the **Royal Orchid Sheraton** hotel is the 1820s **Portuguese Embassy**, the city's oldest. It is best viewed from the riverside.

ABOVE: the elegant Authors' Lounge at the Oriental.
BELOW: the Sala Rim Naam restaurant at the Mandarin Oriental Hotel puts on a nightly show of traditional Thai dance-drama accompanied by a Thai set dinner.

Mandarin Oriental ❷

Further south, the legendary Mandarin Oriental Hotel *(see page 243)* was founded in the 1870s, and is now consistently rated as one of the world's best. A riverside retreat for the influential and wealthy, the Mandarin Oriental's grandeur has endured despite the boxy exteriors of two newer buildings – the Garden Wing (added 1958) and River Wing (1976) – which detract from the classic look of the original Authors' Wing. To best imbibe the old-world atmosphere, have afternoon tea in the elegant **Authors' Lounge** and muse over the literary greats, such as Somerset Maugham, Noel Coward and Graham Greene, who have passed through its doors. The **Riverside Terrace** is another charming spot to settle down with a drink.

Assumption Cathedral ❸

Address: 23 Charoen Krung Soi 38
Tel: 0-2234 8556
Opening Hrs: daily 6am–9pm
Entrance Fee: free
Transport: Oriental pier

Turn right outside the Oriental Hotel towards the river; a side road on the left leads to a small tree-lined square dominated by the **Assumption Cathedral**. Built in 1910, the red-brick cathedral is surrounded by a Catholic mission. Its rococo interior has stained-glass windows and gilded pillars topped with a domed ceiling. Looming behind it in stark contrast is the unmistakable State Tower *(see opposite)*.

Oriental Hotel area

Continue to the Tha Oriental ferry point; just to its left is the whitewashed and Venetian-inspired **East Asiatic Company ❹**. Erected in 1901, it was once the most visible riverside structure in this area; today, it awaits redevelopment. To the left of the Oriental hotel are two early 20th-century buildings, one of which houses the elegant **China House** restaurant (run by the Oriental hotel). A side road to the left leads to the charming **OP Place**. Dating from 1905, this old-world building was one of the city's first department stores. Today, it is mostly filled with shops selling pricey arts and crafts, jewellery and Thai silk. Close by are the home-decor shops of the new **OP Garden** in a beautiful Rama V wooden complex.

Continue past Haroon Mosque to the recently restored **French Embassy**, hidden behind high walls and an imposing gate. Then head towards the riverside where the crumbling but wonderfully atmospheric

19th-century **Old Customs House** stands. Currently used as a fire station, plans are afoot for its development into a boutique hotel or an arts centre. Both of these sights are best viewed from the river.

Thanon Silom

Taking its name from irrigation windmills (*si lom*) that used to occupy the area, Thanon Silom and its former parallel canal once transported people and goods from farms and orchards to the river. Today, it is a busy urban commercial district, where shopping and nightlife are the principal attractions. The Skytrain (BTS) and metro (MRT) lines intersect at the top of Thanon Silom (with Thanon Rama IV). The Skytrain's westward line was extended across the river in 2009, and now serves two stations in Thonburi.

Standing tall at the river-end junction of Thanon Silom and Thanon Charoen Krung, the ostentatious, faux-classical **State Tower** ❺ contains the upmarket Lebua hotel and a spectacular 200-metre (656ft) -high drinking and dining complex called **The Dome**. On the 63rd-floor rooftop, **Sirocco** *(see page 174)* has some of Bangkok's best panoramas, and claims to be the world's highest outdoor eatery. The Greco-Roman setting – all Doric columns topped by a gold dome – seems incongruous seen from the streets on the edge of Chinatown, but Euro-Asian architecture has a pedigree stretching back over 100 years and is, in fact, very Bangkok.

Heading up Thanon Silom, on the right at corner of Silom Soi 23 is the three-storey **Bangkok Shell Museum** (daily 10am–9pm; charge), which was opened in 2009 by a seashell collector who had gained small fame as a TV quiz show winner on the subject. It has around 3,000 shells, including a giant clam species that can weigh 200kg (440lbs) and gastropods used as jewel-

ABOVE: the imposing gates of the French Embassy. Take a peek from the outside, as entry is forbidden.

Bangrak and Silom

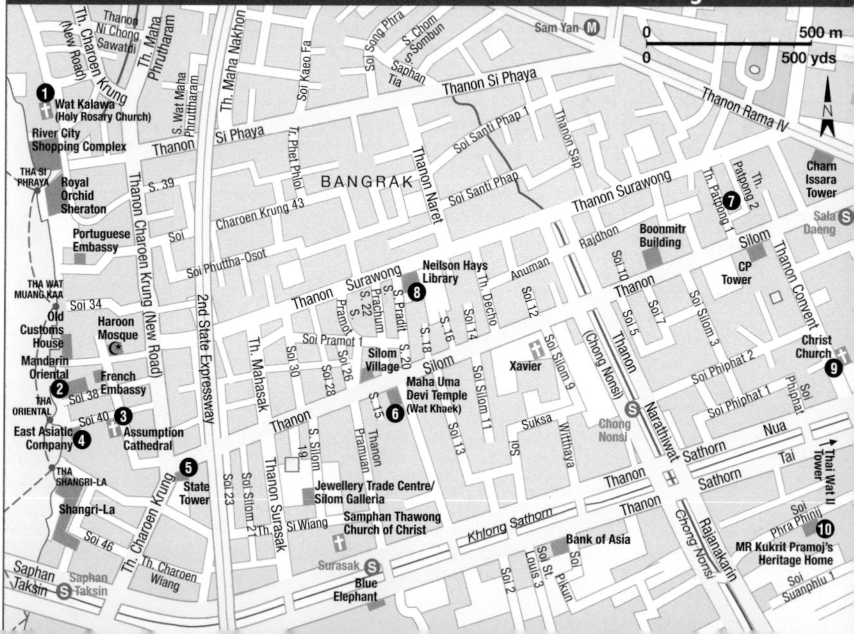

Wat Kalawa (Holy Rosary Church)
River City Shopping Complex
Royal Orchid Sheraton
Portuguese Embassy
Old Customs House
Haroon Mosque
Mandarin Oriental
French Embassy
Assumption Cathedral
East Asiatic Company
State Tower
Shangri-La
Neilson Hays Library
Silom Village
Maha Uma Devi Temple (Wat Khaek)
Jewellery Trade Centre/ Silom Galleria
Samphan Thawong Church of Christ
Blue Elephant
Xavier
Bank of Asia
Boonmitr Building
CP Tower
Charn Issara Tower
Christ Church
MR Kukrit Pramoj's Heritage Home
Thai Wat II Tower
BANGRAK
Thanon Rama IV
Thanon Si Phaya
Thanon Surawong
Thanon Silom
Thanon Sathorn Nua
Thanon Sathorn Tai
Thanon Charoen Krung (New Road)
2nd State Expressway
Sam Yan
Sala Daeng
Chong Nonsi
Surasak
Saphan Taksin
0 500 m
0 500 yds

ABOVE: the towering entrance facade of the Maha Uma Devi Temple.

lery. Information panels tell how shells were historically used as currency and how some have inspired inventors.

Continuing along Silom, also on the right, at No 919/1, is the soaring **Jewellery Trade Centre**, the heart of Thailand's significant precious-stone market. The connecting **Silom Galleria** houses art galleries and jewellery and antiques shops over several levels.

Further up the road, on the left, is the tourist-oriented **Silom Village**, brimming with shoppers and diners. It has traditional music and dance performed in a couple of its establishments.

Maha Uma Devi Temple ❻

Address: 2 Thanon Pan
Tel: 0-2238 4007
Opening Hrs: daily 6am–8pm
Entrance Fee: free
Transport: (BTS) Chong Nonsi

About a quarter of the way up Thanon Silom on the right, on the corner of Soi Pan, is this vibrantly coloured Hindu temple. Named after Shiva's consort, Uma Devi, **Maha Uma Devi** was established in the 1860s by the Tamil community, whose presence is still strong in the area. Thais know it as Wat Khaek, meaning "guests' temple" (*khaek* is also a less welcoming term used by locals for anyone from the Asian subcontinent).

On holy days, the temple is busy with a lively spectrum of worshippers, including many Indian, Thai and Chinese, who, in addition to the Buddha, find devotional comfort in the images of the Hindu images Vishnu and Uma Devi's son Ganesh. The structure has a prominent 6-metre (20ft) -high facade, adorned with an ornate diorama of religious statuary.

Patpong ❼

Come nightfall, the upper end of Thanon Silom throbs with nightlife,

SHOPPING

Bangrak has market stalls galore, with the most famous being those of Patpong's night market.

Antiques

OP Place
Soi 38 Th Charoen Krung. Tel: 0-2266 0186. p273, E4
A cute upmarket mall that offers some exquisite antiques and reproductions from many regions of southeast Asia, India and China. There are a few cheaper crafty shops mixed in.

River City
23 Trok Rongnamkaeng. Tel: 0-2237 0077. www.rivercity.co.th p274, E4
The lower floors are mainly touristy art galleries and tailors, but climb the stairs for art and antiques. Auctions are held monthly in the Auction House.

Fabrics

Jim Thompson Thai Silk
9 Th Surawong. Tel: 0-2632 8100-4. www.jimthompson.com p274, B3
The flagship store of this famous silk company deals in contemporary fabrics, clothing, accessories and home furnishings. The prices match its international brand profile, but the quality is beautiful. There are several branches around the city.

Home

OP Garden
Charoen Krung Soi 39. Tel: 0-2266 0186. p273, E3
This sister of OP Place occupies a Rama V period complex and has a good range of outlets with textiles, crafts and home decor from around Thailand. There are also a couple of nice cafés to relax in.

Jewellery

Jewellery Trade Centre
Silom Galleria, 919/1 Th Silom. Tel: 0-2630 0944-50. www.jewelrytradecenter.com p274, A4
One of many jewellery shops in the Silom Galleria mall and in the surrounding streets. Also home to the Asian Institute of Gemological Sciences, where you can have gemstones graded.

Markets

Patpong
Patpong Soi 1, Th Silom. p274, B3
A must-see for many visitors is this busy neon-lit alley of stalls surrounded by the infamous Patpong go-go scene. Bargain hard here for knock-off watches, jeans and football shirts. The stalls extend into Thanon Silom for several blocks.

most famously in the go-go bars of **Patpong** (Soi 1 and Soi 2). In the 1960s and 1970s this former banana plantation tempted American GIs from Vietnam, but now, depending on your tolerance levels, there's a surprisingly unsleazy ambience. You still get hustle from touts flashing menu cards with a list of notorious ping-pong acrobatics, but these – along with girls pole dancing in bikinis – have become prime tourist attractions, enhanced by a busy night market. This type of invitation card has a long history. In 1923, the writer Somerset Maugham recorded a man giving him a card offering the services of "Miss Pretty Girl", who would "put him in dreamland with perfumed soap".

Vendors set up the **night market** in Patpong Soi 1 and Silom Soi 2–8, selling counterfeit watches, fake name-brand bags and clothes, CDs and DVDs, as well as a strong line in binoculars and knives, presumably aimed at wannabe combat heroes.

The adjacent **Patpong 2** is an alley of box-shaped beer and hostess bars that also accommodates the 24-hour supermarket Foodland.

A few lanes east of Patpong, the mainly gay **Silom Soi 4** also attracts straights, mainly for the people-watching opportunities at the outdoor tables. The place becomes a colourful riot of camp and cross-dressing during occasional *soi* parties, such as Gay Pride Week and the Soi 4 Olympics. Nearby **Silom Soi 2** is clubbier and more hard-core gay-oriented. Further towards Thanon Rama IV, the Japanese-friendly **Soi Thaniya** is lined with sushi joints and karaoke bars, where hostesses stand outside greeting tourists with loud choruses of "*Irrashai Mase Dozo!*" (Hello, welcome, please come in). Sometimes on Thaniya, on the left, discreetly placed beyond the entrance to a car park, there's an illicit moonshine stall where you can buy *ya dong* (pickled medicines) and possibly virility drinks such as *phaya chang sarn* (Power of the Great Elephant).

Neilson Hays Library 8

Address: 195 Thanon Surawong, www.neilsonhayslibrary.com
Tel: 0-2233 1731
Opening Hrs: Tue–Sun 9.30–4pm
Entrance Fee: free
Transport: (BTS) Chong Nonsi

Many of Thanon Silom's even-numbered lanes cut through to parallel **Thanon Surawong**, which

SHOP

The market vendors around Patpong are more unscrupulous than elsewhere in the city, quoting prices that are some 50–75 percent higher than what they are actually prepared to accept. Bargain hard!

LEFT: Patpong in the flesh. **BELOW:** Patpong T-shirt stall.

ABOVE: MR Kukrit Pramoj's Heritage Home.

TIP

If you would like to be a dab hand at Thai cookery, sign up for cookery lessons at the Blue Elephant restaurant *(see page 174)*. Priced at B2,996 per person, four dishes are taught during the half-day hands-on sessions (tel: 0-2673 9353; www.blueelephant.com/bangkok).

has seen less of the district's commercial development. Of interest to bookworms is the early 20th-century **Neilson Hays Library**, named after Jennie Neilson Hays, a founder of the Bangkok Ladies Library Association. It is stacked with over 20,000 books, and also exhibits works by contemporary artists in the small **Rotunda Gallery**.

Soi Convent area

Amid the odd numbered *sois* of Silom, and opposite Soi 4, is **Soi Convent**, a busy tree-shaded lane that starts with a barrage of food stalls and continues with several restaurants catering for various tastes – from Irish pub grub to fancy fusion. Just at the corner with Thanon Sathorn is the Anglican **Christ Church** ❾ (daily 8am–5pm; free). Originally built as the English Chapel in the mid 19th-century, the present Gothic-style building was built in 1905.

Thanon Sathorn

Thanon Sathorn grew on either side of a central canal towards the end of the 19th century, and in turn encouraged the growth of an affluent neighbourhood of colonial-style mansions for the city's local and foreign elite. Modern Sathorn evokes little of this historic charm, though the odd period piece still exists – like the stylish **Blue Elephant** Thai restaurant *(see page 174)*, which once housed the Thai–Chinese Chamber of Commerce.

Building continues apace, with offices, condos and hotels now lining virtually the whole stretch of Thanon Sathorn, from Thanon Rama IV to the river. Several noteworthy buildings stand out, including the slim **Thai Wah II Tower** with its gaping arch, standing tall between two of the capital's hippest boutique hotels, the **Sukhothai** and **Metropolitan**.

Looking more like a creation of a child's fantasy than a bank headquarters, the **Bank of Asia**, at the corner of Thanon Sathorn and Soi Pikun, was designed by one of the country's foremost modern architects, Dr Sumet Jumsai, and is affectionately dubbed the "robot building".

MR Kukrit Pramoj's Heritage Home ❿

Address: Soi Phra Phinij
Tel: 0-2286 8185
Opening Hrs: Sat–Sun 10am–5pm
Entrance Fee: charge
Transport: (BTS) Chong Nonsi

Tucked away on a lane halfway down Thanon Sathorn is a former residence-turned-museum. Born of royal descent (signified by the title Mom Ratchawong – MR), the late Kukrit Pramoj had a brief stint as prime minister during the disruptive 1970s, but is better remembered as a prolific author and cultural preservationist. This splendid wooden home comprises five stilt buildings that are fine examples of the traditional architecture of the Central Plains. The museum contains antique pottery, memorabilia and photos of the famous statesman, while the ornate garden adds to the sense of serenity. ❑

BEST RESTAURANTS AND BARS

Restaurants

Chinese

China House
Mandarin Oriental Hotel, 48 Oriental Ave. Tel: 0-2659 9000. www.mandarinoriental.com Open: daily L and D. **$$$** 55 p273, E4
Beautiful 1930s Shanghainese Art Deco interior that is a wonderful setting for good-quality dishes like hot-and-sour soup filled with fresh herbs and sweet lobster meat.

Mei Jiang
Peninsula Hotel, 333 Th Charoen Nakhorn. Tel: 0-2861 2888. www.peninsula.com Open: daily L and D. **$$$** 56 p273, D4
Cantonese restaurant on the river with an elegant interior of glass chandeliers, silk upholstered teak furniture and beautiful wall hangings. Delicious courses like duck smoked with tea and grouper with soy sauce, complemented by good wines and a selection of teas.

French

Le Bouchon
37/17 Patpong Soi 2. Tel: 0-2234 9109. Open: Mon–Sat L and D. **$$–$$$** 57 p274, B3
Atmospheric seven-table bistro that gains frisson from its Patpong location – slightly naughty like a Marseille dockyard diner. Popular with local French for its simple home cooking and friendly banter at the small bar where diners sip Pastis.

D'Sens
Dusit Thani Hotel, 946 Th Rama IV. Tel: 0-2236 9999. Open: Mon–Fri L and D, Sat D only. **$$$$** 58 p274, C3
This franchise of the three-Michelin-starred Le Jardin des Sens in Montpellier, France, is full of delicate surprises like cep mushrooms and duck liver ravioli in frothy truffle sabayon. The retro decor includes Paul Smith striped carpets and three are good views.

Le Normandie
Mandarin Oriental Hotel, 48 Oriental Ave. Tel: 0-2659 9000. www.mandarinoriental.com Open: Mon–Sat L and D, Sun D only. **$$$$** 59 p273, E4
Formal dining option with jacket and tie required for men. But you don't mind dressing up for concoctions such as goose liver dome with Perigord truffles, and sole fillets with Oscietra caviar cream sauce that can verge on brilliance. The interior has crystal chandeliers and floor-to-ceiling windows overlooking the river.

Indian

Indian Hut
311/2-5 Th Surawong. Tel: 0-2237 8812. Open: daily 11am–11pm. **$$** 60 p273, E4
Rich north Indian food served on two floors. The *murg malai tikka* (chicken in fresh cream and cheese) and the spicy *murg lazeez* (chicken in a tomato and onion sauce) are both mouthwatering.

Tamil Nadu
Silom Soi 11. Tel: 0-2235 6336. Open: daily 11.30am–9.30pm. **$** 61 p274, A4
Simple café serving the south Indian community close to Bangkok's most ornate Indian temple. The speciality is *masala dosa*, a pancake made of rice flour and *urad dal*, stuffed with potato and onion curry and served with coconut chutney.

International/Fusion

Eat Me
Fl 1, 1/6 Piphat Soi 2, off Th Convent. Tel: 0-2238 0931. www.eatmerestaurant.com Open: daily 3pm–1am. **$$$** 62 p274, B4
Very popular restaurant with art exhibitions and modern Australian dishes such as charred scallops with mango, herb salad, pickled onion and citrus dressing. Low lighting and a fragmented layout lend intimacy. On cool nights ask for a table on the terrace.

Prices per person for a three-course meal without drinks:
$ = under B300
$$ = B300–800
$$$ = B800–1,600
$$$$ = over B1,600

RIGHT: the decorative interior of Le Normandie.

Maison Chin
Bandara Suites, 75/1 Soi Saladaeng. Tel: 0-2266 0505. www.chinhouse.com Open: daily L and D. **$$–$$$** (63) p274, C4
British-Chinese TV chef Ken Hom is consultant at this "modern Asian" restaurant. Standout dishes are Wagyu beef carpaccio with tamarind and sesame dressing, and crab and prawn coriander ravioli in a subtle Chinese herb broth.

Panorama
Pan Pacific Bangkok, Th Rama IV. Tel: 0-2632 9000. www.panpacific.com Open: daily L and D. **$$$–$$$$** (64) p275, C4
The open kitchen breaks up a huge restaurant area that's high on expensive, high-quality products like rack of Colorado lamb. Foie gras ice cream is also worth a try. The adjoining Deck is a comfortable bar with good views and a tolerance for smokers.

Sirocco
Fl 63 Lebua at State Tower, 1055 Th Silom. Tel: 0-2624 9555. www.thedomebkk.com Open: daily D. **$$$–$$$$** (65) p273, E4
Spectacularly high outdoor rooftop late-night restaurant with magnificent views over the river. Greco-Roman architecture and a jazz band add to the sense of occasion. In the same complex, there's the classy Distil Bar, the Italian Mezzaluna, and the alfresco pan-Asian restaurant Breeze.

V9
Fl 37 Sofitel Silom Bangkok, 188 Th Silom. Tel: 0-2238 1991. www.sofitel.com Open: daily D. **$$** (66) p274, A4
The retail wine prices are a big pull here. Add 37th-floor views and you can have a very affordable romantic dinner until 1am. The food is served in "tasting trees" with six dishes, such as roast duck salad with Vietnamese dressing, or lobster with three pepper sauces in each.

LEFT: the spectacular view from Sirocco.

Italian

Concerto
661 Fl 1–2 Th Silom. Tel: 0-2266 5333. www.niusonsilom.com Open: daily D. **$$$** (67) p274, A4
The intimate, candle-lit restaurant at Niu's on Silom jazz bar serves modern dishes, including tian of Scottish salmon, pike perch and burrata with tomato confiture, into the small hours. Also has terrace seating.

La Scala
Sukhothai Hotel, 13/3 Th Sathorn Tai. Tel: 0-2344 8888. www.sukhothai.com Open: daily L and D. **$$$** (68) p275, C4
An Asian modernist interior with an open kitchen where diners sit around to watch culinary theatre. Dishes like roasted fillet of turbot with fennel, black olives and dill, sit alongside pizzas fresh from the wood-fired oven.

Zanotti
Gnd fl, Saladaeng Colonnade, 21/2 Soi Saladaeng. Tel: 0-2636 0002. www.zanotti-ristorante.com Open: daily L and D. **$$$** (69) p274, C3
People come here for the buzz as much as the homey Italian fare. Good selection of wines by the glass. Vino di Zanotti, opposite, also serves a full menu and has live jazz.

Japanese

Aoi
132/10–11 Silom Soi 6. Tel: 0-2235 2321/2. Open: daily L and D. **$$** (70) p274, B3
Cool, calm, unfussy restaurant serving well-prepared Japanese food. Downstairs is a sushi bar, with two floors of private and semi-private rooms available for a surcharge. As usual, set meals are much cheaper than the à la carte options.

Korean

Nam Kang
5/3–4 Silom Soi 3. Tel: 0-2233 1480. Open: daily 11am–10pm. **$$** (71) p274, B4
A favourite with Korean expatriates, Nam Kang serves many *yangban* dishes usually associated with upper-class dining. The speciality is the herbal cure-all *samgyetang* (whole chicken stuffed with rice and ginseng and served in soup).

Thai

The Blue Elephant
233 Th Sathorn Tai. Tel: 0-2673 9353. www.blueelephant.com/bangkok Open: daily L and D. **$$–$$$** Off map.

Prices per person for a three-course meal without drinks:
$ = under B300
$$ = B300–800
$$$ = B800–1,600
$$$$ = over B1,600

Part of a Belgian-owned international chain, the menu mixes Thai standards with a few fusion dishes like foie gras in tamarind sauce. The flavours are slightly toned down to suit Western palates. Housed in a beautiful restored building.

Café de Laos
16 Silom Soi 19. Tel: 0-2635 2338/9. www.cafedelaos.com Open: daily L and D. **$–$$** 72 p274, A4
A cute place in a handsome, 100-year-old wooden house, it serves all the famous Isaan dishes like green papaya salad *(som tam)* and *laab* (spicy minced meat salad with ground roasted rice). Photos of old Laos on the walls add a nice touch.

Harmonique
22 Charoen Krung Soi 34. Tel: 0-2237 8175. Open: Mon–Sat 10am–10pm. **$–$$** 73 p273, E4
Charming restaurant occupying several antique-filled Chinese shophouses with leafy courtyards. Popular with Western diners, the spices are fairly quiet by Thai standards, but the food is generally good.

Jim Thompson's Saladaeng Café
120/1 Saladaeng Soi 1. Tel: 0-2266 9167. www.saladaengcafe.com Open: daily 11am–11pm. **$** 74 p274, C4
Drink mulberry tea straight from the farms of the famous Thai silk merchant in this predictably elegant little restaurant. The small menu has Thai salads and curries, plus pastas, sandwiches and burgers. Garden seating is arranged around a small lotus pond.

Kalpapruek
27 Th Pramuan. Tel: 0-2236 4335. Open: Mon–Sat 8am–6pm, Sun 8am–3pm. **$** 75 p274, A4
This royally connected restaurant is pleasingly modest and features some of the Western influences brought to Thai cooking through palace kitchens. On the street is a small, popular café-restaurant, and inside, a covered garden area and a bakery with good cakes.

Krua Aroy Aroy
Th Pan, Silom. Tel: 0-2635 2365. Open: daily 10am–6pm. **$** 76 p274, A4
Opposite Maha Uma Devi Temple, with a sign reading "Delicious, Delicious, Delicious", this wooden-stool café features regional dishes. Curries include *nam ya ka ti* (minced fish in coconut milk); noodles come deep-fried *(mee krob)* or cold *(khanom jeen)*.

Nahm
Metropolitan Hotel, 27 Th Sathorn. Tel: 0-2632 3333. Open: daily L and D. **$$$$** 77 p274, C4
This 2010 newcomer is an outlet of Europe's only Michelin-starred Thai restaurant, run by Australian chef David Thompson. The ultra-traditional menu includes intriguing flavours that are becoming harder to find in modern Thai cooking, in dishes like jungle curry with snakehead fish.

Bars

The Barbican
9/4–5 Soi Thaniya. Tel: 0-2233 4141-2. 9 p274, B3
Split-level pub/wine bar full of leather, teak and brushed concrete. Good Western and Thai food; friendly atmosphere and occasional DJ nights.

Distil
State Tower, 1055 Th Silom. Tel: 0-2624 9555. www.thedomebkk.com 10 p273, E4
Sixty-four floors up, Distil has spectacular views from its small balcony and a very chilled vibe inside, where high flyers quaff champagne and oysters.

Met Bar
Metropolitan Hotel, Th Sathorn. Tel: 0-2625 3399. 11 p275, C4
They're quite relaxed about the members-only policy at this slick, minimalist bar, which has occasional film and fashion shows and visiting international DJs.

Opus
64 Pan Rd, Silom. Tel: 0-2637 9896. 12 p274, A4
Chic wine bar with a walk-in cellar of 300 wines, including ten by the glass and a full Italian food menu.

Roadhouse BBQ
942/1–4 Th Rama IV. Tel: 0-2236 8010. www.roadhousebarbecue.com 13 p274, B3
US-style pub on three floors with a good menu of wings and things, excellent beers, a pool table, shuffleboard, table football and several screens showing sport.

Sphinx
100 Silom Soi 4. Tel: 0-2234 7249. 14 p274, B3
Gay bar also frequented by straights for its menu of well-prepared Thai and Western food. Good choices include northern specialities *laab* and *khao soy*. Serves food late and has outside tables.

Noodi
Th Silom. Tel: 0-2632 7989. Open: daily 11–4am. **$** 78 p274, B3
One of a new generation of cafés that sell cheap Asian street food in funky fast-food surrounds. It's just an average pan-Asian noodle menu, but handy after the bars shut.

Silom Village
286 Th Silom. Tel: 0-2234 4448. www.silomvillage.co.th Open: daily 11am–11.45pm. **$$** 79 p274, A4
Better than you might expect at this touristy theatre-restaurant. The music and dance cultural shows from 8pm nightly account for the inflated prices. Nearby stalls sell souvenirs and local produce.

Somboon Seafood
169/7–11 Th Surawong. Tel: 0-2233 3104. Open: daily 4–11pm. **$$$** 80 p274, A3
No-frills café of tubular metal furniture and good Chinese-style seafood. Fat curried crabs and prawns with spicy *nam jim* dipping sauce are ace, along with whole fish cooked every-which-way. The canteen-like service won't win awards, but the food just might.

SUKHUMVIT

The leafy back lanes off Thanon Sukhumvit are flush with condos for expats and the Thai middle class. For food and fun they're spoilt for choice, as the neighbourhood offers the widest range of restaurants and bars in the city

Main Attractions

KAMTHIENG HOUSE
BENJAKITTI PARK
THAILAND CREATIVE AND DESIGN CENTRE
SOI THONGLOR

Maps and Listings

MAP OF SUKHUMVIT, PAGE 178
SHOPPING, PAGE 179
RESTAURANTS AND BARS, PAGES 180–3
ACCOMMODATION, PAGES 245–6

Bustling, traffic-clogged Thanon Sukhumvit pushes the urban sprawl eastwards, and continues some 400km (250 miles) all the way to Trat, close to the Cambodian border. Once a dirt track surrounded by marshland, the road was built in the 1930s and became Thailand's first proper highway, transporting people beyond the capital. Today it's the efficient Skytrain that provides the fastest means of transport between the upmarket shops, restaurants and entertainment venues that line the Bangkok segment of Thanon Sukhumvit, located mainly around the Nana, Asok, Phrom Phong and Thong Lo stations.

Although thin on key tourist attractions, visitors do come. This is a major residential area, home to many of Bangkok's expanding middle classes and the ever-increasing numbers of European, American and Asian expatriates; plush condo towers line the sometimes quite leafy *sois* that splay either side of the main road, and there are also several top-flight hotels. In short, there's a lot of disposable income around, and, consequently, a lot to spend it on. An excellent range of restaurants and cafés, including Italian, Indian and Middle Eastern, provide early evening fuel stops, and some of Bangkok's best clubs let people party on late into the night.

Sukhumvit's side roads

About 100 metres/yds from the expressway, on the right, is Soi 4, where the raucous go-go bars of the three-storey **Nana Entertainment Plaza** ❶ are in full swing every night. Working girls and *katoeys* (ladyboys) solicit customers on the street here, particularly after hours, from 1am-ish, and the area is seedier than Patpong, though it is also a good place to try the local delicacy of deep-fried insects

LEFT: outdoor sculpture at Benjakitti Park.

from street stalls. Opposite is Soi 3, known as "**Soi Arab**" for its lanes of Lebanese cafés and shisha pipes, smoked streetside, like downtown Cairo. Further on Soi 3 is **Bumrungrad Hospital**, the prime beneficiary of Thailand's boom in health tourism. People come here from all over the world for the low-priced, good-quality care in everything from dental work to cosmetics and major surgery. The booming sector has knock-on effects for the country's government hospitals, which are increasingly struggling to find medical staff.

These *sois* mark the beginning of Sukhumvit's profusion of tailors, pool halls, beer bars and hotels. A night market crowds the pavements from these early blocks, proffering tourist souvenirs, fake-label bags, T-shirts and watches.

Two of the city's best clubs are found on Soi 11, where **Q Bar** and **Bed Supperclub** are pick-up spots for all manner of people who like hip hop with their vodka shots. Close by is **Cheap Charlie's**, a bar that proves Bangkok's variety, with its complete lack of roof or walls.

Further along, Soi 21 (Soi Asoke) has another pole-dancing neon strip, **Soi Cowboy**, located on the right, while on the left is the more genteel ambience of the Siam Society.

Siam Society

The headquarters of the **Siam Society** at Sukhumvit Soi 21 (Soi Asoke) is situated in one of Sukhumvit's oldest buildings. It was founded in 1904 to promote the study and preservation of Thai culture (tel: 0-2661 6470-77; www.siam-society.org; Tue–Sat 9am–5pm), and has an excellent library full of rare books on Thai history, plus old manuscripts and maps. For visitors with more than just passing curiosity, look out for the society's regular lectures on regional history and culture. Non-members may attend by paying a nominal fee.

Kamthieng House ❷

Address: 131 Sukhumvit Soi 21, www.siam-society.org
Tel: 0-2661 6470
Opening Hrs: Tue–Sat 9am–5pm
Entrance Fee: charge
Transport: (BTS) Asok, (MRT) Sukhumvit

In the same grounds as the Siam Society is this 150-year-old building, which was a wooden home on the banks of Chiang Mai's Mae Ping river before being transported to Bangkok, carefully reassembled and opened as an ethnological museum. It is reputedly still inhabited by the ghosts of three former residents. Presentations include audio-visual displays on northern folk culture and daily life.

Sukhumvit's parks

Still on Soi Asoke (Soi 21), south of the Sukhumvit intersection is **Queen Sirikit National Convention Centre** (QSNCC), which hosts mainly large-scale business, cultural and entertainment events. The centre looks out over **Benjakitti Park** ❸ (daily 5am–8pm; free), an activity-orientated green space overlooking the artificial **Lake Ratchada**. Part of the park is shaded by trees, including a children's play area, and it's enhanced by large fountains and cascading water displays. In the early morning and evening a crowd of joggers and cyclists circles the lake on two designated paths. It's very close to the MRT station and refreshments are available in the QSNCC.

Further east, near Soi 24 and Emporium shopping mall, is **Benjasiri Park** ❹ (daily 5am–8pm; free). Opened in celebration of the present queen's 60th birthday, the small garden has a large pond, fountains and sculptures by some of the country's most respected artists. There are also basketball courts, a skate

TIP

Sukhumvit's odd and even streets *(soi)* are out of synch. For instance Soi 24, beside Emporium mall, is opposite Soi 39, on the other side of the street.

BELOW: the stylish Indus bar.

park and a swimming pool with Thai pavilions to relax under. The front of the park is often busy with *tai chi* enthusiasts.

Emporium and Soi Thonglor

On the corner of Soi 24, beside the Phrom Phong Skytrain station, is Sukhumvit's premier shopping mall, **Emporium**, with its six floors of upmarket furniture, clothes and decor shops, bakeries, coffee bars and restaurants. At the top are several cinema screens and the **Thailand Creative and Design Centre**, which is a favourite with art and design enthusiasts for exhibitions ranging from Japanese bamboo crafts to the marketing of Thai streetfood. There are also occasional film shows in its café.

Soi Thonglor

Further east, just off Thong Lo Skytrain station is **Sukhumvit Soi 55**, or **Soi Thonglor**. Opposite the mouth of the *soi*, Sukhumvit Soi 38 is a great place for streetfood, as it has lots of different stalls to try, and just down 38 on the left is the classy Face Bar. Thonglor itself and the *sois* off it (Thonglor is also the name of the area) have flourished in the last decade and there are now several small enclaves with shopping, clubs, bars and restaurants. It has a boutique, out-of-town-ambience that appeals to both Thais and expats. The clubs and bars are modern and edgy, certainly influenced by the MTV generation's exposure to international entertainment, but with a stronger local feel than many of their downtown counterparts. Easy Skytrain access means people travel from all over the city to get here. Popular clubs include **Old Skool** and **Demo**, while shoppers drop by the bijou **H1** mall for coffees and frocks, and the sub *sois* are filling with trendy restaurants, like **Harvey's**, **Red** and **To Die For**. ❑

SHOPPING

All kinds of shops feed this middle-class residential area, from one of the city's best malls to boutique fashion outlets in trendy Thonglor.

Books

Dasa Book Café
714/4 Th Sukhumvit (between Soi 26 and 28). Tel: 0-2661 2993. www.dasabookcafe.com Off map.
Second-hand books in a cosy environment with drinks and desserts to fuel your page thumbing and a useful online database.

Kinokuniya
3rd Fl, Emporium, Th Sukhumvit. Tel: 0-2664 8554. Off map.
The second, but still very large, outlet of this Japanese chain store (the other branch is in Siam Paragon *(see page 160)*; between them they have probably the most comprehensive list in town. Art and design, Thai history and travel all feature strongly.

Department Stores

Robinson
Sukhumvit Soi 19. Tel: 0-2252 5121. Off map.
The chain's most popular branches are Thanon Sukhumvit and Thanon Ratchadaphisek. The quality of goods is not as high as Central, but they are inevitably cheaper.

Malls

Emporium
622 Th Sukhumvit, corner with Soi 24. Tel: 0-2664 8000. Off map.
This mall has lots of fashion and home-decor stores and there's an electronics section too, along with cinemas and a good food hall. The department store, also named Emporium, is one of the city's classiest.

H1
998 Sukhumvit Soi 55 (Soi Thonglor). Tel: 0-2714 9578. Off map.
A low-rise boutique mall, with restaurants run by film directors, esoteric art bookshops and stores selling funky interiors and collectables.

Markets

Sukhumvit
Sukhumvit Sois 3-13. p275, E1/2
The odd-numbered side of the street is lined with touristy stalls and shops selling crafts, CDs, T-shirts, watches and pretty much anything else that is souvenir-friendly. Open all day, but liveliest at night.

Fashion

Greyhound
2nd Fl, Emporium, Sukhumit Soi 24. Tel: 0-2664 8664. www.greyhound.co.th Off map.
This trendy fashion label, self-described as "chic and simple", has three sub-brands: Greyhound Original, Playhound and Grey. It has 15 branches and seven restaurants and café outlets around Bangkok, plus outlets in other Asian cities.

It's Happened to Be a Closet
2nd Fl, Emporium Mall, Th Sukhumvit. Tel: 0-2664 7211. Off map.
Designer Siriwan Tharananithikul has graduated from a Siam Square boutique to this sleek fashion parlour café in just a few short years. It's a cluttered grandma's attic of retro bags, blouses and Indian inspirations. They have a hair salon, too.

Textiles

Almeta Silk
20/3 Sukhumvit Soi 23. Tel: 0-2258 4227. www.almeta.com BTS Off map.
The original store of a brand that does made-to-order home furnishings and fashion items in handwoven silk designs.

Jim Thompson Factory Outlet
153 Sukhumvit Soi 93. Tel: 0-2332 6530. www.jimthompson.com p274, B3
The silk pioneers have shops now all over Thailand, selling beautiful fashion and decor items and printed fabrics by designers like Ed Tuttle, Richard Smith and Ou Baholyodhin. The best prices are found at its factory outlet stores.

RIGHT: the plush interior of Emporium shopping mall.

BEST RESTAURANTS AND BARS

Restaurants

American

Bourbon Street
29/4–6 Washington Sq, Sukhumvit Soi 22. Tel: 0-2259 0328-9. www.bourbonstbkk.com Open: daily 6am–midnight. **$$$** Off map.
Bar-restaurant with Cajun-Creole recipes like jambalaya, barbecued pork ribs, blackened chicken and crayfish pie, followed by traditional pecan pie for dessert. Hearty American breakfasts are also available, with pancakes and homemade sausages.

New York Steakhouse
JW Marriott Hotel, 4 Sukhumvit Soi 2. Tel: 0-2656 7700. www.marriott.com Open: daily D only. **$$$$** 81 p275, E1
Top-notch restaurant with a relaxed atmosphere, despite the formal trappings of club-like dark woods and high-backed leather chairs. Try Manhattan clam chowder before grain-fed Angus beef from a silver trolley, sliced at the table. Long martini list.

French

Le Banyan
59 Sukhumvit Soi 8. Tel: 0-2253 5556. www.le-banyan.com Open: Mon–Sat D only. **$$$** 82 p275, E2
Great little French restaurant where formal maitre d' Bruno Bischoff is the perfect foil for the slightly crumpled demeanour of chef Michel Binaux, who prepares many dishes tableside. Try pressed duck or pan-fried foie gras with apple and morel mushrooms.

Le Beaulieu
50 Sukhumvit Soi 19. Tel: 0-2204 2004. www.le-beaulieu.com Open: daily L and D. **$$$–$$$$** Off map.
With plates like slow-cooked mushroom ragout and New Zealand roast tenderloin in a sauce of veal jus, shallots, white port and pancetta, chef Hervé Frerard has forged one of the best reputations in town for French cuisine. The cosy stone tiling and Mediterranean blue decor sets a relaxing tone to enjoy wine along with a good range of imported cheeses.

Philippe Restaurant
20/15–17 Sukhumvit Soi 39. Tel: 0-2259 4577/8. www.philipperestaurant.com Open: Mon–Sat L and D. **$$$** Off map.
Small restaurant with very good classic French fare. The mini grand staircase sweeping from the mezzanine and nicotine colour scheme make a comfortable setting for delicious roast lamb loin with duck liver sauce or trout with lemon butter and almond.

German

Bei Otto
1 Sukhumvit Soi 20. Tel: 0-2262 0892. www.beiotto.com Open: daily 11am–midnight. **$$$** Off map.
This is a bar, restaurant and bakery run by long-time resident Otto Duffner. Good homemade Turinger and Nuremburger sausages, home-baked breads and apple strudel. The cooked meat platter, which will satisfy two hearty appetites, is ideal ballast for German beer.

Indian

Akbar
1/4 Sukhumvit Soi 3. Tel: 0-2253 3479. Open: daily 10.30am–midnight. **$$** 83 p275, E1
One of the oldest Indian restaurants in Bangkok, it serves reliable tandooris, vindaloos and kormas, on two floors charmingly decorated like an over-the-top curio shop, with Arabic lanterns, Indian rugs and fairy lights.

Hazara
29 Sukhumvit Soi 38. Tel: 0-2713 6048-9. www.facebars.com Open: daily D only. **$$$** Off map.
Tasty north Indian fare, such as peppery *khadai kheenga* (shrimps stir-fried with bell peppers), in a glorious setting

LEFT: the funky interior of the Greyhound café.

Prices per person for a three-course meal without drinks:
$ = under B300
$$ = B300–800
$$$ = B800–1,600
$$$$ = over B1,600

embellished with Asian antiques and artefacts. It is housed in a traditional Thai cluster complex and includes the trendy Face Bar *(see page 183)*.

Rang Mahal
Rembrandt Hotel, 19 Sukhumvit Soi 18. Tel: 0-2261 7100. Open: daily L and D. **$$$** Off map.
Feast on city views in silk-upholstered rooms with Indian wood-carved panelling, lots of mirrors and live music while dining on mouthwatering Mogul specialities. Great curries, huge tandoori prawns and a choice of meat and vegetable *thali* and set meals for the indecisive.

Red
124 Thonglor Soi 9. Tel: 0-2259 7590. Open: daily L and D. **$$–$$$** Off map.
Contemporary Indian food in an attractive detached Thai house, where the chefs concoct surprises like lobster masala flambéed in cognac and curry spiced seafood risotto with shavings of Parmesan. They even drizzle some dishes with balsamic and olive oil. It's good, too.

International

Bed Supperclub
26 Sukhumvit Soi 11. Tel: 0-2651 3537. www.bedsupperclub.com Open: daily D only. **$$$$** 84 p275, E1
This extraordinary tubular construction has an all-white interior of beds and cushions that diners lounge on while they eat inspired fusion cuisine until 1am on weekends. Mixed-media shows accompany meals on multi-choice three-course set menus including dishes like Moroccan cous cous with chilli jam, and tuna steak coated in the North African marinade *chermoula*. Next door is Bed Bar, one of the city's top clubs.

Crêpes and Co
18 Sukhumvit Soi 12. Tel: 0-2251 2895. www.crepes.co.th Open: Mon–Sat 9am–midnight, Sun 8am–midnight. **$$$** 85 p275, E2
Reliable crêperie that specialises in unusual fillings. Also has tajine stews and other Moroccan dishes, and Greek favourites like the tomato and chicken casserole *kotopolou*. Tasteful wooden interior with Berber-style tented ceiling and world music on the sound system.

Greyhound
Fl 2 Emporium, Th Sukhumvit. Tel: 0-2664 8663. www.greyhound.co.th Open: daily 11am–9.15pm. **$$** Off map.
Trendy café with blackboard menus of European-influenced dishes such as Thai anchovy spaghetti with chilli, and glass-fronted displays of mouthwatering cakes. The all-white interior has *de rigueur* exposed ceiling pipes and there are balcony views of the Emporium mall shoppers.

Harvey
Thonglor Soi 9. Tel: 0-2712 9911. Open: daily 11.30am–2pm, 6–11pm. **$$$** Off map.
Comfortable, relaxed restaurant in a townhouse, serving dishes like *tagliolini* with sweet Scottish langoustine and black truffle sauce, and pan-fried foie gras on a bed of chestnut puree with raspberry and mango coulis. Fantastic wine list to suit all pockets.

Kuppa
39 Sukhumvit Soi 16. Tel: 0-2663 0450. Open: Tue–Sun 10am–11pm. **$$–$$$** Off map.
Bangkok's sophisticated thirtysomethings browse magazines and enjoy their *tête-à-tête* over espressos in a huge room of comfortable sofas, blond wood and brushed metal, with a giant coffee roaster in the corner. Decent international and Thai food. Art gallery upstairs.

The Seafood Bar
41 Somerset Lake Place, Sukhumvit Soi 16. Tel: 0-2663 8863. Open: Tue–Sun L and D. **$$$** Off map.
Fantastic imported seafood like Alaskan King Crab and 20 varieties of oyster, which come with tasting notes. Spicy, crusted Bali monkfish served with pork belly and a bed of white beans is typical of what they do very well here.

To Die For
H1 Place, 998 Sukhumvit Soi 55 (Soi Thonglor). Tel: 0-2381 4714. Open: daily 11–2am. **$$$** Off map.
French-Italian bar-restaurant set in a funky warehouse interior. Celebrity owners, like film director Nida Sudasna, help draw customers for homey meals of beef pockets stuffed with anchovy and capers, or asparagus and Parma ham deep-fried in filo pastry.

Italian

Enoteca
39 Sukhumvit Soi 27. Tel: 02-258-4386. www.enotecabangkok.com Open: daily D only. **$$$** Off map.
A very good menu in a small place with exposed brickwork, blackboard menu and arty posters. Saffron risotto flecked with liquorice, suckling pig with coffee-laced chestnut puree, and chocolate foam on rum-seasoned crushed ice are typically clever touches.

Giusto
Sukhumvit Soi 23. Tel: 0-2258 4321. www.giustobangkok.com Open: daily L and D. **$$$** Off map.
Stylish restaurant split into a bar and an octagonal, glass-walled main dining space. Specialities include foie gras terrine and grilled portobello mushrooms with soft cheese and truffle caviar. Interesting wine list that's also available in the attached wine bar.

Pizzeria Limoncello
17 Sukhumvit Soi 11. Tel: 0-2651 0707. Open: daily L and D. **$$–$$$** 86 p275, E1
Pizza parlour with the signature buzz of owner Gianmaria Zanotti of Zanotti *(see page 174)*. It throws big tasty pizzas from the wood-fired oven

to eat in its summery lemon and blue interior. The place is full most nights, so it's best to book ahead.

Rossini's
Sheraton Grande Sukhumvit, 250 Th Sukhumvit. Tel: 0-2649 8888. www.sheratongrandesukhumvit.com Open: daily D only. **$$$** 87 p275, E2
A faux medieval castle interior with cobbled floor, brick-arched doorway and domed ceiling gives a relaxed formality for grilled scallop and shrimp with borlotti bean sauce, *wagyu* rib-eye in balsamic sauce and other fine Italian fare.

Japanese

Koi
26 Sukhumvit Soi 20. Tel: 0-2663 4990/1. www.koirestaurantbkk.com Open: Tue–Sun D only. **$$$–$$$$** Off map.
Branch of a celebrity hang-out in Los Angeles serving Japanese-Californian fusions like miso-bronzed black cod and spicy seared albacore. Also has a glass-and-teak bar where catwalk models on free drinks raise the temperature four nights a week.

Korean

Jang Won
202/9–19 Sukhumvit Plaza, cnr Sukhumvit Soi 12. Tel: 0-2251 2636. Open: daily 10am–11pm. **$$** 88 p275, E2
One of many Korean cafés in this plaza. Diners sit in family-sized booths to enjoy Seoul food such as *ugeoji haejangguk* (spicy beef and vegetable soup), *dolsot bibimbap* (rice and beef cooked in hot stone pots) and sizzling *bulgogi* beef.

Middle Eastern

Nasir Al-Masri
4/6 Sukhumvit Soi 3/1. Tel: 0-2253 5582. Open: daily 24 hrs. **$$** 89 p275, E1
This area, nicknamed "Soi Arab", has numerous Middle Eastern joints selling kebabs and Lebanese dips and smokes of shisha. "Nasir the Egyptian" adds specialities from home, such as *fuul* (mashed beans in oil) and *molokhaya* (a spinach-like vegetable mixed with garlic).

Swiss

Chesa
5 Sukhumvit Soi 20. Tel: 0-2261 6650. www.chesa-swiss.com Open: daily 11am–11pm. **$$$** Off map.
Modern take on a traditional Swiss restaurant-bar complete with a *stammtisch* (a large communal table). Feast on very tasty Steinpilz risotto (with boletus mushrooms), cheese fondue or raclette with baby potatoes and pickles.

Thai

Baan Khanitha
36/1 Sukhumvit Soi 23. Tel: 0-2258 4181. Open: daily L and D. **$$$** Off map.
This first outlet of Baan Khanitha (second restaurant at 69 Th Sathorn Tai) in a charming old house is busy for its tasty foreigner-friendly flavours ranging from Chiang Mai sausage and spicy salads to curries like red duck with grapes.

Basil
Sheraton Grande Sukhumvit, 250 Th Sukhumvit. Tel: 0-2649 8888. www.starwood.com/bangkok Open: Mon–Sat L and D, Sun 11.30am–3pm (brunch). **$$$** 90 p275, E2
A hotel restaurant with a clean-lined modern elegance, that doesn't over-compromise local flavours for tourists. For something unusual, why not pick the stir-fried wild boar with chilli paste or papaya salad with bananas from the extensive menu of mainly traditional staples.

Bo.lan
42 Soi Pichai Ronnarong, Sukhumvit Soi 26. Tel: 0-2260-2962. www.bo.lan.com. Open: Tue–Sun D only; **$$$** Off map.
Cute townhouse operation run by alumni of London's Michelin-starred Thai restaurant Nahm. Very traditional recipes run through mysterious regional flavours in dishes like sweet cured pork in coconut cream and deep-fried fish with an eye-watering spicy-sour dipping sauce.

Cabbages and Condoms
10 Sukhumvit Soi 12. Tel: 0-2229 4610. Open: daily 11am–11pm. **$$–$$$** 91 p275, E2
This two-storey restaurant with a courtyard serves only average Thai standards, but it's a pleasant fairy-lights-in-the-trees environment and famous because of its work towards AIDS awareness. They give you free condoms as you leave.

Kalpapruek on First
Fl 1, Emporium, cnr Sukhumvit Soi 24. Tel: 0-2664 8410-1. Open: daily 11am–9.30pm. **$** Off map.
This clone of the all-white industrial design trend is notable for its fusion-style meals, such as spicy pork casserole. Dishes are prepared at the original restaurant off Thanon Silom *(see page 175)*.

Lemon Grass
5/1 Sukhumvit Soi 24. Tel: 0-2258 8637. Open: daily L and D. **$$** Off map.
This place is a little faded now, but still has the attractive setting of a house with antiques and garden. The food, despite being less fiery than purists would demand, is dependable. Try the pomelo salad or minced chicken with ginger and cabbage leaves.

Long Table
Fl 25, The Column Residence, Sukhumvit Soi 16. Tel: 0-2302 2557-9. www.longtablebangkok.com. Open: daily 11am–2am. **$$$** Off map.

Prices per person for a three-course meal without drinks:
$ = under B300
$$ = B300–800
$$$ = B800–1,600
$$$$ = over B1,600

Fantastic city views and a long communal table are focal points as you dine to a funky soundtrack. Lobster and avocado with a smoky *nam prik* and green mango salad and foie gras with dried shrimp and tamarind are both standouts.

Mahanaga
2 Sukhumvit Soi 29. Tel: 0-2662 3060. www.mahanaga.com Open: daily D only. **$$$** Off map.
The beautiful interior of Thai statuary, North African accents and Indian glass mosaics make this a popular visit despite its less-than-inspired fusion dishes such as lamb chop in *massaman* curry.

Rosabieng
3 Sukhumvit Soi 11. Tel: 0-2253 5868. Open: daily 11am–11pm. **$** 92 p275, E1
A white townhouse with alfresco seating in the spotlit garden, where a band plays pop and jazz standards. The food consists of standard Thai curries and plates like crispy fried morning glory, and shrimp and mango salad. A giant TV screen shows soccer.

Ruen Mallika
189 Sukhumvit Soi 22. Tel: 0-2663 3211-2. www.ruenmallika.com Open: daily 11am–10.30pm. **$$** Off map.
Rama I period wooden house with garden tables and traditional floor-cushion seating inside. Options include *kaeng tai pla* (pungent southern-style fish-stomach curry), which tastes better than it sounds, *mee krob* (sweet and herby crispy noodles) and deep-fried flowers.

Seafood Market and Restaurant
89 Sukhumvit Soi 24. Tel: 0-2661 1252-9. www.seafood.co.th Open: daily 11.30am–midnight. **$$$** Off map.
Bright, 1,500-seat dining hall with counter displays of fresh tiger shrimp, mud crab, giant sea perch and other seafood. Choose your products at the "market", then ask for them to be steamed, grilled or stir-fried as you like. Touristy and expensive, but fun dining.

Spring/Summer
199 Soi Promsri 2, Sukhumvit Soi 39. Tel: 0-2392 2747–8. www.springnsummer.com Open: daily L and D (Spring), noon–midnight (Summer), D only (Winter). **$$** Off map.
Three pleasing venues: Spring, in a glass-and-metal Art Deco house, has tasty modern Thai dishes like rice noodle rolls with fried seabass; Summer serves desserts amid aromas of chocolate and berries; and there's a bar, Winter, with beanbag seating on the lawn.

Vientiane Kitchen
8 Sukhumvit Soi 36. Tel: 0-2258 6171. www.vientiane-kitchen.com Open: daily noon–midnight. **$$** Off map.
Lao-Isaan food in a *sala* complex where musicians play traditional music under trees laden with fairy lights. This is a fun dining experience, with rice whisky, spicy salads, grilled marinated chicken and countryside faves like *kai mot daeng* (red-ant eggs).

Bars

Bull's Head
Sukhumvit Soi 33/1. Tel: 0-2259 4444. www.greatbritishpub.com Off map.
A loyal group of expats sup bitter at this long-standing English pub. Hosts a chess club, quiz nights and the bi-monthly Punchline Comedy Club, with international comedians.

Cheap Charlie's
1 Sukhumvit Soi 11. Tel: 0-2253 4648. 15 p275, E1
This legendary boozing hole takes the minimalist concept to new heights, by having only a bar – no roof, no walls – and a few stools in the street. It's cheap, and typical of the local penchant for setting up business wherever the mood takes you.

Face Bar
29 Sukhumvit Soi 38. Tel: 0-2713 6048-9. www.facebars.com Off map.
Face Bar is part of a highly tasteful Thai villa complex full of antiques and objets d'art. There's a mellow vibe in the bar and Indian and Thai restaurants to dine in.

Indus
71 Sukhumvit Soi 26. Tel: 0-2258 4900. www.indusbangkok.com Off map.
This Indian bar and restaurant in a 1960s house and garden is good for cocktails and conversation over hits of shisha pipe. DJs play bhangra sounds.

Londoner Brew Pub
Sukhumvit Soi 33. Tel: 0-2261 0238-40. www.the-londoner.com Off map.
The main draw at this cavernous basement pub is the microbrewed beer, which comes in several varieties, including a pleasant, sweetish English-style bitter. Has live bands and shows major sports on TV.

Thai Food Stalls

Sukhumvit Soi 38
Open: daily 4pm–2am. **$** Off map.
There's a good mix of rough-and-tumble food stalls at the entrance of this *soi*. Try rice gruel, spring rolls, spicy crab salad, crispy pork, *nam kaeng sai* (desserts with ice) and countless others. Wash them down with fruit juice or beer.

Vegetarian

Govinda
6/5/6 Sukhumvit Soi 22. Tel: 0-2663 4970. Open: Wed–Mon L and D. **$$** Off map.
High-standard, all-vegetarian Italian food that includes a variety of pastas, thin-crust pizzas, risottos and bakes. Even desserts such as tiramisu and cheesecake are egg-free. Also serves bread and ice cream made on the premises, and imported beers.

BANGKOK'S SUBURBS

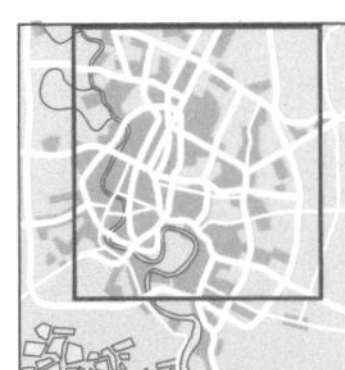

Accessible getaways from the big city's relentless pace are sleepy Nonthaburi by the river, delightfully green Rama IX Royal Park, child-friendly Dream World and sprawling Chatuchak Weekend Market – where incurable shopaholics are in seventh heaven

Main Attractions

CHATUCHAK WEEKEND MARKET
KO KRET
DREAM WORLD
SAFARI WORLD
PRASART MUSEUM

Maps and Listings

MAP OF BANGKOK'S SUBURBS, PAGE 186

There are some surprisingly rural retreats very close to the city centre, where the pace of life is a slow amble. But first there are the strobe lights of Bangkok's biggest dance clubs.

Ratchadaphisek

North along Sukhumvit Soi 21 is Ratchadapisek, an area served by Pra Ram 9 MRT station, and one of the city's designated Nightlife Zones. Most revellers head to the huge clubs of Royal City Avenue (RCA), although a few smaller bars along Thanon Ratchadapisek also draw young Thais. People come here, too, for the cultural shows of **Siam Niramit** (19 Thanon Tiamruammit, Huaykwang; tel: 0-2649 9222; www.siamniramit.com; shows at 8pm; charge) and the **Thailand Cultural Centre**, one of Bangkok's major venues for jazz and classical music concerts.

Chatuchak Weekend Market ❶

Next to Kamphaeng Phet MRT station, and the final stop on the Skytrain's northern line at Mo Chit station, is the sprawling **Chatuchak Weekend Market** (Sat–Sun 7am–6pm). Reputed to be the world's biggest flea market, Chatuchak's sheer scale and variety awes even the least enthusiastic of the estimated 400,000 shoppers that weave through the maze-like alleys every weekend. It's a heady assault on the senses, and an early start (arrive by 9am) is recommended to beat the soaring heat and crowds. Stumbling across gems of kitsch or culture is a great adventure, and you will find anything from crafts, home decor and clothing to flowers, snakes and violins.

Numerous cafés, snack and juice

LEFT: silk shawls on sale at the Chatuchak Weekend Market.

bars are dotted throughout the market with many staying busy long after the stalls pack up for the day. After sunset, the edge of the market on Thanon Kamphaengphet comes alive with a string of bars and coffee shops.

If the market overwhelms then retreat to the nearby **Chatuchak Park** (daily 4.30am–9pm; free). Built on land once owned by the State Railway, the park has a small **Hall Of Railway Heritage** museum (Sat–Sun 7am–3pm; free), with displays of old steam locomotives as well as other forms of transport, like London taxis. Alternatively, **Queen Sirikit Park** contains a botanical garden and the **Children's Discovery Museum** (Thanon Kamphaeng Phet 4; tel: 0-2615 7333; charge) with a playground, interactive displays and classes in things like cooking, music and car maintenance.

Nonthaburi 2

The provincial riverside town of **Nonthaburi**, some 10km (6 miles) north of Bangkok, feels a world away from the hectic city. To get there, take an express boat (around 45 mins) to the end of the line at Tha Nonthaburi pier. The journey passes under bridges and weaves past tiny tugboats, gilded temples and communities of stilted houses.

At Nonthaburi, spend some time exploring the streets and markets, or charter a longtail boat to explore the island of Ko Kret *(see below)* or the scenic canal of Khlong Om. A canal trip along Khlong Om takes you past durian *(see page 70)* plantations and water-bound communities. Five minutes upriver from Nonthaburi pier brings you to the temple of **Wat Chalerm Phra Kiet**, a beautifully restored 19th-century monastery seemingly set in the middle of nowhere.

Ko Kret 3

Further upstream from Nonthaburi is the car-free island of **Ko Kret**. Best reached by chartered longtail boat from Nonthaburi to Tha Pa Fai pier on Ko Kret, the island makes for a laid-back half-day tour, allowing tourists to soak up a relaxed pace of life more typical of the rest of Thailand. The island has no roads, and can be walked round in less than two hours. While there are no spe-

ABOVE: making clay lids in Nonthaburi.

Market Spread

Chatuchak opened in 1982, when the market was moved from Sanam Luang to make room for the Bangkok Bicentennial celebrations, and now its stalls spill onto surrounding streets. On Thanon Pahon Yothin, heading towards Saphan Khwai Skytrain station, traders sell Buddhist amulets; the workshops on the opposite side of Thanon Kamphaengphet 2 have reclaimed teak furniture; and on Thanon Kamphaengphet 1 is Or Tor Kor, possibly Bangkok's best fresh produce market. The streets lining Chatuchak's perimeter fence are busy with stalls selling CDs and DVDs, footwear and clothing. Vendors of food and drink are good places to stock up before you enter the market itself.

TIP

Most people get around Ko Kret either on foot or by bicycle, which are B40 a day at various spots en route. In many places, the path is only wide enough for two people abreast, so progress is at a gentle pace. Quicker options are motorbike taxis (there are no cars on the island) or river taxis, which cost about B20 to hop between each pier.

EAT

En route to Dream World, stop off at one of the flotilla of restaurant barges that moor up along Khlong Rangsit canal beside Thanon Rangsit Nakorn Nayok. They all specialise in a delicious noodle dish found only in this area.

cific attractions, the island is famous for its earthenware pottery studios. The villagers are primarily from the ethnic Mon group, a people of Indo-Burmese origin, who migrated to Central Thailand and were a strong regional influence from the 6th to the 11th centuries.

Air Force Museum ❹

Dedicated plane spotters will appreciate the nostalgic **Royal Thai Air Force Museum**, tucked away in several hangars at the Royal Thai Air Force Base behind Bangkok Airport (171 Thanon Phahonyothin; tel: 0-2534 1853; daily 8am–4pm; free).

The rare planes on display include the only Model I Corsaire in existence, one of only two Japanese Tachikawas left, and Thailand's first domestically built aircraft, the 1920s Model II Bomber Boripatr. There are also helicopters and jetfighters on display. The museum is geared more towards organised groups than the occasional wandering tourist, with little English-language signage to guide you around.

Dream World ❺

Those who have visited Disney World or other major US and European theme parks aren't going to be rendered speechless by Bangkok's **Dream World** (Km 7, Thanon Rangsit Nakorn Nayok; tel: 0-2533 1152; www.dreamworld.th.com/english; Mon–Fri 10am–5pm, Sat–Sun 10am–7pm; charge).

Nevertheless, the park, located west of Bangkok Airport, is worthwhile if you have a bunch of teenagers with you. The park comprises Dream World Plaza, Dream Garden, Fantasy Land and Adventure Land. A sightseeing train circles Dream Garden, while a cable car and monorail offer nice views of the park and surrounding rural areas.

Thrill seekers should head for Adventure Land, the most stomach-

BELOW: the main hall at Wat Thammamongkhon.

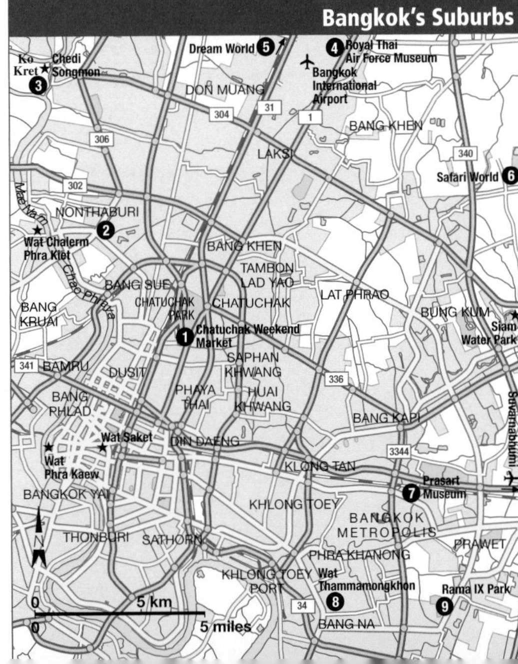

churning section of the park. Along with the two fairly tame rollercoasters, there is a Viking swinging ship, Super Splash log flume and Grand Canyon water ride. In Snow Town, locals get to experience frosty weather, with sled rides down a slope made of artificial snow.

Safari World 6

Some 45km (28 miles) northeast of Bangkok near Minburi is **Safari World**, a popular destination for Bangkok families (99 Thanon Ramindra; tel: 0-2914 4100-19; www.safariworld.com; daily 9am–5pm; charge).

The area is laid out as a safari park and a marine park, and you can either drive your car in or take an organised minibus tour with an English-speaking guide. Animals include giraffes, zebras, ostriches, rhinos and camels, while dolphins and sea lions perform acrobatics. Other attractions include water and jungle rides, stunt shows and animal feeding.

Prasart Museum 7

Little visited, partly because of its rather remote location in Huamak, is the **Prasart Museum** (9 Soi 4A Krungthep Kreetha; tel: 0-2379 3601; visits only by appointment Thur–Sun 10am–3pm; charge). Housed within a garden, the collection of antique Thai arts and crafts on display belong to a private collector, Prasart Vongsakul. The artefacts are contained in several magnificent buildings, all of which are replicas inspired by the region's architectural classics. These elegant structures include a European-style mansion, a Khmer shrine, teak houses from Thailand's North and Central regions, as well as a Thai and a Chinese temple.

Wat Thammamongkhon 8

At the eastern reaches of Thanon Sukhumvit at Soi 101 is the **Wat Thammamongkhon**, unique for its 95-metre (312ft) -high *chedi*, which at 14 storeys is the tallest in Bangkok and offers commanding views of the low-rise eastern suburbs (daily 6am–6pm; free). Built in 1963, the *chedi* is modern in design, containing study rooms for novice monks and a lift to the top circular shrine room. At its base is the Will Power Institute, which runs classes in Buddhist meditation. The three-level glass pavilion beside the temple houses a 14-tonne Buddha image and a 10-tonne sculpture of the Chinese goddess Guanyin, both carved from one solid slab of jade.

ABOVE: an afternoon escapade at the Rama IX Royal Park.
BELOW: stacks of crockery in Chatuchak Weekend Market.

Rama IX Royal Park 9

One of the city's largest green spaces, the 81-hectare (200-acre) **Rama IX Royal Park** offers a welcome escape from the city (daily 5.30am–6.30pm; charge). Unfortunately, the park's suburban locale in Sukhumvit 103 means taking a 20-minute taxi ride from the last Skytrain station at On Nut. In a city desperately thin on public greenery, the park's opening in 1987 as a 60th birthday tribute to the king was a welcome addition.

With a dome-covered botanical garden, canals and bridges, and a water lily pond, as well as Chinese and Japanese ornamental gardens, the park is a delight to explore. ❑

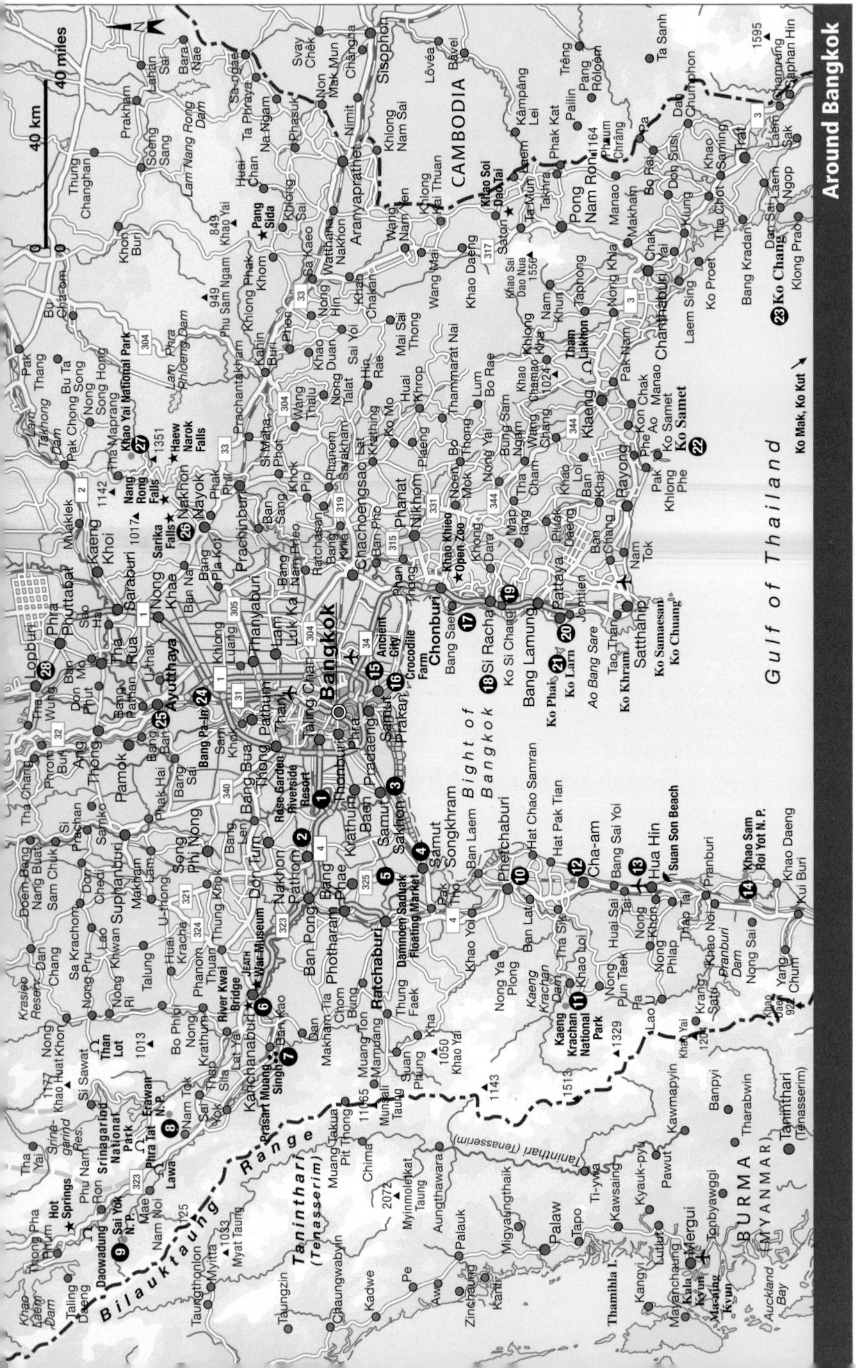
Around Bangkok
0 40 km
0 40 miles
Bangkok
Gulf of Thailand
Bight of Bangkok
CAMBODIA
BURMA (MYANMAR)
Bilauktaung Range
Tanintharí (Tenasserim)
Ayutthaya
Lopburi
Saraburi
Nakhon Nayok
Prachinburi
Chachoengsao
Chonburi
Si Racha
Pattaya
Rayong
Chanthaburi
Trat
Ko Samet
Ko Chang
Kanchanaburi
Ratchaburi
Nakhon Pathom
Samut Sakhon
Samut Songkhram
Samut Prakan
Phetchaburi
Cha-am
Hua Hin
Pranburi
Suphanburi
Aranyaprathet
Sa Kaeo
Khao Yai National Park
Sai Yok N.P.
Erawan N.P.
Srinagarind National Park
Kaeng Krachan National Park
Khao Sam Roi Yot N.P.
Ko Mak, Ko Kut

BANGKOK'S SURROUNDINGS

When Bangkok becomes overwhelming, an easy three to four hours' drive from the city offers a complete change of scene. Choose from ancient city ruins, sandy beaches dotted with sleepy villages or picturesque national parks and waterfalls

Bangkok has much to offer, but when you tire of its charms, there is an array of attractions within a few hours' drive, and some, especially beach destinations, can be extended into leisurely week-long stays. Getting around Thailand is relatively easy and cheap. There is a good network of flights to many provincial centres, and a regular, if slow, rail network. Buses are another alternative, although drivers can be reckless. Roads are usually decent, if you want to drive yourself *(see pages 238–9 for details on getting there)*.

The nearest and most accessible areas from Bangkok are in the flat, fertile Central Plains, which contain the remnants of former kingdoms and several expansive national parks. To the west are attractions like the Rose Garden cultural shows, the world's largest Buddhist shrine at Nakhon Pathom, and Kanchanaburi, with its legendary Bridge on the River Kwai. The area around Kanchanaburi has river rafting, trekking and waterfalls. South of Bangkok, towards Hua Hin, is where royalty and wealthy Thais have kept holiday homes for over a century.

The Eastern Seaboard has beach escapades, all the way from scandalous Pattaya, through Ko Samet, to the white sands of Ko Chang. And to the north, the ancient city of Ayutthaya is a grand repository of faded ruins, dating to the 14th century, when it functioned as Thailand's capital. Some say the best part about Ayutthaya is getting there – on a teakwood barge winding up the sinuous Chao Phraya river.

To the northeast of Bangkok, the main attraction is Khao Yai National Park, a favourite spot for Thais seeking picturesque mountains, waterfalls and a break from the city heat. ❑

PRECEDING PAGES: the three Khmer-style *prang* of Prang Sam Yot at Lopburi. **ABOVE LEFT:** fishing boat in Ban Bang Bao, Ko Chang. **ABOVE RIGHT:** Bang Pa-In summer palace.

WEST OF BANGKOK

Home to the world's tallest Buddhist monument, the historic River Kwai Bridge and spectacular waterfalls in rainforest-clad national parks, this region offers attractions for both history and culture enthusiasts as well as nature lovers

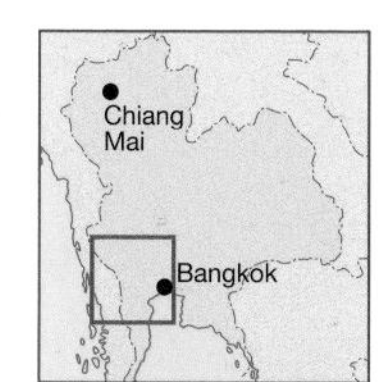

Main Attractions

ROSE GARDEN RIVERSIDE RESORT
PHRA PATHOM CHEDI
DAMNOEN SADUAK FLOATING MARKET
RIVER KWAI BRIDGE
PRASART MUANG SINGH
ERAWAN FALLS

Maps and Listings

MAP OF AROUND BANGKOK, PAGE 190
TRANSPORT INFORMATION, PAGE 239
ACCOMMODATION, PAGE 246

Further afield, in Bangkok's neighbouring provinces are a number of attractions that can be visited on day trips or as pleasant overnight breaks. The western provinces are only a short distance from the capital and share a border with nearby Burma (Myanmar). Most people heading in this direction make a brief stop in Nakhon Pathom province to gawk at the huge *chedi* that dominates the town, before heading to Kanchanaburi province, famous for its so-called "Bridge over the River Kwai" and its tragic wartime associations. However, equally fascinating are the seldom-visited coastal provinces of Samut Sakhon and the lush lowlands of Samut Songkhram.

Trains to Nakhon Pathom and Kanchanaburi leave from Bangkok Noi Railway Station daily. Buses run from Bangkok's southern bus terminal to all destinations in this chapter, and you can hop between them by bus or by hiring taxis or *songthaews*, which will gather at tourist sites and transport terminals. If you plan to make many stops it may be cheaper to hire a car *(see page 238)*.

LEFT: Erawan Falls at Erawan National Park, Kanchanaburi. **RIGHT:** bamboo dance demonstration at Rose Garden.

Rose Garden ❶

Some 32km (20 miles) west from Bangkok on Route 4 towards Nakhon Pathom is the **Rose Garden Riverside Resort** (tel: 0-3432 2588; www.rose-gardenriverside.com; daily 8am–6pm; charge). It has well-landscaped gardens with roses and orchids in addition to a resort-style hotel, a cultural centre, restaurants, tennis courts, an artificial lake with paddleboats, a spa and an excellent golf course.

The premier attraction here is the Thai Village Cultural Show

The Jumbo Queen contest which takes place at Samphran Elephant Ground annually on 1 May seeks a "well-padded" lady who "best exhibits the characteristics of the majestic pachyderm to persuade people to support the cause of elephant conservation in Thailand". Strange but true. More details at www.jumboqueen.com.

held daily in the garden. In a large arena, costumed actors perform folk dances to live traditional music and re-enact a traditional wedding ceremony and a Thai boxing match. Outside, after this, elephants put on their own show, moving huge teak logs as they would in the forests of the north. The elephants then carry tourists around the compound for a small fee. Otherwise, spend time browsing at the Cultural Village, with gift shops and demonstrations by weavers creating thread from silkworm cocoons.

Samphran Elephant Ground and Zoo

Just a stone's throw from the Rose Garden is the **Samphran Elephant Ground and Zoo**, another family-oriented attraction that provides a chance to trek on an elephant, feed the crocs and learn about the pachyderm's importance in Thai culture (tel: 0-2284 1873; www.elephantshow.com; daily 8am–5.30pm; charge). Other fauna on view include gibbons, macaques, pythons and a diverse flock of local birds.

At the Crocodile Show, men wrestle with these scaly creatures, while the Elephant Show explains Thailand's historical relationship with its national symbol. The war re-enactments are exciting displays, but the elephants' majesty somewhat diminishes when they're made to do silly things, like dance, race and play football in oversized shirts. After the show, you can feed the elephants or go on a 30-minute elephant trek.

BELOW: resident elephant at Samphran Elephant Ground and Zoo. **RIGHT:** the towering Phra Pathom Chedi.

Phra Pathom Chedi

Just 56km (35 miles) west of Bangkok, beyond the Rose Garden on Route 4, is the town of **Nakhon Pathom ❷**, known for the colossal **Phra Pathom Chedi** (Thanon Khwa Phra ; tel: 0-3424 2143; daily 6am–6pm; charge). Measuring 130 metres (420ft) in height, this golden landmark is claimed as the tallest Buddhist monument in the world, and possibly the oldest Buddhist site in the country.

The original small Sri Lankan-style *chedi* was erected to commemorate the arrival of Indian Buddhist missionaries who supposedly brought Buddhism to Thailand via Burma in 3 BC. The town Nakhon Pathom was settled in the 6th–11th centuries AD by the Dvaravati empire, a Mon civilisation whose culture flourished in Burma and Thailand. In the early 11th century the Khmers invaded from Angkor, overrunning the city and replacing the original *chedi* with a Brahman-style *prang*.

Then in 1057, King Anawrahta of Burma besieged the town, leaving the religious edifice in ruins. When King Mongkut (Rama IV) visited the old *chedi* in 1853, he was so impressed by its historical significance that he ordered the restoration of the temple. A new *chedi* was built, covering the older one; the present structure was completed by King Chulalongkorn (Rama V).

Set in a huge square park, the massive *chedi* rests upon a circular terrace and is accented with trees associated with the Buddha's life. Located in the compound is **Phra Pathom Chedi National Museum** (tel: 0-3424 2500; www.thailandmuseum.com; Wed–Sun 9am–4pm; charge), which is worth seeing for its artefacts, including tools, carvings and statuary from the Dvaravati period.

In former times, a visit to Nakhon Pathom was more than a day's journey, so it's not surprising that a number of palaces and residences were built for visiting royalty. One of them is **Sanam Chan Palace** (www.palaces.thai.net; Thur–Sun 9am–4pm; charge). Located 2km (1 mile) west of Phra Pathom Chedi along Thanon Rajamankha Nai, the palace comprises several buildings, including a Thai-style pavilion that is now used as government offices, and a building in the English Tudor style. The palace was commissioned by King Vajiravudh (Rama VI) in 1907. Be sure to see the **Yaleh Monument**, which honours Yaleh, the pet dog of Vajiravudh. The fierce dog, unpopular with the court, was poisoned by the king's attendants. Even as a statue, Yaleh looks insufferable.

Samut Sakhon ❸

A good way to approach the coastal port of **Samut Sakhon** (Ocean City), 28km (17 miles) from Bangkok, is by the Mae Khlong Railway line that connects to Thonburi in Bangkok. The line carries passengers on the 40-minute journey through the capital's suburbs, then through thriving vegetable gardens, groves of coconut and areca palms, and rice fields. A busy fishing port, Samut Sakhon (also called Mahachai) lies at the meeting of the Tachin River, the Mahachai Canal and the Gulf of Thailand. The main landing stage on the riverbank has a clock tower and a seafood restaurant.

At the fish market pier, it's possible to hire a boat for a round-trip to Samut Sakhon's principal temple, **Wat Chong Lom** at the mouth of the Tachin river. Most of the temple structures are modern, except for an old *viharn* (sermon hall) immediately to the right of the temple's river landing. The *viharn* dates back about a century. The extensive grounds overlooking the water are nicely laid out with shrubs and flowering trees.

ABOVE: close-up of gold-leaf offerings covering a Buddha image at Phra Pathom Chedi. **BELOW:** schoolchildren at Phra Pathom Chedi.

There is also a bronze statue of King Chulalongkorn commemorating his visit to the temple.

Samut Songkhram ❹

From Samut Sakhon, cross the river to the railway station on the opposite side. Here, board a second train for another 40-minute trip to the province of **Samut Songkhram**, 74km (46 miles) southwest from Bangkok, on the banks of the Mae Khlong river. The journey goes through broad salt flats, with their picturesque windmills slowly being turned by the sea breezes. Thailand's smallest province, Samut Songkhram has abundant fruit orchards. Pomelo, jackfruit, rose apple, lychee, mango, as well as the more ubiquitous banana and coconuts, are harvested here before being loaded onto the ice-packed vending carts that trundle the streets of Bangkok.

Samut Songkhram itself is just another fishing town; wandering around its wharf is an olfactory and visual experience. Teak barges can be hired for private dinner cruises up the river (ask at riverside restaurants), and the area is known for swarms of fireflies that magically illuminate the shoreline of lamphu trees in the evenings.

ABOVE: Damnoen Saduak Floating Market. **BELOW:** Samut Sakhon railway station.

King Buddhalertla Naphalai Memorial Park

From Samut Songkhram, you can make a fairly short detour by bus or taxi to the Amphawa District to visit **King Buddhalertla Naphalai Memorial Park**, also known as Rama II Historical Park (park daily 9am–6pm; museum Wed–Sun 9am–4pm; charge), situated at the birthplace of Rama II. This small museum houses displays of art and crafts from the early Rattanakosin period in four beautifully reconstructed teakwood stilted houses, illustrating how Thai people lived during the rule of King Rama II. In the well-maintained gardens around the museum are rare species of trees, some of which are mentioned in classical Thai literature.

Also found in Amphawa is the **Amphawa Floating Market**, which anchors in front of the old Wat Amphawa each Friday, Saturday and Sunday afternoon. About a 10-minute walk from the historical park, the market is smaller and more authentic than Damnoen Saduak *(see page 197)*.

Don Hoi Lot

Another option, accessible by car or longtail boat from Samut Songkhram, is **Don Hoi Lot**, at the mouth of the Mae Khlong River. Don Hoi Lot is in fact a bank of fossilised shells that has become a popular attraction with locals. It's a great place to enjoy fresh seafood and tube-like clams (*hoi lot* in Thai means straw clams). In the late afternoon when the tide is low, villagers enthusiastically search the muddy estuary for clam burrows. They spread a little bit of lime powder at the entrance of the holes, and when the clams become agitated and come out of the ground, they are eagerly fished out.

Damnoen Saduak Floating Market ❺

From Samut Songkhram, hire a longtail boat for a trip up the Mae Khlong river to **Damnoen Saduak Floating Market** (daily 7am– 1pm). An early morning departure is necessary if you want to beat the tour buses from Bangkok, 65km (40 miles) away, that flock to this famous floating market in Ratchaburi province by 10am.

While it is possible to walk along the bankside lined with souvenir stands, it's better to hire a longtail boat to get a better sense of the water-bound commercial bustle. Be prepared though for the worst: this 100-year-old market is little more than a sideshow today, with tourists clambering to snap pictures of the colourful fruit- and vegetable-laden wooden vessels, oared by smiling sun-beaten women wearing wide-brimmed straw hats.

If you've hired your own longtail boat, it might be worthwhile asking the boatman to take you deeper into the canals where you can get a glimpse of the canal communities.

KANCHANABURI

Located around 130km (75 miles) west of Bangkok, the sleepy provincial town of **Kanchanaburi** ❻ is well worth the two-hour drive it takes to get there. It can be done as a busy day trip but, better yet, plan for a more relaxing overnight, with an evening spent on the banks of the Kwae Yai river.

Kanchanaburi received widespread publicity in the last half-century for its infamous railway, which was built during World War II by Allied POWs and Asian labourers, under the watch of the Japanese occupying army. Thousands of lives were lost as the ill-equipped prisoners struggled in appalling conditions to complete over 400km (249 miles) of railway track, called the "Death Railway", linking Thailand with Burma. Despite its association with the war and the railway, Kanchanaburi remains a laid-back provincial town.

ABOVE: Damnoen Saduak Floating Market. **BELOW:** the famous bridge spanning the Kwai River.

TIP

Instead of staying at a land-based hotel in Kanchanaburi, opt for a floating guesthouse moored by the riverbank instead. Be warned though: while these are atmospheric, they can also get very noisy during weekends, thanks to discos and karaoke boats packed with drunken young Thais on a night of revelry.

ABOVE: JEATH War Museum. **BELOW:** only the eight curved sections of the "Bridge over the River Kwai" are original; the rest of it was rebuilt after World War II.

Situated close to the Burmese border, it has several interesting temples, as well as nearby caves, waterfalls, forests and the remnants of a 13th-century Khmer palace.

River Kwai Bridge

Spanning the Kwae Yai river (also known as Kwai Yai), the latticed steel **Bridge over the River Kwai** (which takes its name from a movie of the same name) has become a memorial for the fallen. It can be reached by boat or rickshaw from Kanchanaburi town. The bridge has lost some of its significance to tourist commercialisation, but walking across it is a sobering experience. A steam locomotive used shortly after the war is displayed beside the tiny Kanchanaburi station platform, along with an ingenious Japanese supply truck that could run on both road and rail. Floating restaurants and hotels line both banks of the river.

The bridge itself was the second of two bridges, built side by side, crossing the river; the earlier wooden structure was completed in 1942, with the sturdier steel bridge erected by May 1943. Both bridges became a constant target for Allied bombers and were eventually bombed out of action in 1945. Only the eight curved segments on each side of the current structure are original; the rest was rebuilt after the war as part of Japan's war reparations.

The tragic saga of the bridge was represented on celluloid in the 1957 Film *Bridge over the River Kwai*, directed by David Lean and starring the late Sir Alec Guinness. Winner of seven Academy Awards, this version contains several historic inaccuracies, the most blatant of which was that the bridge was destroyed by commandos, when in fact it was bombed by allied planes.

Today, most of the old railway tracks have been removed, except for a section that runs from Kanchanaburi west to the terminus at **Nam Tok** near Burma. The 50km (30-mile) journey takes about 90 minutes to complete and the train passes over the reconstructed bridge, the old wooden tracks creaking beneath.

World War II Museum

Located near the bridge is the **World War II Museum** (395–403 River Kwai Road; tel: 034-512 596; daily 7am–6pm; charge), also known as the Art Gallery and War Museum. It contains

Death Railway

The Japanese began work on a railway between Thailand and Burma in 1942. For most of its 400km (260-mile) length, the railway followed the river valley because this allowed its construction simultaneously in different areas. In the end, nearly 15km (9 miles) of bridges were completed. The Japanese forced some 250,000 Asian labourers and 61,000 Allied POWS to construct 260km (160 miles) of rail on the Thai side, leading to the Three Pagodas Pass on the Thai–Burmese border. An estimated 100,000 Asian labourers and 16,000 Allied pows lost their lives during 1942–5 from beatings, starvation and disease. It is said that one prisoner died for every sleeper laid.

an odd mixture of exhibits, some of which have nothing to do at all with the war. But if you are into kitsch, there's plenty to interest you. Among life-sized statues of significant war figures like Hitler, Churchill and Hirohito are murals of past winners of the Miss Thailand pageant.

JEATH War Museum

The small but informative **JEATH War Museum** (tel: 034-515 203; daily 8am–6pm; charge), tucked away in the grounds of Wat Chaichumpol on Thanon Pak Phraek in the southern end of Kanchanaburi town, will give you a better appreciation of the enormous obstacles the prisoners faced. Its peaceful locale on the banks of the Mae Khlong river (the larger river which splits into the two tributaries of Kwae Yai and Kwae Noi), shadowed by a 500-year-old *samrong* tree, provides for a quiet moment of poignant reflection.

The acronym JEATH comes from the first letter of some of the principal countries that were involved in this regional conflict during World War II, namely Japan, England, America, Thailand and Holland. The museum is split into two buildings, the larger of which is a long bamboo hut similar to those that housed the POWs during their construction of the Siam–Burma railway. Inside is a collection of poignant photographs, sketches, paintings, newspaper clippings and other war memorabilia, giving you an idea of the harsh conditions they endured.

Death Railway Museum

Equally fascinating is the **Death Railway Museum** (73 Jaokunnen Road; tel: 034 512 721; www.tbrconline.com; daily 9am–5pm; charge) at the Thailand–Burma Railway Centre, just adjacent to the Allied War Cemetery *(see page 200)*. The museum has eight galleries that trace the history and recount the sufferings of the people involved, without making biased judgement. It even has a full-scale replica of the original wooden bridge. The museum was founded by Australian Rod Beattie, the local supervisor of the Commonwealth War Graves Commission.

ABOVE AND BELOW: bomb display and archive photographs at the JEATH War Museum.

ABOVE: over the years, trees and vegetation have grown and embedded their roots in the ruins of Prasart Muang Singh. **BELOW:** Allied War Cemetery, Kanchanaburi.

Allied War Cemetery

At the **Kanchanaburi Allied War Cemetery** (daily 7am–6pm; free) nearly 7,000 Allied soldiers are buried or commemorated, representing less than half of the 16,000 who lost their lives in the war. Immaculate green lawns planted with colourful flowers add a sense of serenity to the graves of the British, Australian and Dutch soldiers lined row upon row (the US dead were repatriated). Look at the grave markers and you'll notice that most of the young men who died for their countries were under the age of 30. Its location, however, beside noisy Thanon Saengchuto detracts from the solemnity of the place.

Located in a more tranquil setting is the **Chung Kai Allied War Cemetery**, found southwest of Kanchanaburi town across the river (daily 7am–6pm; free). Another 1,750 POWs are buried at this site.

AROUND KANCHANABURI

For those who opt to stay overnight in Kanchanaburi, the surrounding countryside holds plenty of surprises. There are a couple of cave temples found within limestone crags on the southern outskirts of Kanchanaburi, some requiring nimble legwork in order to navigate the claustrophobic passageways that lead to eerily-lit meditation cells filled with Buddha images. While they are generally safe, don't venture into the more remote caves unaccompanied: in 1996 a British female tourist was murdered by a drug-crazed monk at Wat Tham Kao Pun.

One of the frequently visited cave temples is that of **Wat Tham Mangkhon Thong**, primarily known for its "floating nun" (daily 8am–5pm; charge). An old nun, who has since passed away, used to float on her back in a pool of water while in a state of meditation. Today, a young disciple gives her own interpretation of the ritual – in return for a fee – for busloads of gaping Asian tourists.

Prasart Muang Singh ❼

Located 43km (27 miles) west of Kanchanaburi, the Khmer ruins of **Prasart Muang Singh** (daily 8am–5pm; charge) are situated in a manicured park. The site makes for a great picnic as it is beside the picturesque Kwae Noi river (a smaller tributary of the Kwae Yai). The central sanctuary of this 13th-century temple complex points east, and is in direct alignment with its more grandiose sister, Angkor Wat in Cambodia. Although nowhere near as impressive or intricate as Angkor Wat, Prasart Muang Singh is still a fascinating testament to just how far west the Khmer empire stretched at the height of its power. On the same site is a small exhibition hall containing duplicates of Khmer sculptures, while near the river is a Neolithic burial site displaying partially uncovered skeletons.

Erawan National Park 8

Alternative trips in the vicinity include the spectacular seven-tiered **Erawan Waterfall**, found in **Erawan National Park** (daily 8am–4.30pm; charge). The falls are best visited during and just after the rainy season (May–Nov), when the water is at full flow. Situated some 70km (40 miles) north of Kanchanaburi, Erawan Falls can become quite congested with locals who visit the park at weekends and on public holidays.

The route to the waterfall starts from the national park office. The climb up to level five of the waterfall is manageble; getting up to the slippery sixth and seventh levels is not recommended unless you are fit and have enough derring-do. You can cool off at the inviting natural pools (don't forget your swimsuit) at the base of each of the tiers. The rocks at the highest level are said to resemble the three-headed elephant Erawan, hence its name.

There are several hiking trails in the park, which covers some 550 sq km (212 sq miles) and comprises mainly deciduous forests with limestone hills rising up to 1,000 metres (3,281ft). One of the more popular hiking trails is the 90-minute Khanmak–Mookling trail; the 1,400-metre/yd-long circular trail starts from the national park office. Also taking 90 minutes, the Wangbadan Cave trail takes you through bamboo and evergreen forest along a 1,350-metre/yd-long route.

ABOVE: Erawan National Park.

Sai Yok National Park 9

Less visited is **Sai Yok Waterfall** in **Sai Yok National Park** (daily 8am–4.30pm; charge). The waterfall is a little more remote at 100km (62 miles) northwest of Kanchanaburi and best undertaken on an overnight tour. The national park itself covers over 500 sq km (193 sq miles) of mainly teak forests, with one side of it bordering Myanmar (Burma). Apart from the stunning cascade (again best seen in the rainy season, or just after), the park is known as the habitat of the smallest known mammal in the world – Kitti's Hog-Nosed Bat, also known as the Bumblebee Bat. Found in Sai Yok's limestone caves in 1974, the creature, which weighs a mere 2 grams (and hardly larger than a bumblebee), has been declared an endangered species.

More adventurous travellers should enquire in lodges and hotels in these national park areas about organised kayaking, rafting and mountain biking trips. ❑

TIP

There are some 140 gazetted national parks in Thailand, a number of which are easily accessed from Bangkok, like Erawan, Sai Yok, Kaeng Krachan and Khao Sam Roi Yot. For more information on Thai national parks, look up www.thaiparks123.com or www.trekthailand.net.

SOUTH OF BANGKOK

A few hours' journey south of the capital brings you to exclusive beach retreats and spa resorts. Meanwhile, large mammals find sanctuary in the mountains and rainforests of Kaeng Krachan, the largest national park in Thailand

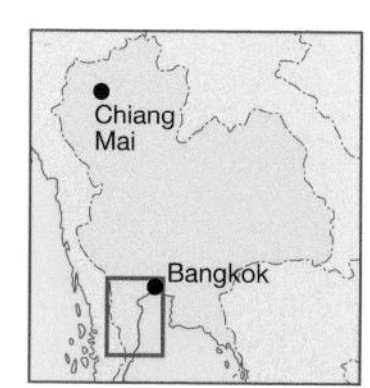

Main Attractions

WAT YAI SUWANNARAM
KHAO WANG
CHA-AM
KAENG KRACHAN NATIONAL PARK
HUA HIN

Maps and Listings

MAP OF BANGKOK'S SURROUNDINGS, PAGE 190
TRANSPORT INFORMATION, PAGE 239
ACCOMMODATION, PAGES 246–7

The diverse towns of Cha-am and Hua Hin, south of Bangkok, are popular hangouts for the city's twenty-somethings, for upper class socialites, for expats and holiday-homers in Thailand on spa leave. The trend started with royalty as far back as 1860 when King Mongkut built a summer palace in Phetchaburi. The king also liked to visit the nearby forested areas, now designated national parks. The current royal family has its own summer palace in the region, in Hua Hin.

There are several trains daily from Hualamphong Station to Petchaburi and Hua Hin, and buses from the Southern Bus Terminal to Cha-am, Phetchaburi and Hua Hin.

Phetchaburi ⑩

Historically rich **Phetchaburi**, some 120km (75 miles) south of Bangkok, is one of Thailand's oldest towns and has been an important trade and cultural centre since the 11th century. Lying on the Phetchaburi river, the town has come under the influence of the Mon, Khmers and Thais at various times, and has over 30 temples that reflect the different cultures and architectural styles of its past invaders.

Some of the more important religious sites in Phetchaburi – usually pronounced "Petburi" – include the laterite Khmer *prang* of **Wat Kamphaeng Laeng**, and **Wat Yai Suwannaram**, thought to have once been a residence of King Suea. It is very evocative of its 17th-century heritage, with many ornately tiled buildings in a low-walled complex. Its fine murals are among the oldest in Thailand, while the stucco work is of a style that predates the symmetric Ayutthayan influences that came to dominate

LEFT: tourists making the trek up to Khao Wang. **RIGHT:** the distinctive Khmer structures of Wat Kamphaeng Laeng.

ABOVE: rope swing and suspension bridge spanning the river at Kaeng Krachan National Park.
BELOW: Phra Nakon Kiri Historical Park.

Thai architecture. The old library building on stilts in the middle of the pond illustrates an early method of protecting manuscripts from termites. Another key temple is **Wat Mahathat**. This 14th-century site has relics of the Buddha enshrined, but is probably better known for the intricate depictions of angels and other mythical creatures in the low-relief stucco on the gables of the main buildings. It's easy to hire a tuk-tuk to hop between temples in Phetchaburi.

Just west of town is a 92-metre (302ft) -high hill, locally known as **Khao Wang**, topped by the summer palace of King Mongkut (Rama IV). Commissioned in 1860, the complex is also known as the **Phra Nakhon Khiri Historical Park** and contains a mélange of Eastern and Western architectural styles; many of its buildings offer fabulous panoramas of the vicinity, especially at sunset.

The hilltop buildings include three throne halls (two of which have been turned into a museum housing furniture and collectables that belonged to King Mongkut), an observatory (the king was a keen astronomer), a large white *chedi* and the **Wat Maha Samanaram** (daily 8am–4pm; free). The steep trail to the summit winds through woods populated by monkeys, though the easier option is to take the cable tram to the top.

An interesting excursion only 5km (3 miles) from town is the **Khao Luang** cave, which is adorned with stalactites, small *chedi* and Buddha images and is illuminated by shafts of sunlight that filter down from holes in the roof. Beside the cave's mouth is **Wat Bunthawi**, a temple with wonderfully carved wooden door panels.

As the railway line south brought greater access to this part of Thailand, a number of palaces were erected for the royal family in times past. Situated beside the Phetchaburi river, **Ban Puen Palace** (daily 8am–4pm; charge) built in 1910 for King Chulalongkorn (the same year in which he died), this stately home was designed by a German architect and would look more at home in Germany's Black Forest than the coastal flats of Phetchaburi. The grandiose palace has a luxurious interior and is surrounded by a manicured garden.

Kaeng Krachan National Park ⓫

Located some 60km (37 miles) southwest of Phetchaburi town is the vast 3,000-sq-km (1,158-sq-mile) **Kaeng Krachan National Park** (daily 6am–6pm; charge). The park – the largest in Thailand – covers almost half of Phetchaburi province and is a haven for numerous species of large mammals, including tigers, elephants, leopards, bears, deer, gibbons and monkeys. The topography varies between rainforest and savannah grasslands, and includes a freshwater lake and rugged mountain ranges.

It is possible to ascend the park's tallest peak, the 1,207-metre (3,960ft) **Phanoen Tung**, for superb views of the lush countryside, or trek to the 18-tier **Tho Thip Waterfall**. Swimming and boating in the vast reservoir created by **Kaeng Krachan Dam** are other popular activities.

On the southern edge of Kaeng Krachan, towards the mountain range that divides Thailand from Burma, is the spectacular **Pala-U Waterfall**. Best seen during the rainy season, the falls have 11 tiers and are surrounded by dense forest.

Considering Kaeng Krachan's proximity to Bangkok, surprisingly few tourists venture here. Trekking is the main activity in the park, with forestry officials for hire as guides at the park's headquarters at the end of the road beyond Kaeng Krachan Dam. Accommodation consists of basic park lodgings, but the easiest way to visit the park is on a tour organised by many hotels in nearby Hua Hin *(see page 206)*.

Cha-am 12

The weekend getaway of **Cha-am** is a long stretch of beach that has become popular with groups of young Bangkokians. Around 40km (25 miles) south of Phetchaburi, the resort is very peaceful during weekdays, with plenty of delicious seafood restaurants to choose from. Outside of Thailand's university breaks, the resort is very quiet, so if a little more nightlife suits you, then Hua Hin is better geared up.

Roughly 10km (6 miles) south of Cha-am, heading towards Hua Hin, is the grand seaside abode called **Marukhathayawan Palace** (daily 8am–5pm; charge). Built in 1923 from golden teakwood, the airy stilted structures are European in style and have been beautifully renovated and painted in summery pastel shades. Interconnected by raised covered walkways, the palace buildings were a retreat for King Vajiravudh (Rama VI) for the last two years before he died.

Hua Hin 13

Prachuap Kiri Khan is Thailand's narrowest province and its coast is fringed with mountains and lovely quiet beaches, the most popular of which is the 5km (3-mile) -long sandy beach at **Hua Hin**. Located 203km (126 miles) from Bangkok and taking less than four hours by road or rail, the former fishing village of Hua Hin has long had an air of exclusivity, thanks to its residences maintained by the Thai royalty and Bangkok's wealthy elite. Partly because of this it retains more of a family ambience than most other beach destinations in Thailand.

The royal connection can be seen at the seafront teakwood summer abode called **Klai Kangwon Palace**, which means "far from worries". Built

TIP

Organised tours to Kaeng Krachan National Park usually include a stop at the Wildlife Rescue Centre (daily 8am–5pm) in Phetchaburi, where you can visit rescued gibbons and hear about the centre's uphill battle to save local wildlife.

LEFT: Hua Hin railway station. **BELOW:** makeshift stalls at Cha-am beach.

in 1926 at the northern end of Hua Hin beach by command of King Rama VII, the Spanish-style villa is still regularly used by the royal family and is not open to the public.

One of the country's first rail lines linked Bangkok to Hua Hin at the start of the 20th century, transporting the capital's wealthy to the southern shores. Hua Hin thus had the aura of a European spa town, with the royals coming here for the clean air. Today, the coastal town is beginning to reclaim that mantle as several exclusive spa retreats – like the award-winning Chiva Som – cater to the holistic needs of international jetsetters. A string of brand-name resorts like Hilton, Hyatt and Marriott are also represented here, along with local (and equally expensive) concerns like Dusit and Anantara.

After the palace, **Hua Hin Railway Station** is perhaps the second most famous building in town. Although the bucolic lane in which it sits is now busy with 21st-century traffic, the dainty, traditional Thai teak structure maintains enough charm to evoke the 1923 scene of its creation.

ABOVE: Hua Hin is blessed with bountiful seafood and fine restaurants that serve dishes like this grilled squid salad. **BELOW:** one of the Hua Hin station staff.

Five hundred metres/yds towards the beach is another historic landmark, the 1922 colonial-style **Hotel Sofitel Central**, formerly the Railway Hotel, which masqueraded as the Phnom Penh Hotel in the 1984 movie *Killing Fields*.

Today, the sweeping run of Hua Hin beach is backed by opulent summer homes along with a slew of faceless condo developments. Hua Hin is fast gaining an international reputation as a place to retire, and more and more condos and beach houses are being built to accommodate the upsurge in interest. The beach lacks the character of Thailand's palm-fringed island bays, but is great for long strolls. Pony rides set off from near the main drag. The beaches south of town, **Suan Son** and **Khao Tao**, are rather nicer and more secluded.

Hua Hin activities

Although Hua Hin's nightlife has picked up in the last few years, it is still relatively quiet, with the restaurants and bars clustered mainly in a small area around Thanon Naresdamri and on the parallel Thanon Phunsuk. Soi Bintabaht has the highest concentration of beer bars, and the pier restaurants on Naresdamri grill some of the best seafood in

town, in the most atmospheric spot.

Along with this upsurge in nightlife, a number of new restaurants have appeared too. While Hua Hin has always been known as a place for fresh seafood, the diversity of culinary options has expanded beyond just Thai, with Japanese, Korean, Scandinavian, German, French and Italian, reflecting the nationality of tourist arrivals.

Hua Hin sees a lot of activities and events, usually organised at weekends so that the Bangkok crowds can join in. These include the annual **Hua Hin Jazz Festival** in June and the **Hua Hin Regatta**, which attracts sailors to the town each July or August.

Outside Hua Hin

Visible a few kilometres south of town is **Khao Takiab** (Chopstick Hill). This rocky outcrop has a steep climb to its summit but the views of the surrounding coast are worth the sweat. Of course, it's incredibly hot, and no one would blame you for taking a tuk-tuk. There's an unremarkable temple at the top with a large Buddha statue standing facing the sea, around which are resident troops of boisterous macaques.

The beaches further south of Hua Hin down towards **Pranburi** are also starting to see a number of tastefully designed boutique resorts, like the **Evason** and **Aleenta**, making for a stylish, if expensive, escape from Bangkok.

Located around 50km (31 miles) south of Hua Hin, **Khao Sam Roi Yot National Park** ⓮ translates as "Three Hundred Mountain Peaks" and refers to the limestone pinnacles jutting up from the park's mangrove swamps to heights above 600 metres (1,900ft). Carved from the rugged coastline and a haven for kayakers, the park has superb beaches, marshes, forest walks and caves. Wildlife includes a multitude of birdlife, crab-eating macaques and the rare serow – a mountain goat-antelope.

Tham Phraya Nakhon is the most famous attraction here; the huge cave has a large sinkhole that allows shafts of light to shine down and illuminate the grand Thai-style pavilion (*sala*) built in the 1890s for a visit by King Chulalongkorn. Other noteworthy caves are **Tham Sai** and **Tham Kaeo**, the latter meaning "Jewel Cave" and named after its glistening stalactite and rock formations. ❑

LEFT: brown gibbon, Khao Sam Roi Yot National Park (**ABOVE**).

In 1868, King Mongkut, an astute astronomer, visited Khao Sam Roi Yot National Park to view a total eclipse of the sun, which he had foretold. The king's prediction, to the astonishment of local astrologers, was only four minutes off the mark. Sadly, Mongkut contracted malaria from this trip and died a week after his return to Bangkok.

SINGHA

EASTERN SEABOARD

Southeast of Bangkok there are diverse attractions that include an extraordinary architectural model of the whole country, wildlife parks with tigers, the touristy anything-goes beach town of Pattaya and unspoilt palm-fringed islands such as Ko Samet and Ko Chang

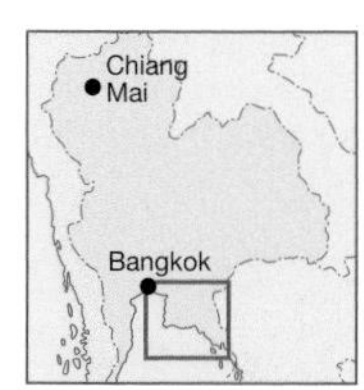

Main Attractions

ANCIENT CITY
SRIRACHA TIGER ZOO
PATTAYA
THE SANCTUARY OF TRUTH, PATTAYA
KO SAMET
KO CHANG

Maps and Listings

MAP OF BANGKOK'S SURROUNDINGS, PAGE 190
TRANSPORT INFORMATION, PAGE 239
ACCOMMODATION, PAGES 246–7

In Samut Prakan Province, 30km (20 miles) or about half an hour's drive southeast of Bangkok, are two attractions – Muang Boran, or Ancient City, and the Crocodile Farm and Zoo, which claim to be the world's biggest open air museum and the world's largest crocodile farm, respectively.

Beyond Samut Prakan is Thailand's Eastern Seaboard, which runs from Chonburi province all the way to Trat province, near the Cambodian border, from the ugliness of the country's largest industrial zone, known as "The Detroit of the East", to some beautiful beaches and scenic islands.

Take a bus from Bangkok's Eastern Bus Terminal to reach Samut Prakan, then hire a *songthaew* or take a local bus to the Ancient City. All other destinations in this chapter are on a different route to Samut Prakan, but the quickest access to these is also from the Eastern Bus Terminal.

Ancient City ⓯

One of Bangkok's best-value tourist attractions is the surprisingly under-visited **Ancient City** or Muang Boran (tel: 0-2323 9253; www.ancientcity.com; daily 8am–5pm; charge). The park officially changed its name to Ancient Siam in 2008, although everyone (including the website) still calls it by the original name. The parkland site is loosely shaped to represent Thailand, with over 100 monuments, palaces and other buildings placed approximately in their correct geographical location. Some are life-size or near life-size reproductions of both existing and long-lost structures, notably royal complexes from the ruins of the former capital, Ayutthaya. Others are completely relocated buildings that

LEFT: lounging at Ao Thian (Candlelight Beach) in Ko Samet. **RIGHT:** Sanphet Prasat Palace in the Ancient City.

TIP

The Erawan Museum is a good stop-off on the way from Bangkok to the Ancient City.

would otherwise have been demolished. The result is an educational celebration of Thai history and architecture. And, while these may be idealised tableaux, there's not an ounce of Disney about any of it. Its size means it's not practical to tour the Ancient City on foot. You can drive around it (charge), rent bicycles or golf carts at the gate, or take a tram tour, which is available with an English-speaking guide (charge).

It's rewarding to wander round the whole place, which could take around four hours, but for highlights head to the Central region, where the centrepiece is the 15th-century Sanphet Prasat Palace, the main royal residence of the early Ayutthaya period. It was notable at the time because it heralded a new architecture that differed from the earlier Khmer and Sukhothai styles in details such as tapering pillars, pedimented doorframes and overlapping roofing. The style became known as the Ayutthaya School and was to dominate the landscape well into the Rattanakosin era four centuries later. The palace was completely destroyed when the Burmese sacked Ayutthaya in 1767. Superb craftsmanship has been allied to painstaking research, using archaeological remains, contemporary accounts and drawings, and details from similar period buildings, to produce an exquisite structure in its own right, even down to interior murals and ornamentation. Close by are other replica monuments of the country's rich "Rice Bowl", such as the beautiful Dusit Maha Prasat Palace and the Phra Kaew Pavilion from the current Grand Palace in Bangkok.

RIGHT: Buddha statue, Ancient City.

The site also has period houses of various styles, statues depicting famous battles, and mock-ups of regional villages with local crafts for sale. There are small open-air cafés around the grounds serving Thai food, with several near the Floating Market. Aside from the monuments, the park offers a peaceful and secluded environment – particularly if you go mid-week – and one of the charms is that you are left free to wander in and out of buildings at will, with no staff, barriers or stuffy formalities. It's a real treasure.

The Erawan Museum

Lek Viriyaphant, the businessman–philanthropist who built both the Ancient City and The Sanctuary of Truth *(see page 214)*, left another cultural legacy in the shape of The Erawan Museum (Sukhumvit Soi 119, Samut Prakan; tel: 0-2371 3135; www.erawan-museum.com; daily 8am–3pm; charge). Housed in an extraordinary 43-metre (140ft)-high, three-headed elephant that represents Erawan, the animal ridden by the god Indra in Hindu mythology, the museum is divided into three sections. The basement "Underworld" contains mainly Chinese and Thai pieces from the founder's private antiques collection. The middle section, "Earth", has a stained-glass domed ceiling and examples of Thai art styles from the country's most celebrated craftsmen. These include stucco work from Phetchaburi, hammered tin plating from Nakhon Si Thammarat and ceramics from Ampawa. In the hollow interior of the elephant's belly, "Heaven" is an odd, hippy-esque purple room with abstract murals and antique Buddha statues. Because the museum contains many Buddha images it has assumed the level of religious pilgrimage for many people, who come to a shrine in the gardens to make merit and pray for good luck.

Crocodile Farm and Zoo ⓰

Samut Prakan's **Crocodile Farm and Zoo** (tel: 0-2387 0020; daily 7am–

6pm; charge) is located a short distance from the Ancient City on the old Sukhumvit Highway (Route 3). The farm has South American caimans and Nile River crocodiles, plus over 60,000 freshwater and saltwater local varieties. It claims to be both the largest crocodile farm in the world, and to have the world's largest captive crocodile, the 6-metre (20ft) -long and 1,114kg (2,456lbs) Chai Yai.

Highlights are the eight daily shows (hourly 9am–4pm, reptile feeding 4–5pm), in which handlers enter a pond teeming with crocodiles to wrestle them and place their heads in their mouths. The farm's shops do a nice line in handbags, belts, shoes and other products made from crocodile and fish skins, which are certified by CITES (Convention on International Trade in Endangered Species). They also sell stewed crocodile meat, purportedly a tonic and aphrodisiac in traditional Chinese medicine.

Other attractions include a Dinosaur Museum, an amusement park and a zoo featuring tigers, ostriches, camels and elephants.

Chonburi

The sprawling town of **Chonburi**, 80km (50 miles) from Bangkok, is the gateway to the Eastern Seaboard, and is usually a brief stop, at most, for visitors on the way to Pattaya and beyond. However, Chonburi has its fair share of attractions. Just outside of town is **Wat Buddhabat Sam Yot** (daily 8am–6pm; free). Built by an Ayutthayan king and renovated during the reign of King Chulalongkorn, this hilltop monastery holds a cast of what is supposedly the Buddha's footprint. The climb to the top of the hill is rewarded with coastal panoramas.

Near the centre of Chonburi, a gold-mosaic image of the Buddha dominates the Chinese **Wat Dhamma Nimitr** (daily 8am–6pm; free). The largest image along this coastline, and the only one in the country depicting the Buddha in a boat, the 40-metre (135ft) -high statue recalls the story of the Buddha's journey to the cholera-ridden town of Pai Salee.

Bang Saen ⓱

Continuing south from Chonburi past the town of Ang Sila, the 2km (1-mile) -long beach at **Bang Saen** springs to life each weekend as hordes of middle-class Bangkok residents descend in cars and buses. The nearest stretch of beach from the capital, it's covered with beach umbrellas and inflatable inner tubes, and the surf is filled with bobbing bodies dressed head-to-toe in clothes to avoid getting a tan (Thais associate tanned skin with poor manual labourers who toil in the sun).

Tucked inland near Bang Phra Reservoir, and operated by Bangkok's Dusit Zoo *(see page 142)*, is **Khao Khieo Open Zoo** (tel: 0-3829 8187-8; daily 8am–8pm; charge). It exhibits deer, elephants and other animals, and includes a Night Safari (daily 6–8pm; charge).

ABOVE: stained glass in the Earth section of the Erawan Museum. **BELOW:** wrestling a reptile at Samut Prakan's Crocodile Farm and Zoo.

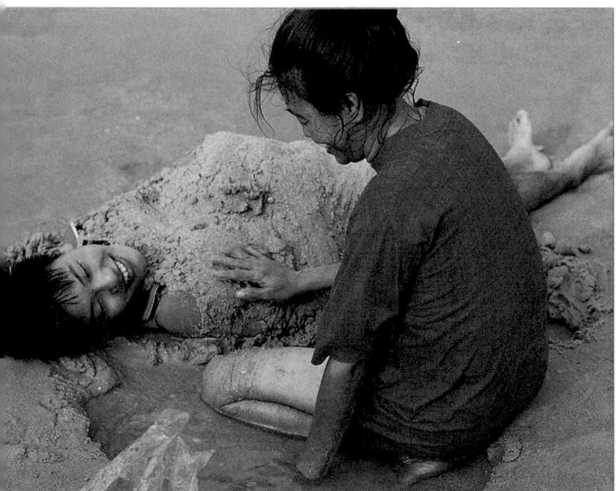

ABOVE: family fun on the beach at Ko Si Chang. **RIGHT:** carving in the Sanctuary of Truth at Pattaya.

Si Racha ⓲

The coastal town of **Si Racha** is the original home of one of Thailand's most famous relishes – Si Racha Sauce (*nam prik si racha*), into which diners dip fresh shrimp, crab, oyster and mussels at the town's waterfront restaurants.

The **Sriracha Tiger Zoo**, 9km (6 miles) to the south, claims to be the largest tiger zoo in the world (tel: 0-3829 6556-8; www.tigerzoo.com; daily 8am–6pm; charge). The zoo has over 100 Bengal tigers in captivity – visitors can attend the nursery to hold and feed the young cubs. In addition there is a menagerie of other animals, like crocodiles, elephants, ostriches and chimps. While the tigers are the star attraction in the daily circus shows, there is crocodile wrestling, an elephant show and even pig racing.

TIP

If you have time to kill at Si Racha, visit the offshore rock of Ko Loi. It is connected to the mainland by a bridge and supports a picturesque temple with Thai and Chinese elements. A Buddha footprint, cast in bronze, graces the temple along with pictures of the Goddess of Mercy, Kuan Yin, and the Monkey God.

Ko Si Chang ⓳

A short boat ride from Si Racha's shore is the small island of **Ko Si Chang**, known primarily as a coastal retreat for King Chulalongkorn (Rama V). The king built his summer palace here in the 1890s, although little remains of the palace grounds, and the palace itself was dismantled and rebuilt in Bangkok as the Vimanmek Mansion (*see page 141*). The gardens and ponds are still recognisable. The king used to meditate in the now dilapidated Wat Atsadang.

The island has a couple of reasonably good beaches, though certainly not Thailand's best or cleanest, and it is busy at weekends with Thai day-trippers. Once a transfer point for cargo ships unloading onto smaller vessels to sail up the Chao Phraya river, Ko Si Chang's surrounding seas are still crowded, these days with large freighters.

Pattaya ⓴

Pattaya's reputation as a centre of sex tourism is not undeserved, despite ongoing efforts by hotels and other local businesses to clean up its image. So, it's something of a surprise that this resort is a popular destination for families as well as single men. The reason is that Pattaya has an abundance of accommodation options at all prices, plenty of international restaurants and a wide range of attractions and activities for all ages on both land and sea, although its beaches are less pristine than those in

the southern islands and are narrow, packed with parasols and too close to the main road for comfort.

The town's notoriety dates back to the Vietnam War when boatloads of American GIs flocked to the then quiet beaches and bars for a spot of R&R. Today, with the Thai Navy still operating from the nearby port at Satthahip, occasional battalions of visiting US Marines still descend on the resort – to the delight of Pattaya's entertainment establishments. And this buzzing, salacious nightlife has become a tourist attraction in itself for many visitors, even if they play no part in the action.

Located 147km (91 miles) from Bangkok, (just over two hours by road), the seaside town has long been popular with Thai youth and families. In recent years, apart from Europeans, visitors from China, Hong Kong and Taiwan are Pattaya's most visible foreign tourists, along with significant numbers of Russians.

It is also a popular spot for condos and beach homes, mainly used as weekend getaways for Bangkok expats, and as winter homes for retirees from Europe. Property prices rise at an astonishing rate, and improvements to infrastructure, especially international schools, are drawing in more respectable residents. But Pattaya's seedy reputation also attracts a strong criminal element, and a browse through the English-language newspaper the *Pattaya Mail* reads like a police alert for Thailand's most wanted. This underworld, however, is rarely visible to the average tourist, and Pattaya feels as safe as anywhere else in Thailand.

The waterfront starts at the fishing village of **Hat Naklua** to the north of town, leading down to the crescent-shaped **Hat Pattaya**, followed by a nicer and slightly wilder 6km (3½-mile) stretch at **Hat Jomtien**, to the south. Pattaya and Jomtien are good locations for watersports fans, with equipment for windsurfing, sailing, snorkelling and diving available for rent, along with jet skis, water scooters and water-skiing equipment. The brave may try parasailing, strapped into a parachute harness and towed aloft by a speedboat.

Pattaya's land attractions

Pattaya's land-based attractions include everything from golf courses and paintball parks to go-karting, bungee jumping and parachuting. In addition, there are several sights that may be worth seeing.

At the Royal Garden Plaza is a branch of **Ripley's Believe It or Not!**, with its collection of bizarre oddities (tel: 0-3871 0294; www.ripleysthailand.com; daily 11am–11pm; charge). At Thanon Sukhumvit is the **Pattaya Elephant Village** with its elephant shows and rides (tel: 0-3824 9818; www.elephant-village-pattaya.com; daily 8.30am–7pm; charge).

At **Pattaya Park**, the young ones will enjoy the cable car rides as well as the exciting waterslides and whirlpools at this large water amusement facility (tel: 0-3825 1201; www.pattaya

TIP

The most popular beach in Ko Si Chang is Hat Tham Phang (Collapsed Cave Beach) on the western part of the island. The privately run website www.ko-sichang.com has more info on where to stay and eat, and tips on what to do on this tiny island.

BELOW: parasailing is a popular activity off the beaches at Pattaya.

ABOVE: elephant show at Nong Nooch Village.
BELOW: sex worker outside Pattaya's Kitty bar.

park.com; daily 9am–6pm; charge).

The **Sanctuary of Truth** on Naklua Soi 12 (tel: 0-3822 5407; www.sanctuaryoftruth.com; daily 8am–6pm; charge) appears like a fairytale castle right on the edge of the sea. Standing over 100 metres (330ft) high, with a central dome of 42 tons, it is made entirely of hardwoods, intricately carved both inside and out with figures of gods and spirits representing Asian religions. Begun in 1981, construction is still ongoing, with surrounding workshops full of carpenters and wood carvers. You can watch them work and take up tools yourself if you want to learn a few moves. The sanctuary also offers horse riding and dolphin shows.

About 18km (11 miles) south of Pattaya is **Nong Nooch Tropical Garden**, a 243-hectare (600-acre) landscaped parkland enclosing two lakes (tel: 0-3870 9360; www.nongnoochtropicalgarden.com; daily 8am–6pm; charge). It offers a variety of activities, including a mini-zoo, with animals such as gibbons, tigers, and ostriches, a butterfly park, a huge orchid garden and cultural shows featuring traditional dances, Thai boxing and elephants.

Pattaya's nightlife

Pattaya's nightlife clusters along or off Beach Road and Walking Street in South Pattaya. There is a stagger-

TIP

PETA, People for the Ethical Treatment of Animals, campaigns against cruel treatment used in training elephants. They estimate that nearly 80 percent of Thailand's 5,000 elephants are owned privately for use in performances and to give rides at elephant camps. See www.peta.org.

ing range of bars, Irish pubs, German brew houses and nightclubs, as well as an overwhelming saturation of go-go bars and massage parlours (Pattaya heaves with sex workers, both female and male). The international mix here means at least one of the bars now features Eastern European lap dancers. The strip called Boys' Town (Pattayaland Soi 3) is where the gay crowd gathers. Pattaya also has lip-synching Vegas-style cabaret shows which feature a pageant of stunning lady-boys or *katoey* (transsexuals). Tiffany's (tel: 0-3842 1700; www.tiffany-show.th) is the most popular.

A more family-oriented option is **Alangkarn Theatre** in Thanon Sukhumvit, which stages a show combining traditional Thai dancers and elephants with lasers and pyrotechnics (tel: 0-3825 6007; www.alangkarnthailand.com; Thur–Tue at 6pm; charge). It is kitschy but makes for a fun evening with dinner thrown in.

Ko Larn ㉑

Offshore from Pattaya, **Ko Larn** – identified in brochures as Coral Island but whose name translates as Bald Island – used to be known for its coral reefs. These have long since been destroyed by fishermen using dynamite to stun fish. Yet, glass-bottomed boats still ferry visitors from the mainland to its shore, their passengers peering in vain at the dead grey coral in the hope of seeing something alive and moving. Ko Larn, however, has the wide, soft sand beaches that Pattaya lacks and it's a great place to spend a leisurely day. The shore is filled with good seafood restaurants, and there are watersports facilities for those who want to stir from their beach chairs.

Further south, the coastline continues all the way through **Rayong** and beyond into **Chanthaburi**, with much of it quite undeveloped or with small hotels aimed solely at the domestic market.

Ko Samet ㉒

Located 200km (124 miles) from Bangkok (or over three hours by road) from the capital and a short boat trip across from the fishing harbour of **Ban Phe**, the postcard-perfect island of **Ko Samet** has become a popular weekend getaway for Bangkok residents. The island is famous among Thais as the place where Sunthorn Phu (1786–1855), a flamboyantly romantic court poet, retired to compose some of his works. Born in nearby Klaeng on the mainland, Sunthorn called the island Ko Kaeo Phisadan, or "island with sand like crushed crystal", and it was here that he set his best-known work, *Phra Aphaimani*, a tale about a prince and a mermaid. A weathered statue stands as tribute on the rocky point at the end of the main beach of Hat Sai Kaew.

From a quiet poetic retreat, the island has gained popularity as a superb resort, helped by the fine white sand beaches and turquoise blue waters. Most activity here is relaxed – sunbathing, beach strolls, swimming and snorkelling – though jet skis and inflatable banana boats

ABOVE: spectacular undersea life awaits divers in the waters around Ko Samet.
BELOW: longtail boat off Phuket.

TIP

While the regular fishing boat ferries are much cheaper, taking a speedboat across to Ko Samet (around B800 per boat) from the mainland is much faster, drops you at the bay of your choice, and usually means you escape paying the National Park entry fee of B200 per foreigner, which is pretty steep compared to the B20 that Thais are charged.

BELOW: sunset over Ko Chang.

do occasionally interrupt the peace. The island is part of a national marine park (entry fee upon arrival at the pier), so, technically, most of the resort and bungalow operations are illegal. However, development along the coast has progressed despite the law, though as yet it remains fairly unobtrusive, with simple single-storey huts and bungalows. But as a sign of things to come, a couple of resorts have upgraded their facilities, and the west coast's only beach of **Ao Phrao** has a few upmarket resorts nestled into this small scenic bay.

Almost all the island's sandy beaches run down the east coast, starting near the larger northern tip with **Hat Sai Kaew** (Diamond Sand), and gradually getting less isolated as the island narrows to the southernmost bay of **Ao Karang**. The island is relatively small and can be walked from top to bottom in just a few hours, though the coastal track traverses some rocky headlands. The single road turns to bumpy dirt track fairly quickly. Hat Sai Kaew is where Thais prefer to stay, having more air-conditioned rooms and seafood restaurants, whereas foreign visitors like the bays of **Ao Phai** and **Ao Hin Khok**.

The island is best avoided on public holidays, when visitors outnumber beds, and tents are pitched on any spare patch of land. Evenings are relatively low-key, with restaurants setting up fresh seafood beach barbeques, and the restaurant-bars at small hotels like **Naga** (Ao Hin Khok) and **Silver Sand** (Ao Phai) the only spots to focus on music, late-night partying and the obligatory fire juggling. The mosquitoes on Ko Samet are known to be monsters, so repellent is a must.

Further down at picturesque **Ao Wong Deuan**, the scene, unfortunately, has become more akin to Pattaya, with European males being pampered by their hired female "guides", raucous bars on the land and noisy jet skis on the waters. **Ao Thian** (Candlelight Beach), the next bay, is a quieter spot and the facilities are more basic.

Ko Chang ㉓

Ko Chang (Elephant Island), at 492 sq km (190 sq miles), is Thailand's

second-largest island after Phuket. It is part of the Ko Chang Marine National Park which includes some 50 islands. You can drive here in around five hours from Bangkok. Alternatively, the flight to Trat, on the mainland, takes 45 minutes. Either way there is an hour's boat crossing from **Laem Ngop** pier, 20 minutes from the airport.

The verdant island, which is part of Trat province (close to the Cambodian border), has managed to escape the rapid development of Phuket and Ko Samui, despite the government's promotion of Ko Chang as a playground for the rich. There has been a rapid increase in hotel construction and infrastructure in the last decade (including an upgrade of the road that loops practically the whole island), and the opening of Trat airport in 2003. There is now a yachting marina and a greater choice of stylish resorts and spas than there used to be, although still nothing in the luxury class, and the island remains a firm favourite with backpackers.

As the island becomes more popular, the single road is increasingly busy, but despite this it still has a relatively untouched hilly interior, mangroves and some lovely beaches lined up along the west coast. The most developed is **Hat Sai Khao** (White Sand Beach), which is just south of the idyllic stretch of sand at **Hat Khlong Phrao**. Next, you reach **Hat Kai Bae**, and then the last vestige of Ko Chang's hippie traveller scene, **Hat Tha Nam** (Lonely Beach). As more resorts edge in, the last no longer has quite the solitude implied by its name.

Popular activities include snorkelling and diving, including trips to some of the smaller islands, kayaking, and treks to the island's numerous waterfalls. Visit the southern stilted fishing village of **Ban Bang Bao** to get an idea of how local communities live (and how their lifestyles are changing). The island's nightlife is still relatively subdued, with each beach having its own preferred watering holes. However Hat Sai Khao is still where the main action is.

ABOVE: soaking up the rays on Ko Chang.
BELOW: seashells from the beach at Ko Chang.

Islands near Ko Chang

If Ko Chang still feels a little too well trodden, the string of islands off the southern tip are much quieter and worth exploring. The tiny **Ko Wai** has limited and basic accommodation, but the vibe here is very relaxed, the views of the surrounding islands are spectacular, and there is a lovely coral reef just a short swim from the main beach.

An hour by speedboat from the mainland pier of Laem Ngop, the flat island of **Ko Mak** is dense with coconut plantations and has two nice main beaches, where tourists are sparse. The island lies about halfway between Ko Chang and the second-largest island in the archipelago, **Ko Kut**, which attracts a lot of organised tour groups to resorts that mainly cater to all-inclusive packages. ❑

NORTH OF BANGKOK

The undisputed capital city of the Thai kingdom more than 600 years ago, Ayutthaya is a time capsule that captures the faded grandeur of that violent era. To its west lies Khao Yai National Park, a huge expanse of greenery that's also worth exploring

Main Attractions

Maps and Listings

Bang Pa-In became a favourite royal retreat from the reign of King Chulalongkorn, over 100 years ago. It is a picturesque stopover before reaching the main event, the ruins of Ayutthaya, the once-powerful old capital of Thailand. Also in this area there are waterfalls and a national park near Nakhon Nayok, wild animal spotting in Khao Yai and more (wildish) animals in the ancient city of Lopburi, where monkeys cause mischief at Prang Sam Yot.

Trains from Hualamphong Station stop at Bang Pa-In, Ayutthaya and Lopburi. Buses to Ayutthaya leave from Bangkok's Northern Bus Terminal, stopping at Bang Pa-In en route. Separate buses leave the same station for Lopburi

Bang Pa-In ㉔

Drive north from Bangkok for about 50km (32 miles) and you reach **Bang Pa-In**, an eclectic collection of palaces and pavilions once used as a royal summer retreat (tel: 0-3526 1673-82; www.palaces.thai.net; daily 8.30am–4.30pm; charge).

The palace buildings one sees today at Bang Pa-in date from the late 19th- and early 20th-century reigns of King Chulalongkorn (Rama V) and King Vajiravudh (Rama VI), who came here to escape the mid-year rains in Bangkok. Under the instruction of Chulalongkorn, the manicured grounds contain several buildings that feature Italian Baroque, European Gothic, Victorian and Chinese architectural styles. Only parts of the royal quarters are open to public view, providing a glimpse into Chulalongkorn's penchant for European furniture and decor.

LEFT: the stone Buddha's head embedded in a tree at Ayutthaya. **RIGHT:** exploring the ruins on an elephant is a novel option.

TIP

Most day trips that visit Ayutthaya from Bangkok include Bang Pa-In as a brief stopover either on the way there or back. For more details on tours to Ayutthaya and Bang Pa-In, see page 239 of the Travel Tips section.

The palace buildings of note at Bang Pa-In include the two-storey Chinese-style **Wehat Chamrun Palace** and the nearby islet with the **Withun Thatsana** observation tower, as well as the Italianate **Warophat Phiman Hall**. The 1876 **Aisawan Thipphaya-at**, a Thai-style pavilion in the middle of the adjacent lake near the entrance, is regarded as one of the finest surviving examples of Thai architecture.

Across the river and slightly south of the palace, **Wat Niwet Thammaprawat** looks more like a Gothic Christian church than a Buddhist temple, and is topped by a spire. Worthy of an hour's stop on the way to Ayutthaya, the pleasant gardens are embellished with canals, ponds, fountains, bridges and a topiary of large elephant-shaped hedges. Coach tours to Ayutthaya stop off here in the morning, so to avoid the crowds it's better to drop by in the afternoon.

RIGHT: Aisawan Thipphaya-at.

AYUTTHAYA ㉕

Even if one were ignorant of the importance and history of **Ayutthaya**, one would still be impressed by the beauty and grandeur of this city – built by 33 Ayutthayan kings over 400 years. From the ruins, it is easy to appreciate the genius of the kings who built it. Located 85km (55 miles) north of Bangkok, Ayutthaya was laid out at the junction of three rivers: Chao Phraya, Pa Sak and

Ayutthaya

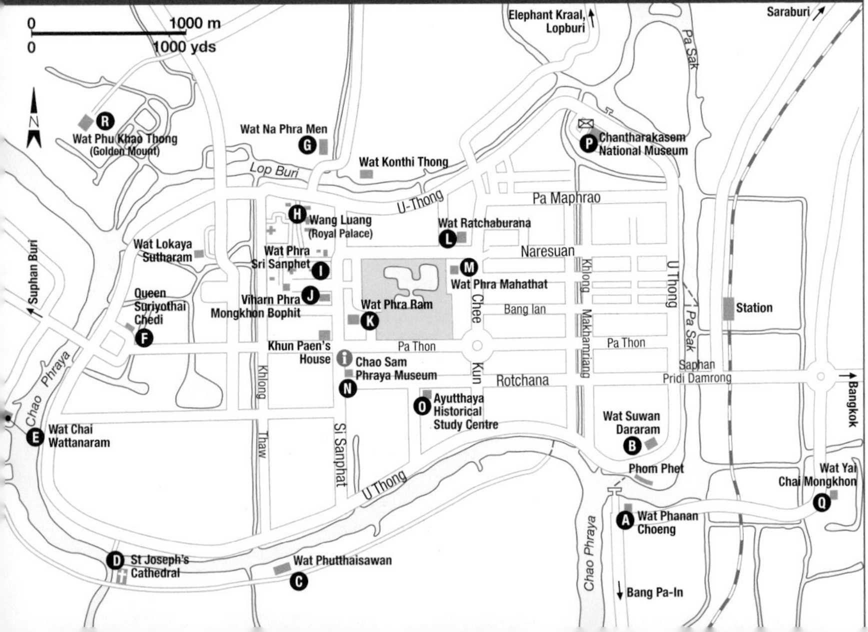

0 1000 m
0 1000 yds
N
Elephant Kraal, Lopburi
Saraburi
Pa Sak
R Wat Phu Khao Thong (Golden Mount)
G Wat Na Phra Men
P Chantharakasem National Museum
Wat Konthi Thong
Lop Buri
U-Thong
Pa Maphrao
H Wang Luang (Royal Palace)
L Wat Ratchaburana
Wat Lokaya Sutharam
Wat Phra Sri Sanphet I
Naresuan
M Wat Phra Mahathat
Suphan Buri
Queen Suriyothai Chedi F
Viharn Phra Mongkhon Bophit J
K Wat Phra Ram
Chee Kun
Bang Ian
Khlong Makhamriang
U Thong
Pa Sak
Station
Khun Paen's House
Pa Thon
Pa Thon
Chao Sam Phraya Museum N
Rotchana
Saphan Pridi Damrong
Bangkok
Chao Phraya
Khlong Thaw
O Ayutthaya Historical Study Centre
Wat Suwan Dararam B
E Wat Chai Wattanaram
Si Sanphat
Phom Phet
Wat Yai Chai Mongkhon Q
U Thong
A Wat Phanan Choeng
Chao Phraya
D St Joseph's Cathedral
Wat Phutthaisawan C
Bang Pa-In

ABOVE: Wat Chai Wattanaram.

Lopburi. Engineers had only to cut a canal across the loop of the Chao Phraya River to create an island. A network of canals – few of which exist today – acted as streets, and palaces and temples were erected alongside. The Europeans dubbed this city "Venice of the East", and even today, chartering a longtail boat for a trip around the natural moat is the most ambient way to see many of the riverbank ruins. As a Unesco World Heritage site, Ayutthaya is a must visit. Several boat operators from Bangkok organise regular trips by river from the capital to the historic city, conveying them in either modern express boats or traditional teakwood barges *(see page 239)*.

Ayutthaya's foundations

Ayutthaya was founded around 1350 by Prince U-Thong (later known as King Ramathibodi I). Thirty years later, the northern kingdom of Sukhothai was placed under Ayutthayan rule, which then spread its control to Angkor in the east, and to Pegu, in Burma, to the west. It was one of the richest and most cosmopolitan cities in Asia by the 1600s – exporting rice, animal skins and ivory – and had a population of 1 million, greater than that of London at the time. Merchants came from Europe, the Middle East and elsewhere in Asia to trade in its markets, with many eventually settling there. Today, there is a plaque to mark the former Portuguese settlement and a memorial hall and gate to mark the Japanese settlement. Europeans wrote awed accounts of the fabulous wealth of the courts and of the 2,000 temple spires clad in gold.

Thirty-three kings left their mark on the old capital. Although in ruins, very impressive remnants of Ayutthaya's rich architectural and cultural achievements can still be seen today. As fast as it rose to greatness, it collapsed, suffering destruction so complete that it was never rebuilt. Burmese armies had been pounding on its doors for centuries before occupying it for a period in the 16th century. Siamese kings then expelled them and reasserted independence. In 1767, however, the Burmese triumphed again. In a mad rampage, they burned and

In the 1950s, unscrupulous locals plundered Ayutthaya's hidden treasures and Buddha images. The Thai government recently realised that some of Ayutthaya's most important treasures are now housed in overseas museum collections, and they are trying to reclaim these stolen artefacts.

ABOVE: Wat Phanan Choeng.

looted, destroying most of the city's monuments and enslaving, killing and scattering the population.

Within a year, Ayutthaya was nearly a ghost town, its population reduced to fewer than 10,000 inhabitants as the royal court resettled south near the mouth of the Chao Phraya river in what today is Bangkok. Even after the Burmese garrison was defeated, Ayutthaya was beyond repair, a fabled city left to crumble into dust. Today, the ruins, collectively known as the **Ayutthaya Historical Park** (daily 8am–5pm; charge) stand on the western half of the island, with the modern city of Ayutthaya on the eastern side.

By the riverside

Start close to the junction of the Nam Pa Sak and Chao Phraya rivers, passing by the imposing **Wat Phanan Choeng** Ⓐ. Records suggest that the temple was established 26 years prior to Ayutthaya's foundation in 1350. The temple houses the statue of a giant seated bronze Buddha, so tightly pressed against the roof that the statue appears to be holding it up. With an unmistakably Chinese atmosphere, Wat Phanan Choeng was a favourite with the Chinese traders of the time, who prayed there before setting out on long voyages. The temple also holds the Mae Soi Dok Mak shrine, a tribute to a Chinese princess who supposedly killed herself on this spot after an icy reception from her suitor, an Ayutthayan king.

The foundations of Wat Suwan Dararam's bot *dip in the centre, in emulation of the graceful deck line of a boat. This typical Ayutthayan decoration is meant to suggest a boat that carries pious Buddhists to salvation.*

Ayutthaya was at one time surrounded by fortress walls, only portions of which remain today. One of the best-preserved sections is at **Phom Phet**, across the river from Wat Phanan Choeng. Near Phom Phet is the restored **Wat Suwan Dararam** Ⓑ, built near the close of the Ayutthaya period. Destroyed by the Burmese in 1767, the temple was rebuilt by Rama I, with the wall murals dating from the reign of Rama III; later, a more unconventional (1925–35) mural depicting King Naruesan's famous battle with the Burmese was added. Still used as a temple, the *wat* is magical in the early evening as the monks chant prayers.

Upstream from Wat Phanan Choeng by the river bank is the restored **Wat Phutthaisawan** Ⓒ. Seldom visited, it is quiet, and the landing is an excellent place to enjoy the river's tranquillity in the evenings. Further upstream, the **Cathedral of St Joseph** Ⓓ is a Catholic reminder of the large European population that lived in the city at its prime.

Where the river bends to the north is one of Ayutthaya's most romantic ruins, **Wat Chai Wattanaram** Ⓔ, erected in 1630. Modelled after the Angkor Wat complex in Cambodia, the dramatically placed temple is a photographer's favourite, especially at sunset. Restored in the 1990s, the temple was built by King Prasat Thong, and has a large central Cambodian-style *prang* fringed by several smaller *chedi*. Perched high on a pedestal in front of the ruins, a Buddha keeps solitary watch. This extraordinary temple with rows of headless Buddhas makes a fine contrast to the less impressive white-and-gold **Queen**

Suriyothai Chedi Ⓕ on the city side of the river. The shrine commemorates the life of Ayutthayan Queen Suriyothai, one of the most famous heroines of Thai history. She was the wife of King Maha Chakapat (1548–69), and legend states that when her husband went to engage the invading Burmese armies in the first year of his reign, Queen Suriyothai disguised herself as a man and rode into battle with him. The king, his elephant wounded, was in mortal danger, when the queen rode her elephant between him and his attacker and was herself killed. In 2001, a movie about her called *Suriyothai* was the most expensive film ever made in Thailand and was a huge box office hit. Francis Ford Coppola edited the US release.

Across a river bridge from Wang Luang stands the restored temple of **Wat Na Phra Men** Ⓖ. Used as a strategic attack post by the Burmese when they descended on the old city, the temple is one of Ayutthaya's only monasteries not to have been ransacked. Here, a large stone Buddha is seated on a throne, a sharp contrast to the yoga position of most seated Buddhas. Found in the ruins of Wat Phra Mahathat *(see page 225)*, the statue is believed to be one of five that originally sat in the recently unearthed Dvaravati-period complex in Nakhon Pathom. The main hall or *bot* contains an Ayutthayan-style seated Buddha in regal attire, which is very unlike the more common monastic dress of Buddha representations.

Royal Palace

The **Wang Luang** Ⓗ (Royal Palace) was of substantial size, if the foundations for the stables of some 100 elephants are any indication. Established by King Borommatrailokanat in the 15th century, it was later razed by the Burmese. The bricks were removed to Bangkok to build the city's defensive walls, so only remnants of the foundations survive to mark the site.

A part of the original palace grounds, next door stands the three Ceylonese-style *chedi* of **Wat Phra Sri Sanphet** Ⓘ. The royal temple would have held as much importance as the Temple of the Emerald Buddha (Wat Phra Kaew) in Bangkok *(see page 102)* does today. Two

ABOVE: statue of a sitting Buddha at the Wat Yai Chai Monkhon temple in Ayutthaya.
BELOW: Wat Phra Sri Sanphet.

ABOVE: Wat Phra Sri Sanphet. **RIGHT:** stupas, Wat Phra Mahathat.

of the *chedi* were built in 1492 by King Borommatrailokanat's son, Ramathibodi II, to hold the ashes of his father and brother. The third was added in 1540 to hold the ashes of Ramathibodi II. The three spires have become the archetypal image of Ayutthaya.

Around the Royal Palace

For two centuries after Ayutthaya's fall, a huge bronze Buddha sat unsheltered near Wat Phra Sri Sanphet. Its flame of knowledge (on the top of its head) and one of its arms had been broken when the roof, set on fire by the Burmese, collapsed. Based on the original, a new building called **Viharn Phra Mongkhon Bophit** ❶ was built in 1956 around the restored statue. Dating back to the 15th century and over 12 metres (39ft) tall, it is one of Thailand's largest bronze images and seems rather cramped in this sanctuary.

Following the defeat of Ayutthaya, King Taksin was desperate for funds to build the new capital in Thonburi. He authorised treasure hunts in the old city, looking for the riches buried by the city's merchants before they fled. Finders were allowed to keep half the loot for themselves.

In the park just south of Viharn Phra Mongkhon Bophit is **Khun Paen's House** (Thanon Pa Thon; daily 8.30am-4.30pm; charge), which although empty of furnishings is a good example of a traditional Thai "cluster" dwelling. It shows the three separate houses of the extended family arranged around a communal verandah for socialising and dining. People habitually ate on the floor – the original reason for taking your shoes off when entering a Thai building. It was restored here in 1940, the location of the original city jail.

Across the road to the east, **Wat Phra Ram** Ⓚ is one of Ayutthaya's oldest temples. Founded in 1369 by the son of Ayutthaya's founding king, Prince U-Thong, its buildings, dating from the 1400s, have been restored twice. Elephant gates punctuate the old walls, and the central terrace is dominated by a crumbling *prang* to which clings a gallery of stucco *naga*, *garuda* and Buddha statues. The reflection of Wat Phra Ram's *prang* shimmers in the pool that surrounds the complex, making it one of Ayutthaya's most tranquil settings.

Ayutthaya's best temples

Two of Ayutthaya's finest temples stand side by side across the lake from Wat Phra Ram. The first is **Wat Ratchaburana** Ⓛ, built in 1424 by the seventh king of Ayutthaya, King Borom Rachathirat II (1424–48) as a memorial to his brothers who died as a result of a duel for the throne. Excavations during its restoration in 1957 revealed a crypt below the tow-

ering central *prang*, containing a stash of gold jewellery, Buddha images and other art objects, among them a magnificent ceremonial sword and an intricately decorated elephant statue – all probably the property of the interred brothers. The narrow, claustrophobic and dimly lit crypt can be accessed through a doorway in the *prang*, leading down steep stairs to some barely visible wall paintings.

The second temple, across the road, is **Wat Phra Mahathat** Ⓜ (Temple of the Great Relic), once one of the most beautiful temple complexes in Ayutthaya, and one of its oldest, dating from the 1380s. It was also one of the most important temples in Ayutthaya's heyday: the seat of the Supreme Patriarch, the focal point for religious ceremonies, and where King Ramesuan (1388–95) resided. Its glory was its huge laterite *prang*, which originally stood 46 metres (150ft) high. The *prang* later collapsed, but its foundations are still there, circled by restored *chedi*. A much revered symbol here is a stone Buddha head that is embedded in the gnarled roots of an old banyan tree. Around the ruins are numerous headless statues, with just the crossed legs of meditation hinting at the positions they once assumed. The souvenir shops at the entrance here mark this as one of the most visited (and most atmospheric) temples, but the Wat Mahathat grounds are large enough to gain serene moments even when accompanied by coach parties.

Next door, the government has built a model of how the royal city may have once looked.

Ayutthaya's museums

While looters quickly made off with a great many of Ayutthaya's glories, the remaining treasures of what was probably Thailand's greatest archaeological discovery are now kept in the **Chao Sam Phraya Museum** Ⓝ just to the south (tel: 0-3524 1587; www.thailandmuseum.com; Wed–Sun 9am–4pm; charge).

Nearby is another museum, the **Ayutthaya**

ABOVE: Wat Ratchaburana.

BELOW: one of the best ways of exploring the widely spread ruins of Ayutthaya is on bicycle. These can be rented for about B50 a day at many guesthouses in Ayutthaya. If you can't be bothered to expend your energy, hire a motorised tuk-tuk with driver for about B180 an hour.

ABOVE: Wat Yai Chai Mongkhon.
BELOW: seated Buddha images at Wat Yai Chai Mongkhon in Ayutthaya.

Historical Study Centre Ⓞ (tel: 0-3524 5124; Mon–Fri 9am–4.30pm, Sat–Sun 9am–5pm; charge). Funded by the Japanese government and on land that was once part of Ayutthaya's Japanese quarter, the modern building houses hi-tech exhibits which guide visitors through 400 years of Ayutthaya's development, trade, administration and social changes. There are also models of the city in its glory days, a Chinese junk and small tableaux of village life.

To the northeast is **Chantharakasem National Museum** Ⓟ, formerly known as the Chantharakasem Palace (tel: 0-3525 5124; www.thailandmuseum.com; Wed–Sun 9am–4pm; charge). It was originally constructed outside the city walls, close to the confluence of the rivers and the canal. King Maha Thammaracha built it for his son Prince Naresuan (later king), and it became the residence for future heirs apparent. In 1767, the Burmese destroyed the palace, but King Mongkut (Rama IV) resurrected it in the 19th century as a royal summer retreat for escaping the lowland heat. Today, it looks out on the noisiest part of modern Ayutthaya. The palace's collection isn't that impressive but is still worthy of a perusal.

To its rear is the European-style four-storey **Pisai Sayalak** tower, built by King Mongkut for stargazing. Across the street from the palace is the boat pier for trips around the island, and the night market, with food stalls set up beside the water. It's a good spot to eat cheap local food and unwind at the end of the day.

Ayutthaya's outskirts

Southeast of Ayutthaya is **Wat Yai Chai Mongkhon** Ⓠ, originally established in the mid-1300s. The immense *chedi*, built to match that of Wat Phu Khao Thong *(see below)*, celebrates the victory of King Naresuan, in single-handed combat on elephant back, over the crown prince of Burma in 1592. Rows of yellow-sashed Buddha images skirt the inner walls. Also of interest is the statue of a huge white reclining Buddha, which, unusually, has its eyes open.

About 2km (1 mile) northwest of Ayutthaya is **Wat Phu Khao Thong** Ⓡ, better known as the **Golden**

Mount. Its 80-metre (260ft) -high *chedi* rises amidst the rice fields, its upper terraces commanding a panoramic view of the countryside. While the *wat* dates from 1387, the *chedi* was built by the Burmese after their earlier and less destructive conquest in 1569. In 1957, to mark 2,500 years of Buddhism, a 2,500-gram (5½lb) gold ball was mounted on top of the *chedi*, only to be stolen almost immediately after.

Nakhon Nayok ㉖

The most scenic route to the northeast province is Route 305, which branches off Route 1 (Friendship Highway) just north of Rangsit, 30km (20 miles) north of Bangkok. This wide road runs northeast along a lovely canal, passing rice paddy fields and small rivers to reach the provincial capital of **Nakhon Nayok**, some 140km (90 miles) from the capital. Nakhon Nayok has long been overshadowed by the more famous tourist destinations in Thailand, but Thai visitors recognise its abundant nearby attractions – natural forests, craggy gorges and tumbling waterfalls – which offer a respite from the chaos of the city.

Other than a glimpse of a typical rural centre, however, the town of Nakhon Nayok itself has little to offer. From the town centre, Route 33 heads northwest and then, after just a few kilometres, a second road leads off to the right towards two waterfalls, one of which is **Sarika Falls**. Surrounded by dense forest, the nine-tier waterfall is in full force towards the end of the rainy season (September to November). But remember to wear sturdy shoes: the stone paths are slippery.

Wang Takrai National Park

Due north of Nakhon Nayok is the **Wang Takrai National Park**, established by Prince Chumbhot (of Suan Pakkad Palace fame in Bangkok, *see page 161*) in the 1950s (daily 6am–6pm; charge). His wife, Princess Chumbhot, a keen horticulturalist, planted many varieties of flowers and trees, including some imported

ABOVE: countryside around Nakhon Nayok.

TIP

A common end to a day at Khao Yai National Park is a walk to Khoa Luk Chang Bat Cave at dusk to watch thousands of bats fly out as they head off in search of food.

ABOVE: Phra Narai Ratchaniwet ruins.
BELOW: harvesting grapes in a Khao Yai vineyard.

species. Cultivated gardens sit among tall trees, which line both banks of the main stream flowing through the 2km (1-mile) stretch of the 80-hectare (195-acre) park. For those wishing to stay overnight in the area, bungalows are available for rent.

Just outside the park entrance, the road on the left crosses a river and continues 5km (3 miles) to **Nang Rong Falls**, an inviting three-tiered cascade located in a steep valley.

Khao Yai National Park ㉗

Khao Yai National Park, one of Thailand's oldest and most popular nature reserves, lies 200km (125 miles) northeast of the capital (daily 6am–6pm; charge). It is Thailand's second-largest national park at 2,168 sq km (837 sq miles) and cuts across four different provinces.

Most of Khao Yai is located 400 metres (1,300ft) above sea level, making it a pleasant escape from the hot, humid lowlands of Central Thailand. Most people visit during the dry season from November to February; be sure to bring warm clothes during this period as temperatures can plummet to as low as 10°C (50°F) at night. Alternatively, the rainy season is one of the best times for animal spotting and waterfalls, although you'll need to cover up bare legs and arms, as leeches are common then.

Often clad in mist, Khao Yai's highest peaks lie in the east along a landform known as the Korat Plateau. **Khao Laem** (Shadow Mountain) is 1,350 metres (4,430ft) high while **Khao Khiew** (Green Mountain) rises to a height of 1,020 metres (3,350ft). Evergreen and deciduous trees, palms and bamboo blanket the park, and unlike much of Thailand, patches of indigenous rainforest can still be seen here. Khao Yai is home to some 200 elephants, while monkeys, gibbons, deer, langurs, boar and gaurs are also commonly spotted. Bears are less often seen, and big cats such as leopards and tigers are rare. In addition, over 300 species of migrant birds have been identified, with regular sightings of great hornbills.

Wine Country

Bacchus has discovered Thailand in the past few years, and wines from local vineyards are beginning to grow in both popularity and quality. Khao Yai region's favourable climate is supposed to be ideal for grape cultivation, with vineyards such as PB Valley Khao Yai (tel: 0-2562 0858), GranMonte Family Vineyard (tel: 0-2653 1522) and Village Farm & Winery (tel: 0-4422 8407) getting into the act. The word from connoisseurs is that while these wines are eminently palatable, they still need considerable refinement before they will be ready to compete with international wines. Tours, tastings and, in some places, accommodation can be arranged.

More than 50km (30 miles) of marked trails criss-cross the park, most of them originally forged and still used by elephants. In several clearings, there are observation towers where you can watch animals feed. Park rangers have information about the area, but few speak English, so it might be worth getting a guide, (try **Jungle Planet**; tel: 88 9282 2280; www.khaoyaijungleplanet.com) from the nearest town, Pak Chong, or from one of the surrounding resorts. The guides are handy because the better ones carry spotting scopes for you to use, and they can explain what you're looking at. They may even have guidebooks on wildlife, flora and fauna for more in-depth information. On longer overnight treks you may sleep in a tent close to ranger stations.

Other attractions in the park include the three-level **Heaw Narok** waterfall, southeast of the park headquarters, which rises to a height of 150 metres (492ft), and, further north, the 20-metre (66ft) -high **Heaw Suwat** waterfall, which Leonardo di Caprio jumped off in the film *The Beach*.

Near the entrance to the park are numerous lodges and bungalows, including the luxury Kirimaya, a boutique resort in the vein of African safari camps with tented villas. Other pursuits include teeing off at internationally designed golf courses and jungle rides on ATVs (all-terrain vehicles).

LOPBURI ㉘

Lopburi lies 150km (100 miles) north of Bangkok, a two- to three-hour drive through the fertile rice bowl of Thailand. Centuries before Lopburi became the favoured summer residence for Ayutthayan King Narai, the town was known as Lavo and had been a part of the Mon Dvaravati kingdom (6th–10th centuries). From the 10th to 13th centuries, the strategic town became a Khmer outpost for the Angkor empire; later it came under the influence of the Sukhothai kingdom to the north. Lopburi had its heyday in the mid-1600s when Ayutthaya flourished as a bustling capital city of more than 1 million people. It was where King Narai retreated each summer to escape from Ayutthaya's heat. When the Dutch imposed a naval blockade on Ayutthaya from the Gulf of Siam, King Narai decided to install Lopburi as a second capital, running his court

A contentious figure in Thai history, Constantine Phaulkon (1648–88) was undone by a rumour that he had converted King Narai's adopted son to Christianity, and intended to eventually seek succession to the Thai throne. He was arrested and executed in 1688, barely a month after King Narai died.

LEFT: the macaques in Lopburi's Prang Sam Yot are honoured (or pacified) in late November with a feast of fruit, veggies and other foods in a spectacle known as the Monkey Buffet. **BELOW:** headless Buddha image at Prang Sam Yot.

from there. It was said that, while his throne was in Ayutthaya, his heart belonged to Lopburi; indeed, after his new palace was completed he began spending more and more time there.

Wat Phra Si Rattana Mahathat

Just across from Lopburi's main train station is **Wat Phra Si Rattana Mahathat** (daily 8am–6pm; charge). Originally a Khmer temple with a tall stucco-decorated laterite *prang*, around the 12th century King Narai added a large *viharn* (sermon hall) that infused elements of European and Persian architecture, the latter influence coming from the strong Persian presence at the Ayutthayan court. On the grounds are several smaller *chedi*.

Phra Narai Ratchaniwet

Just northwest, the grounds of **Phra Narai Ratchaniwet** (or Lopburi Palace), built between 1665 and 1677, are enclosed by massive walls, which still dominate the centre of the modern town (daily 8am–6pm; charge). Built in a mélange of Thai, Khmer and European styles, the palace grounds have a complex of official, ceremonial and residential buildings in three sections.

The outer grounds contained facilities for utilities and maintenance. The middle section enclosed the **Chanthara Phisan Pavilion**, the first structure built by King Narai, later restored by King Mongkut. On its south side is the **Dusit Maha Prasat Hall**, built for the audience granted by King Narai in 1685 to the French ambassador of Louis XIV.

Narai National Museum

To the left is the **Phiman Mongkut Pavilion**, a three-storey colonial-style mansion. It was built in the mid-19th century by King Mongkut, who wanted to restore the entire palace. The immensely thick walls and high ceilings averted the summer heat. The mansion, small but full of character, now functions as the **Narai National Museum** (tel: 0-3641 1458; www.thailandmuseum.com; Wed–Sun 9am–4pm; charge). It has a display of bronze statues, Chi-

ABOVE: Phiman Mongkut Pavilion.
BELOW: Wat Phra Si Rattana Mahathat.

nese and Sukhothai porcelain, coins, Buddhist fans and shadow-play puppets. Some of the pieces, particularly the Ayutthaya bronze heads and Bencharong porcelain, are superb. The inner courtyard housed the private chambers of King Narai, but not much is left except the foundations and the **Suttha Sawan Pavilion**, nestled amid gardens and ponds.

Baan Vichayen

North of Phra Narai Ratchaniwet are the remains of **Baan Vichayen** palace, said to have belonged to Constantine Phaulkon (daily 8am–6pm; charge). Phaulkon was a Greek adventurer who arrived in Siam in 1678 to work for the English East India Company. He settled in quickly, becoming fluent in Siamese and gaining favour with King Narai, who promoted him to be his most senior minister. However, he antagonised many of the other foreign settlers in Ayutthaya, as well as Thai nobles who felt threatened by a foreigner wielding so much influence. Phaulkon forged strong ties with the French, but when more Catholic missionary priests started arriving in Siam, local Buddhists believed the Greek was conspiring with King Louis XIV to convert Siam to Christianity. As King Narai lay on his deathbed, his successors had Phaulkon arrested and later executed for treason. The following period saw the Siamese court become more wary of foreign influence.

The palace buildings show strong European influences, with straight-sided walls and decorations over Western-style windows.

Prang Sam Yot

To the east are the three laterite towers of **Prang Sam Yot** (daily 8am–6pm; charge). This much-photographed sight is of interest as the towers were originally built by the Khmers as a Hindu shrine honouring the gods Brahma, Vishnu and Shiva. It was later converted into a Buddhist shrine, incorporating a hodge-podge fusion of Brahman, Khmer and Buddhist elements that is often dubbed the Lopburi style. Beware of the annoying monkeys at this site. ❑

ABOVE: riding past the Narai National Museum.
BELOW: Baan Vichayen.

1 Nov 08
ZEN

INSIGHT GUIDES TRAVEL TIPS
BANGKOK

Transport

Accommodation

Activities

A – Z

Language

Further Reading

Transport

Getting There and Getting Around

Getting There

By Air

Bangkok is not only a key gateway between Asia and the West, but also a major transportation hub for the rest of Southeast Asia.

Suvarnabhumi Airport

Bangkok International Airport, Suvarnabhumi (pronounced "su-wa-na-poom") Airport (www.airportthai.co.th) is located about 30km (19 miles) east of Bangkok in Samut Prakan province. It takes about 45 minutes to get to the airport from the city by taxi, depending on traffic conditions. The airport handles all international flights to Bangkok as well as many domestic connections.

Suvarnabhumi has one main passenger terminal with seven concourses, easily capable of handling 76 flights per hour, according to the Airport Authority of Thailand (AOT). The airport has its fair share of complaints, usually sparse toilet facilities, a congested arrival hall and long walks between gates. But the experience is pretty hassle-free, the main bugbear being rogue taxis *(see below)*.

The airport has a good range of facilities, including foreign exchange outlets, ATMs, a Tourism Authority of Thailand (TAT) office, medical centre, Internet facilities and a wide array of shops and restaurants.

For more details check the airport website or call any of the following:

Airport Call Centre
Tel: 0-2132 1888
Arrivals
Tel: 0-2132 9328–9
Departures
Tel: 0-2132 9324–7

In line with the practice of major airports the world over, the airport tax for international flights out of Suvarnabhumi is now incorporated into the price of your air ticket.

Don Muang Airport

The old **Don Muang Airport** (tel: 0-2535 1111; www.airportthai.co.th) re-opened in March 2007 following the teething problems that Suvarnabhumi was experiencing. A small number of THAI domestic flights and all domestic flights operated by Nok Air and Orient Thai use Don Muang Airport.

Don Muang is about 30km (19 miles) north of the city centre. It takes about 40–45 minutes by taxi, depending on traffic, to get to or from the airport.

Note: if making a flight connection between Suvarnabhumi and Don Muang airports, be sure to allow for sufficient time as taxi travel time between the two airports could take up to 1½ hours.

Flying from UK and US

Even if you don't plan to spend any time in Thailand, Bangkok is the most convenient (and sometimes the only) way to transfer to neighbouring countries like Laos, Cambodia and Burma. The recent introduction of low-cost airlines to Thailand means that domestic and regional flights to nearby destinations like Malaysia and Singapore and even destinations in southern China have become incredibly cheap – if booked in advance.

Passengers from UK and Europe can fly direct to Bangkok in about 12 hours, though it is considerably cheaper to take an airline that makes a stopover in Europe, the Middle East or Asia. Airlines that fly non-stop include British Airways, Qantas, THAI and EVA Airways. Many travellers to Australia and New Zealand choose Bangkok as a transit point on their journey.

Travel time from the US is considerably longer. Flying from the West Coast usually takes around 18 hours (not including transit time) and often involves a connection in North Asia – Japan, Korea or Taiwan; the East Coast route via Europe takes about 19 hours in the air.

By Rail

The **State Railway of Thailand** (tel: 0-2222 0175, hotline: 1690; www.railway.co.th) operates trains that are generally clean, cheap and reliable, if a little slow. There are three entry points by rail into Thailand. Two are from Malaysia, the most popular of which is the daily train that leaves Butterworth near Penang at 1.15pm for Hat Yai (south Thailand) and arrives in Bangkok's Hualamphong Station at 10.50am the next morning. Trains leave Hualamphong daily at 2.45pm for Malaysia. In 2009, a short line opened from Nong Khai in northeastern Thailand to Thanaleng, in Laos. It will eventually run to Vientiane.

If you like to travel in style and prefer not to fly, then plump for the **Eastern and Oriental Express** (www.orient-express.com). Travelling several times a month between Singapore, Kuala Lumpur and Bangkok, the 22-carriage train is a very expensive but very elegant way to travel.

By Road

Malaysia provides the main road access into Thailand, with crossings near Betong and Sungai Kolok. From Laos, it is possible to cross from Vientiane into Nong Khai in northeast Thailand by using the Friendship Bridge across the Mekong River. From Cambodia, the most commonly used border crossing is from Poipet, which connects to Aranyaprathet, east of Bangkok. One other option is overland from Kompong Cham in Cambodia, crossing over to Hat Lek in Thailand.

GETTING AROUND

From the Airport

The journey from Suvarnabhumi Airport to the city centre takes about 45 minutes, depending on traffic conditions (the worst period is between 4 and 9pm). Negotiating an exit from the Arrival Hall, however, can be more daunting. If you are on a business trip, you'll understand why it is the norm for Bangkok hosts to deploy a personal greeter and escort. Emerging in the Arrival Hall, you may be harangued by taxi (and hotel) touts both inside and outside the barriers. Never volunteer your name or destination to these people. If you already have a reservation at a hotel, a representative will have your name written on a sign, or at least a sign bearing the name of your hotel. If you haven't made prior arrangements, use one of the following modes to get to the city.

ABOVE: Hualamphong Station.

By Taxi

Operating 24 hours daily, all taxis officially serving the airport are air-conditioned and metered. When you exit the Arrival Hall, there is an official taxi booth outside on the fourth-floor concourse. Join the queue and tell the person at the desk where you want to go. A receipt will be issued, with the licence plate number of the taxi and your destination in Thai written on it. Make sure the driver turns on the meter. At the end of your trip, you need to pay what is on the meter plus a B50 airport surcharge. If the driver uses the expressway to speed up the journey, he will ask for your approval first. If you agree, you will have to pay the toll fees, which will be around B70 in total. Depending on traffic, an average fare from the airport to the city centre is around B300 (excluding toll fees and airport surcharge).

By Limousine

There are two limousine operators stationed at the Arrival Hall. **Airports of Thailand Limousines** (tel: 0-2134 2323-6) operates a variety of standard vehicles that can take you to the city centre for B950–B1,100. Luxury cars include Mercedes E Class at B1,600 and 7-series BMW at B2,200. Rates to Pattaya start at around B2,600, depending on the vehicle used. **Thai Airways Limousines** (mobile tel: 081-652 4444; www.thaiairways.com) also operates a premium car service. Prices are similar to that charged by AOT.

By Airport Bus

The Airport Bus passes the main hotels in downtown Bangkok. You must first get on the free airport shuttle to the Public Transportation Centre, which is separate from the main terminal building. Buses depart every 15 minutes from 5.30am to 12.30am, and the cost is B150 per person.

Airport Bus Routes:

AE-1 – to Silom via Pratunam, Thanon Phetchaburi, Thanon Ratchadamri, Thanon Silom and Thanon Surawong.

AE-2 – to Banglamphu via Thanon Phetchaburi, Thanon Lan Luang and Thanon Khao San.

AE-3 – to Sukhumvit (Nana) via Bangna, Thanon Phrakhanong, Ekkamai, Asok, Thanon Ratchadamri, Thanon Phetchaburi and Thanon Sukhumvit.

AE-4 – to Hualamphong Railway Station via Victory Monument, Thanon Ploenchit, Thanon Rama, Thanon Phaya Thai and Thanon Rama IV.

By Rail

The 28km (17-mile) Suvarnabhumi Airport Rail Link (SARL) connecting the airport to the city opened in 2010. The high-speed system has two services. The 24-hour City Line to Phaya Thai calls at eight stations en route – Lat Krabang, Ban Thap Chang, Hua Mak, Ramkhamhaeng, Asoke, Makkasan, Ratchaprarop and Phaya Thai – and takes 30 minutes for the full journey. It links to the Skytrain system at Phaya Thai. The Express Line (6am–1am) runs direct to Bangkok City Air Terminal, at Makkasan (a 15-minute journey), where passengers can check in and drop their luggage. Makkasan will eventually link to Phetchaburi Metro station. Tickets: B15–40 (City Line), B150 (Express Line).

Orientation

Bangkok is a flat, low-lying city that sprawls over 1,565 sq km (602 sq miles) in the heart of Thailand's fertile Central Plains delta. It sits almost in the middle of the country's north–south length, at the mouth of Thailand's longest river, the Chao Phraya, which separates Thonburi to its west from Bangkok to its east.

The modern city has no definitive centre, with major business and shopping areas now occupying Pathumwan, Silom and Sukhumvit. Rattanakosin, the Old City and Chinatown hold most of the city's historic architecture. Dusit mixes the palatial grandeur of European-influenced royal buildings with tiny lanes of the homes of immigrant Vietnamese and Cambodian refugees. Across the river, Thonburi, despite its urban sprawl, offers trips through countryside canals.

Walking is hot work, but the colourful streets give an insightful peek into everyday life as you pick your way through hawker stalls. Ease your progress with water or chopped fresh fruit, served in a bag with a cocktail stick, so it makes it easy to eat on the move.

Street Name Confusion

Note that **Wireless Road** (a street full of embassies and hotels) is more commonly known by its Thai name, **Thanon Withayu**. Similarly, **Sathorn Road**, a main thoroughfare divided into north and south which runs between Lumphini Park and the river, is often referred to as **Sathorn Nua** (north) and **Sathorn Tai** (south). With no standard translated English spellings for the Thai language, it is common to find a street or area spelt with several variants and broken or joined syllables. Even more confusing, some streets have as many as four names, based on old and new official names and landmarks. Skytrain station names often differ from the street sign spelling, so Chidlom district becomes Chit Lom station, Thanon Asoke becomes Asok station, and Soi Thonglor becomes Thong Lo.

Public Transport

Skytrain (BTS)

BTS Tourist Information Centre: tel: 0-2617 7340; hotline: tel: 0-2617 6000; www.bts.co.th.

The Bangkok Transit System's (BTS) elevated train service, better known as Skytrain, is the perfect way of beating the city's traffic-congested streets. It consists of two lines. The **Sukhumvit Line** runs from Mo Chit station in the north to On Nut in the southeast. The **Silom Line** runs from National Stadium, near Siam Square, south to Wongwian Yai station, across the river in Thonburi. The lines intersect at Siam station.

The Skytrain is fast, frequent and clean, but suffers from overcrowding during peak hours. Accessibility too is problem for the disabled and aged as there aren't enough escalators or lifts.

Trains operate from 6am to midnight (3 minutes peak; 5 minutes off-peak). Single-trip fares vary according to distance, starting at B15 and rising to B40. Self-service ticket machines are found at all station concourses. Tourists may find it more useful to buy the unlimited ride 1-Day Pass (B120) or the 30-Day Adult Pass (which comes in three types: B440 for 20 rides, B600 for 30 and B800 for 40) – all available at station counters.

BTS Tourist Information Centres are found on the concourse levels of Siam, Nana and Saphan Taksin stations (daily 8am–8pm).

Metro (MRT or Subway)

Customer Relations Centre: tel: 0-2624 5200; www.bangkokmetro.co.th.

Bangkok's metro line was launched in July 2004 by the Mass Rapid Transit Authority (MRT). The line has 18 stations, stretching 20km (12 miles) between Bang Sue in the northern suburbs of Bangkok and the city's main railway station, Hualamphong, at the edge of Chinatown. Three of its stations – Silom, Sukhumvit and Chatuchak Park – are interchanges, where passengers can transfer to the BTS network, though you need to pay separately for each service.

Operating from 6am to midnight, the air-conditioned trains are frequent, with never more than a few minutes' wait (2–4 minutes peak, 4–6 minutes off-peak). Fares start at B16, increasing by B2–3 every station, with a maximum fare of B41.

Unlike the BTS, coin-sized plastic tokens are used instead of cards, with self-service ticket machines at all stations. Also available at station counters are passes with unlimited rides: the 1-Day Pass (B120), 3-Day Pass (B230), 15-Day Pass (B600) and the stored-value Adult Card (B200, which includes a B50 deposit).

Taxis

Taxis are in Bangkok are metered, air-conditioned, inexpensive and comfortably seat 3–4 persons. It's best to hail them on the streets, as those parked outside hotels often hustle for a no-meter fare. Metered taxis are recognisable by the sign on their roof, and they have an illuminated red light above the dashboard indicating whether it's available for hire or not.

The flag-fall is B35 for the first kilometre, then B5–8.50 per kilometre, depending on distance travelled. If stuck in traffic, a small per-minute surcharge kicks in. If your journey crosses town, ask the driver to take the expressway. The network of elevated multi-lane roads can cut the journey time by more than half. The toll fare of B25–50 is given to the driver at the payment booth, not at the end of the trip.

Before starting, check that the meter has been reset and turned on. Generally, drivers are far better than their reputation in this regard, but will try it on occasionally. This happens particularly if there is heavy rain, when it is sometimes wise to negotiate, otherwise you may be stuck for some time but the meter will keep ticking. Fares, however, are negotiated for longer distances outside Bangkok: for instance, to Pattaya (B1,200), Koh Samet (B1,500) or Hua Hin (B1,500–2,000). Often, drivers don't speak much English, but should know the locations of major hotels. It is a good idea to have a destination written in Thai.

The following taxi companies take bookings (there's a B20 surcharge):

Siam Taxi, hotline: 1661
Nakhornthai Transportation, tel: 02-878 9000

Tuk-Tuks

Tuk-tuks are the brightly coloured three-wheeled taxis, whose name comes from the incessant noise their two-stroke engines make. Few tuk-tuk drivers speak English, so make sure your destination is written down in Thai. Negotiate the fare before you set off. Expect to pay B30–50 for short journeys of a few blocks or around 15 minutes or less, and B50–100 for longer journeys. A B100 ride should get you a half-hour ride across most parts of downtown. Be sure to negotiate the fare beforehand. Although they can be a fun experience, unless you bargain hard, tuk-tuk fares are rarely lower than metered taxi fares and you are surrounded by traffic fumes.

Motorcycle Taxis

Motorcycle taxi stands are noticeable by their drivers – a gathering of men in fluorescent numbered vests found at the mouth of many *sois*, at busy intersections, buildings and markets. Hire only a driver who provides a passenger helmet, and negotiate fares beforehand. For longer journeys motorcycle taxis are rarely cheaper than taxi fares for the same distance travelled, but they are a great way to beat the traffic and economical for short journeys, such as the length of a street, which will cost B10–20. Longer rides (B80–100 should get you a half-hour trip across most parts of downtown) are more expensive during rush hour (8–10am, 4–6pm). Hold on tight and keep your knees tucked in (Thai women usually ride side-saddle, with their hands clasped between their knees for modesty). If the driver is going too fast, ask him to slow down in Thai: "*cha-cha*".

Buses

Buses are very cheap but with little English either spoken by staff or on signage, finding the right bus can be frustrating. They come in air-conditioned or non-air-conditioned varieties and the Bangkok Metropolitan Authority (BMA)have made attempts to clean up the surrounding air by banning buses with heavy exhaust fumes. Municipal and private operators all come under the charge of the Bangkok Mass Transit Authority (tel: 0-2246 0973; www.bmta.co.th). Free maps found at the airport and tourist centres often have bus routes marked.

Boats

The most common waterborne transport is The **Chao Phraya Express Boat Company** (tel: 0-2623 6143; www.chaophrayaboat.co.th), which runs several services between Nonthaburi pier in the north to Ratburana in the south. Boats run every 15 minutes from 6am to 9pm, and stop at different piers according to the coloured flag on top of the boat. Yellow and green flags are fastest, but stop at only 12 piers, while orange flags are slowest but stop at every pier. Sat and Sun have only orange flags. Tickets cost B17–34 and are purchased from the conductor on board or at some pier counters.

The **Chao Phraya Tourist Boat** (tel: 0-2623 6143; www.chaophrayaboat.co.th) operates daily from 9.30am to 3pm and a trip costs B120. After 3.30pm, you can use the ticket on regular express boats. A useful commentary is provided on board, plus a small guidebook and a bottle of water. The route begins at the Sathorn pier and travels upriver to the Phra Athit pier, stopping at 10 major piers along the way. Boats leave every 30 minutes and you can get off at any pier and pick up another boat later on this hop-on-hop-off service.

Transport Etiquette

While it is quite normal to let an elderly person stand up on a crowded bus or train, legions of locals are quick to vacate their seats if a young child steps aboard. On buses, the two seats nearest the door must be vacated for monks; female passengers should not sit next to a monk on any kind of transport. Queuing is still a novel concept to most Thais, so don't expect any orderly behaviour at bus stops or boat piers. At rush hours on the Skytrain and metro, you often see commuters standing in front of train doors blocking passengers from getting off while squeezing to get in.

River **ferries** are used for getting from one side of the river to the other. They can be boarded close to the jetties that service the Chao Phraya River Express Boats; cost from B2.50 per journey; and operate from 5am to 10pm or later.

Longtail boat taxis ply the narrow inner canals, carrying passengers from the centre of town to the outlying districts. Many of the piers are located near road bridges. Be sure to tell the conductor your destination, as boats do not stop otherwise. Tickets cost B5–10, depending on distance, with services operating roughly every 10 minutes until 6–7pm. While there are routes serving Thonburi's canals and Bangkok's outskirts, tourists will probably only use the main downtown artery of Khlong Saen Saep, which starts from the Saphan Phan Fah pier near Wat Saket, into the heart of downtown and beyond to Bang Kapi. It's useful if going to the Old City, Jim Thompson's House, Siam Paragon and the Thanon Ploenchit malls or all the way to Thonglor and Ekkamai.

If you wish to explore the canals of Thonburi or Nonthaburi, **private longtail boats** can be hired from most of the river's main piers. A 90-minute to two-hour tour will take you into the quieter canal communities. Negotiate rates beforehand and get an agreement on what sites will be included and which route the boat will take. On the journey ask to pull up and get out if anything interests you. An hour-long trip should cost B700–800, rising to B1,000 and more for two hours. The price is for the entire boat, which seats up to 16 people, not per person.

Above: the busy and colourful streets of Bangkok.

Rental Cars

Driving in Bangkok has some frustrations, but with a few adjustments and *jai yen* (a cool heart), the experience is generally comfortable. The problems include: drivers will often cut in front of you with little warning, side streets are very narrow and busy, signalling is rarely used, motorbikes are everywhere, and again have little road discipline, so use of wing mirrors needs to be constant. It might sound scary, but drivers generally stick to their lane, at least, and if you're used to city driving there should be little to worry about. If you park on the street at night, someone may approach you for a parking fee (usually B40) to watch your car. This is unofficial, but it is better to pay, otherwise your car will be keyed. An international driver's licence is necessary to drive a car; these are available for hire from around B800 a day, including insurance.

Avis: 2/12 Thanon Withayu; tel: 0-2255 5300-4; and Bangkok International Airport Building 2; tel: 0 84 700 8157-9; www.avisthailand.com.

Hertz: Soi 71, Thanon Sukhumvit; tel: 0-2266 4666; www.hertz.com.

Sathorn Car Rent: 6/8–9 Thanon Sathorn; tel: 0-2633 8888.

Trips Out of Bangkok

By Road

Thailand has a good road system with over 50,000km (31,000 miles) of motorways and more being built every year. Road signs are in both Thai and English and you should have no difficulty following a map. An international driver's licence is required.

Driving on a narrow but busy road can be a terrifying experience, with right-of-way determined by size. It is not unusual for a bus to overtake a truck despite the fact that the oncoming lane is filled with vehicles. A safer option is to hire a car or a van with driver for trips outside of Bangkok. A reliable option is www.thaicarhire.com, with rates from around B1,400 per day.

You can get to several places outside Bangkok, like Pattaya and Hua Hin, by simply flagging a taxi on the street or booking one beforehand. Be sure to negotiate a flat rate before boarding; don't use the meter *(see pages 236–7)*.

By Air

Thai Airways International (THAI) services a domestic network, with as many as 14 daily flights to the more popular destinations such as Chiang Mai and Phuket. **Bangkok Airways** is the second-largest domestic operator. In recent years, a slew of low-cost airlines – like **Air Asia** and

One-Two-Go – have entered the market, flying to the main tourism centres in Thailand.
Air Asia: Bangkok International Airport, tel: 0-2215 9999; www.air-asia.com.
Bangkok Airways: 99 Moo 14 Thanon Vibhavadi Rangsit; tel: 1771; www.bangkokair.com.
Nok Air: Bangkok International Airport, tel: 1318 (Call Centre); www.nokair.com.
One-Two-Go Airlines: 222 Thanon Vibhavadi Rangsit; tel: 1126 (Call Centre); www.fly12go.com.
Orient Thai Airlines: 222 Thanon Vibhavadi Rangsit; tel: 0-2229 4260; www.orient-thai.com.
Thai Airways International: Bangkok International Airport; tel: 0-2134 5483; www.thaiair.com.

By Bus

Air-conditioned buses service many destinations in Thailand. VIP coaches with extra leg room are the best for overnight journeys. All buses are operated by the **Transport Company Ltd** (www.transport.co.th), with terminals at the following locations:
Eastern (Ekamai) Bus Terminal: Thanon Sukhumvit opposite Soi 63, tel: 0-2391 8097.
Northern and Northeastern Bus Terminal: Thanon Khampaengphet 2, Northern: tel: 0-2936 2841–48; Northeastern: tel: 0-2936 2852–66 ext. 611.
Southern Bus Terminal: Thanon Boromrat Chonnani, Thonburi, tel: 0-2435 1200.

By Train

State Railway of Thailand (tel: 0-2222 0175, hotline 1690; www.railway.co.th) operates three principal routes – north, northeast and south – from **Hualamphong Railway Station** (Thanon Rama 4; tel: 0-2225 0300). Express and rapid services on the main lines offer first-class air-conditioned or second-class fan-cooled carriages with sleeping cabins or berths. In addition, some trains depart from **Bangkok Noi Station** (tel: 0-2411 3102) in Thonburi.

West

Kanchanaburi
By Train: Take the Southern line from Bangkok Noi Station to Kanchanaburi or to the Kwai River Bridge (via Nakhon Pathom). Two departures daily (7.45am and 1.55pm) for the 2½-hour journey.
By Bus: Although Kanchanaburi is west of Bangkok, buses leave from the Southern Bus Terminal every 20 minutes from 5am to 10.30pm. Journey time: 2½ hours.

South

Hua Hin
By Taxi: A taxi ride from Bangkok to Hua Hin, taking 3 hours, can be negotiated for a flat rate of B1,500–2,000.
By Train: There are 12 daily departures between 8.05am to 10.50pm for Petchaburi and Hua Hin from Hualamphong Station. The journey takes around 4 hours.
By Bus: Buses leave from the Southern Bus Terminal every 30 minutes between 6.30am and 5.30pm, stopping at Petchaburi and Cha-am before arriving at Hua Hin. The journey takes around 3½ hours.

Eastern Seaboard

Pattaya
By Taxi: A taxi ride from Bangkok to Pattaya can be negotiated for a flat rate of B1,200. The ride will take 90 minutes.
By Bus: Buses leave every 40 minutes from 5am to 11pm from the Eastern Bus Terminal. The journey takes around 2 hours.

Ko Samet
By Taxi: A Bangkok taxi will make the 3-hour ride to Ban Phe pier in Rayong province for a flat rate of B1,500.
By Bus: Buses leave every hour from 5am to 9pm from Eastern Bus Terminal to Ban Phe pier. Travel time is 3½ hours.
By Boat: Once in Ban Phe pier, fishing boats leave every 30 minutes to an hour (or when there are enough passengers) for the short ride to Na Dan pier on Ko Samet. If there are a few of you, hiring a speedboat is much faster (B800–B1,000).

Ko Chang
By Bus: Buses leave from Eastern Bus Terminal to Trat every 90 minutes between 6am to 11.30pm. The journey takes around 5 to 6 hours. From Trat bus station take a *songthaew* (van with bench seats) to Laem Ngop pier.
By Air: Bangkok Airways has three 50-minute flights a day to Trat airport. From the airport take a 20-minute taxi ride to Laem Ngop pier.
By Boat: From Laem Ngop pier, ferries leave nine times a day between 7am and 5pm for Tha Dan Kao pier in Ko Chang.

North

Ayutthaya
By Train: There are 11 daily departures from Hualamphong from 7am to 10pm. The journey takes around 2 hours.
By Bus: Buses leave every 30 minutes from the Northern Bus Terminal between 5am and 8pm. The journey takes 90 minutes.
By Boat: Several companies operate canal cruises to Ayutthaya; some return the same day, while others take a leisurely 2 to 3 days. The **Chao Phraya Express Boat** (tel: 0-2623 6001) operates a day trip every Sunday at 8am. The **River Sun Cruise** travels one way by coach and returns by boat (tel: 2266 9125; www.riversuncruise.com). More expensive is the overnight trip on board a restored teakwood barge by **Manohra Cruises** (tel: 0-2477 0770; www.manohracruises.com).

Lopburi
By Train: 11 daily departures from Hualamphong from 7am to 10pm. Journey time: 3 hours.
By Bus: Buses leave every 30 minutes from the Northern Bus Terminal between 5am and 8pm daily. The journey to Lopburi takes about 3 hours.

Accommodation

Some Things to Consider Before You Book The Room

Choosing a Hotel

Hotels in Bangkok, with their first-rate service and complete range of facilities, are among the best in the world. The Mandarin Oriental hotel has consistently been rated as one of the world's best, but nipping at its heels are the top-class Peninsula, Shangri-La and Sukhothai hotels. Many moderately-priced hotels in Bangkok would be considered first-class in Europe, and even budget hotels will invariably have a swimming pool and at least one decent food outlet.

Those on a tight budget will find numerous guesthouses offering decent accommodation. Once of primary interest only to backpackers because of their sparse facilities, many have been upgraded to include air-conditioning and en-suite bathrooms. Many of these are found along Thanon Khao San and Sukhumvit Soi 1–15, but there are options all over the city.

Hotel Areas

Downtown Bangkok has the largest number of hotels and is the most convenient for getting around on the BTS (Skytrain) and underground MRT (metro) system. This area includes the prime shopping and entertainment area around Pathumwan and Pratunam, which is home to several mid- to upper-end hotels. Chitlom and Ploenchit have some high-end chains, as do Silom and Sathorn. Heading east along the BTS line, Thanon Sukhumvit has a lot of mid-range accommodation and is packed with dining, drinking and shopping options.

Further west, on the Chao Phraya river, near Saphan Taksin BTS station and Sathorn pier, is where many of city's most luxurious hotels are located – on both sides of the river. The area north along the river towards Chinatown makes for an interesting cultural experience and is quite close to the Old City sights.

Access to the Rattanakosin and the Old City is even easier from the backpacking enclave of Thanon Khao San and Banglamphu. Accommodation options here are principally budget guesthouses; however, new mid-range boutique inns and lodges have also opened for business in these areas.

Prices and Bookings

Thailand has plenty of good-value accommodation, but as more hotels and guesthouses upgrade to compete with new boutique and design-oriented hotels, prices have begun to creep up.

It's worth checking rates again before arrival as there are high, low and peak seasons. Many hotels have recently started adding compulsory gala dinners to the room rate at Christmas and New Year, some of which are exorbitantly priced in return for what is little more than a fancy buffet dinner. Be sure to book a room in advance during the Christmas, New Year or Chinese New Year holiday and, if staying outside Bangkok, during Songkran in mid-April.

Many mid- and top-end hotels add a standard 7 percent VAT and 10 percent service to the bill, so check to see if the rate includes this or not. Increasingly, internet bookings are cheaper than the walk-in or call-up rate. Either check the hotel website directly, or online hotel sites like **Thailand Hotels Association** (www.thaihotels.org).

Serviced Apartments

Another option is to rent a serviced apartment. They're often a great choice for families and have many of the facilities you'd find in a good hotel, such as a gym, swimming pool and often a restaurant. In fact many hotels now offer the service themselves, as do some large shopping malls. You can search for properties by area at **www.sabaai.com**, and rent by the day or get better deals booking by the week or month.

ACCOMMODATION LISTINGS

THONBURI

Luxury

The Peninsula Bangkok
333 Th Charoen Nakorn
Tel: 0-2861 2888
www.peninsula.com
1 p273, D4
Being on the "wrong" side of the river, the hotel's rooms, all of which overlook the Chao Phraya, have views of downtown, and the contemporary international decor has neat Asian undertones. The Chinese restaurant, Mei Jiang, is superb. Free shuttle boat to the Saphan Taksin BTS station.

Expensive

Bangkok Marriott Resort and Spa
257 Th Charoen Nakorn
Tel: 0-2476 0022
www.marriotthotels.com
2 p273, D4
With lush grounds and a pool that fronts the river, this resort feels like an escape from the city as you arrive on the free shuttle boat. It has six restaurants, the Mandara Spa and Thai dinner-dance performances on the Riverside Terrace.

Millennium Hilton Bangkok
123 Th Charoen Nakorn
Tel: 0-2442 2000
www.bangkok.hilton.com
3 p273, D3
The swish Hilton has a stylish modern Asian interior designed by Tony Chi. All rooms have expansive windows with river views and the pool has a resort feel. There's a spa, four restaurants and two bars, plus a complimentary shuttle boat to the Bangkok side.

RATTANAKOSIN, OLD CITY AND DUSIT

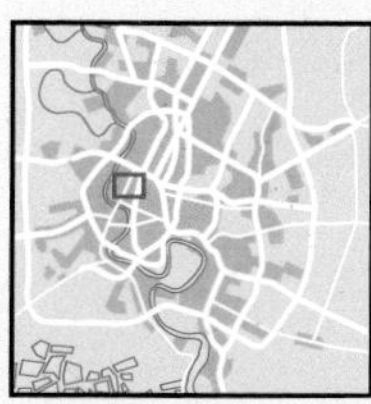

Expensive

Chakrabongse Villa
396 Th Maharat
Tel: 0-2225 0139
www.thaivillas.com
4 p272, B1
This early-20th-century riverside compound was the home of a Thai prince. Its four elegant Thai-style villas overlook Wat Arun. Beautiful gardens and a secluded swimming pool add to its appeal, as does the 15-minute walk to the Grand Palace.

Moderate

Arun Residence
38 Soi Pratoo Nok Yoong, Th Maharat
Tel: 0-2221 9158
www.arunresidence.com
5 p272, B1
A small riverbank hotel with views of Wat Arun and just a short walk from Wat Pho and 100-year-old Chinese shophouses. Its French–Thai restaurant, The Deck *(see page 117)*, is an atmospheric spot for cocktails and dinner.

Buddy Lodge
265 Th Khao San
Tel: 0-2629 4477
www.buddylodge.com
6 p268, C3
Khao San's pioneering boutique hotel in the early noughties, Buddy Lodge has a rooftop swimming pool, fitness room and even a well-run spa. The rooms are more cute than plush, but are ensuite with louvred windows and satellite TV.

Old Bangkok Inn
609 Th Phra Sumen
Tel: 0-2629 1785
www.oldbangkokinn.com
7 p269, C3
With teak furniture and fittings this 10-room hotel is a gem of traditional Thai character, set in a late 19th-century royal home. Some rooms have split-level accommodation, and each one has satellite TV, DVD players, broadband internet and even computers.

Viengtai Hotel
42 Th Rambuttri
Tel: 0-2280 5434–45
www.viengtai.co.th
8 p268, C3
This large, recently renovated hotel has smartly decorated ensuite rooms with cable TV. There are a few family suites, too, plus a small outdoor swimming pool, wireless internet access in the lobby and a buffet restaurant.

Budget

D&D Inn
68-70 Th Khao San
Tel: 0-2629 0526–8
www.khaosanby.com
9 p268, B3
Right in the middle of Khao San, this is more of a hotel than guesthouse, with a rooftop swimming pool, bar and

PRICE CATEGORIES

Price categories for a double room without breakfast and taxes:
Luxury = over B8,000
Expensive = B4,000–8,000
Moderate = B2,000–4,000
Budget = under B2,000

an open *sala* for traditional massage. Rooms are well equipped with bathrooms, air-conditioning, TV, fridge and IDD phone.

Khao San Palace
139 Th Khao San
Tel: 0-2282 0578
www.khaosanpalace.com
⑩ p268, B3
Among the better guesthouses here, this is located just off Khao San down a small alley. The newer rooms are very smart, with en-suite showers, air-con and TV. Good views from the small rooftop pool.

Sawasdee Bangkok Inn
126/2 Th Khao San
Tel: 0-2280 1251
www.sawasdee-hotels.com
⑪ p268, B3
Part of a growing chain run by the Sawasdee group, the decor is an attempt at old Siam. The rooms are clean and most have air-conditioning, hot shower and TV. There is a restaurant, bar, internet access and travel agent on site.

CHINATOWN

Moderate

Grand China Princess
Th Yaowaraj
Tel: 0-2224 9977
www.grandchina.com
⑫ p273, D1
Smart rooms with good river and city views are a major draw, as is the revolving restaurant on the 25th floor. Located amid the Chinatown bustle, it's 10 minutes to the Old City by taxi.

Shanghai Mansion
479–481 Th Yaowaraj
Tel: 0-2221 2121
www.shanghaimansion.com
⑬ p273, D2
A classy boutique hotel with lovely over-the-top chinoiserie, four-poster beds and vibrant saturated hues, many reflecting those you see in the nearby market alleyways; it is *feng-shui* heaven. There is free internet access and a spa, too.

Budget

Bangkok Centre
328 Th Rama IV
Tel: 0-2238 4848
www.bangkokcentrehotel.com
⑭ p273, E2
This budget place on the outskirts of Chinatown is within walking distance of Hualamphong railway station. The smartly furnished air-conditioned rooms have TV, and there's internet access, a swimming pool and three restaurants.

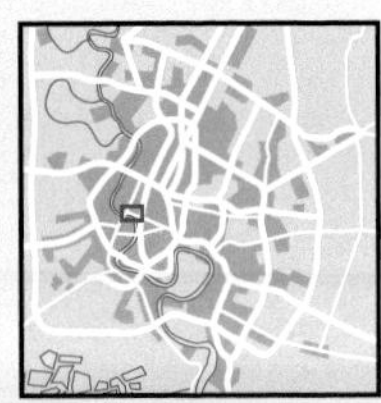

PATHUMWAN AND PRATUNAM

Luxury

Conrad Bangkok
All Seasons Place, 87 Th Withayu
Tel: 0-2690 9999
www.conradhotels.com
⑮ p275, D2
Located next door to the All Seasons Place shopping centre, the Conrad has spacious and contemporary rooms, furnished with Thai silk and woods and large bathrooms with rain showers. Also offers high-speed internet access and an excellent choice of outlets such as the Diplomat jazz bar.

Four Seasons
155 Th Ratchadamri
Tel: 0-2251 6127
www.fourseasons.com/bangkok
⑯ p274, C1/2
Expect five-star luxury including a magnificent lobby decorated with hand-painted silk ceilings and Thai murals by renowned local artists. The hotel also has some of the city's best dining outlets, including the Italian Biscotti.

Grand Hyatt Erawan
494 Th Ratchadamri
Tel: 0-2254 1234
www.bangkok.grand.hyatt.com
⑰ p275, C1
Smack in the middle of downtown's shopping mecca and beside the Erawan Shrine, the Hyatt's imposing formal lobby has huge classical columns. An excellent range of restaurants includes the traditional French restaurant Tables, and the basement restaurant-nightclub Spasso.

InterContinental Bangkok
973 Th Ploenchit
Tel: 0-2656 0444
www.ichotelsgroup.com
⑱ p275, C1
Linked to Chit Lom Skytrain station and Gaysorn Plaza, this hotel has spacious rooms with Internet access and CD players. A rooftop swimming pool has fine city views, and there's a very cute new Italian bistro, called Grossi, in the basement.

Expensive

Amari Watergate
847 Th Petchaburi
Tel: 0-2653 9000-19
www.amari.com/watergate
⑲ p275, C4
This hotel has a great gym, the pampering Sivara Spa and a popular basement Americana bar and grill, Henry J. Beans. It's located just across the Pratunam Market and close to the shopping district around Central World. All rooms have flat-screen TV, DVD

wireless access and floor-to-ceiling windows.

Swissotel Nai Lert Park
2 Th Withayu
Tel: 0-2253 0123
www.swissotel.com
20 p275, D1
Set in a small tropical garden with a landscaped pool, there's a touch of contemporary attitude here in the hip lounge bar Syn, which has a wide range of custom cocktails. The curious can check out the phallic totems at Nai Lert Shrine beside the canal.

Moderate

Asia Hotel
296 Th Phayathai
Tel: 0-2215 0808
www.asiahotel.co.th
21 p270, B4
Joined to Ratchathewi Skytrain station, this hotel is not particularly attractive from the outside but is well maintained within. Many facilities on site, as well as the famous ladyboy cabaret shows and Elvis impersonators.

Novotel Bangkok
Siam Square Soi 6
Tel: 0-2255 6888
www.accorhotels-asia.com
22 p274, B2
Tucked among the buzzy Siam Square, a short walk to shopping malls and the Siam Skytrain station, location is a big draw here. The hotel's large basement entertainment complex, Concept CM2, is a frequently packed local nightspot.

Pathumwan Princess
444 Th Phayathai
Tel: 0-2216 3700
www.pprincess.com
23 p274, B1
This centrally located hotel joined to the huge Mahboonkrong mall is ideal for shoppers. It's a family-friendly place with a large saltwater pool, a gym and comfortable rooms, and offers good value for money.

VIE Hotel
117/39-40 Th Phaya Thai
Tel: 0-2309 3939
www.accorhotels.com
24 p270, B4
This new hotel has modern, elegant rooms fitted with LCD TVs, computers, Wi-fi and lots of nice Asian design touches. It's a few minutes' walk from downtown malls and there's a rooftop pool bar to relax at.

Budget

A-One Inn
13–15 Soi Kasemsan 1, Th Rama I
Tel: 0-2215 3029
www.aoneinn.com
25 p274, B1
The basic rooms here nevertheless have satellite TV and air-con, and the hotel offers value for money so close to Siam Square shops and the SkyTrain. It also has an internet café with Wi-fi and a laundry service. If you can't find space here, this street has other similar options.

Bangkok Palace
1091 New Th Petchaburi
Tel: 0-2253 0510
www.bangkokpalace.com
26 p271, D4
A large, old-style hotel, close to Pratunam Market, Panthip Plaza and the expressway. Some of its recently refurbished rooms have good city views and there's a small gym, sauna and an open-air pool.

BANGRAK AND SILOM

Luxury

Banyan Tree Bangkok
21/100 Th Sathorn Tai
Tel: 0-2679 1200
www.banyantree.com
27 p274, C4
Bangkok's third-tallest hotel has large luxury suites. The Vertigo Grill and Moon Bar are breathtaking alfresco rooftop outlets and the luxurious Banyan Tree Spa (the highest in the city) also offers spectacular views.

The Mandarin Oriental
48 Oriental Avenue
Tel: 0-2659 9000
www.mandarinoriental.com
28 p273, E4
Bangkok's riverside "Grand Dame" has hosted guests since 1876 in its original Authors' Wing, which still has period suites and delightful tea rooms. It also has the excellent Le Normandie French restaurant and Ayurvedic pleasures in the Oriental Spa.

The Metropolitan
27 Th Sathorn Tai
Tel: 0-2625 3322
www.metropolitan.como.bz
29 p275, C4
Expect East–West minimalist chic at this sister to the Met in London. The Met Bar hosts cultural events with good cocktails and DJ grooves and the Como Shambhala Spa offers Asian-influenced treatments.

BELOW: Banyan Tree spa.

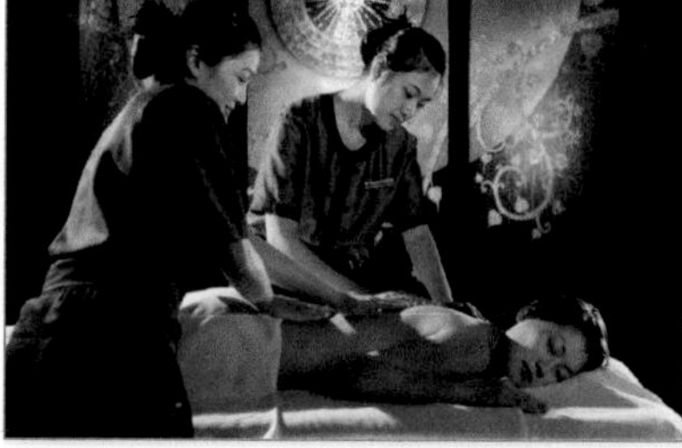

PRICE CATEGORIES

Price categories for a double room without breakfast and taxes:
Luxury = over B8,000
Expensive = B4,000–8,000
Moderate = B2,000–4,000
Budget = under B2,000

There is also a branch of David Thompson's Michelin-starred Thai restaurant Nahm.

The Sukhothai
13/3 Th South Sathorn
Tel: 0-2344 8888
www.sukhothai.com
30 p275, C4
Drawing inspiration from ancient Sukhothai, this place pioneered Asian detailing in a contemporary setting. It has rooms in tropical gardens with a reflecting pool, while on-site distractions include one of Bangkok's best upmarket Thai restaurants, Celadon, and the tastefully attired Zuk Bar.

Expensive

Le Bua at State Tower
State Tower,
1055/111 Th Silom
Tel: 0-2624 9999
www.lebua.com
31 p273, E4
Le Bua has contemporary Asian-style rooms and suites in the 64-storey State Tower, with river- or city-view balconies. The rooftop outlets, collectively called The Dome, feature the top restaurants Sirocco, Mezzaluna and Breeze, and the sophisticated Distil Bar.

Dusit Thani
946 Th Rama IV
Tel: 0-2200 9999
www.dusit.com
32 p274, B3
Situated near Lumphini Park, Patpong nightlife and MRT and Skytrain stations, the Dusit Thani now has some new millennium chic in the Asian-tinged interior. The Devarana Spa is high quality, as is the French dining at the top-floor D'Sens, one of 13 bars and restaurants in this luxury hotel.

Le Meridien Bangkok
40/5 Th Surawong
Tel: 0-2232 8888
www.lemeridien.com/bangkok surawong
33 p274, B3
A fully wired techno vision of brushed concrete, glass and funky nightclub lighting effects just 50 metres/yds from Patpong. Rooms have full wall windows and flat-screen TVs and the Bamboo Chic restaurant fuses Thai, Japanese and Chinese cuisines to a techno soundtrack.

Montien
54 Th Surawong
Tel: 0-2233 7060–69
www.montien.com
34 p274, B3
This 1960s throwback, one of the city's oldest modern hotels, is a stone's throw from the naughty nightlife of Patpong, and Sala Daeng Skytrain station. It's a faded grand hotel with three restaurants and Thai fortune tellers on the first floor.

Royal Orchid Sheraton
2 Captain Bush Lane
Tel: 0-2266 0123
www.royalorchidsheraton.com
35 p274, E3
The Sheraton's recent makeover has given its rooms a much more contemporary feel to match its prime riverfront location. The new Sambal international restaurant, all rooms and the swimming pool overlook the Chao Phraya.

Below: Le Meridien's Bamboo Chic restaurant.

Shangri-La
89 Soi Wat Suan Plu
Tel: 0-2236 7777
www.shangri-la.com
36 p274, E4
The largest of the five-star hotels located along the Chao Phraya, whose highlights include a beautiful free-form pool overlooking the river, the Chi Spa and the Italian restaurant Angelini's.

Moderate

La Residence
173/8-9 Th Surawong
Tel: 0-2266 5400
www.laresidencebangkok.com
37 p274, A3
A small, friendly hotel with funky, individually decorated rooms, including two modest suites, one with garden views. There is no pool but all accommodation has Wi-fi access and it is just a short cab ride to Patpong night market.

Sofitel Silom
188 Th Silom
Tel: 0-2238 1991
www.sofitel.com
38 p274, A4
Stylish 38-storey hotel in the quieter part of Thanon Silom, a short walk to Chong Nonsi Skytrain station. Its wine bar, V9, has good views from the 37th floor, while one floor above is the excellent Shanghai 38 Chinese restaurant.

Tarntawan Place
119/5-10 Th Surawong
Tel: 0-2238 2620-39
www.tarntawan.com
39 p274, B3
This is a gay-friendly hotel located off a quiet *soi*; there's only one restaurant and bar, but the rooms have tasteful Thai detailing and it is close to the Patpong night market and the clubs

and bars of Surawong and Silom.

Budget

Baan Saladaeng
69/2 Saladaeng Soi 3
Tel: 0-2636 3038
www.baansaladaeng.com
40 p274, C4
A very tasteful budget operation with just nine themed rooms with names like Neo Siam, Moroccan Suite and Pop Art Mania. Each has aircon, TV and wireless internet. There's a small coffee bar, and it's a great location for transport, restaurants and nightlife.

Take a Nap
920–26 Th Rama 4
Tel: 0-2637 0015
www.takeanaphotel.com
41 p274, B3
You will find basic but attractively attired rooms here, each with an artistic theme, such as Japanese Waves, Pop Art, and the child-like Happy Forest. There is air-con and a few TV stations, but no fridge or wardrobe. Close to Patpong and Skytrain and subway stations.

Sukhumvit

Luxury

Sheraton Grande Sukhumvit
250 Th Sukhumvit
Tel: 0-2649 8888
www.starwood.com/bangkok
42 p275, E2
Facilities at this deluxe spot include a landscaped swimming pool and an excellent spa, plus excellent Thai and Italian restaurants. The Living Room lounge bar hosts some hot visiting jazz players. Great location with a skywalk to BTS and MRT stations.

Expensive

Emporium Suites
622 Th Sukhumvit Soi 24
Tel: 0-2664 9999
www.emporiumsuites.com
Off map
Located above the Emporium mall and connected to the Phrom Phong BTS station, these stylish serviced apartments comprise studios and 1-bedroom suites up to 3-bedroom apartments. Some rooms have nice views of Benjasiri Park.

The Eugenia
267 Sukhumvit Soi 31
Tel: 0-2259 9011
www.theeugenia.com
Off map
This 12-suite accommodation in a 19th-century home has Old-World colonial charm. All rooms have antique furnishings and many have four-poster beds. The hotel's limousines are a fleet of vintage Jaguars and Mercedes Benz.

JW Marriott
4 Th Sukhumvit Soi 2
Tel: 0-2656 7700
www.marriotthotels.com
43 p275, E1
Close to Sukhumvit's nightlife, this place has a huge fitness centre, efficient business facilities and spacious, well-appointed rooms. Some of the city's best dining is at Tsunami Japanese restaurant and the New York Steakhouse.

Westin Grande Sukhumvit
259 Th Sukhumvit Soi 19
Tel: 0-2207 8000
www.westin.com/bangkok
44 p275, E2
A large, modern hotel offering comfortable rooms and karaoke with a view at Horizons Sky Lounge. Other pluses include an outdoor pool with a swim-up bar, and hydrotherapy bath and aroma steam room at the Vareena day spa.

Moderate

Amari Boulevard
Th Sukhumvit Soi 7
Tel: 0-2255 2930/40
www.amari.com/boulevard
45 p275, E1
This is an oasis in a raucous tourist area filled with markets, noodle shops and girlie bars. Amenities include a sixth-floor swimming pool, fitness centre, restaurants and garden terraces attached to some of the deluxe rooms.

Dream BKK
10 Sukhumvit Soi 15
Tel: 0-2254 8500
www.dreambkk.com
46 p275, E2
Dream offers 100 rooms with clean lines and ambient lighting, plus nice touches like Egyptian-cotton bedsheets and personal iPod players. Its restaurant serves Thai and Western food, and the chill-out Flava Lounge is a good spot for drinks.

Landmark
138 Th Sukhumvit
Tel: 0-2254 0404
www.landmarkbangkok.com
47 p275, E1/2
Easy access to Nana Skytrain station and a good location for bars, restaurants and the market stalls of Sukhumvit. Wide choice of outlets includes a top-floor steak house with good city views, and The Huntsman pub in the basement.

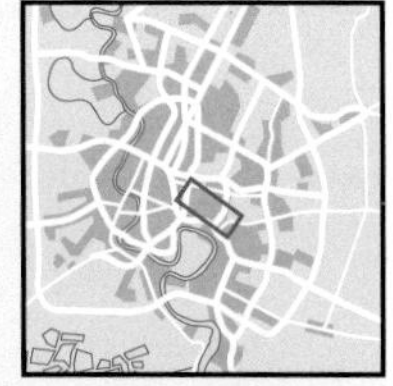

Novotel Lotus
1 Th Sukhumvit Soi 33
Tel: 0-2261 0111
www.accorhotels-asia.comaa
Off map
Very tasteful guest rooms spreading off a Zen-like hotel lobby with an appropriate lotus pond. It has a café and two restaurants, and is close to shopping and Phrom Phong Skytrain station.

President Park
95 Th Sukhumvit Soi 24
Tel: 0-2661 1000
www.presidentpark.com
Off map
Large modern apartment complex with spacious studios. Rooms

Price Categories

Price categories for a double room without breakfast and taxes:
Luxury = over B8,000
Expensive = B4,000–8,000
Moderate = B2,000–4,000
Budget = under B2,000

have plasma TVs and DVD players and a kitchenette attached. There are three large pools and full leisure facilities in its Capitol Club. Daily, weekly and monthly rates available.

Rembrandt
19 Th Sukhumvit Soi 18
Tel: 0-2261 7100
www.rembrandtbkk.com
Off map
A good-value hotel on a small *soi* of shops and eateries. There's a complimentary tuk-tuk shuttle to the end of the *soi* and then it's a short walk to the BTS or MRT station. Has the city's best Indian dining at Rang Mahal, and a Mexican restaurant, Señor Pico.

Windsor Suites
8-10 Th Sukhumvit Soi 20
Tel: 0-2262 1234
www.windsorsuiteshotel.com
Off map
An all-suite hotel with satellite TV and internet access. It has Chinese, Japanese and international restaurants, a spa and a beer garden. A short cab ride to Asok and Phrom Phong Skytrain stations.

Budget

Ambassador
171 Sukhumvit Soi 11
Tel: 0-2254 0444
www.amtel.co.th
Off map
It is huge and rather dated, but this hotel has decent rooms for this price range, and is only a five-minute walk to Nana Skytrain station. There's an on-site spa and outdoor pool and lots of good restaurants and clubs nearby.

Atlanta
78 Th Sukhumvit Soi 2
Tel: 0-2252 1650
www.theatlantahotel.bizland.com
Off map
A quirky 1950s throwback, rich in character, with a period interior, and a strong moral ethos that holds no truck with sex tourists and allows no visitors. There is a pool in landscaped gardens and a good Thai restaurant.

Miami
2 Th Sukhumvit Soi 13
Tel: 0-2253 5611
www.thaimiami.com
Off map
One of several Bangkok hotels modelled on US motels from the 1960s, and the coffee shop still has a retro Miami milk-bar feel. This place may have seen better days, but it's cheap, has a reasonable pool and is close to Sukhumvit's main action.

Sukhumvit 11 Hostel
1/33 Th Sukhumvit Soi 11
Tel: 0-2253 5927
www.suk11.com
Off map
This family-run guesthouse is non-smoking, with bare rooms and with no TV or fridge, but lots of wood and rustic decor. There is internet access in the lobby, plus a common room with TV and DVDs. A short walk from the Skytrain station.

BANGKOK'S SURROUNDINGS

Kanchanaburi

Moderate

Comsaed River Kwai Resort
18/9 Moo 5 Ladya, Kanchanaburi Province
Tel: 0-3463 1443–9
www.comsaedriverkwai.com
Some way outside town in the rolling countryside, with manicured lawns, wooden bridges and riverine views, this hotel is geared up for outdoor activities such as canoeing and biking. Rooms are clean and smart but slightly old-fashioned.

Felix River Kwai
9/1 Moo 3 Thamakham
Tel: 0-3455 1000
www.felixriverkwai.co.th
A comfortable resort, the Felix shows some signs of wear, but it is still the first choice to stay at in town, and the deluxe rooms facing the river are romantic. You can easily walk to the Bridge on the River Kwai from here.

Budget

River Kwai Jungle Rafts
Baan Tahsao, Amphur Saiyoke
Tel: 08-1734 0667, 0-2642 5497 (Bangkok office)
www.serenatahotels.com
For something different, sleep in the floating Jungle Raft's quaint lodgings and eat and drink on the adjoining floating restaurant and bar. You can swim or fish in the river, ride elephants and visit nearby ethnic tribal villages.

Hua Hin/Pranburi

Luxury

Sofitel Centara Hua Hin
1 Damnernkasem Road
Tel: 0-3251 2021
www.sofitel.com
This gorgeous hotel retains its white colonial 1920s elegance. Lush gardens are the backdrop for a choice of villas or handsome rooms, while infinity pools offer prime sunbathing spots in front of the beach.

Expensive

Aleenta
Pranburi Beach
Tel: 0-2514 8112
www.aleenta.com
This intimate beach resort, about 30 minutes' drive from Hua Hin, has atmospheric options including pool and sea-view suites; thatch-roofed bungalows with private balconies and jacuzzis; and a penthouse. There's a bar and spa, and beach dinners can be arranged.

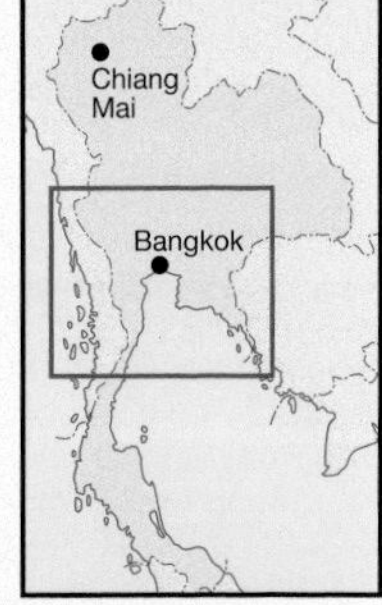

Anantara Resort
43/1 Phetkasem Beach
Tel: 0-3252 0250
www.anantara.com
A luxurious hideaway tucked among verdant gardens and fronting the beach. Rooms have strong Thai silk and teak accents with the more expensive ones facing the beach and the

lagoon. Enjoy the highly rated spa plus Italian and Thai restaurants.

Pattaya

Expensive

Hard Rock Hotel
Pattaya Beach
Tel: 0-3842 8755
www.hardrockhotelpattaya.com
The rooms are fairly standard, with colourful pop colours and music memorabilia typical of Hard Rock outlets, but the vast hotel pool comes complete with boulders and thatched *sala* for shade.

Sheraton Pattaya
437 Th Phra Tamnak
Tel: 0-3825 9888
www.sheraton.com/pattaya
A beautifully landscaped resort with calming water features and a private beach. The rooms are arranged on a terrace running down to the sea and many have their own ocean-facing pavilions. The Amburaya Spa offers the usual pampering.

Moderate

Rabbit Resort
Dongtan Beach, Jomtien
Tel: 0-3825 1730
www.rabbitresort.com
A beach resort with Thai-style houses and bungalows amid pretty palm-tree gardens. All are individually decorated with original artworks and antiques from the owner's collection. Facilities include two pools, a restaurant and an oceanside grill.

Above: view from the Sheraton Pattaya resort.

Ko Samet

Expensive

Ao Phrao Resort
60 Moo 4, Ao Phrao Beach
Tel: 0-3864 4101–7
www.samedresorts.com
The island's most upmarket resort sits on the only beach on the sunset side of Samet. The comfortable bungalows come with cable TV and the resort also has the most expensive restaurant on the island – though don't expect too much.

Le Vimarn
Moo 4, Ao Phrao Beach
Tel: 0-3864 4104–7
www.samedresorts.com
This teakwood resort with infinity pool is under the same ownership as the nearby Ao Prao Resort. Offering an elegant blend of traditional and contemporary local style, you can choose from three types of cottages and villas and try the spa and restaurant.

Moderate

Samed Villa
89 Moo 4, Ao Phai Beach
Tel: 0-3864 4094
www.samedvilla.com
Located at the end of Ao Phai beach on a headland with nice sea views, this popular family-run resort is full most weekends with Bangkok expats. The bungalows are good value with air-con, hot showers and TV.

Ko Chang

Expensive

Amari Emerald Cove Resort
88/8 Moo 4, Ao Khlong Phrao
Tel: 0-3955 2000
www.amari.com
One of the island's biggest and best options has stylish contemporary Asian rooms, a big beachfront pool, three restaurants, a lobby bar and the excellent Sivara Spa.

Moderate

Aiyapura Resort and Spa
29 Moo 3, Ko Chang
Tel: 0-3955 5111
www.aiyapura.com
A secluded resort with pool deck overlooking the sea and rooms with ocean-view terrace, satellite TV, DVD and CD players. It is a great place just to relax, but also offers a range of activities like yoga, meditation, Thai boxing and cooking classes.

Ayutthaya

Budget

Krungsri River Hotel
27/2 Moo 11, Th Rojchana
Tel: 0-3524 4333
www.krungsririver.com
A decent provincial hotel in a town with few options, it has modern facilities, including air-conditioning and cable TV, but is short on ambience. There's a pool, fitness centre, sauna, restaurant and bar.

Khao Yai National Park

Luxury

Kirimaya
1/3 Moo 6, Th Thanarat
Tel: 0-4442 6099
www.kirimaya.com
A very stylish resort that mixes hotel-style rooms with plusher tented villas nestled among plantation-style buildings not far from the park entrance. There's an infinity pool, spa and an 18-hole golf course.

Price Categories

Price categories for a double room without breakfast and taxes:
Luxury = over B8,000
Expensive = B4,000–8,000
Moderate = B2,000–4,000
Budget = under B2,000

Activities

The Arts, Festivals, Nightlife, Sightseeing Tours, Sports and Children's Activities

The Arts

While Thailand's traditional arts and crafts heritage is well identified, there are surprisingly few venues in the capital to appreciate it fully. The modern art scene on the other hand is simmering away in numerous art galleries. There is no distinct cultural enclave in Bangkok: events and sites are dotted throughout the city. See also The Creative Arts chapter *(page 57)*.

Art Galleries

Most contemporary art on view in the capital is created by home-grown artists, several of whom are gaining significant international exposure. For show details check the free monthly Bangkok Art Map (BAM!) available in restaurants, cafés and bars; the *Bangkok Post*; *The Nation* and the website www.rama9art.com.

100 Tonson Gallery
100 Soi Tonson, Thanon Ploenchit
Tel: 0-2684 1527
www.100tonsongallery.com
Attracts some of the country's best artists and holds high-profile exhibitions that create a lot of buzz.

Bangkok Art and Culture Centre
939 Thanon Rama 1
Tel: 0-2214 6630-8
www.bacc.or.th
This vast 500-million-baht centre has areas for multimedia, photography and design, plus performance spaces, and holds regular exhibitions by Thai artists. Art markets on the concourse also feature music, dance and performance from Friday to Sunday *(see page 155)*.

Chulalongkorn Art Centre
7th Floor, Centre of Academic Resources, Chulalongkorn University, Thanon Phayathai
Tel: 0-2218 2964
Showcases some of the country's most prolific artists, as well as influential foreign ones.

H Gallery
201 Soi 12 Thanon Sathorn
Mobile tel: 081-310 4428
www.hgallerybkk.com
Run by an American, this gallery is located in an old converted wooden school building and promotes a young and eclectic stable of commercially viable artists.

National Gallery
4 Thanon Chao Fah
Tel: 0-2281 2224
The permanent collection isn't particularly noteworthy, but it does hold some interesting monthly shows in the annex, mainly by older Thai artists *(see page 110)*.

Numthong Gallery
Room 109, Bangkok Co-op Building, Thanon Toeddamri
Tel: 0-2243 4326
Work by the country's most interesting and successful artists is exhibited in this tiny space.

Queen's Gallery
101 Th Ratchadamnoen Klang
Tel: 0-2281 5360
www.queengallery.org
Five-floor gallery with a steady exhibition schedule of modern and contemporary art, predominantly locally produced works.

Rotunda Gallery
Neilson Hays Library
195 Thanon Surawong
Tel: 0-2233 1731
www.neilsonhayslibrary.com
Hosts monthly shows of mainly conventional art.

Silpakorn University Gallery
31 Thanon Na Phra Lan, opposite the Grand Palace
Tel: 0-2221 3841
www.art-centre.su.ac.th
Thailand's oldest and most prestigious arts university has three galleries displaying works by students, teachers and visiting artists.

Thavibu Gallery
Suite 308, Silom Galleria
Thanon Silom
Tel: 0-2266 5454
www.thavibu.com
Promotes a mixed bag of Thai, Vietnamese and Burmese art.

VER Gallery
2nd Floor, 71/31-35 Klongsarn Plaza, Thanon Charoennakorn
Tel: 0-2861 0933
www.mono.net
Offbeat and funky art space

founded by superstar Thai artist Rirkrit Tiravanija.

Cinema

Bangkok's cinemas are comfortable and tickets are cheap; they usually screen mainstream Hollywood pulp. Thai movies have improved dramatically, and there is more interest in films produced in North Asia. There are numerous large multiplexes but only one independent art cinema, called the **House**, at Royal City Avenue.

EGV Multiplexes
Tel: 0-2812 9999 (all branches)
www.egv.com
6th Floor, Siam Discovery Centre, Thanon Rama I

House Cinema
RCA Plaza, Royal City Avenue
Tel: 0-2641 5177-8
www.houserama.com

Lido Multiplex
Siam Square, Thanon Rama I
Tel: 0-2252 6498
www.apexsiam-square.com

Major Cineplex
Tel: 0-2515 5555 (all branches)
www.majorcineplex.com
Central World Plaza, 7th Floor, Thanon Ratchadamri; Sukhumvit Ekkamai, Soi 61 Sukhumvit; and Ratchayothin, 1839 Thanon Pahonyothin

Paragon Cineplex
5th Floor, Siam Paragon
Thanon Rama I
Tel: 0-2515 5555
www.paragoncineplex.com

Scala
Siam Square Soi 1
Tel: 0-2251 2861
www.apexsiam-square.com

SF Cinemas
www.sfcinemacity.com
7th Floor, Mahboonkrong Centre, 444 Thanon Phayathai, tel: 0-2611 6444; 6th Floor, Emporium, Sukhumvit Soi 24, tel: 0-2260 9333; and 7th Floor Central World, tel: 0-2268 8888

Dinner Dance and Drama

There is traditional *khon* dance-drama, without dinner, at Sala Chalerm Krung *(see below)*, and free performances at the **Erawan Shrine** *(see page 156)* in the Pathumwan area or **Lak Muang** *(see page 109)* near the Grand Palace, both of which have resident dance troupes who are paid by devotees to dance in thanksgiving for having prayers answered.

Otherwise, traditional dance-drama is performed in condensed forms at a few restaurants around the capital, usually by dance-drama students, after a Thai dinner or as vignettes interspersed between the courses.

Riverside Terrace
Marriott Riverside Resort and Spa
257/1-3 Thanon Charoen Nakhon, Thonburi
Tel: 0-2476 0022
Large stone pillars set alight with Olympic-style flames frame a stage fringed by a lily pond. It's a great setting for the nightly 7.30–9pm dance performances that look out over the river.

Ruen Thep Room
Silom Village, 286 Thanon Silom
Tel: 0-2234 4581
A large hall of dark wood and Thai paintings and sculptures creates the right ambience for the nightly hour-long performance at 8.30pm.

Sala Rim Nam
opposite Oriental Hotel
48 Oriental Avenue
Tel: 0-2437 6211
A very grand riverside restaurant decorated in traditional Thai style with set dinner accompanied by entertaining dance-drama performances at 8.30pm nightly.

Siam Niramit
19 Thanon Tiamruammit
Tel: 0-2649 9222
www.siamniramit.com
A beautifully costumed extravaganza that traverses the country's history and diverse cultures in three acts. Nightly performance at 8pm. Pre-show buffet dinner available at its restaurant.

Studio 9
69/1 Soi Wat Rakang
Tel: 0-2866 2144
This riverside restaurant has performances on Friday and Saturday of small productions of classical and contemporary dance drama, plus puppetry, readings and music. They also have some art shows and during the week you might catch impromptu rehearsals.

Performing Arts Venues

Aksra Theartre
8/1 Rangnam
Tel: 0-2677 8888
www.aksratheatre.com
This 600-seat theatre mixes Thai and other Asian puppetry with

BELOW: traditional dancers perform scenes from the Ramakien.

cultural performances scheduled around events like cock fighting and *muay thai*. Located in the King Power duty-free complex, so you can shop for gifts after the show (Tue–Fri 7pm; Sat–Sun 1pm and 7pm).

Joe Louis Theatre
Suan Lum Night Bazaar
1875 Thanon Rama IV
Tel: 0-2252 9683
www.thaipuppet.com
The award-winning puppet handlers are themselves trained dancers and perform alongside their puppets. A puppet gallery in the foyer is free to view. Shows daily at 8pm.

National Theatre
Thanon Ratchini
Tel: 0-2224 1342
A grossly underused facility, with few productions or performances ever staged in this grand old theatre. Hosts traditional music and dance performances every month.

Patravadi Theatre
69/1 Soi Wat Rakhang, Thanon Arun Amarin, Thonburi
Tel: 0-2412 7287
www.patravaditheatre.com
This is the nucleus of the Thai contemporary theatre scene, led by Patravadi Medchudhon, who artfully melds traditional and modern dance and drama in either her open-air theatre or the riverside Studio 9 *(see above)*.

Sala Chalerm Krung
66 Thanon Charoen Krung
Tel: 0-2222 1854
A convenient space to hear some Thai classical music, as it hosts *khon* masked drama performances every Friday and Saturday evening from 7pm. It's unusual to see this in a theatre setting; most other shows are in hotel restaurants and lobbies or themed tourist spots.

Thailand Cultural Centre
Thanon Ratchada Phisek
Tel: 0-2247 0028
www.thaiculturalcenter.com
Stages everything from pop concerts to works by the Bangkok Opera (www.bangkokopera.com) and the Bangkok Symphony Orchestra, and is also the main venue for the International Festival of Dance and Music from August to September.

Festivals

The dates for the traditional festivals listed here change from year to year. Check dates on the Tourism Authority of Thailand's website at www.tourismthailand.org. Also see page 261 for a list of public holidays. In addition to these traditional festivals, the calendar is jam-packed with secular events of all sorts, with many new ones added every year. These range from the high-brow (the International Festival of Dance and Music) to the glitzy (Bangkok International Motor Show) and the sexually-liberating, on-off Bangkok Pride Festival.

January/February

Chinese New Year (late Jan/early Feb): Chinatown comes alive as the capital's large Thai–Chinese community celebrates with typical mayhem – expect firecrackers, lion and dragon dances, and feasting galore.

February/March

Makha Puja (late Feb/early Mar): The full moon of the third lunar month marks the gathering of 1,250 disciples to hear the Buddha preach before he entered Nirvana. In the evening, Thais gather at temples for a candle-lit procession with offerings of incense and flowers.

April

Chakri Day (6 Apr): Celebrates the founding of the Chakri dynasty (which presently rules Thailand) in 1782. The festivities are confined to the palace. Most Thais celebrate it as a day off from work.

Songkran (13–15 Apr): Thailand's official New Year. In days gone by people would celebrate by visiting temples and sprinkling water on each other's heads. Nowadays it's a different story, as people get wet and wild on the streets with water pistols the size of machine guns. No one is exempt as revellers careen around the streets in open trucks with barrels of water, drenching everyone in sight. Sanam Luang *(see page 109)* is one of the best places to witness the festivities. Nearby Thanon Khao San is a relentless party zone where both Thais and Westerners dance and douse each other with gallons of water.

Above: Chinese New Year.

May/June

Royal Ploughing Ceremony (early May): Held at Sanam Luang in early May, this Brahman ritual is presided over by King Bhumibol and marks the official start of the rice-planting season. Crimson-clad attendants lead buffaloes drawing a plough over specially consecrated ground.

Visakha Puja (late May/early June): The most important Buddhist day, marking the birth, enlightenment and death of Lord Buddha. Thai people visit temples to listen to sermons by the monks. In the evenings candle-lit processions are held at temples.

July/August

Asanha Puja and Khao Phansa (late July/early Aug): Asanha Puja marks the day when the Buddha preached to his first five disciples. It is celebrated on the full-moon night in similar manner to Magha Puja and Visakha Puja. Immediately afterwards, the three-month Buddhist Lent (Khao Pansa) begins, when monks start a season of prayers and meditation known as the Rains Retreat. Most Thai men will at some time in their lives enter a monastery, even for a brief time, and this is the most common period.
HM The Queen's Birthday (12 Aug): Often dubbed "Mother's Day", this celebration is in honour of Her Majesty Queen Sirikit's birthday. Thais decorate their houses and public buildings with flags and pictures of the Queen.

October

Ok Phansa: October full moon marks the end of the three-month Buddhist Lent, and the beginning of the *kathin* season when Buddhists visit temples to present monks with new robes.
Chulalongkorn Day (23 Oct): Honours King Rama V (1868–1910), who led Thailand into the modern era.

November

Loy Krathong: On the full-moon night of November, Thais everywhere launch small floats with candles, incense and flowers into rivers, canals and ponds, asking for blessings from the water spirits.

December

Trooping of the Colour (3 Dec): Presided over by the king and queen, this annual event is a brilliant spectacle. Amid pomp and ceremony, the Royal Guards swear allegiance to the Royal family.
King's Birthday Celebrations (5 Dec): Dubbed "Father's Day" in honour of King Bhumibol's birthday. Thai people all over the country decorate homes and buildings with flags and lights, and there are firework displays at night.

Nightlife

Bangkok's reputation as a centre for sex of every persuasion frequently overshadows its other nighttime offerings. While there has been no reduction in the number of massage parlours and bars, there has been an upsurge in other activities to meet the needs of the new breed of travellers. Jazz clubs, cool bars and chic clubs abound, attracting young Thais and visitors in droves.

Clubs

Unheard of a decade ago, a cover charge is now charged by several clubs to keep out the riff-raff (particularly cruising working girls) and keep the crowd chic and trendy. The law requires you to be over 20 to enter a club, and most ask for ID at the door. A photocopy of your passport is fine. For more details on nightlife, see chapter on Bangkok After Dark *(page 81)*.

808
RCA Block C
Tel: 0-2203 1043
www.808bangkok.com
Very popular club with brick-and-steel decor, an ace sound system and leather seats on the mezzanine for chill-out moments. A regular influx of international DJs such as Grandmaster Flash.

Bed Supperclub
26 Sukhumvit Soi 11
Tel: 0-2651 3537
www.bedsupperclub.com
This striking, elliptically shaped building hides a pumping bar-club that has people queuing down the street. Popular themed parties include Model Nights, and there's a monthly roster of imported DJs. One of the best in town. The other half is a funky restaurant where diners lie on beds to eat.

The Club
123 Thanon Khao San
Tel: 0-2629 1010
www.theclubkhaosan.com
A fairy-tale castle interior throbs to crowds of young Thais and foreign backpackers dancing to house, techno and electro with occasional live musicians and professional dancers.

Club Culture
Thanon Sri Ayutthaya
Tel: 0-2653 7216
www.club-culture-bkk.com
This refurbished former Thai theatre venue attracts international DJs with a certain funky edge. Eclectic music ranges from electro, garage and drum 'n' bass to hip hop, house and disco; one of Bangkok's hot spots.

Demo
Thonglor Soi 10
Tel: 0-2711 6970
Graffiti-covered walls help the urban warehouse ambience at this new Thonglor hot spot. It serves an exclusive menu of house music in all its forms, and a long list of stiff drinks. Great sound system, mock classical French furniture and a very cool crowd indeed.

Narz
112 Sukhumvit Soi 23
Tel: 0-2664 0373
www.narzbangkok.com
The huge old Narcissus has undergone a name change and split into three zones: Narcissus for trance; Zealot plays urban; and live bands plug in at Ripper.

Q Bar
34 Sukhumvit Soi 11
Tel: 0-2252 3274
www.qbarbangkok.com

Nightlife Listings

Two good sources of information about what's going on are the *Bangkok Post* and *The Nation*, both of which have daily listings sections and weekend entertainment supplements. The weekly magazine *BK* is found in coffee shops around town.

Modelled after a New York lounge bar, this stylishly dark and seductive two-floored venue hosts some of the city's coolest dance music. The nightly line-up of DJs runs the gamut of modern sounds and the impressive drinks list includes 50 brands of vodka alone.

Route 66
Royal City Avenue
Tel: 0-1916 2989
Divided into two zones: East has breakbeat, hip hop and R&B; West pumps house, funk, disco and pop. Despite the lack of dance space – Thais often like to shuffle around tables – the place is crammed.

Tapas Café and Tapas Room
Soi 4 Thanon Silom
Tel: 0-2632 0920-1
A true survivor in the city's party scene, this compact two-floored stylish dance bar is packed with beautiful twentysomething locals and expats, downing jugs of icy margaritas. Choice of two music genres with different DJs on the downstairs deck and above.

Gay Venues

9 Night Club
90-96 Silom Soi 4
Tel: 02-226 6368
www.9nightclub.com
Hot and trendy club opened in 2009 with nightly shows – usually starting around midnight – that feature gay men and *katoey* dance routines.

Babylon
34 Soi Nantha, Sathorn Soi 1
Tel: 0-2679 7984/5
www.babylonbangkok.com
Not quite a nightlife spot but legendary as a gay meeting place. An all-in-one complex housing accommodation, gym, sauna, massage, restaurant and café, plus an ongoing schedule of entertainment and party nights.

Balcony
86-88 Soi 4 Thanon Silom
Tel: 0-2235 5891
www.balconypub.com
Longstanding lively bar with a mixed party crowd who spill out onto the street.

Above: the Bamboo bar.

Bearbie
82 Silom Soi 4
Tel: 0-2632 8446
www.bearbiebar.com
Hang-out and karaoke joint where would-be George Michaels can strut their stuff against a backdrop of white sofas and cuddly teddy bears.

Boy's Bangkok
894/11-13 Soi Pratuchai
Duangthawee Plaza
Tel: 0-2237 2006
One of the better gay go-go bars, on a strip of several such places.

Dick's Café
894/7-8 Soi Pratuchai
Duangthawee Plaza
Tel: 0-2637 0078
www.dickscafe.com
Jazz on the sound system and regular exhibitions of paintings by local artists create a mellow mood at this laid-back bar.

DJ Station
8/6-8 Silom Soi 2
Tel: 0-2266 4029
www.dj-station.com
Bangkok's most popular gay club is packed all night long. The atmosphere is electric and patrons often dress outrageously. On theme nights, the crowd wears costumes that could show Sydney's Mardi Gras a thing or two.

Kathoey Cabaret

For a night of campy fun, see a Vegas-style lip-synching show performed by transsexuals known as ladyboys or *kathoey*.

Calypso
Asia Hotel, Thanon Phayathai
Tel: 0-2216 8937-8
www.calypsocabaret.com
Twice-nightly shows at 8.15pm and 9.45pm, with each divided into bite-sized segments featuring anything from Marilyn Monroe impersonators to Thai classical dance. Tickets cost B1,000, including one drink.

Mambo
59/28 Thanon Rama III
Tel: 0-2294 7381
www.mambocabaret.com
The decor is less glam than the acts, which are glitzy pro routines of Hollywood show tunes and pop divas. Daily performances at 7.15pm, 8.30pm and 10pm; a ticket costs B800.

Live Jazz Venues

Bamboo Bar
Mandarin Oriental Hotel,
48 Oriental Avenue
Tel: 0-2659 9000
www.mandarinoriental.com

The perfect place to soak up jazz, this cosy, intimate bar with its wicker furnishings evokes a bygone era. The band is almost on your lap as they play laid-back jazz classics, usually fronted by US women singers.

Brown Sugar
231/20 Thanon Sarasin
Tel: 0-2250 1826
Long established, intimate and slightly grungy two-floor jazz bar that attracts various local bands and musicians for jam nights.

Diplomat
Conrad Hotel, 87 Thanon Withayu
Tel: 0-2690 9999
One of the city's best bars, this is a great warm-up spot for the hotel's other hip hang-out spot, the 87 Plus club. Sit at the circular bartop in the middle and be mesmerised by seductive jazz singers.

Living Room
Sheraton Grande Sukhumvit
205 Thanon Sukhumvit
Tel: 0-2653 0333
www.starwood.com/bangkok
There's a very good house band at this open-plan, circular venue, plus occasional resident singers and overseas visitors like Ernie Watts and The Preservation Hall Jazz Band.

Niu's on Silom
661 Fl 1-2 Silom Rd
Tel: 0-2266 5333
www.niusonsilom.com
Intimate lounge bar with leather armchairs and great acoustics. Bands plays most styles from Latin to post-bop, with occasional top international acts. An annual outdoor festival launched in 2009 featured the likes of Richard Bona and James Carter. The Concerto Italian restaurant is upstairs.

Other Live Music Venues

Ad Here
13 Thanon Samsen
Tel: 08-9769 4613
Musicians turn up to jam blues and jazz in a bar the size of a guitar case. You sometimes get pleasant surprises like Charlie Musselwhite playing when they're in town. As it is situated close to Khao San Road, there's a laid-back vibe and a good mix of Thai and *farang* punters.

Brick Bar
265 Thanon Khao San
Tel: 0-2629 4499
A large stage hosts three bands a night playing mostly original rock, ska, reggae and blues. Thai and Western food includes spicy salads, stir-fries and pizzas. Good atmosphere.

Overtone
29/70-72 RCA Block D
Tel: 0-2203 0423
www.prartmusic.com/overtone
Signed guitars displayed on the walls by rock guitar heroes like Yngwie Malmsteen and photos of Hendrix and Zappa spell out the rock credentials of this small but serious music bar run by local promoter Prart Aroonrungsi. Some of Thailand's better acts, such as Silly Fools and the Olarn Project, play here, and jazz guitarist John Scofield even marked one of the international nights.

Saxophone Pub
3/8 Thanon Phaya Thai
Tel: 0-2246 5472
www.saxophonepub.com
As much a monument as the neighbouring war memorial, this lively two-floor bar has been packing them in for close to two decades. It hosts great resident bands (at least two a night), who get the whole place jumping and jiving to excellent jazz, R&B, soul and funk.

Spasso
Grand Hyatt Erawan
Thanon Ratchadamri
Tel: 0-2254 1234
www.bangkok.grand.hyatt.com
This basement club and Italian eatery is one of the capital's most consistently popular hotel-based nightspots. International bands play mainly pop, soul and R&B covers. Note: lots of working girls cruise the dance floor.

Tawandang German Brewery
462/61 Thanon Rama III
Tel: 0-2678 1114-5
www.tawandang.com
A vast two-tier pub-cum-theatre with a wide-ranging programme of Thai music, costumed dancers, occasional magic acts and even ballet. The house band – Fong Nam, led by American avant gardist Bruce Gaston, plays a mix of traditional and modern styles. They also have occasional big-name Thai acts like Ad Carabao, and serve good Thai food.

Sightseeing Tours

Unfortunately, Bangkok has very little in the way of organised sightseeing tours. What little is out there is often directed at the domestic market, with guides only speaking Thai. However, all the major hotels have tour desks that can arrange visits (with private guide and car with driver) to the major tourist sites.

The **Chao Phraya Tourist Boat** *(see page 237)* is more of a shuttle service than a tour proper but you do get a running commentary on board about the sights along the Chao Phraya river. For those wishing to explore the canals of Thonburi or Nonthaburi, private **longtail boats** *(see page 238)* can be rented at most of the river's main piers.

Dinner cruises (or evening cocktails) on board an atmospheric teakwood barge is a pleasant way of spending the evening and soaking up the sights along the river.

Loy Nava Dinner Cruise
Tel: 0-2437 4932
www.loynava.com
A teakwood barge was refurbished and converted into the *Tahsaneeya Nava*. Its two-hour dinner cruise (daily 6pm and 8.10pm) starts with a traditional welcome by hostesses. Dinner is a Thai set menu accompanied by live traditional music. You also get a map with the main river sites marked out, and an audio commentary on board. Cost: B1,500 per person.

Manohra Cruises
Tel : 0-2477 0770
www.manohracruises.com

This option uses a restored and converted rice barge called the *Manohra* for dinner cruises from 7.30pm to 10pm. The boat departs daily from the pier at the Bangkok Marriot Resort but can also pick up from Sathorn or Oriental piers. The cost is from B1,250 per person.

Oriental Escape
497 Thanon Sirinthorn, Bang Bamrooh
Tel: 0-2881 8710
www.orientalescape.com
This company offers a wide range of tours (including Thai boxing and Thai dance and dinner shows) of Bangkok and its surroundings.

Real Asia
10/5-7 Soi Aree, Sukhumvit Soi 26
Tel: 0-2665 6364
www.realasia.net
Offers one-day cycling tours (including a ride on a longtail boat) into the capital's more scenic and traffic-free countryside (B1,500 per person). Also has walking and canal boat tours plus an interesting train tour into the countryside at Samut Sakhon.

SPORTS

Participant Sports

Bowling

RCA Bowl
3rd Floor, RCA Plaza
Tel: 0-2641 5870-3
Teenagers come here to rock 'n' bowl to the modern music and disco-like lights. There are 42 lanes open from 10am to 1am.

SF Strike Bowl
7th Floor MBK Centre
Tel: 0-2611 4555
A 28-lane bowling alley, and a Game Zone with pool, table football and air hockey.

Fitness Centres

Most gyms are located within hotels and sell expensive one-day passes to non-guests.

True Fitness
Exchange Tower, 388 Thanon Sukhumvit
Tel: 0-2663 4999; and
Zen@Central World
999/9 Thanon Rama I
Tel: 0-2610 0999
www.truefitness.co.th
Well-equipped, growing chain with personal trainers and fitness instructors available if you need them. Along with a good choice of weights, running and biking facilities, they have classes in yoga, dance and Pilates.

Go-Karting

Easykart.net
2nd Floor, RCA Plaza, Royal City Avenue, Thanon Rama IX
Tel: 0-2203 1205
www.easykart.net
One might think of indoor karting as a room full of petrol fumes, but in fact Easykart's 600-metre (1,968ft) -long race circuit is a cool, clean and well-managed place. The karts are extremely fast and light, reaching a top speed of around 60kph (37mph). The stadium has a hi-tech computerised time clock, highlighting individual fastest laps and printing it out on a time sheet for you to take away.

Golf

Thais are big golfing buffs, going so far as to employ some of the golfing world's stellar architects to design international-class courses. At around B500 to B4,000, green fees are considerably lower than abroad and clubs are not sticky about letting non-guests play.

Bangkok Golf Club
99 Moo 2 Thanon Tivanond
Tel: 0-2501 2828
www.golf.th.com
About 40 minutes from central Bangkok there's an 18-hole course and a nine-hole made up of only par threes, all modelled on famous holes from around the world.

Panya Indra Golf Course
99 Moo 6, Km 9 Kannayao, Thanon Ramindra
Tel: 0-2943 0000
www.panyagolf.com
About 30 minutes from Downtown, this well-kept course has a challenging 27 holes.

Thai Country Club
88 Moo 1, Bangna-Trad Km 35.5
Tel: 0-2651 5300-6
www.thaicountryclub.com
This 343-metre (375yd), 18-hole course regularly hosts top tournaments such as the Volvo Masters Asia. Tiger Woods played here on his only vist to Thailand in 1997.

Muay Thai Training

Sor Vorapin
13 Trok Kasab, near Thanon Khao San
Tel: 0-2243 3651
A simple gym offering *muay thai* lessons. If you turn out to be any good they might even find you fights at local stadiums.

Muay Thai Institute
336/932 Thanon Phahon Yothin, 118 Thanon Vipavadi Prachatipat, Thayaburi Prathumthani, Rangsit
Tel: 0-2992 0096
www.muaythai-institute.net
Instruction on boxing, refereeing, training and first aid. Has accommodation on site.

THAI BOXING

If you enjoy seeing a punch-up, the frenzied sport of *muay thai*, or Thai kickboxing, will keep you on the edge of your seat. Employing not just fists but elbows, feet and knees, in fact almost any part of the body except the head, this highly ritualised sport is accompanied by high-pitched Thai music played by a *phipat* orchestra. Fight nights are divided into several bouts, most consisting of five 3-minute rounds with a 2-minute rest between each round. Before the match begins, the fighters do a *wai kru* and *ram muay*, stylised movements to pay respects to their trainers and appease the ring spirits. The cheers and frantic betting of the audience almost steal the thunder from the action in the ring.

Cooking Classes

Blue Elephant Cookery School
Blue Elephant Restaurant
233 Thanon Sathorn
Tel: 0-2673 9353
www.blueelephant.com
Half-day morning and afternoon sessions in a restored mansion focus on four popular Thai dishes, which you then eat for lunch or dinner. Morning classes include a trip to a local market.

Mandarin Oriental Cookery School
Mandarin Oriental Hotel,
48 Oriental Avenue
Tel: 0-2659 9000
www.mandarinoriental.com
The legendary hotel runs pricey cooking demonstrations rather than hands-on classes, but even this is a fascinating gastronomic experience.

Thai House
32/4 Moo 8, Tambol Bangmaung, Amphoe Bangyai, Nonthaburi
Tel: 0-2903 9611, 2997 5161
www.thaihouse.co.th
Take just the cookery lessons or combine it with a stay in a rustic Thai-style house in the suburb of Nonthaburi. One-, two- and three-day courses are available with market trips and meals.

Racquet Sports

Santisuk Tennis Court
Soi 38 Thanon Sukhumvit
Tel: 0-2391 1830
Five outdoor and three indoor courts that have seen better days but are still popular and cheap.

Soi Klang Racquet Club
Soi 49 Thanon Sukhumvit
Tel: 0-2714 7200
www.rqclub.com
Well-equipped sports centre that has two swimming pools, four tennis courts, three squash courts, 20 badminton courts, rock climbing and a gym.

Waterskiing

Club Taco
Thanon Bangna-Trad Km 13
Tel: 0-2316 7810
Cable-ski (B300 for 2 hours, B500 for the day) is the main activity at this large lake found on the eastern edge of Bangkok. There are a variety of skis and wakeboards to choose from with pulley speeds adjusted to suit different skill levels. Entrance fee includes windsurf boards or water skis. Wakeboards can be hired.

Yoga

Absolute Yoga Bangkok
14th Floor, Unico House Building
Soi Lang Suan
Tel: 0-2652 1333
www.absoluteyogabangkok.com
Specialises in Bikram yoga, but also offers other exercise styles, including Pilates, for all levels.

Yoga Elements Studio
Vanissa Building, 29 Soi Chidlom
Tel: 0-2391 9919
www.yogaelements.com
Popular classes based on Ashtanga Vinyasa that teach everything from elemental procedures like breath control and body alignment to advanced techniques.

Spectator Sports

Muay Thai

Bangkok has two principal places to view Thai boxing, or *muay thai*.

Lumpini Boxing Stadium
Thanon Rama IV
Tel: 0-2251 4303
www.muaythailumpini.com
Matches are on Tue 6.15–11pm, Fri–Sat 5–8pm and 8.30pm–midnight. Tickets at B500, B800 and B1,500.

Ratchadamnoen Boxing Stadium
1 Thanon Ratchadamnoen Nok
Tel: 0-2281 4205
Matches at 6pm on Mon, Wed and Thur, and 5pm on Sun. Tickets: B500, B800 and B1,500.

Takraw

An acrobatic team game of kicking (or heading) a rattan ball over a net, tournaments are held at the **Thai–Japanese Sports Complex** (tel: 0-2465 5325 for dates and times). Otherwise you'll usually find a game being played in **Lumphini Park** *(see page 159)*.

Children's Activities

The city's larger shopping malls often have designated kids' zones, with playgrounds for kids and video arcades for teenagers, a sign of how Bangkok families like to spend their leisure time. Bangkok may be short on green spaces, but all its major parks – Lumphini, Benjasiri, Benjakitti and Chatuchak – have special children's play areas.

The Places section highlights attractions ideal for familes with children. These include **Dusit Zoo** *(page 142)*, **Siam Ocean World** *(page 156)*, **Snake Farm** *(page 158)*, **Dream World** *(page 186)*, **Safari World** *(page 187)*, **Samphran Elephant Ground and Zoo** *(page 194)*, **Ancient City** *(page 209)*, **Crocodile Farm and Zoo** *(page 210)* and **Rose Garden Country Resort** *(page 193)*. Another option is **Siam Park** at 99 Thanon Serithai (tel: 0-2517 0075), a water park with two exciting water rides, a waterfall and a large artificial beach with rolling waves.

Below: Thai cookery classes.

A – Z

AN ALPHABETICAL SUMMARY OF PRACTICAL INFORMATION

Addresses

Given the size of the city and its many twisting alleyways, finding your way around Bangkok can be a bit confusing. The city is mostly laid out with main roads having smaller streets – called *soi* – leading off, each having the main road's name followed by a number. For example, Sukhumvit Road (or Thanon Sukhumvit) has side streets called Sukhumvit Soi 1, Sukhumvit Soi 3, etc, running in sequence, odd and even numbers on opposite sides of the road. *Soi* may be sub-divided using a slash after the number followed by another number. The same system is used for shop and house addresses, a slash separating the block or building number from the shop. So an address might read 36/1 Sukhumvit 33/1. Street names are usually written in Thai and English and most hotels provide business cards with the address written in Thai to show taxi drivers.

Budgeting for your Trip

By Western standards, Bangkok is a bargain. Budget accommodation can be as cheap as B200 a night, with a delicious streetside meal and beer around B120. Five-star hotels cost from B6,000, and a three-course meal may be had for B1,000 without drinks (although wine is expensive and one bottle will at least double that price). In bars, refreshments start around B60, and even in posh clubs they may be as little as B200. Bus fares cost B7 to B22, a Skytrain or Metro ride from B16 to B40 and taxi meters start at B35. If you live frugally, you can get by on B500 a day.

Business Travellers

As Thailand strives to become a regional business hub, the capital hosts an increasing number of business travellers. Most hotels have business centres with communications and secretarial services in several languages. Elsewhere in Bangkok, it is possible to lease small offices with shared clerical staff. Interpreter services are also available.

A good starting point for overseas business people wanting to start a company in Thailand is the **Board of Investment** (BOI), tel: 0-2537 8111; www.boi.go.th. They are authorised to grant tax holidays and other incentives to promote certain key industries.

Children

Travelling with children is not especially difficult in Thailand, although Bangkok footpaths are often in disrepair and invariably obstructed by something or someone. Leave the baby stroller at home and bring back- or chest-mounted baby carriers. Many department stores and malls have play areas and baby-changing facilities and some upmarket hotels have baby-sitting services. The tropical heat is intense, so sun block and hats are important, while clean hands help ward off possible stomach bugs.

Climate

There are three official seasons in Thailand: hot, rainy and cool. But to the tourist winging in from more temperate regions, Bangkok has only one temperature: hot, with humidity above 70 percent. There is little wind and the mercury drops only a few degrees during the night. Evenings during the cool season, however, can be very pleasant. Air-conditioning of course makes Bangkok tolerable indoors, at least. These temperature ranges give you an idea of what to expect:

- Hot season (Mar to mid-June): 27–35°C (80–95°F)
- Rainy season (June to Oct): 24–32°C (75–90°F)
- Cool season (Nov to Feb): 18–32°C (65–90°F), but with less humidity.

What to Wear

Clothes should be light and loose and preferably of natural fibres, which "breathe" better. A shirt and tie are expected for business appointments. A hat will offer pro-

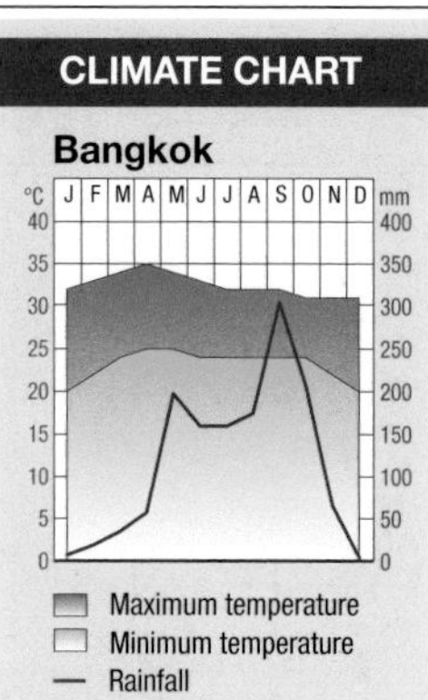

tection from the sun, and it's best to carry an umbrella during the rainy season. Convenience stores sell them if you get caught out.

When to Visit

The cool season is overwhelmingly the best time to visit for most people. The temperature is not only lower, but there is also significantly less humidity. This means walking the city sights is more comfortable, hence you can see more. In addition there is hardly any rain then. When it rains in Bangkok, it happens suddenly and ferociously, which hampers many a plan. That said, even in the rainy season, parts of most days will be sunny. Waterfalls in national parks such as Khao Yai will be at their fullest in the rainy season or in the early cool season.

Crime and Safety

Bangkok, like all cities, has an underbelly of violent crime, but tourists rarely encounter it and the streets are generally very safe. The biggest risk to travellers is from scams and con artists. If you do run into trouble in Bangkok, there are Tourist Police specially assigned to assist travellers, though much of the time there is little they are able to do but record the details of the crime and provide a report for insurance purposes.

Tourist Police: Tourist Service Centre, TAT headquarters, 4 Thanon Rachadamneon Nok, tel: 0-2281 5051; hotline: 1155.

Most members of the force speak some English. Tourist Police booths can also be found in tourist areas including Lumphini Park (near the intersection of Rama IV and Silom) and Patpong (at the Surawong intersection).

Common Scams

- Touts on Patpong offering live sex shows upstairs. Once inside, you are sometimes handed an exorbitant bill and threatened if you protest. Pay, take the receipt, and go immediately to the Tourist Police, who will usually take you back and demand a refund.
- Don't take free or very cheap boat rides into the canals. Once you are well into the canal, you are given the choice of paying a high fee or being stranded.
- Don't follow touts who offer to take you to a gem factory for a "special deal". The gems are usually synthetic or of substandard quality and there is no way to get your money back.
- There are no tuk-tuk rides for B10. If a driver takes you on one, you will end up stopping at every gem, silver and tailor shop in the city, where he will collect commission for wasting your day.

Bear in mind that in Thai culture, strangers rarely approach and engage foreigners in conversation, so if you find yourself on the receiving end, be on guard no matter how polite and innocent they appear to be. Feel free to be rude and walk away, even if it goes against the rules of polite behaviour.

Customs Regulations

In Thailand the import or export of drugs, dangerous chemicals, pornography, firearms and goods displaying the Thai flag are prohibited. Attempting to smuggle heroin or other hard drugs in or out may be punishable by death. Scores of foreigners are serving very long prison terms for this offence.

Foreign currency exceeding US$20,000 either entering or leaving the country should be declared. Thai currency leaving the country is restricted to B50,000. Foreign guests are allowed to bring in 200 cigarettes and one litre of wine or spirits tax free.

Buddha images, antiques and art objects can only leave the country with a Department of Fine Arts permit *(see page xxx)*. For more information contact the National Museum, Bangkok (tel: 0-2224 1333).

For more details check the Thai **Customs Department** website at www.customs.go.th, or call the hotline: 1164.

Disabled Travellers

Bangkok falls short on accommodating the disabled. The uneven pavements are studded with obstructions and few buildings have wheelchair ramps. Traffic is relentless and drivers generally unsympathetic to pedestrians. However, there have been signs of improvement in recent years. Although only a few Skytrain stations have lifts, the Metro has them at every station, and pricier hotels and shopping malls will often have disabled access and modified toilets. Taxi drivers, if arranged beforehand, can be quite cooperative. As it is a challenge for a lone disabled traveller, a companion may be preferable.

Electricity

Electrical outlets are rated at 220 volts, 50 cycles and accept flat-pronged or round-pronged plugs. Adaptors can be purchased at department or hardware stores.

Emergencies

Police: 191
Tourist Police: tel: 1155 or tel: 0-2281 5051/2664 0222
For hospitals, *see opposite*.

Embassies and Consulates

Bangkok

Australia: 37 Thanon Sathorn Tai, tel: 0-2344 6300. Visas: Mon–Fri 8.15am–12.15pm.
Canada: 15/F, Abdulrahim Place, Thanon Rama IV, tel: 0-2636 0540, 2254 2530.
New Zealand: M Thai Tower, 14th Fl, All Seasons Place, 87 Thanon Withayu, tel: 0-2254 2530.
Singapore: 129 Thanon Sathorn Tai, tel: 0-2286 1434.
UK: 1031 Thanon Ploenchit, tel: 0-2305 8333. Visas: now handled by post via Hong Kong.
US: 120-122 Thanon Withayu, tel: 0-2205 4000. Visas: Mon–Fri 7.30–10am.

Overseas

UK: Royal Thai Embassy, 29–30 Queen's Gate, London SW7 5JB tel : 020 7589 2944; www.thaiembassyuk.org.uk. Visas: Mon–Fri 9.30am–12.30pm.
US: Royal Thai Embassy, 1024 Wisconsin Ave, N.W. Washington D.C. 20007; tel: (202) 944 3600, www.thaiembdc.org. Visas: Mon– Fri 9am–1pm.

Etiquette

Thais are remarkably tolerant and forgiving of foreigners' eccentricities, but there are a few things that upset them.

Buddhism

In general, it is impolite to point your feet at Buddha images or to have bare legs or shoulders when visiting temples. Monks have taken vows of celibacy, and women should avoid physical contact with them, including passing items directly to them. Instead, place the object somewhere to be picked up.

Head and Feet

The Hindu religion, which has had a strong influence on Thai Buddhism *(see page 49)*, regards the head as the wellspring of wisdom

Above: Thai Royal Family.

and the feet as unclean. For this reason, it is insulting to touch another person on the head (children are an exception), to point one's feet at anything or to step over another person. In formal situations, when wishing to pass someone who is seated on the floor, bow slightly while walking and point an arm down to indicate the path to be taken, and a path will be cleared.

Public Behaviour

Two decades ago, Thai couples showed no intimacy in public. That has changed due to modernisation and foreign influence on the young, but even these days, intimacy rarely extends beyond holding hands. As in many traditional societies, displaying open affection in public, such as kissing, is a sign of bad manners.

The Royal Family

Thais have a great reverence for the monarchy, and disapprove of any disrespect directed towards members of the royal family. Thailand also has lese-majesty laws that, although usually invoked to settle business or political rivalries, may result in jail terms for people convicted of defaming, insulting or threatening royalty. Standing for the National Anthem is expected in cinemas.

Temple Dress Code

Shorts are taboo for women and men who wish to enter some of the more highly revered temples. Women wearing sleeveless dresses and short skirts may also be barred from certain temples. Improperly dressed and unkempt visitors will be turned away from Wat Phra Kaew and the Grand Palace (though some clothing can be borrowed at the entrance).

Terms of Address

Thais are addressed by their first names, usually preceded by the word *khun*, the equivalent of Mr or Ms. For example, Silpachai Krishnamra would be addressed as Khun Silpachai.

Thai Greetings

The common greeting and farewell in Thailand is *sawadee* (followed by *khrap* when spoken by men and *kha* by women). In more formal settings this is accompanied by a *wai* – raising the hands in a prayer-like gesture, the fingertips touching the nose, and bowing the head slightly. In business meetings, the *wai* is often followed by a handshake. Foreigners are not expected to *wai*.

Gay and Lesbian

Foreign gays quickly discover that Thailand is one of the most tolerant countries in the world. The gay nightlife scene is a thriving one. See **Bangkok After Dark** *(see page 81)* and **Gay Venues** *(see page 252)*. The city also hosts an annual on–off Bangkok Gay Pride Festival (www.bangkokpride.org/en) in November, with a similar one taking place in Pattaya in December (www.pattayagayfestival.com).

Utopia at www.utopia-asia.com is Bangkok's major online gay resource. It's a good place to make contacts and to find out what's happening on the gay scene in Thailand and Asia.

Purple Dragon is a travel agency that caters exclusively for gay travellers, located at Tarntawan Place Hotel, 119/5-10 Thanon Surawong, tel: 0-2634 3186, www.purpledrag.com.

Health and Medical Care

Visitors entering Thailand are not required to show evidence of vaccination for smallpox or cholera. Check that your tetanus boosters are up-to-date. Immunisation against cholera is a good idea as are hepatitis A and B innoculations. Malaria and dengue persist in rural areas but generally not in Bangkok. When in the countryside, especially in the monsoon season, apply mosquito repellent on exposed skin at all times – dengue mosquitoes are at their most active in the day.

Many first-time visitors take awhile to adjust to the heat. It is important to drink plenty of water, especially if you've drunk alcohol. Avoid too much sun when out and about and use sunblock – the sun is far more powerful at this latitude than in temperate regions. Tap water in Bangkok has been certified as potable, but bottled water is still safer and is available widely. Within Bangok, ice is clean and presents no health problems.

Buy travel insurance before travelling to Bangkok.

Dental Clinics

Apart from the dental clinics at the BNH and Bumrungrad hospitals above, the **Dental Hospital** at 88/88 Soi 49 Thanon Sukhumvit, tel: 0-2260 5000-15, with its long-standing good reputation, is recommended. It looks more like a hotel than a dental hospital and has the latest equipment.

Hospitals

The level of medical care can be excellent in Bangkok, particularly at the following hospitals, all of which have specialised clinics as well as general medical services and are of international standard. In fact, there has been a growing business in "medical tourism" over the past 10 years, with people coming to Thailand to have procedures performed (including cosmetic surgery and sex changes) that would cost many times more at home or require waiting in a months-long queue. Equipment is up-to-date and the doctors are usually trained overseas and speak English. By Thai standards, these are considered expensive, but the fees are a fraction of what they are in most Western countries. The hospitals listed also have dental clinics.

Bangkok Christian Hospital, 124 Thanon Silom, tel: 0-2233 6981-9, www.bkkchristianhosp.th.com. A medium-sized hospital, a bit less luxurious than the others listed here but with high standards.
BNH Hospital, 9/1 Thanon Convent, Silom, tel: 0-2686 2700; www.bnhhospital.com. This squeaky-clean hospital offers comfortable rooms, top-notch equipment and a large team of specialists. Service is efficient and English is widely spoken.
Bumrungrad Hospital, 33 Soi 3, Thanon Sukhumvit, tel: 0-2667 1000; www.bumrungrad.com. This one is the top of the heap, and looks more like a five-star hotel than a hospital. Offers a huge range of specialised clinics, excellent staff, and a selection of rooms from basic four-bed to luxury suites, the latter at only slightly more than the cost of a similar hotel room.

Medical Clinics

For minor problems, the **British Dispensary**, 109 Thanon Sukhumvit (between Soi 3 and 5), tel: 0-2252 8056, has British doctors on its staff. All the major hotels also have an on-premises clinic, or a doctor on call.

Pharmacies

These are found everywhere in downtown Bangkok. In recent years, official control on prescription drugs has been more strongly applied and requires the presence of a licensed pharmacist on the premises. Nonetheless, most antibiotics and many other drugs that would require a prescription in the West are available without a prescription.

Check the expiry date on all drugs you buy, and, wherever possible, purchase them from an air-conditioned pharmacy. There are several branches of **Boots** and **Watson's** pharmacies in central Bangkok.

Internet

Wi-fi zones at the airport, in some hotels, and some branches of Starbucks are a growing phenomenon. Major hotels usually include in-room internet, and public internet cafés mainly have reasonable speed broadband at around B30 per hour. There are many located around Thanon Khao San. Otherwise, ask in your hotel.

Left Luggage

There are two left-luggage facilities at Bangkok International Airport. One is on the 1st floor of the Arrivals Hall, and the second is on the 3rd floor of the Departures Hall near the currency-exchange counter. The fee is B20 per bag per day. All hotels and guesthouses offer a left-luggage service, usually for a small daily fee.

Lost Property

If you lose any valuable property, report it as soon as possible to the **Tourist Police** either in person *(see page 257)* or on their hotline: 1155, to get an insurance statement.

Airport: For property lost at the airport, contact tel: 0-2535 1254.

Public Transit: BMTA city bus service, tel: 0-2246 0973; **BTS Skytrain**, tel: 0-2617 6000; **MRTA subway**, tel: 0-2624 5200, **Hualamphong Railway Station**, tel: 0-2225 6964, hotline 1690.

Taxis: Taxi drivers frequently listen to **JS100 Radio 100FM**, hotline: 1137, which has set up a lost-property hotline, and it is surprising how often forgetful passengers get their lost items back.

Maps

Basic maps of Bangkok are available free at the Tourism Authority of Thailand (TAT) offices *(see page 263)* and at big hotels. More detailed ones can be found at bookshops. The *Insight Fleximap* and *Nelles Map* of Bangkok are probably the best. Other more funky insights into Bangkok's attractions can be found in Nancy Chandler's *Map of Bangkok* and Groovy Map's *Bangkok by Day* and *Bangkok by Night*.

Media

Magazines

There are several what's on and listings publications in English that cover events, nightlife, art galleries, restaurants, and more, although most are sparsely filled, unreliable and often consist of advertising copy disguised as editorial. The best free sheet is *BK*, which also has a regularly updated website. The small format glossy *Bangkok 101* costs B100, and usually leads with a Bangkok photo feature. It also has a good run-down of art shows and venues, along with events and restaurant and nightlife reviews. See page 263 for website addresses.

Newspapers

Thailand has two longstanding English-language dailies, the *Bangkok Post* and *The Nation*. The *Bangkok Post* is more conservative than *The Nation*, which is more maverick and has had several run-ins with the government. Many big hotels furnish one or the other for free with the room, or they can be purchased at newsstands for B30.

Radio

AM radio is devoted entirely to Thai-language programmes. FM frequencies include several English-language stations with the latest pop hits. Some frequencies have bilingual DJs and play a mixture of Thai and English songs in the same programme.

97 MHz: Radio Thailand has 4 hours of English-language broadcasts each day.

105.5 MHz: Tourism Authority of Thailand offers useful tips to tourists every hour.

Fat FM 104.5: Has the latest on Thailand's thriving indie music.

Eazy FM 105.5 FM: As the name suggests, mostly easy-listening, middle-of-the road music.

FMX 95.5 FM: Contemporary dance and pop hits.

Television

Bangkok has six Thai-language television channels. ITV or Independent Television specialises in news and documentaries. The rest mainly air soaps, songs and game shows with a sprinkling of mostly domestically-orientated news. There is also Truevision, a cable television network that provides subscribers with a wide choice of international channels, including BBC News, HBO, ESPN and MTV Thailand.

Money

The baht is the principal Thai monetary unit. Though it is divided into 100 units called satang, this is becoming outdated; only 50- and 25-satang pieces are used.

Banknotes are of different colours and denominations, and include 1,000 (light brown), 500 (purple), 100 (red), 50 (blue) and 20 (green). There is a 10-baht coin (brass centre with silver rim), a 5-baht coin (silver with copper edge), a 2-baht coin, a 1-baht coin (silver) and two small coins of 50 and 25 satang (both brass-coloured).

At the time of press US$1 was trading at around B32.

ATMs

ATMs are available 24 hours a day at banks, malls, major train and bus stations, and airports. Many accept credit cards and MasterCard and Visa debit cards.

Changing Money

Banking hours are Mon–Fri 9.30am–3.30pm, but nearly every bank maintains money-changing kiosks in tourist areas. Better hotels almost always have exchange kiosks, but generally give poor exchange rates compared to banks.

Credit Cards

American Express, Diner's Club, MasterCard, JCB and Visa are widely accepted throughout Bangkok. Credit cards can be used to draw emergency cash at most banks. If you lose your credit card, call one of the numbers below:
American Express: tel: 0-2273 5222
Diner's Club: tel: 0-2238 3660
Visa: tel: 001-800-441-3485
Mastercard: tel: 001-800-11-887-0663

Warning: Credit-card fraud is a major problem in Thailand. Don't leave your credit card in a safe-deposit box. When making a purchase, make sure that you get the carbon-copies and dispose of them.

Travellers' Cheques

Travellers' cheques can be cashed at all exchange kiosks and banks, and generally receive better exchange rates than cash. There is a nominal charge of B25 for each travellers' cheque cashed.

Tipping

Tipping is not a custom in Thailand, although it is becoming more common in upper-end establishments. However, people will generally leave any change left from their bill, in both cafés and taxis. A service charge of 10 percent is included in the more expensive restaurants and is usually, though not always, divided among the staff.

Opening Hours

Government offices operate Mon–Fri 8.30am–4.30pm. Most businesses are open Mon–Fri 8am–5.30pm, while some are open 8.30am–noon on Sat. Banks are open Mon–Fri 9.30am–3.30pm. Money-changing kiosks in the city are open until 8pm daily.

Department stores are open 10.30am–9pm daily, though larger stores are open as late as 10pm. Ordinary shops open at 8.30am or 9am and close between 6pm and 8pm, depending on location and type of business.

Small open-air coffee shops and restaurants open at 7am and close at 8.30pm, though some stay open past midnight. Large restaurants generally close by 10pm, though some in Bangkok stay open later on Friday and Saturday. Most hotel coffee shops close at midnight; some stay open 24 hours, and the city has several outdoor restaurants that are open as late as 4am for post-bar-hopping suppers. Clubs and bars are subject to loosely applied licensing laws and may close anywhere between midnight and 5am, depending on location and political and policing climate.

Photography

With more than 10 million visitors per year, Thailand is much photographed. The country and its people are very photogenic, and everything the photographer may need is readily available. Camera shops and photo development outlets are commonly found in the tourist areas, and most now offer digital transfers onto CD and hard-copy photos from digital. Prices are cheaper than many other countries at B3–4 per print, with bigger enlargements working out to be a real bargain.

Postal Services

The Thai postal service is reasonably reliable, though mail seems to go more astray upcountry and at Christmas time. The odds for domestic mail can be improved by registering or sending items by **EMS** for a fee of B20 for a business-sized letter. EMS is supposed to guarantee that a letter reaches a domestic destination in one day, and it generally does, particularly in Bangkok. If you wish to send valuable parcels or bulky documents overseas, it is better to use a courier service.

The **General Post Office** at Thanon Charoen Krung, tel: 0-2233 1050, is open from Mon to Fri 8am to 8pm, and Sat, Sun and holidays 8am to 1pm.

Post offices elsewhere in Bangkok usually open at 8am and close at 4pm on weekdays. The GPO and many larger offices sell packing boxes and materials.

You can find mini post offices in some office buildings and hotels. Look for a red sign in English. These outlets offer basic mail services and accept small packages, but have no telecommunications services. Kiosks along some of the city's busier streets sell stamps and also ship small parcels.

Courier Services

The usual global courier services are available in Bangkok. You can call direct or book online.
DHL: tel: 0-2345 5000; www.dhl.co.th.

Public Holidays

1 Jan: New Year's Day
Jan/Feb: (full moon) Magha Puja. Note: Chinese New Year is not an official holiday but many businesses close for several days.
6 Apr: Chakri Day
13–15 Apr: Songkran
1 May: Labour Day
5 May: Coronation Day
Late May/June: (full moon) Visakha Puja
Late July/Aug: (full moon) Asanha Puja and Khao Pansa
12 Aug: Queen's Birthday
23 Oct: Chulalongkorn Day
5 Dec: King's Birthday
10 Dec: Constitution Day

FedEx: tel: 0-2229 8800, or hotline: 1782; www.fedex.com/th.
UPS: tel: 0-2712 3300; www.ups.com/th.

Religious Services

Buddhists will find no lack of temples to worship at. There are also several mosques, one major Hindu temple, the Maha Uma Devi *(see page 170)*, a few churches and at least one synagogue.

Anglican

Christ Church Bangkok, 11 Convent Rd; tel: 0-2234 3634. Sunday services at 7.30am, 10am and 5pm.
International Church of Bangkok, 67 Soi 19, Thanon Sukhumvit, tel: 0-2258 5821. Services at 8am.

Catholic

Holy Redeemer Church, 123/19 Soi Ruam Rudi, Thanon Withayu, tel: 0-2256 6305. Sunday Mass at 8.30am, 9.45am, 11am and 5.30pm.
St Louis Church, 215/2 Thanon Sathorn Tai, tel: 0-2211 0220. Sunday Mass at 6am, 8am, 10am and 5.30pm.

Jewish

Even Chen Synagogue, Chao Phraya Office Tower, Shangri-La Hotel, Charoen Krung Soi 42/1; tel: 0-2236 7777. Services: Mon–Thur 8am, Fri 8am and 6.15pm, Sat 9am–noon, Sun 8.30am–9.30am.

Muslim

Assalafiyah Mosque, 2827 Thanon Charoen Krung; tel: 0-2688 1481. Service times vary.

Tax

Thailand has a Value-Added Tax (VAT) of 7 percent. This is added on to most goods and services (but not goods sold by street vendors and markets). It is possible to get the 7 percent VAT refunded from your shopping if you purchase goods from stores displaying the "VAT Refund for Tourists" sign. Refunds can only be claimed on single purchases of B2,000 or more, with a minimum overall expenditure of B5,000. At the time of purchase, present your passport and ask the sales assistant to complete the VAT refund form. Before departure at the airport, present your goods together with the VAT refund form and sales invoice to the Customs officers for inspection. After approval, present your claim to the Revenue officers at the airport's VAT Refund Counter.

Refunds under B30,000 will be made in cash (in baht) or by bank draft or credit to your credit-card account. Those over B30,000 cannot be made in cash. There is an administrative fee of B100 for cash refunds; bank drafts and card refunds will incur extra charges. See www.rd.go.th for more details.

All major hotels add 10 percent tax plus service charge to the room rate. At top-class restaurants, 10 percent service charge is added to the bill on top of VAT.

TIME ZONE

Thailand is 7 hours ahead of GMT. Since it gets dark between 6 and 7pm, uniformly throughout the year, Thailand does not observe daylight savings time.

Telephones

International Calls

The country code for Thailand is 66. When calling Thailand from overseas, dial your local international access code, followed by 66 and the 8-digit number (without the preceding 0) in Thailand.

To make an international call from Thailand, dial 001 or 009 before the country and area codes followed by the telephone number (again, without the preceding 0). If you need international call assistance, call the local operator at tel: 100.

Peak-hour calls made 7am–9pm cost the most; non-peak rates are charged 5–7am and 9pm–midnight. The lowest call rates are midnight–5am.

Prepaid international phone cards (called Thaicard) with values of B300, B500 and B1,000 can be used to make international calls. These can be bought at post offices, certain shops that carry the Thaicard sign or the office of the **Communications Authority of Thailand**, tel: 0-2950 3712, www.cat.or.th.

Local Calls

Area codes in Thailand have been merged with phone numbers and in theory don't exist anymore.

The prefix 0 must be dialled for all calls made within Thailand, even when calling local numbers in Bangkok. Services such as bus companies and airlines increasingly have four-digit hotline numbers that link directly to customer services. If you need local directory assistance, dial 1133.

Any local number that begins with the prefix 08 denotes a mobile number.

Mobile Phones

Only users of **GSM 900** or **GSM 1800** mobile phones with international roaming facility can hook up automatically to the local Thai network. Check with your service provider if you're not sure, especially if coming from US, Korea or Japan. Your phone will automatically select a local service provider, and this enables you to make calls within Thailand at local rates. However if someone calls your number, international call rates will apply. Charges will be billed to your account in your home country.

If you're planning to travel in Thailand for any length of time, it's more economical to buy a local SIM card with a stored value from a mobile-phone shop. You will be assigned a local number and local calls to and from the phone will be at local rates. Inter-

national rates will apply if you make overseas calls.

Public Phones

Public telephones accept B1, B5 and B10 coins. Phone cards for local calls in denominations of B50, B100, B200 and B400 can be purchased at convenience shops throughout the city.

Toilets

There are few public toilets in Bangkok, though the city is beginning to address this in tourist areas. Restrooms are usually very dirty and often of the squat-toilet variety, a tricky experience for the uninitiated. Your best bet is usually to sneak into fast-food outlets, which are very easy to find. Shopping malls usually have clean toilets as well, particularly near the food courts. Sometimes a small fee of a few baht applies.

Tourist Information

The **Tourism Authority of Thailand** (TAT) have information outlets in several countries and service kiosks within Thailand that offer maps and other promotional materials as well as advice on things to do and places to see.

Bangkok

TAT Call Centre: tel: 1672. Open daily 8am–8pm.
Airport Information Counter: Arrival Hall, Suvarnabhumi Airport; tel: 0-2132 1888. Open: daily 24 hrs.
Tourism Authority of Thailand Main Office: 1600 Thanon Phetchaburi, Makkasan, Bangkok 10400; tel: 0-2250 5500. Open daily 8.30am–4.30pm.
TAT Tourist Information Counter (Ratchadamnoen): 4 Thanon Ratchadamnoen Nok; tel: 0-2283 1500, ext. 1620. Open daily 8.30am–4.30pm.

Overseas Offices

Australia and New Zealand: Suite 20.02, Level 20, 56 Pitt Street, Sydney, NSW 2000; tel: 61-2 9247 7549; fax: 61-2 9251 2465.
UK: 3rd Floor, Brook House, 98–99 Jermyn Street, London SW1 6EE; tel: 44-20 7925 2511; fax: 44-20 7925 2512.
US: 61 Broadway, Suite 2810, New York, NY 10006; tel: 1-212 432 0433; fax: 1-212 269 2588; and 611 North Larchmont Blvd, 1st Floor, Los Angeles, CA 90004; tel: 1-323 461 9814; fax: 1-323 461 9834.

Visas and Passports

Visa regulations vary for different nationalities. For updated information, check with a Thai embassy or consulate or on the Thai Ministry of Foreign Affairs website (www.mfa.go.th).

All foreign nationals entering Thailand must have passports with at least six month's validity. You can get 60-day tourist visas at the Thai embassy in your home country prior to arrival, or at the airport. Nationals from most countries can get a visa on arrival, valid for 15–90 days, depending on the country. Visas can be extended for 30 days at a time for B1,000 or you can leave the country (even for half an hour) and return to receive another visa on entry.

In total, tourists are allowed to stay in Thailand for a cumulative period not exceeding 90 days within any six-month period from the date of first entry. Overstaying can carry a fine of B500 daily, up to a maximum of B20,000, on leaving the country, but if the police catch you before you leave you may face imprisonment.

Thai Immigration Bureau
Government Centre Chaengwattana, 120 Moo 3, Chaengwattana Road; tel: 0-2141 9889; www.imm.police.go.th; Mon–Fri 8.30am–4.30pm.

Websites

www.tourismthailand.org
The official website of the Tourism Authority of Thailand.
www.bangkokpost.com
Daily news from the *Bangkok Post* daily newspaper.
www.nationmultimedia.com
Daily news clips from *The Nation* newspaper.
www.bangkoktourist.com
Information on Bangkok from the Bangkok Tourist Bureau.
www.langhub.com/en-th
Audio and video files to help foreigners learn Thai, and vice versa.
www.bkmagazine.com
Website of weekly free listings mag with features, events and restaurant reviews.
www.khaosanroad.com
Backpackers resource with accommodation, work advice, upcountry travel, forums etc.

Weights and Measures

Thailand uses the metric system, except for their traditional system of land measurement (1 rai = 1,600 sq metres) and gold (1 baht = 15.2 grams).

Women Travellers

Thailand is generally safe for women travellers, even those travelling alone. Thais tend to be non-confrontational, and the country is generally safe in terms of both casual harassment and serious assault. That said, there have been sporadic cases of rape, particularly when walking alone at night on island beaches.

Below: essential Thai vocab.

Transport
Accommodation
Activities
A – Z
Language

Language

Understanding The Language

Origins and Intonation

For centuries the Thai language, rather than tripping from foreigners' tongues, has been tripping them up. Its roots go back to the place Thais originated from in the hills of southern China, but these are overlaid by Indian influences. From the original settlers come the five tones that seem designed to frustrate visitors. One sound can have five different tones: high (h), low (l), mid (m), rising (r) and falling (f), and each of these means a different thing from the other *(see text box)*.

Therefore, when you mispronounce a word, you don't simply say a word incorrectly, you say another word entirely. It is not unusual to see a semi-fluent foreigner standing before a Thai and running through the scale of tones until suddenly a light of recognition dawns on his companion's face. There are misinformed visitors who will tell you that tones are not important. These people do not communicate with Thais – they communicate at them in a one-sided exchange that frustrates both parties.

Phonology

The way Thai consonants are written in English often confuses foreigners. An "*h*" following a letter like "*p*" and "*t*" gives the letter a soft sound; without the "*h*", the sound is more explosive. Thus, "*ph*" is not pronounced "*f*" but as a soft "*p*"; without the "*h*", the "*p*" has the sound of a very hard "*b*". The word *thanon* (street) is pronounced "*tanon*" in the same way as "Thailand" is not meant to sound like "*Thighland*". Similarly, final letters are often not pronounced as they look. A "*j*" on the end of a word is pronounced "*t*"; "*l*" is pronounced as an "*n*". To complicate matters further, many words end with "*se*" or "*r*", which are not pronounced.

Vowels are pronounced as follows: **i** as in *sip*, **ii** as in *seep*, **e** as in *bet*, **a** as in *pan*, **aa** as in *car*, **u** as in *pool*, **o** as in *so*, **ai** as in *pie*, **ow** as in *cow*, **aw** as in *paw*, **iw** as in *you*, **oy** as in *toy*.

In Thai, the pronouns "I" and "me" are the same word, but it is different for males and females. Men use the word *phom* when referring to themselves, while women say *chan* or *diichan*. Men use *khrap* at the end of a sentence when addressing either a male or a female to add politeness, or in a similar manner as "please" (the word for "please", *karuna*, is seldom used directly), ie *Pai* (f) *nai, khrap* (h) (eg Where are you going, Sir?). Women add the word *kha* to their statements, as in *Pai* (f) *nai, kha* (h).

To ask a question, add a high tone *mai* to the end of the phrase ie *rao pai* (we go) or *rao pai mai* (h) (shall we go?). To negate a statement, insert a falling tone *mai* between the subject and the verb ie *rao pai* (we go), *rao mai pai* (we don't go). "Very" or "much" are indicated by adding *maak* to the end of a phrase ie *ron* (hot), *ron maak* (very hot), or *phaeng* (expensive), *phaeng maak* (very expensive), and the opposite *mai phaeng* (not expensive).

Thai Names

From the languages of India have come polysyllabic names and words, the lexicon of literature. Thai names are among the longest in the world. Every Thai

The Five Tones

Mid tone (m): Voiced at the speaker's normal, even pitch.
High tone (h): Pitched slightly higher than the mid tone.
Low tone (l): Pitched slightly lower than the mid tone.
Rising tone (r): Sounds like a questioning pitch, starting low and rising.
Falling tone (f): Sounds like an English speaker suddenly understanding something: "Oh, I see!"

person's first and surname has a meaning. Thus, by learning the meaning of the name of everyone you meet, you would acquire a formal, but quite extensive vocabulary.

There is no universal transliteration system from Thai into English, which is why names (and street names) can be spelled in three different ways. For example, the surname Chumsai is written Chumsai, Jumsai and Xoomsai depending on the family. This confuses even the Thais. If you ask a Thai how they spell something, they may well reply, "how do you want to spell it?" So, Bangkok's thoroughfare of Ratchadamnoen is also spelled Ratchadamnern. Ko Samui can be spelled Koh Samui. The spellings will differ from map to map, and from book to book.

To address a person one has never met, the title *khun* is used for both male and female. Having long and complicated surnames, Thais typically address one another by their first name only and preceded by the title *khun* for formality, ie Hataichanok Phrommayon becomes *Khun* Hataichanok. Thais usually adopt nicknames from birth, often accorded to their physical or behavioural attributes as a baby, eg *Lek* (small), *Yai* (big), *Daeng* (red), *Moo* (pig) etc. If the person is familiar – a friend, relative, or close colleague – then according to the senior age relationship between both persons, they are addressed *Pii* (if older) or *Nong* (if younger). So an older friend would be addressed *Pii Lek*, or if younger *Nong Lek*.

Numbers

0 *soon* (m)
1 *nung* (m)
2 *song* (r)
3 *sam* (r)
4 *sii* (m)
5 *haa* (f)
6 *hok* (m)
7 *jet* (m)
8 *bet* (m)
9 *kow* (f)
10 *sip* (m)
11 *sip et* (m, m)
12 *sip song* (m, r)
13 *sip sam* (m, r) and so on
20 *yii sip* (m, m)
30 *sam sip* (f, m) and so on
100 *nung roi* (m, m)
1,000 *nung phan* (m, m)

Useful Words and Phrases

Days of the Week

Monday *wan jan*
Tuesday *wan angkan*
Wednesday *wan phoot*
Thursday *wan pharuhat*
Friday *wan sook*
Saturday *wan sao*
Sunday *wan athit*
today *wan nii* (h)
yesterday *meua wan nii* (h)
tomorrow *prung nii* (h)

Colours

white *sii kao*
black *sii dum*
red *sii daeng*
yellow *sii leuang*
blue *sii num ngern*
green *sii keeow*
orange *sii som*
pink *sii chompoo*

Short Phrases

Hello/goodbye *Sawadee* (a man then says *khrap*; a woman says *kha*: thus *sawadee khrap* or *sawadee kha*)
How are you? *Khun sabai dii, mai* (h)
Well, thank you *Sabai dii, khopkhun*
Thank you very much *Khopkhun maak*
May I take a photo? *Thai roop* (f) *noi, dai* (f) *mai* (h)
Never mind *Mai* (f) *pen rai*
I cannot speak Thai *Phuut Thai mai* (f) *dai* (f)
I can speak a little Thai *Phuut Thai dai* (f) *nit* (h) *diew*
Where do you live? *Khun yoo thii* (f) *nai* (r)
What is this called in Thai? *An nii* (h), *kaw riak aray phasa Thai*
How much? *Thao* (f) *rai*

Directions and Travel

go *pai*
come *maa*
where *thii* (f) *nai* (r)
right *khwaa* (r)
left *sai* (h)
turn *leo*
straight ahead *trong pai*
Please slow down *Cha cha noi*
Stop here *Yawt thii* (f) *nii* (f)
fast *raew*
slow *cha*
hotel *rong raem*
street *thanon*
lane *soi*
bridge *saphan*
police station *sathanii dtam ruat*
ferry *reua*
longtail boat *reua haang yao*
train *rot fai*
bus *rot may*
skytrain *rot fai faa*
metro/subway *rot fai tai din*
pier *tha reua*
bus stop *pai rot may*
station *sathanii (rot may, rot fai, rot fai faa)*

Other Handy Phrases

yes *chai* (f)
no *mai* (f) *chai* (f)
Where's the toilet? *Horng narm yoo tee nai*
Do you have...? *Mii...mai* (h)
expensive *phaeng*
Do you have something cheaper? *Mii arai thii thook* (l) *kwa, mai* (h)
Can you lower the price a bit? *Kaw lot noi dai* (f) *mai* (h)
Do you have another colour? *Mii sii uhn mai* (h)
too big *yai kern pai*
too small *lek kern pai*
Do you have any in a bigger size? *Mii arai thii yai kwa mai* (h)
Do you have any in a smaller size? *Mii arai thii lek kwa mai* (h)
Do you have a girlfriend/ boyfriend? *Mii faen mai* (h)
I don't want it *Mai ao*
hot (heat hot) *rawn* (h)
hot (spicy) *phet*
cold *yen*
sweet *waan* (r)
sour *prio* (f)
delicious *aroy*
I do not feel well *Mai* (f) *sabai*

FURTHER READING

General

Mai Pen Rai Means Never Mind by Carol Hollinger. Amusing book describing hilarious experiences in Thailand half a century ago.
Travellers' Tales Thailand edited by James O'Reilly and Larry Habegger. A stimulating collection of observations and true stories from around 50 writers.

Fiction

Bangkok Haunts by John Burdett. More hard-boiled capers with the half-Thai, half-American Buddhist policeman of Bangkok 8 fame.
The Beach by Alex Garland. The beach read that inspired the movie staring Leonardo Dicaprio about a group of backpackers trying to find their own paradise. Bangkok's Khao San area features prominently.
The Big Mango by Jake Needham. An action-adventure story about a search for millions of dollars in cash that went missing during the fall of Saigon in 1975.
Evil in the Land Without by Colin Cotterill. A gripping novel about Detective John Jessel being threatened by a serial killer called "The Paw".
A Killing Smile by Christopher G. Moore. A gripping thriller set in the capital city of Thailand.
Sleepless in Bangkok by Ian Quartermaine. A tough and funny erotic thriller, based on actual events, about an ex-SAS security consultant on a covert assignment to Siam.

History and Society

The King Never Smiles: A Biography of Thailand's Bhumibol Adulyadej by Paul M. Handley. An unauthorised portrait of the current King Bhumibol. As monarchy matters are taken very seriously, the book is banned in the kingdom and throughout Southeast Asia.
A History of Thailand, second edition, by Dr Pasuk Phongpaichit and Chris Baker. Concise and well-informed history, mainly of the Rattanakosin period.
A History of Southeast Asia by D.G.E. Hall. The classic history text.
Jim Thompson: The Legendary American by William Warren. The intriguing story of the American Thai silk magnate, Jim Thompson.
The Revolutionary King: The True-Life Sequel to The King and I by William Stevenson. An intimate portrait of the current King Bhumibol Adulyadej. As monarchy matters are taken very seriously here, the book is unavailable in the kingdom.
Bangkok Then and Now by Steve Van Beek. A hardcover book with many photos both old and new showing how the city has changed in many ways, but also remained the same in others.
The Balancing Act: A History of Modern Thailand by Joseph Wright. Accessible and detailed history of modern Thailand from 1932 to 1991.

Art and Culture

Thai Folk Wisdom: Contemporary Takes on Traditional Proverbs by Tulaya Pornpiriyakulchai and Jane Vejjajiva. Dual-language coffee table book that looks at society through 50 proverbs. Illustrated with paintings by leading Thai artists.
Very Thai: Everyday Popular Culture by Philip Cornwel-Smith. If you've ever wondered why every compound in Thailand has a spirit house or why insect treats are such a hit, this book is for you. A must-read for tourists and residents.
Flavours: Thai Contemporary Art by Steven Pettifor. Brimming with colourful illustrations, this is the only book that offers insights into Thailand's burgeoning contemporary visual arts scene.
The Arts of Thailand by Steve Van Beek and Luca Tettoni. Beautifully illustrated and includes the minor arts.
Things Thai by Tanistha Dansilp and Michael Freeman. Coffee-table book that presents quintessential Thai objects and artefacts.
The Grand Palace by Nngnoi Saksi, Naengnoi Suksri and Michael Freeman. Beautifully illustrated and detailed account of Bangkok's Grand Palace and its surroundings.

Religion

A History of Buddhism in Siam by Prince Dhani Nivat. Written by one of Thailand's most respected scholars.
What the Buddha Taught by Walpola Rahula. Comprehensive account of Buddhist doctrine.

Cookery

Thai Food by David Thompson. Almost 700 pages of traditional recipes and food background from the chef at Europe's only Michelin-starred Thai restaurant.

Other Insight Guides

The Insight Guides series includes several titles on Thailand, including *Thailand*, *Thailand's Beaches and Islands*, *Smart Guide Bangkok*, and *Fleximap Thailand*.

BANGKOK STREET ATLAS

The key map shows the area of Bangkok covered by the atlas section. An index of street names and places of interest shown on the maps can be found on the following pages. For each entry there is a page number and grid reference

Map Legend

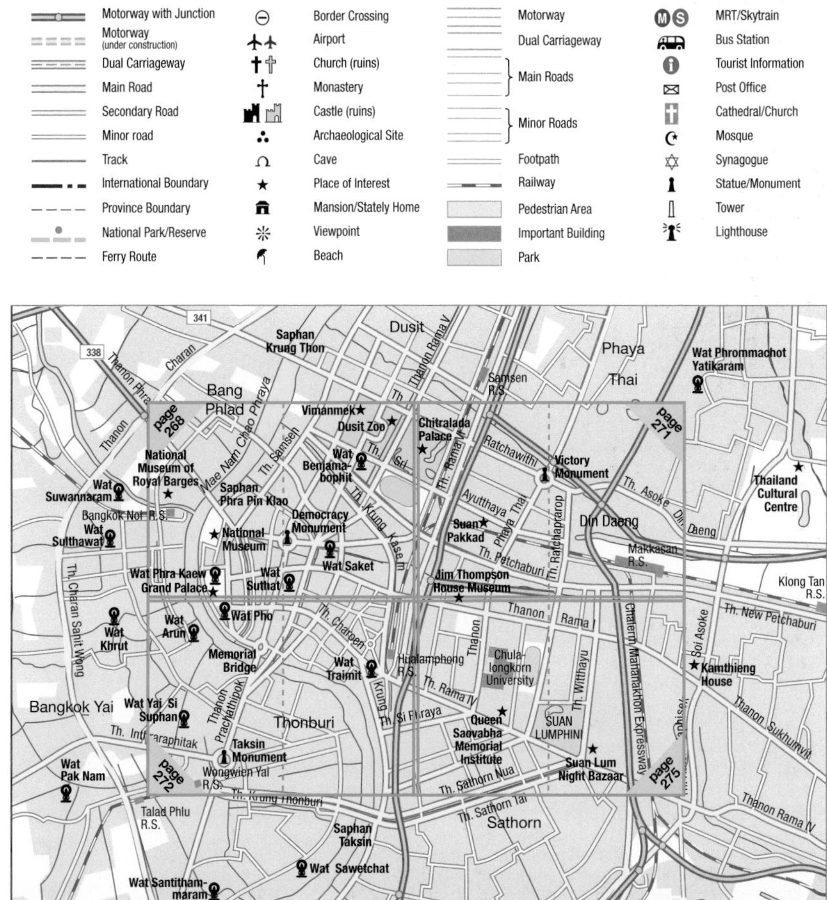

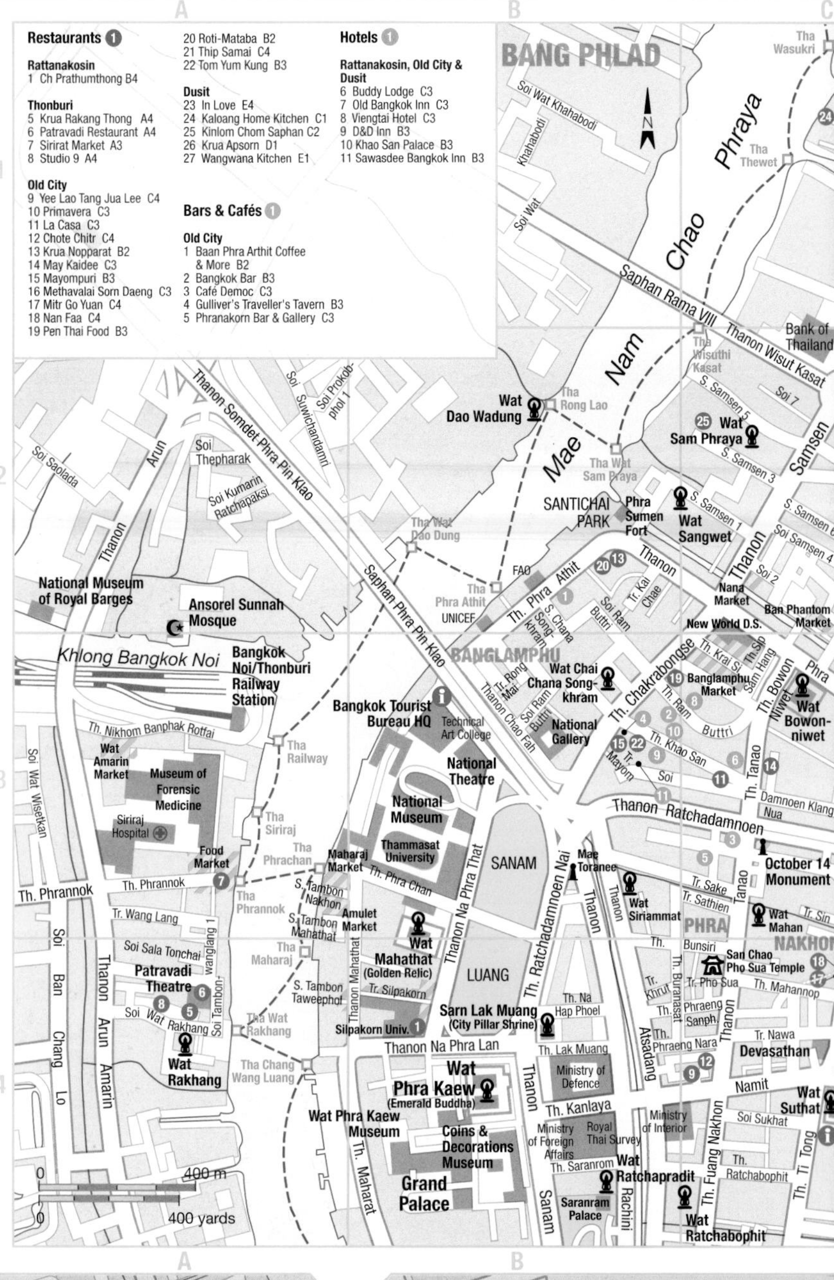
Restaurants 1
Rattanakosin
1 Ch Prathumthong B4
Thonburi
5 Krua Rakang Thong A4
6 Patravadi Restaurant A4
7 Sirirat Market A3
8 Studio 9 A4
Old City
9 Yee Lao Tang Jua Lee C4
10 Primavera C3
11 La Casa C3
12 Chote Chitr C4
13 Krua Nopparat B2
14 May Kaidee C3
15 Mayompuri B3
16 Methavalai Sorn Daeng C3
17 Mitr Go Yuan C4
18 Nan Faa C4
19 Pen Thai Food B3
20 Roti-Mataba B2
21 Thip Samai C4
22 Tom Yum Kung B3
Dusit
23 In Love E4
24 Kaloang Home Kitchen C1
25 Kinlom Chom Saphan C2
26 Krua Apsorn D1
27 Wangwana Kitchen E1
Bars & Cafés 1
Old City
1 Baan Phra Arthit Coffee & More B2
2 Bangkok Bar B3
3 Café Democ C3
4 Gulliver's Traveller's Tavern B3
5 Phranakorn Bar & Gallery C3
Hotels 1
Rattanakosin, Old City & Dusit
6 Buddy Lodge C3
7 Old Bangkok Inn C3
8 Viengtai Hotel C3
9 D&D Inn B3
10 Khao San Palace B3
11 Sawasdee Bangkok Inn B3
A
B
C
1
2
3
4
BANG PHLAD
Mae Nam Chao Phraya
Tha Wasukri
Tha Thewet
Saphan Rama VIII
Thanon Wisut Kasat
Bank of Thailand
Wat Dao Wadung
Tha Rong Lao
Wat Sam Phraya
Tha Wat Sam Phraya
SANTICHAI PARK
Phra Sumen Fort
Wat Sangwet
Thanon Somdet Phra Pin Klao
Saphan Phra Pin Klao
Tha Wat Dao Dung
Tha Phra Athit
National Museum of Royal Barges
Ansorel Sunnah Mosque
Khlong Bangkok Noi
Bangkok Noi/Thonburi Railway Station
Tha Railway
Tha Siriraj
Bangkok Tourist Bureau HQ
Technical Art College
BANGLAMPHU
Wat Chai Chana Song-khram
National Gallery
National Theatre
National Museum
Thammasat University
Banglamphu Market
New World D.S.
Nana Market
Ban Phantom Market
Wat Bowon-niwet
Thanon Ratchadamnoen
Th. Khao San
Wat Amarin Market
Museum of Forensic Medicine
Siriraj Hospital
Food Market
Th. Phrannok
Tha Phrannok
Tha Phrachan
Maharaj Market
Amulet Market
Wat Mahathat (Golden Relic)
SANAM LUANG
Mae Toranee
October 14 Monument
Wat Siriammat
Wat Mahan
PHRA NAKHON
San Chao Pho Sua Temple
Patravadi Theatre
Wat Rakhang
Tha Wat Rakhang
Tha Maharaj
Tha Chang Wang Luang
Silpakorn Univ.
Thanon Na Phra Lan
Sarn Lak Muang (City Pillar Shrine)
Wat Phra Kaew (Emerald Buddha)
Wat Phra Kaew Museum
Coins & Decorations Museum
Grand Palace
Ministry of Defence
Ministry of Foreign Affairs
Royal Thai Survey
Ministry of Interior
Wat Ratchapradit
Saranram Palace
Wat Ratchabophit
Devasathan
Wat Suthat
0
400 m
0
400 yards

272

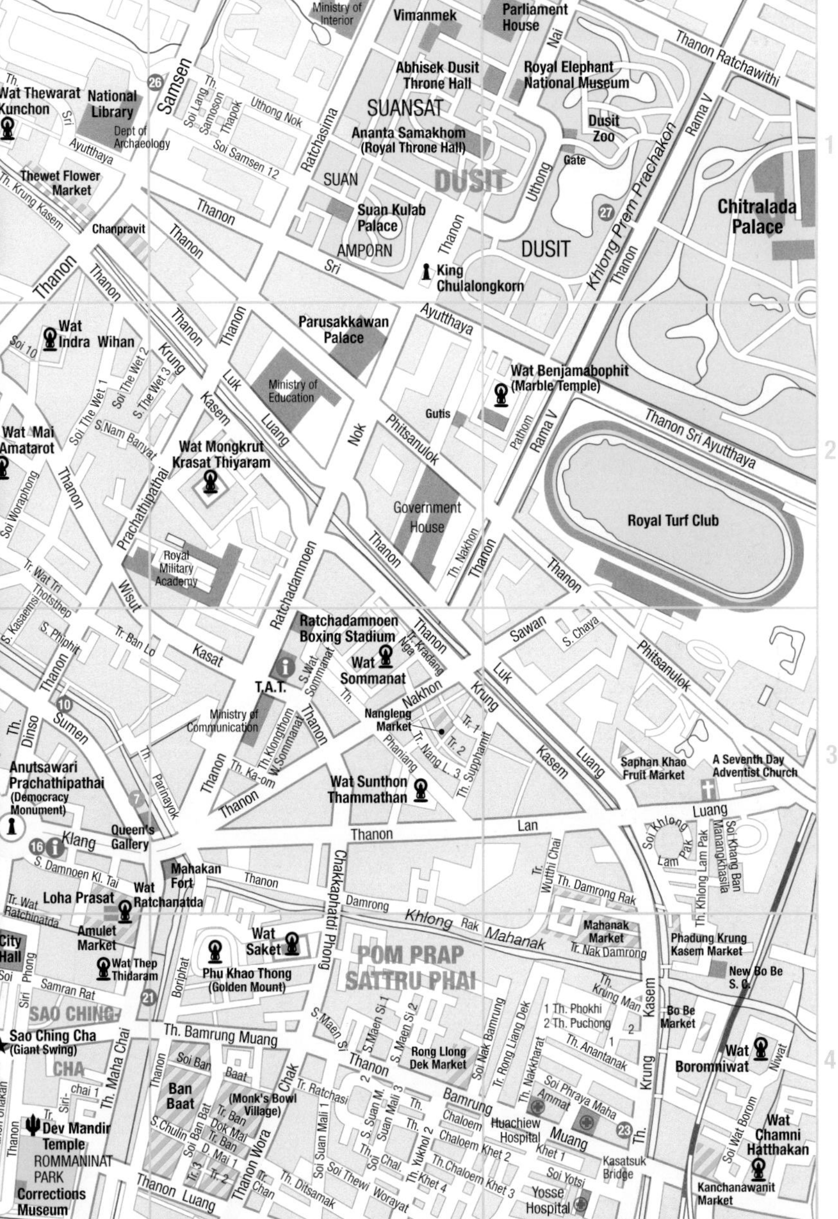
D
E
1
2
3
4
C
D
E
Ministry of Interior
Vimanmek
Parliament House
Thanon Ratchawithi
Abhisek Dusit Throne Hall
Royal Elephant National Museum
Nai
Rama V
Wat Thewarat Kunchon
National Library
Dept of Archaeology
26
Samsen
Soi Lang
Th. Samoson
Thapok
Uthong Nok
Soi Samsen 12
Ratchasima
SUANSAT
Ananta Samakhom (Royal Throne Hall)
Dusit Zoo
Gate
Khlong Prem Prachakon
SUAN
DUSIT
Uthong
Sri
Ayutthaya
Thewet Flower Market
Th. Krung Kasem
Thanon
Suan Kulab Palace
AMPORN
27
Chitralada Palace
Chanpravit
Thanon
DUSIT
Thanon
King Chulalongkorn
Sri
Thanon
Thanon
Wat Indra Wihan
Soi 10
Thanon
Thanon
Parusakkawan Palace
Ayutthaya
Krung
Soi The Wet 2
Soi The Wet 1
S.The Wet 3
Luk
Kasem
Ministry of Education
Luang
Nok
Phitsanulok
Gutis
Wat Benjamabophit (Marble Temple)
Pathom
Rama V
Thanon Sri Ayutthaya
Wat Mai Amatarot
S.Nam Banyat
Wat Mongkrut Krasat Thiyaram
Prachathipatai
Soi Woraphong
Thanon
Government House
Royal Turf Club
Royal Military Academy
Ratchadamnoen
Thanon
Th. Nakhon
Thanon
Thanon
Tr. Wat Tri Thotsthep
Wisut
S. Kasaemsi
S. Phiphit
Tr. Ban Lo
Kasat
Ratchadamnoen Boxing Stadium
Thanon
Tr. Kradang Nga
Wat Sommanat
S. Wat Sommanat
Th.
Sawan
S. Chaya
Phitsanulok
270
Thanon
10
T.A.T.
Luk
Krung
Sumen
Th. Dinso
Ministry of Communication
Th. Klongthom W.Sommanat
Thanon
Nakhon
Nangleng Market
Tr. 1
Tr. 2
Phaniang
Tr. Nang L. 3
Th. Supphamit
Kasem
Luang
Saphan Khao Fruit Market
A Seventh Day Adventist Church
Anutsawari Prachathipatai (Democracy Monument)
Th.
Parinayok
Thanon
Th. Ka-om
Thanon
Wat Sunthon Thammathan
7
Queen's Gallery
Klang
16
Thanon
Lan
Luang
Soi Khlong Lam Pak
Soi Khang Ban Manangkhasila
Th. Khlong Lam Pak
S. Damnoen Kl. Tai
Mahakan Fort
Thanon
Chakkaphatdi Phong
Tr. Wutthi Chai
Th. Damrong Rak
Tr. Wat Ratchinatda
Loha Prasat
Wat Ratchanatda
Damrong
Khlong
Rak
Mahanak
Mahanak Market
Tr. Nak Damrong
Phadung Krung Kasem Market
City Hall
Amulet Market
Wat Saket
POM PRAP SATTRU PHAI
New Bo Be S. C.
Soi Phong
Wat Thep Thidaram
Boriphat
Phu Khao Thong (Golden Mount)
Th. Krung Man
Kasem
Samran Rat
Siri
21
SAO CHING-CHA
S.Maen Si
S.Maen Si 1
S.Maen Si 2
Soi Nak Bamrung
Tr. Rong Liang Dek
1 Th. Phokhi
2 Th. Puchong
1
2
Bo Be Market
Sao Ching Cha (Giant Swing)
Th. Maha Chai
Th. Bamrung Muang
Soi Ban Baat
Thanon
Rong Llong Dek Market
Th. Anantanak
Krung
Wat Borommiwat
Niwat
Thanon Unakan
Siri-chai 1
Tr.
Ban Baat
(Monk's Bowl Village)
Chak
Tr. Ratchasi
S. Suan M. 3
Suan Mali 3
Th.
Bamrung
Th. Nakkharat
Soi Phraya Maha Ammat
Th.
Wat Chamni Hatthakan
Soi Wat Borom
Thanon
Dev Mandir Temple
ROMMANINAT PARK
S.Chulin
Soi Ban Bat
Tr. Ban Dok Mai
Tr. Ban D. Mai 1
Wora
Soi Suan Mali 1
S. Suan M. 2
Th.
Chaloem
Chaloem Khet 2
Huachiew Hospital
Muang
23
Khet 1
Kasatsuk Bridge
Corrections Museum
Thanon Luang
Tr. 3
Tr. 2
Thanon
Tr. Chan
Th. Ditsamak
Soi Thewi Worayat
Th. Chal.
Soi
Th. Yukhol 2
Th. Khet 4
Th.Chaloem Khet 3
Soi Yotsi
Yosse Hospital
Kanchanawanit Market

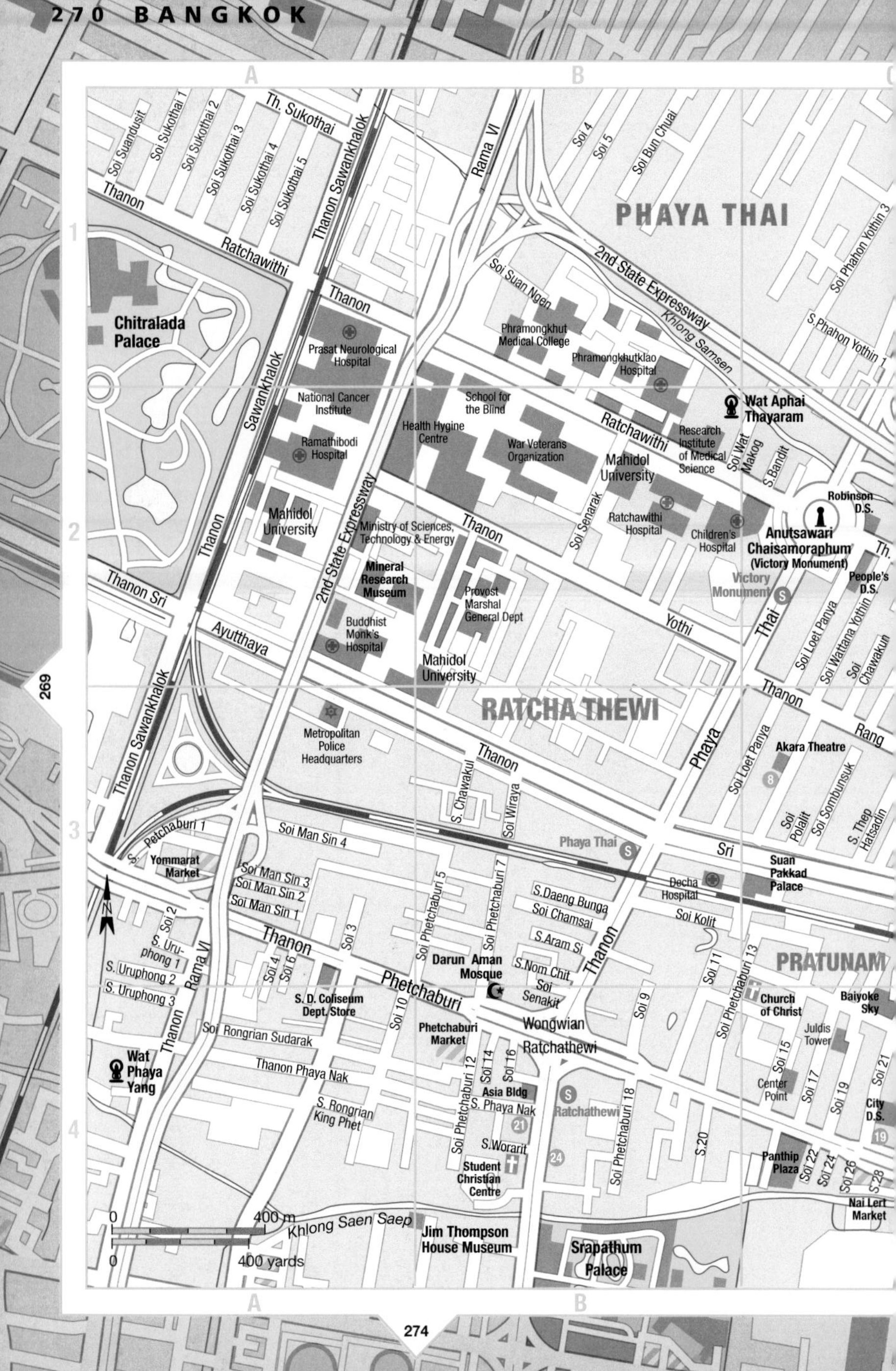
A
B
1
2
3
4
PHAYA THAI
RATCHA THEWI
PRATUNAM
Th. Sukothai
Soi Suandusit
Soi Sukothai 1
Soi Sukothai 2
Soi Sukothai 3
Soi Sukothai 4
Soi Sukothai 5
Thanon Sawankhalok
Rama VI
Soi 4
Soi 5
Soi Bun Chuai
Thanon Ratchawithi
Chitralada Palace
2nd State Expressway
Khlong Samsen
Soi Suan Ngen
Soi Phahon Yothin 3
S.Phahon Yothin 1
Thanon
Prasat Neurological Hospital
Phramongkhut Medical College
Phramongkhutklao Hospital
Wat Aphai Thayaram
National Cancer Institute
School for the Blind
Health Hygine Centre
War Veterans Organization
Ratchawithi
Research Institute of Medical Science
Soi Wat Makog
S.Bandit
Ramathibodi Hospital
Mahidol University
Sawankhalok
Robinson D.S.
Ratchawithi Hospital
Children's Hospital
Anutsawari Chaisamoraphum (Victory Monument)
Soi Senarak
Mahidol University
Ministry of Sciences, Technology & Energy
Thanon
Thanon
Th.
2nd State Expressway
Mineral Research Museum
Victory Monument
People's D.S.
Thanon Sri
Provost Marshal General Dept
Yothi
Thai
Soi Loet Panya
Soi Wattana Yothin
Soi Chawakun
Ayutthaya
Buddhist Monk's Hospital
Mahidol University
Thanon
Rang
Thanon Sawankhalok
Metropolitan Police Headquarters
Thanon
Phaya
Soi Loet Panya
Akara Theatre
Soi Sombunsuk
S. Chawakul
Soi Wiraya
Soi Polalit
S. Thep Hatsadin
Petchaburi 1
Soi Man Sin 4
Phaya Thai
Sri
Suan Pakkad Palace
Yommarat Market
Soi Man Sin 3
Soi Man Sin 2
Soi Man Sin 1
Soi Phetchaburi 5
Soi Phetchaburi 7
S.Daeng Bunga
Soi Chamsai
Decha Hospital
Soi Kolit
Soi 2
S. Uru-phong 1
S. Uruphong 2
S. Uruphong 3
Thanon
Soi 3
Soi 4
Soi 6
S.Aram Si
Thanon
Soi 11
Soi Phetchaburi 13
Rama VI
Darun Aman Mosque
S.Nom Chit
Soi Senakit
Phetchaburi
S. D. Coliseum Dept. Store
Soi 10
Soi 9
Church of Christ
Baiyoke Sky
Thanon
Soi Rongrian Sudarak
Phetchaburi Market
Wongwian Ratchathewi
Juldis Tower
Soi Phetchaburi 12
Soi 14
Soi 16
Soi 15
Soi 17
Soi 19
Soi 21
Wat Phaya Yang
Thanon Phaya Nak
Asia Bldg
S. Phaya Nak
Ratchathewi
Soi Phetchaburi 18
Center Point
City D.S.
S. Rongrian King Phet
21
S.Worarit
24
S.20
Panthip Plaza
Soi 22
Soi 24
Soi 26
S.28
19
8
Student Christian Centre
0
400 m
0
400 yards
Khlong Saen Saep
Jim Thompson House Museum
Srapathum Palace
Nai Lert Market
N

269

274

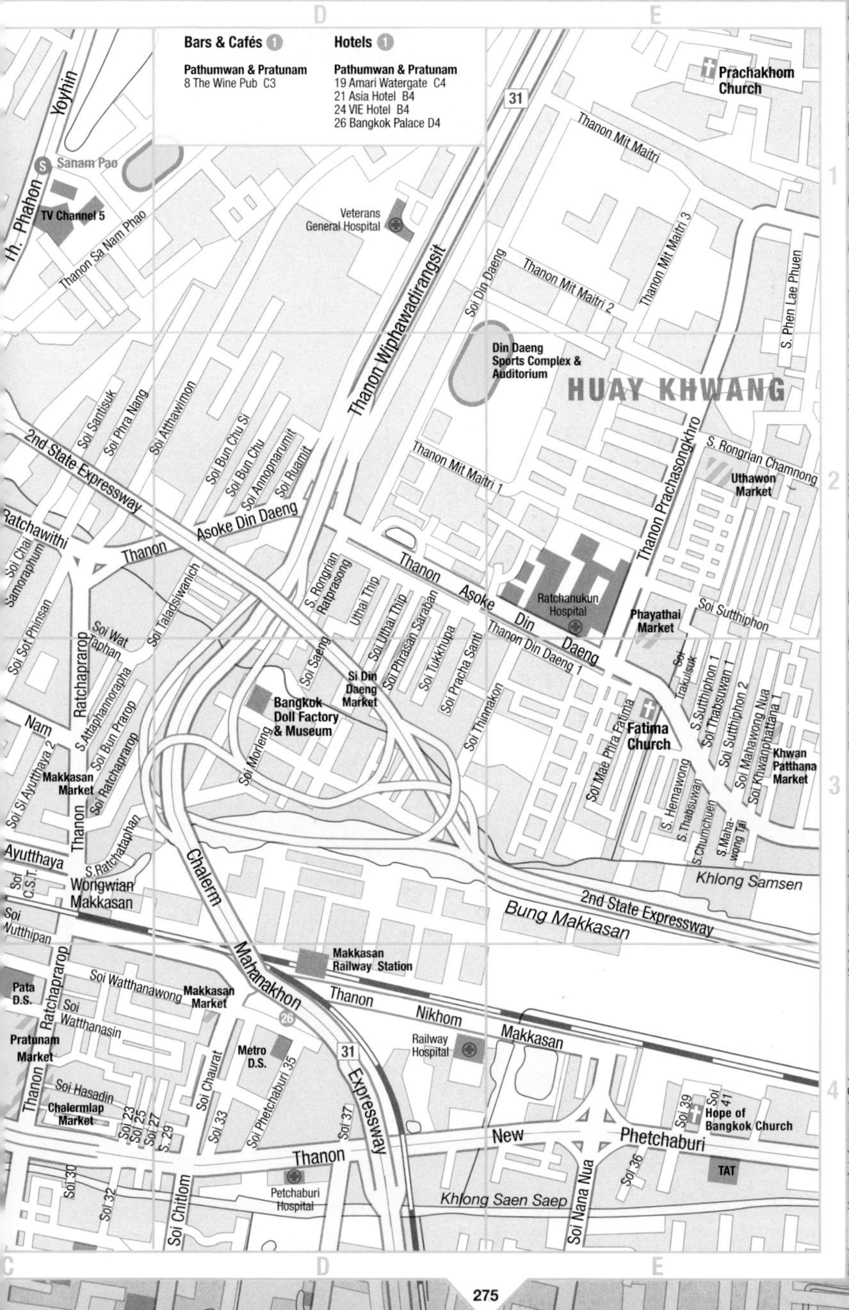

Bars & Cafés
Pathumwan & Pratunam
8 The Wine Pub C3
Hotels
Pathumwan & Pratunam
19 Amari Watergate C4
21 Asia Hotel B4
24 VIE Hotel B4
26 Bangkok Palace D4
Prachakhom Church
Thanon Mit Maitri
Sanam Pao
TV Channel 5
Th. Phahon Yoyhin
Thanon Sa Nam Phao
Veterans General Hospital
Thanon Wiphawadirangsit
Soi Din Daeng
Thanon Mit Maitri 2
Thanon Mit Maitri 3
S. Phen Lae Phuen
Din Daeng Sports Complex & Auditorium
HUAY KHWANG
Thanon Prachasongkhro
S. Rongrian Chamnong
Uthawon Market
Thanon Mit Maitri 1
2nd State Expressway
Ratchawithi
Soi Santisuk
Soi Phra Nang
Soi Atthawimon
Soi Bun Chu Si
Soi Bun Chu
Soi Annopnarumit
Soi Ruamit
Thanon Asoke Din Daeng
Soi Chai Samoraphum
Soi Taladsiwanich
S. Rongrian Ratprasong
Uthai Thip
Soi Uthai Thip
Soi Phrasan Saraban
Soi Tukkhupa
Soi Pracha Santi
Ratchanukun Hospital
Phayathai Market
Soi Sutthiphon
Thanon Din Daeng 1
Soi Sot Phinsan
Soi Wat Taphan
Soi Saeng
Si Din Daeng Market
Bangkok Doll Factory & Museum
Soi Thinnakon
Soi Mae Phra Fatima
Fatima Church
Soi Trakulsuk
S. Sutthiphon 1
Soi Thabsuwan 1
Soi Sutthiphon 2
Soi Mahawong Nua
Soi Khwanphattana 1
Khwan Patthana Market
Nam
Ratchaprarop
S. Attaphannorapha
Soi Bun Prarop
Soi Ratchaprarop
Soi Si Ayutthaya 2
Makkasan Market
Soi Morleng
S. Hemawong
S. Thabsuwan
S. Chumchuen
S. Maha-wong Tai
Ayutthaya
S. Ratchataphan
Wongwian Makkasan
Soi C.S.T.
Soi Nutthipan
Chalerm Mahanakhon
Khlong Samsen
2nd State Expressway
Bung Makkasan
Makkasan Railway Station
Pata D.S.
Soi Watthanawong
Makkasan Market
Soi Watthanasin
Thanon Nikhom Makkasan
Railway Hospital
Pratunam Market
Metro D.S.
31
Expressway
Soi Hasadin
Chalermlap Market
Soi 23
Soi 25
Soi 27
S. 29
Soi Chaurat
Soi 33
Soi Phetchaburi 35
Soi 37
Soi 39
Soi 41
Hope of Bangkok Church
Thanon New Phetchaburi
TAT
Soi 30
Soi 32
Soi Chitlom
Petchaburi Hospital
Khlong Saen Saep
Soi Nana Nua
Soi 36
C
D
E
1
2
3
4

275

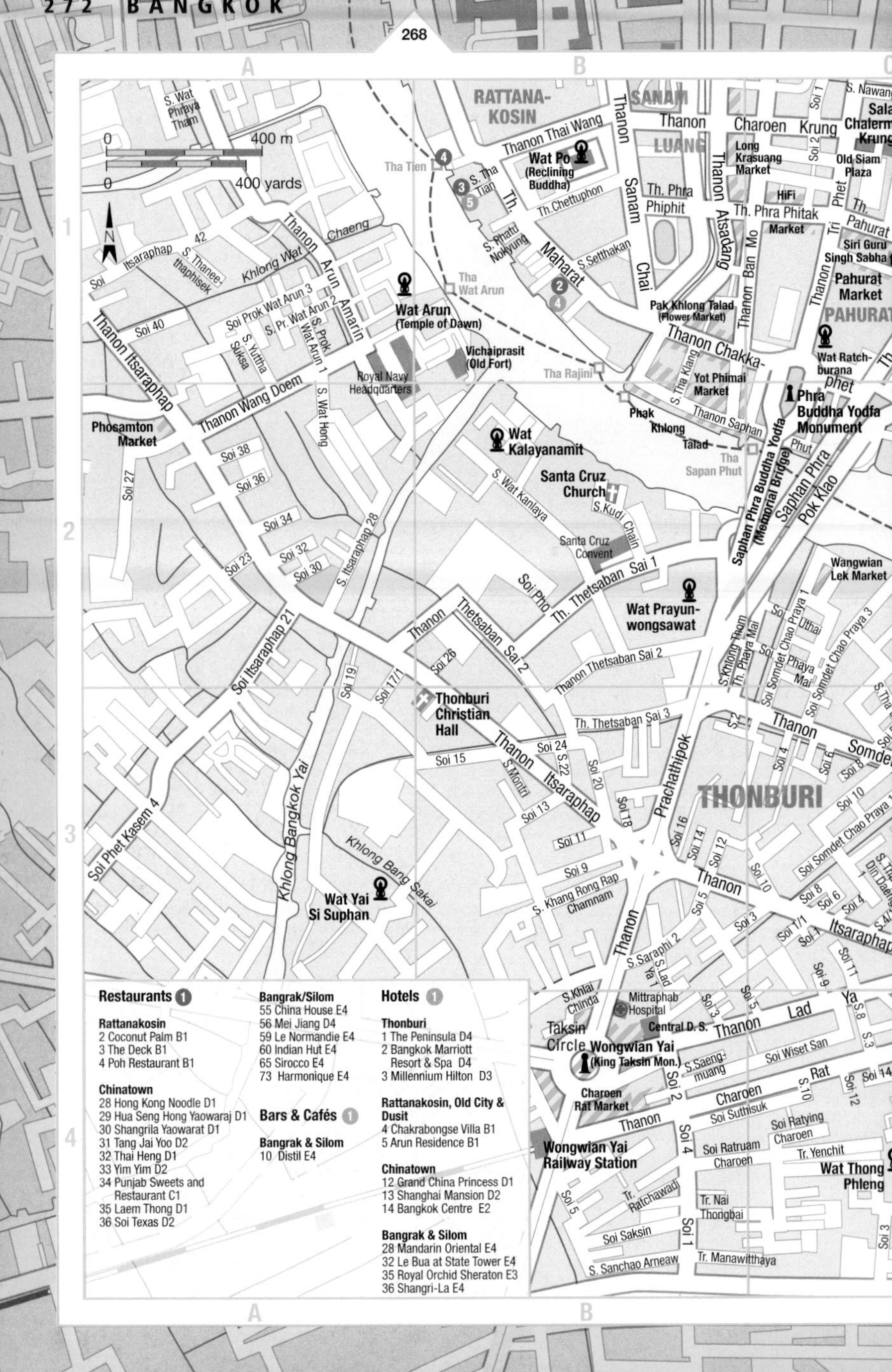
268
A
B
C
1
2
3
4
0
400 m
0
400 yards
RATTANA-
KOSIN
SANAM
LUANG
Thanon Thai Wang
Wat Po
(Reclining
Buddha)
Tha Tien
S. Tha
Tian
Th.Chettuphon
Th.
Maharat
S. Phatu
Nokyung
S.Setthakan
Thanon
Sanam
Chai
Thanon
Charoen
Krung
Long
Krasuang
Market
Th. Phra
Phiphit
Thanon
Atsadang
Thanon Ban Mo
Th. Phra Phitak
Market
HiFi
Old Siam
Plaza
Sala
Chalerm
Krung
S. Nawang
Soi 1
Soi 2
Phet
Th.
Pahurat
Siri Guru
Singh Sabha
Pahurat
Market
PAHURAT
Thanon Tri
Pak Khlong Talad
(Flower Market)
Thanon Chakka-
phet
Wat Ratch-
burana
Yot Phimai
Market
S. Tha Klang
Thanon Saphan
Phak
Khlong
Talad
Tha
Sapan Phut
Phra
Buddha Yodfa
Monument
Phut
Saphan Phra Buddha Yodfa
(Memorial Bridge)
Saphan Phra
Pok Klao
Tha Rajini
Tha
Wat Arun
Wat Arun
(Temple of Dawn)
Vichaiprasit
(Old Fort)
Royal Navy
Headquarters
Thanon
Arun
Amarin
Chaeng
Khlong Wat
S. Wat
Phraya
Tham
S. Thanee-
thaphisek
Soi Itsaraphap 42
Soi Prok Wat Arun 3
S. Pr. Wat Arun 2
S. Prok
Wat Arun 1
S. Yuttha
Suksa
Soi 40
Thanon Itsaraphap
Thanon Wang Doem
S. Wat Hong
Phosamton
Market
Soi 38
Soi 36
Soi 34
Soi 32
Soi 30
Soi 27
Soi 23
S. Itsaraphap 28
Wat
Kalayanamit
S. Wat Kanlaya
Santa Cruz
Church
S.Kudi Chain
Santa Cruz
Convent
Soi Pho
Th. Thetsaban Sai 1
Wat Prayun-
wongsawat
Wangwian
Lek Market
Thanon
Thetsaban
Sai 2
Thanon Thetsaban Sai 2
Th. Thetsaban Sai 3
Soi 26
Soi Itsaraphap 21
Soi 19
Soi 17/1
Thonburi
Christian
Hall
Soi 15
Thanon
Itsaraphap
Soi 24
S.22
Soi 20
S.Montri
Soi 13
Soi 11
Soi 9
Soi 18
S. Khang Rong Rap
Chamnam
Thanon
Prachathipok
THONBURI
Soi 16
Soi 14
Soi 12
Soi 10
Soi 8
Soi 6
Soi 4
Soi 5
Soi 3
Soi 1/1
Soi 1
Thanon
Itsaraphap
Thanon
Somdet
S. Khlong Thom
Th. Phaya Mai
Soi Somdet Chao Praya 1
Soi Somdet Chao Praya 3
Soi Somdet Chao Praya 12
Soi Phaya
Mai
Soi Uthai
S.Tha Din Daeng
Soi Phet Kasem 4
Khlong Bangkok Yai
Khlong Bang Sakai
Wat Yai
Si Suphan
S.Saraphi 2
S.Lad
Ya 1
S.Khlai
Chinda
Mittraphab
Hospital
Central D. S.
Taksin
Circle
Wongwian Yai
(King Taksin Mon.)
S.Saeng-
muang
Soi Wiset San
Thanon
Lad
Ya
Charoen
Rat Market
Thanon
Charoen
Rat
Soi Suthisuk
Soi Ratying
Charoen
Soi Ratruam
Charoen
Tr. Yenchit
Wat Thong
Phleng
Wongwian Yai
Railway Station
Tr.
Ratchawadi
Tr. Nai
Thongbai
Soi Saksin
S. Sanchao Arneaw
Tr. Manawitthaya
Soi 2
Soi 4
Soi 1
Soi 5
S.10
Soi 12
Soi 14
S.8
S.3

Restaurants 1
Rattanakosin
2 Coconut Palm B1
3 The Deck B1
4 Poh Restaurant B1
Chinatown
28 Hong Kong Noodle D1
29 Hua Seng Hong Yaowaraj D1
30 Shangrila Yaowarat D1
31 Tang Jai Yoo D2
32 Thai Heng D1
33 Yim Yim D2
34 Punjab Sweets and
Restaurant C1
35 Laem Thong D1
36 Soi Texas D2
Bangrak/Silom
55 China House E4
56 Mei Jiang D4
59 Le Normandie E4
60 Indian Hut E4
65 Sirocco E4
73 Harmonique E4
Bars & Cafés 1
Bangrak & Silom
10 Distil E4
Hotels 1
Thonburi
1 The Peninsula D4
2 Bangkok Marriott
Resort & Spa D4
3 Millennium Hilton D3
Rattanakosin, Old City &
Dusit
4 Chakrabongse Villa B1
5 Arun Residence B1
Chinatown
12 Grand China Princess D1
13 Shanghai Mansion D2
14 Bangkok Centre E2
Bangrak & Silom
28 Mandarin Oriental E4
32 Le Bua at State Tower E4
35 Royal Orchid Sheraton E3
36 Shangri-La E4

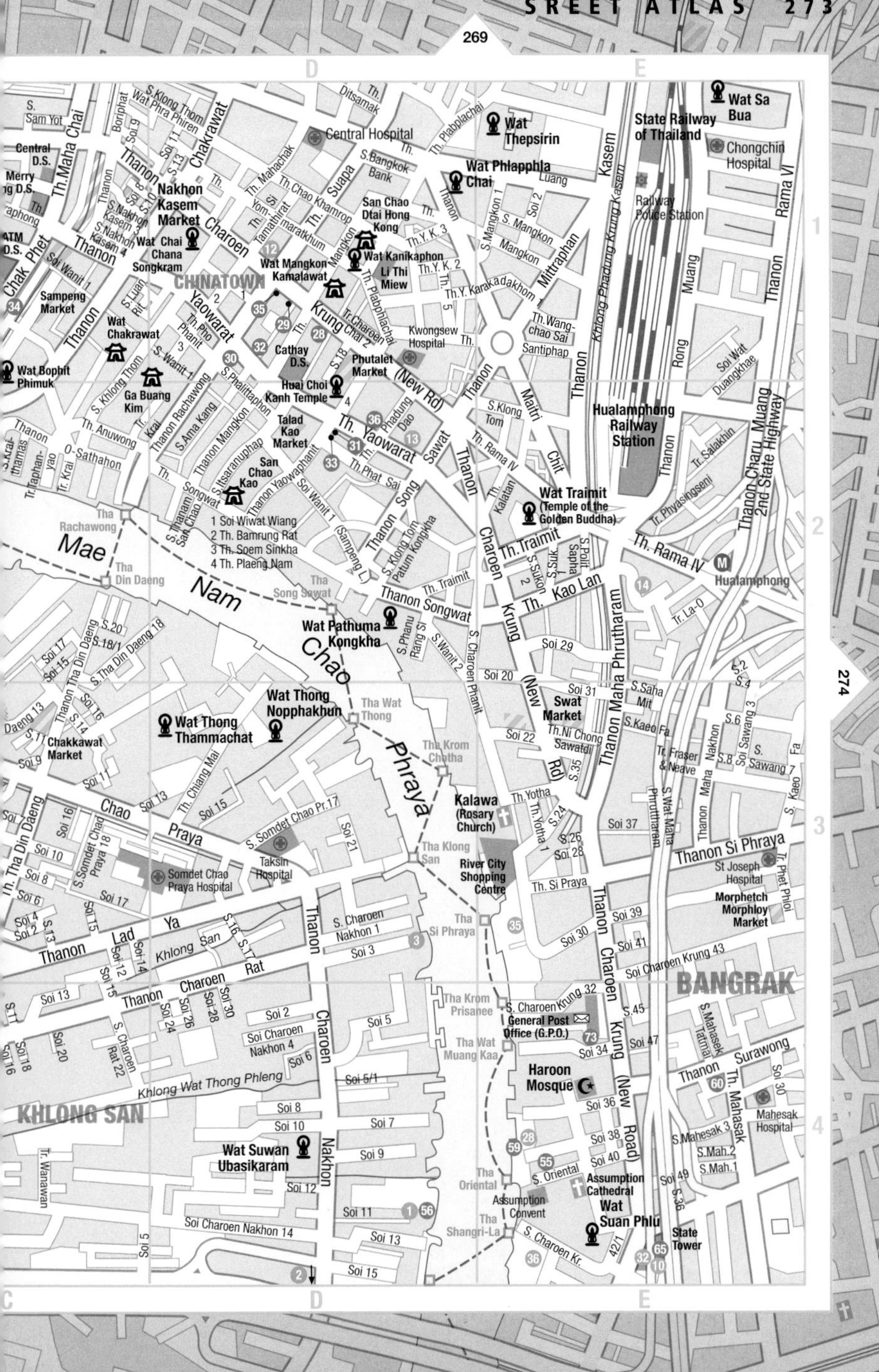
269
274
D
E
C
1
2
3
4
CHINATOWN
BANGRAK
KHLONG SAN
Mae Nam Chao Phraya
Wat Sa Bua
State Railway of Thailand
Chongchin Hospital
Wat Thepsirin
Central Hospital
Wat Phlapphla Chai
Railway Police Station
Central D.S.
Merry D.S.
Nakhon Kasem Market
Wat Chai Chana Songkram
San Chao Dtai Hong Kong
Wat Kanikaphon
Li Thi Miew
Wat Mangkon Kamalawat
Sampeng Market
Wat Chakrawat
Cathay D.S.
Kwongsew Hospital
Phutalet Market
Wat Bophit Phimuk
Ga Buang Kim
Huai Choi Kanh Temple
Talad Kao Market
San Chao Kao
Hualamphong Railway Station
Wat Traimit (Temple of the Golden Buddha)
Hualamphong
Tha Rachawong
Tha Din Daeng
Tha Song Sawat
Wat Pathuma Kongkha
Tha Wat Thong
Wat Thong Nopphakhun
Wat Thong Thammachat
Chakkawat Market
Tha Krom Chotha
Swat Market
Kalawa (Rosary Church)
River City Shopping Centre
Tha Klong San
Taksin Hospital
Somdet Chao Praya Hospital
St Joseph Hospital
Morphetch Morphloy Market
Tha Si Phraya
Tha Krom Prisanee
General Post Office (G.P.O.)
Tha Wat Muang Kaa
Haroon Mosque
Mahesak Hospital
Wat Suwan Ubasikaram
Tha Oriental
Assumption Convent
Assumption Cathedral
Wat Suan Phlu
Tha Shangri-La
State Tower
1 Soi Wiwat Wiang
2 Th. Bamrung Rat
3 Th. Soem Sinkha
4 Th. Plaeng Nam
Th. Maha Chai
Chakrawat
Thanon Charoen Krung (New Rd)
Th. Yaowarat
Yaowarat
Thanon Song Sawat
Thanon Songwat
Thanon Rama IV
Th. Rama IV
Mittraphan
Maitri Chit
Kasem
Khlong Phadung Krung Kasem
Thanon Rong Muang
Thanon Rama VI
Thanon Charu Muang
2nd State Highway
Th. Traimit
Th. Kao Lan
Thanon Maha Phrutharam
Thanon Si Phraya
Thanon Surawong
Th. Mahasak
Thanon Chao Praya
Thanon Lad Ya
Thanon Charoen Rat
Thanon Charoen Nakhon
Khlong San
Khlong Wat Thong Phleng
Soi Charoen Nakhon 14
Soi Charoen Krung 43
S. Charoen Krung 32
S. Oriental
S. Charoen Kr.
Th. Si Praya
Th. Yotha
Th. Phlabphlachai
Th. Chao Khamrop
Th. Mahachak
Th. Anuwong
Th. Phat Sai
Th. Phadung Dao
Thanon Rachawong
Thanon Mangkon
Thanon Yaowaphanit
Santiphap
Th. Wang-chao Sai
Th. Luang
Tr. Wanawan

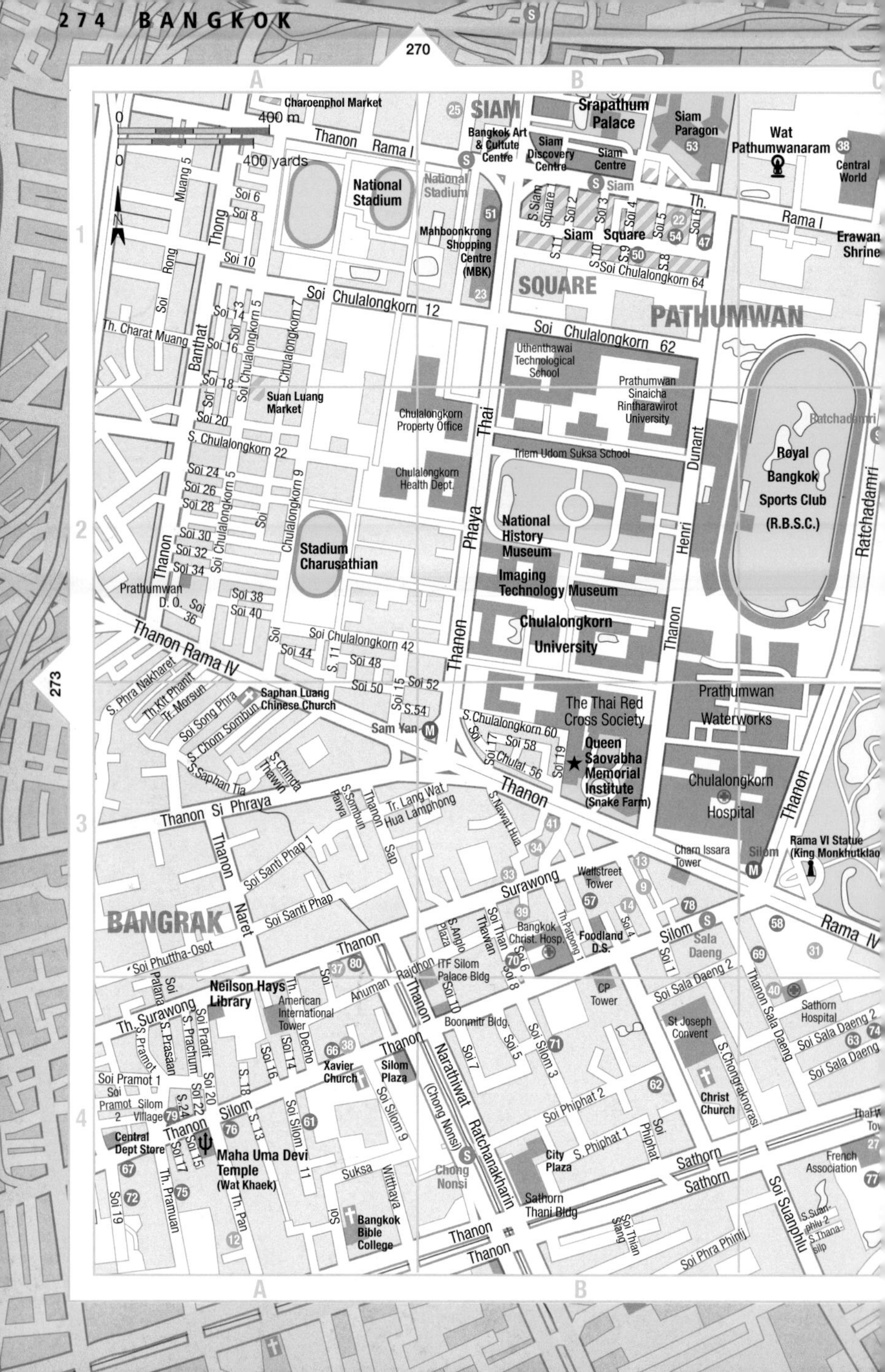
270
273
A
B
C
1
2
3
4
0
400 m
400 yards
SIAM
SQUARE
PATHUMWAN
BANGRAK
Charoenphol Market
Thanon Rama I
National Stadium
Bangkok Art & Culture Centre
Siam Discovery Centre
Srapathum Palace
Siam Centre
Siam Paragon
Wat Pathumwanaram
Central World
Erawan Shrine
Siam
Siam Square
Mahboonkrong Shopping Centre (MBK)
Soi Chulalongkorn 64
Soi Chulalongkorn 12
Soi Chulalongkorn 62
Th. Charat Muang
Thanon Banthat Thong
Soi Rong Muang 5
Suan Luang Market
Utenthawai Technological School
Prathumwan Sinaicha Rintharawirot University
Chulalongkorn Property Office
Chulalongkorn Health Dept.
Triem Udom Suksa School
Royal Bangkok Sports Club (R.B.S.C.)
Ratchadamri
Thanon Ratchadamri
Thanon Henri Dunant
Thanon Phaya Thai
National History Museum
Imaging Technology Museum
Chulalongkorn University
Stadium Charusathian
Prathumwan D. O.
Thanon Rama IV
Soi Chulalongkorn 42
S. Chulalongkorn 22
Saphan Luang Chinese Church
Sam Yan
S. Chulalongkorn 60
The Thai Red Cross Society
Queen Saovabha Memorial Institute (Snake Farm)
Prathumwan Waterworks
Chulalongkorn Hospital
Rama VI Statue (King Monkhutklao)
Silom
Charn Issara Tower
Thanon Si Phraya
Tr. Lang Wat Hua Lamphong
Soi Santi Phap
Thanon Surawong
Wallstreet Tower
Bangkok Christ. Hosp.
Foodland D.S.
Sala Daeng
Soi Sala Daeng 2
Thanon Naret
Soi Phuttha-Osot
Neilson Hays Library
American International Tower
ITF Silom Palace Bldg
CP Tower
Boonmitr Bldg.
St Joseph Convent
Sathorn Hospital
Thanon Sala Daeng
Xavier Church
Silom Plaza
Thanon Narathiwat Ratchanakharin (Chong Nonsi)
Christ Church
Soi Pramot 1
Soi Pramot 2
Silom Village
Central Dept Store
Maha Uma Devi Temple (Wat Khaek)
Chong Nonsi
City Plaza
Sathorn Thani Bldg
Thanon Sathorn
Soi Suanphlu
French Association
Bangkok Bible College
Soi Phra Phinij
Soi Phiphat 2
Th. Pramuan
Th. Pan
Suksa Witthaya

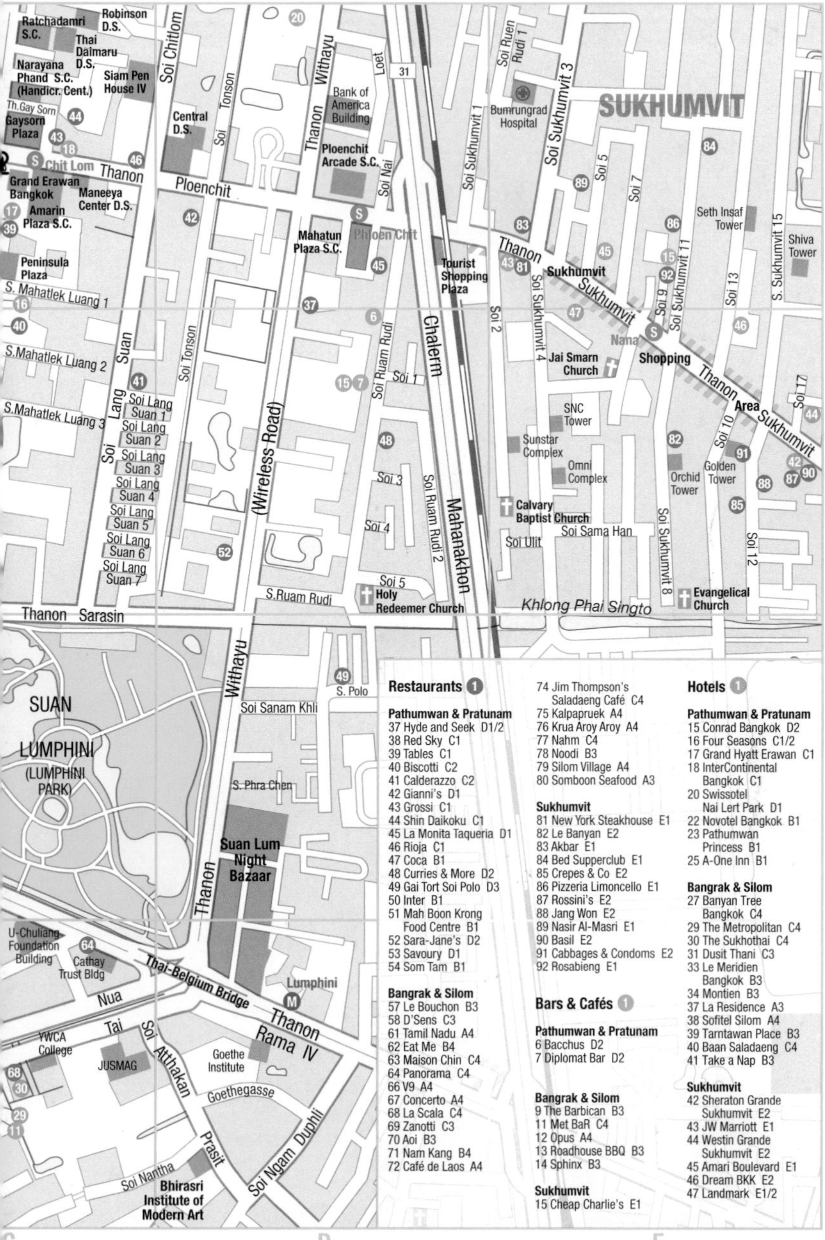

Restaurants 1

Pathumwan & Pratunam
37 Hyde and Seek D1/2
38 Red Sky C1
39 Tables C1
40 Biscotti C2
41 Calderazzo C2
42 Gianni's D1
43 Grossi C1
44 Shin Daikoku C1
45 La Monita Taqueria D1
46 Rioja C1
47 Coca B1
48 Curries & More D2
49 Gai Tort Soi Polo D3
50 Inter B1
51 Mah Boon Krong Food Centre B1
52 Sara-Jane's D2
53 Savoury D1
54 Som Tam B1

Bangrak & Silom
57 Le Bouchon B3
58 D'Sens C3
61 Tamil Nadu A4
62 Eat Me B4
63 Maison Chin C4
64 Panorama C4
66 V9 A4
67 Concerto A4
68 La Scala C4
69 Zanotti C3
70 Aoi B3
71 Nam Kang B4
72 Café de Laos A4
74 Jim Thompson's Saladaeng Café C4
75 Kalpapruek A4
76 Krua Aroy Aroy A4
77 Nahm C4
78 Noodi B3
79 Silom Village A4
80 Somboon Seafood A3

Sukhumvit
81 New York Steakhouse E1
82 Le Banyan E2
83 Akbar E1
84 Bed Supperclub E1
85 Crepes & Co E2
86 Pizzeria Limoncello E1
87 Rossini's E2
88 Jang Won E2
89 Nasir Al-Masri E1
90 Basil E2
91 Cabbages & Condoms E2
92 Rosabieng E1

Bars & Cafés 1

Pathumwan & Pratunam
6 Bacchus D2
7 Diplomat Bar D2

Bangrak & Silom
9 The Barbican B3
11 Met BaR C4
12 Opus A4
13 Roadhouse BBQ B3
14 Sphinx B3

Sukhumvit
15 Cheap Charlie's E1

Hotels 1

Pathumwan & Pratunam
15 Conrad Bangkok D2
16 Four Seasons C1/2
17 Grand Hyatt Erawan C1
18 InterContinental Bangkok C1
20 Swissotel Nai Lert Park D1
22 Novotel Bangkok B1
23 Pathumwan Princess B1
25 A-One Inn B1

Bangrak & Silom
27 Banyan Tree Bangkok C4
29 The Metropolitan C4
30 The Sukhothai C4
31 Dusit Thani C3
33 Le Meridien Bangkok B3
34 Montien B3
37 La Residence A3
38 Sofitel Silom A4
39 Tarntawan Place B3
40 Baan Saladaeng C4
41 Take a Nap B3

Sukhumvit
42 Sheraton Grande Sukhumvit E2
43 JW Marriott E1
44 Westin Grande Sukhumvit E2
45 Amari Boulevard E1
46 Dream BKK E2
47 Landmark E1/2

STREET INDEX

Art and Photo Credits

Adam Baker 231T
AKG London 27, 28B
Alamy 63T
Art Archive 32B
AWL Images, 6MR, 17R, 23B, 223T
Avlxyz/flickr 121
Banyan 242
Karen Blumberg 68, 71, 144, 151
Allie Caulfield 141
Steve & Jemma Copley 70L
Corbis 33B, 34T, 37B, 38B/T, 39B, 40B/T, 41T, 42T, 44, 59
Andrew Crump 134
Devarana Spa 88
Divan 90BR
APA Francis Dorai 104T, 124/T, 136, 169
Mary Evans 26B
Fotolia 6/7, 67BL
Getty Images 33T, 34B, 39T, 41, 45
Harsha KR 22B
HellyKelly 87B
APA jack Hollingsworth 149T
Istockphoto 6TL, 60B, 192, 201, 209, 210, 211T, 221, 226/T
Oskari Kettunen 64
Peter Knocke 263
Kobal 63B
Lukas Kurtz 61T
Kurvenalbn/flickr 227
Emilio Labrador 14/15, 77, 110, 111B
APA Jason Lang 8M, 10MR, 18, 19, 20L, 80, 84L, 94/95, 102, 103, 107B, 108, 109T, 111, 125, 130, 131B, 133/T, 141T, 147, 152, 153, 154, 155, 156TR, 166, 167, 176, 179, 184, 186, 187, 188/189, 191L, 194/T, 195/T, 198B, 200T, 202, 203, 204, 205/T, 206B/TR, 207, 208, 212/T, 214B, 215, 216, 217/T, 228, 229/T
Courtesy Mandarin Oriental 7CL, 173, 252
Divya Manian 139
Eric Molina 138B
APA Jock Montgomerie 199T
Museum of Siam 116/T
On Asia 7TR, 9B, 24/T, 28T, 42B, 43, 60TL, 78/T, 82R, 85T, 109, 185, 196, 228B, 230
Courtesy Oriental Hotel 67, 168/T
Courtesy the Peninsula 11ML, 89T, 90BL
Photoshot 113
Kevin Poh 86
M.C. Piya Rangsit 33L, 35
Courtesy Red Sky 162
Rex Features 29B/T
Spa 91
Pittaya Sroilong 62/T
Courtesy Starwood Hotels 240, 244, 247
APA Peter Stuckings 4T, 5, 6BL, 9T, 10BL/BR/ML//T, 11BL/BR, 12/13, 16, 17L, 20R, 21, 22, 23T, 29M, 52/T, 56, 57, 58/T, 60TR, 65, 66L/R/T, 69/T, 70R/T, 73, 74L/R, 75B, 76/T, 79, 81, 82L, 83, 84R, 87T, 90T, 92/93, 96, 97L/R, 101, 104, 106T, 107, 108B, 110T, 113B, 114/T, 115B, 117, 120, 129, 134T, 135B, 137, 145, 157, 158, 159/T, 161/T, 171B, 172, 174, 177, 180, 187B, 191R, 196T, 197/T, 198, 199, 200, 204B, 206TL, 218, 219, 220T, 222, 223, 224/T, 225/T, 232, 234, 235, 238, 248, 249, 255, 258, 264
Superstock 46/47, 51, 53B
Luca Invernizzi Tettoni 31, 33R
the uff da! Chronicles 53T, 148
US Library of Congress 37T
APA Marcus Wilson Smith 4B, 8B/T, 25, 30, 48, 49, 50L/R, 61B, 72, 75T, 85B, 100, 105, 106, 115, 122, 128, 131/T, 132/T, 135TL/TR, 140, 142, 143, 146, 148T, 149, 150/T, 156B/TL, 158T, 170, 171T, 193, 211, 213, 214, 215T,
David Wong 250
David Woo 138T

Photo Features

54/55: APA Peter Stuckings
54/55, APA Marcus Wilson Smith 54B/M, 54BM/T, APA Francis Dorai 55BL, APA Derrick Lim 55BR

118/119: Photolibrary 118/119, Corbis 118M/TL, Superstock 118B, Pictures Colour Library 119M, Scala 119B
126/127: APA Jason Lang 126/127, David Henley CPA 105T, Istockphoto 127BL, APA Peter Stuckings 126BL/BR/T, 127BR/M

164/165: All Pictures APA Peter Stuckings except Michael Freeman 165TR

Map Production: original cartography Berndtson & Berndtson, updated by Apa Cartographic Department

Production: Linton Donaldson

General Index

N

Restaurants

Bars and Cafés

INSIGHT GUIDE
BANGKOK

Picture Manager
Steven Lawrence
Series Manager
Rachel Fox
Series Editor
Rachel Lawrence

Distribution

UK & Ireland
GeoCenter International Ltd
Meridian House, Churchill Way West
Basingstoke, Hampshire RG21 6YR
sales@geocenter.co.uk

United States
Langenscheidt Publishers, Inc.
36–36 33rd Street 4th Floor
Long Island City, NY 11106
orders@langenscheidt.com

Australia
Universal Publishers
1 Waterloo Road
Macquarie Park, NSW 2113
sales@universalpublishers.com.au

New Zealand
Hema Maps New Zealand Ltd (HNZ)
Unit 2, 10 Cryers Road
East Tamaki, Auckland 2013
Tel: (64) 9 273 6459
sales.hema@clear.net.nz

Worldwide
Apa Publications GmbH & Co. Verlag KG (Singapore branch)
7030 Ang Mo Kio Avenue 5
08-65 Northstar @ AMK
Singapore 569880
Tel: (65) 6865-1600
apasin@singnet.com.sg

Printing
CTPS – China

First Edition 1988
Fifth Edition 2011

www.insightguides.com

About This Book

What makes an Insight Guide different? Since our first book pioneered the use of creative full-colour photography in travel guides in 1970, we have aimed to provide not only reliable information but also the key to a real understanding of a destination and its people.

Now, when the internet can supply inexhaustible (but not always reliable) facts, our books marry text and pictures to provide that more elusive quality: knowledge. To achieve this, they rely on the authority of locally based writers and photographers.

This new edition of *City Guide Bangkok* was commissioned by Series Editor **Rachel Lawrence**. The book was thoroughly updated by **Howard Richardson**, who has lived in Thailand since 1996. An award-winning feature writer, he contributed a monthly column to the Thai Airways inflight magazine *Sawasdee* for six years and has written for publications such as *GQ* and the BBC's food magazine *Olive*. He was previously the editor of *Bangkok Metro*, then Thailand's biggest selling English-language magazine. Richardson has worked on numerous Insight Guides – he wrote *Smart Guide Bangkok* and *Step-by-Step Bangkok* and recently contributed to *Insight Guide Thailand*.

This edition builds on the success of earlier editions produced by **Francis Dorai** and **Steven Pettifor**. The text of writers who contributed to previous editions has been updated for this book. They include **Sarah Rooney**, who wrote the People and Shopping chapters; **Chami Jotisalikorn**, who compiled the chapter on Spas and Wellness Centres; and **Dr Andrew Forbes** who condensed Bangkok's history into a riveting read.

Among the talented photographers whose images bring Bangkok to life are **Jason Lang** (whose work has been featured in *Wallpaper* and *Travel and Leisure*), **Peter Stuckings** and **Marcus Wilson-Smith**.

The book was copy-edited by **Naomi Peck**, proofread by **John King** and indexed by **Helen Peters**.

Send Us Your Thoughts

We do our best to ensure the information in our books is as accurate and up-to-date as possible. The books are updated on a regular basis using local contacts, who painstakingly add, amend, and correct as required. However, some details (such as telephone numbers and opening times) are liable to change, and we are ultimately reliant on our readers to put us in the picture.

We welcome your feedback, especially your experience of using the book "on the road". Maybe we recommended a hotel that you liked (or another that you didn't), or you came across a great bar or new attraction that we missed.

We will acknowledge all contributions, and we'll offer an Insight Guide to the best letters received.

Please write to us at:
Insight Guides
PO Box 7910, London SE1 1WE
Or email us at:
insight@apaguide.co.uk